LEADERS COUNT

Leaders Count

The Story of BNSF Railway

Lawrence H Kaufman

CUSTOM PUBLISHING

Texas Monthly Custom Publishing
P.O. Box 1569
Austin, Texas 78767-1569
www.emmiscustompublishing.com

Distributed by Texas A&M University Press
John H. Lindsey Building, Lewis Street
4354 TAMU
College Station, Texas 77843-4354
www.tamu.edu/upress

The opinions expressed by contributors to this book are solely those of the individual contributors and do not necessarily reflect the opinions or views of Burlington Northern Santa Fe Corporation or BNSF Railway Company.

Excerpt from the book *Comes Now the Interstate Commerce Practitioner,* by Frank N. Wilner, is reprinted with permission from the Association of Transportation Logistics, Law, and Policy.

Excerpt from the book *Railroad Mergers: History, Analysis, Insight,* by Frank N. Wilner, is reprinted with permission from the author.

Cover design: Methodologie. Book design: David Timmons.
ISBN 0-9724495-2-3 cloth
ISBN 0-9724495-4-X paper
First printing 2005
1 2 3 4 5 6 7 8 9 10   09 08 07 06 05

Contents

Preface

THROUGHOUT THE NEARLY 200 YEARS that railroads have operated in America, people have been captivated by what has become known as the romance of railroading. Perhaps it was the belching steam and the raw power of the locomotives pulling huge amounts of freight and large numbers of people from one place to another. Perhaps it was the mystery of where the train was coming from and where it was going. Whatever the reason, people to this day still are thrilled by the sight of passing trains.

And for the people who work in the railroad industry there also is a romance to what they do for a living. Railroading is in the blood of many of the people who work in the industry. Only dedicated employees would tolerate conditions in which they are on call 24 hours a day, seven days a week. The romance extends from generation to generation, as sons, and now daughters, of railroaders follow their fathers and grandfathers into the industry.

Fascination with the romance of railroading is such that many people—inside and outside the industry—forget that it is first and foremost a business. In fact, the railroad was the first capital-intensive network business. It also was the first business in which labor—ordinary employees—took the owners' capital out of the sight and control of the owners of the enterprise.

By necessity railroads needed to develop business practices that were detailed and exact. Once there was more than one train operating over a set of tracks, it took explicit rules and precise timekeeping to prevent trains from colliding. It was the railroad industry that fostered the development of standard time in the United States, so trains could be directed safely over the track systems. The business continues, exact and explicit, to this day.

Railroads also were the first businesses that were large enough to require more capital than traditional business owners could provide on their own, which led to development of the corporate form of business organization, the sale of stocks and bonds to finance construction and operation of the new transportation form, and the further development of securities markets that made it easier for promoters to raise capital and for investors to move their capital into and out of the enterprise easily. Financial historians credit the railroads with having effectively created the modern stock markets with their instantaneous execution of buy and sell orders.

The largest contributors to a tumultuous business environment, the railroads also were the first to be regulated by government, with the passage of the Interstate Commerce Act (ICA) in 1887, the first antitrust law in the United States. Amended many times, the ICA still exists, and railroads still must consider potential government and regulatory consequences of many things they do. Virtually all industries today are subject to antitrust laws.

Finally, mergers affected railroads in ways that few other industries experienced, and in the last 50 years mergers have absolutely dominated the business directions of American railroads. Today, after 175 years, the U.S. railroad industry has evolved into seven large systems known as Class 1 railroads and some 550 regional and short-line railroads. A merger between any two of the seven largest railroads undoubtedly will trigger competing mergers and a final round of consolidation that will leave North America with just two massive rail systems. Whether a final consolidation occurs or not, there is diminishing opportunity for railroads to grow by the traditional acquisition of connecting lines. Railroads like the BNSF Railway must focus on internal growth and are entering a new paradigm.

The geographic system of today is likely to be the system of tomorrow. With geographic growth behind them, the managerial focus of railroad leaders now is on improving service quality so that a new era of growth can occur. Where railroads have spent a half century fighting the trucking industry that steadily took traffic away from them, they now are working with their competitors to capture service-sensitive business that once was believed to be gone forever. New times demand innovative strategies that the railroad pioneers could not envision.

Walk down the halls of the corporate headquarters of the BNSF Railway Company, the second-largest railroad system in North America, and you'll see display cases filled with fascinating memorabilia of the railroad's past, from the fine china of the passenger era to the original mercury clocks with legendary accuracy that helped establish our concepts of time and service. You'll see paintings of the Grand Canyon, Glacier National Park, and the Native Americans of the Southwest by some of the nation's finest artists, including Thomas Moran, Eanger Irving Couse, and John Fery. These paintings, first displayed in train depots to promote train travel in the early 1900s, line the halls of the railroad headquarters today, a reminder of the railroad's role in settling the West.

It is easy to sense the impact of this particular business on lives and fortunes in the past. We are less likely to consider the impact of those same railroads on our lives today.

As one of the largest and most successful of U.S. railroads, BNSF is a living example of today's freight railroad industry. Although we will look briefly at the colorful and fascinating history of railroads in general and the five railroads making up the present-day BNSF in particular, our focus will be on the critical decisions and strategies that ensured the railroad's survival, the growing impact of railroads on our lives today, and the continuing challenges for the future. For, as we have said, railroads are businesses, and today's railroads are very big businesses. BNSF operates 32,000 route miles in 28 states and two Canadian provinces, and it connects at several gateways to the Mexican rail system. The company handles about one-fourth of all the freight moved by rail in the United States.

BNSF is typical of U.S. railroads in that it is a combination of many smaller railroads. In all, BNSF comprises 390 smaller railroads, the earliest dating back to 1849. In addition to BNSF, there are several large regional rail systems and a few hundred smaller regional and short-line railroads. These represent a combination of the survivors of more than 2,000 railroad companies that have offered freight and passenger service during the first 175 years of the industry's history in North America.

BNSF's success as one of the industry survivors reflects the wise and fortuitous decisions of its founders, as well as many other leaders during its 153-year history. In fact, a close look reveals several common threads woven throughout that history—management philosophies and themes that reappear frequently and at crucial times. These started first with the perseverance and commitment to a dream by men like James J. Hill, who built the Great Northern (GN), and Cyrus K. Holliday, the founder of what was then known as the Atchison, Topeka, and Santa Fe Railroad, both predecessors of today's BNSF. Both men pushed their respective railroads—the

GN across the northern tier of states, and the Santa Fe across the southern—through barren prairies, over the Rocky Mountains, and on to the Pacific Coast.

The leadership style and priorities of the railroad's founders shaped the corporate culture that grew and often thrived in the years that followed. The leadership also included its share of disappointments and misguided decision makers. Efforts to drive needed cultural change following deregulation in 1980 were heavy-handed and negatively affected morale throughout the organization. Remarkably, though, among companies of such age, BNSF's history really includes no broad instances of scandal or dishonesty. Unlike other rail ventures that were promoted by men who intended to make their fortunes building railroads or promoting the sale of railroad stock to a gullible public, the BNSF predecessor railroads avoided the worst transgressions of the 19th-century promoters and robber barons who fostered scandals like the Credit Mobilier construction of the Union Pacific.

The decisions made today in those halls and offices at BNSF headquarters, decorated by the art and artifacts reflecting the glorious days of the railroad's past, have critical consequences not only for BNSF but also for the rail industry and the U.S. transportation infrastructure. Thus has it ever been. At every point in their history, BNSF railroad leaders have faced tremendous challenges, whether the physical challenges of building the railroads, the logistical challenges of managing a rapidly growing industry at the heart of a growing nation's economy, or the economic challenges of continuing to grow a mature industry. There have been missteps along the way, but overall the strength and relevance of the company have been maintained. The future is less certain. The direction that BNSF and the other railroads take in the future not only may reflect on the health and future of the rail industry but also may have much to say about the future of the U.S. and world economies.

And behind it all will remain the men and women who now, as then, shape that future as well as their own present.

Edward Ripley took over the presidency of the Santa Fe in 1896 and saved the line from crumbling under the economic pressures of the day. Ripley combined a solid operating knowledge with the qualities of integrity, honesty, and leadership as he extended the Santa Fe line to San Francisco at the request of farmers and growers who until the arrival of the Santa Fe were at the mercy of a Southern Pacific monopoly.

J. Frank Jarrell, who started as the editor of the Santa Fe's agricultural newspaper, the *Earth*, designed and led a series of "demonstration trains" in the 1920s and 1930s throughout Kansas, Texas, and Oklahoma. He enthusiastically led a team that taught crop diversification, soil preparation, crop rotation, insect control, and farming safety to tens of thousands of wheat farmers. Jarrell's sense of mission not only increased the Santa Fe Railway's grain and agricultural markets but also arguably revolutionized agricultural practices that built the nation's farming belt.

The Northern Pacific opened up the Northwest, bringing population to a once-barren part of the country. With nearly fifty million acres of land grant, the railway's founders had three options: retain the land for future speculation; sell it in bulk for grazing or other development; or sell it to individuals. The third option offered the promise of settlers and freight, both of which the railroad needed to justify the expense of building a two-thousand-mile railroad from Duluth at the head of the Great Lakes to Seattle and Portland on the Pacific.

John Budd of the Great Northern was one of the more visionary rail leaders of his time. He was the driving force who obtained regulatory and court approval of the five-company merger that created the Burlington Northern (BN) in 1970. It was the only one of several railroad mergers at that time that was an unqualified success.

Credit for much of the BN merger's success goes to Budd, who determined that people were to be treated fairly when the merger took place. He established formulas for determining who would get the top jobs in each department. And he decreed that if the head of a department had been a Great Northern officer, for example, that the deputy must come from one of the other railroads.

While the existence of huge low-sulfur coal deposits in Wyoming and Montana long had been known, it was Budd and Louis W. Menk in the 1970s who foresaw the growing demand by utilities for environmentally friendly coal. They invested billions of dollars to upgrade a railroad that had been designed to haul grain into one that could handle millions of tons of Powder River Basin coal annually, moving it over longer distances than ever before.

The current generation of rail leaders must deal with the reality that unlike their predecessors, who had a virtual monopoly on the interstate movement of America's production, they represent a minority of that movement today. A vibrant trucking industry exists, one that provides flexible, reliable door-to-door service to customers who want to receive raw materials and finished goods in smaller lots than in the past.

The less regulated environment in which the railroads operate today makes it essential that railroad executives find ways to compete both with other railroads and with other forms of transportation. Unlike their forebears, who had to worry more about dealing with government regulators than with customers, executives today must find ways to differentiate their services in the marketplace.

BNSF is led today by Matthew K. Rose, who was 45 years old when this was written. He rose through a series of key management positions, from his 1993 arrival at the former BN until he was made president and chief operating officer in June 1999. The chief executive officer's title was added in December 2000, and he was elected chairman on March 21, 2002. Industry observers note that Rose is a leader who brings to the railroad a greater understanding of the need for change than more traditional up-through-the-ranks executives might be expected to have. He also brings vitality and the likelihood that he will be in his position long enough to drive the needed changes.

Rose's background is different from that of other railroad executives, most of whom have spent their entire careers in railroading and with the companies they lead. He spent years in the service-driven trucking industry and brings a strong customer-service orientation to BNSF.

Rose heads BNSF at a time when the railroad culture is changing more radically and more rapidly than at any time in the last century and a half. Historically, railroading has featured a command and control management structure and culture. Going back to a time when labor (in the form of the train crew) was taking the owners' capital out of the immediate control of the entrepreneur, the railroad always has worked with sets of very explicit rules and procedures. Penalties for violating rules were certain. Reflecting the changing times, today's rail workers are not as willing as their fathers were to accept either traditional discipline or the lifestyle demands of their jobs. Change has sometimes come slowly in the railroad industry, but the more-progressive leaders such as Rose are trying to foster a cooperative labor-management relationship that better reflects today's realities.

The railroad industry had its greatest period of expansion following the Civil War. Many railroads were planned and developed by former Civil War officers who imposed a militaristic culture on the new industry. Although that may have been acceptable a hundred years ago, it no longer is. Just as the modern military puts a premium on adaptability to change and an ability to think through the resolution of problems, railroads increasingly are encouraging employees to think and act in a more entrepreneurial manner.

Acknowledgments

WHAT STARTED OUT TO BE AN EXERCISE that would occupy my time gainfully while I eased my way into retirement has turned out to be one of the most fascinating and stimulating projects that I have undertaken.

I am deeply indebted to the Burlington Northern Santa Fe Corporation, which underwrote the expenses of researching and writing this book. More important, at no time over the nearly three years that I devoted to it did the BNSF exert any pressure or even steer me to any of the conclusions or interpretations expressed. This book represents the best thinking and analysis of which I am capable, and I am solely responsible for it.

I have been in and around the railroad industry for more than 35 years. In that time, I covered railroads as a journalist for *Business Week* magazine, the *Journal of Commerce,* and several trade magazines and newsletters. In addition, I have been privileged to have worked in the Office of the Secretary of Transportation, where I gained a firsthand view of the dedication of many government officials—and the paralysis of process that so often interferes with government's ability to play a constructive role in developing and carrying out meaningful transportation policies.

There were three other periods of my life that were intimately involved with railroads and during which I gained tremendous knowledge. I worked in the Office of Information and Public Affairs of the Association of American Railroads (AAR) and was the vice president of public affairs when the railroads were substantially deregulated. I was a vice president at the Burlington Northern during some of the periods covered in this book, and while I have relied in part on my own memory of the way things were, I also relied on outside sources. Later, I was the last managing director of corporate communications of the Southern Pacific and then worked as a consultant to the AAR, the Norfolk Southern, and the Canadian National on public policy issues.

In each of these positions, I learned much that stood me in good stead over the years and especially in preparation for writing this book. If I have insights that make this a better history, I owe it to the many dedicated people with whom I have been privileged to work over the years.

I am equally indebted to the many current and former railroad executives who freely shared their time and their experiences with me. They were extremely helpful, and I hope they will agree that I have passed along accurately their invaluable recollections and insights. There are too many of them to name individually, and besides, most of them appear in this book. I hope those who are neither named in the book nor acknowledged here will forgive me. No slight is intended.

I do want to acknowledge separately two men who helped with the book and who since have died. A. Scheffer Lang, the first federal railroad administrator, was a notorious truth-teller and conscience of the railroads in his government work and at the AAR. He became a good friend, and I was fortunate to spend time with him not long before his death. Similarly, Richard C. Grayson was one of the finest executives I ever met and a superb human being to work for. He held his subordinates accountable but provided the tools that made it easy to be accountable. He was quite ill when I last talked with him, and when he died while I still was writing, I realized how fortunate I was to have had that opportunity.

Along the way, I came to appreciate anew what I learned years ago—that railroaders are some of the most sincere and dedicated people in our society. I can think of no group I would rather rely on in an emergency than the people who keep America's railroads in operation. They truly live to the code of keeping the trains on the move and reserve their competitive battles within their organizations and between railroads for other times.

Special thanks go to Richard A. Russack, BNSF vice president of corporate relations, who helped immeasurably. He made resources available and was a "glinty-eyed" first reader of each part of this book. Lynda McCreery, administrative coordinator of BNSF's corporate relations department, was the ever-cheerful, efficient coordinator of the many deadlines and revisions.

Also on the BNSF staff, Kristen Rabe helped coordinate substantive reviews by various experts to ensure accuracy throughout the book, and Darren Natvig quickly and accurately transcribed the many oral history interviews and enabled me to draw on the thinking of so many people who lived the BNSF story.

Last, but certainly not least, I want to acknowledge Donna Kaufman, my wife, who put up with me for the past three years and the many times I started a conversation with "I came across something really interesting today." She was both patient and supportive.

LAWRENCE H (LARRY) KAUFMAN
Golden, Colorado
March 16, 2005

1

Nineteenth-Century Dot-coms

The railroad made America a continental nation and an economic force of immense potential. It changed everything. Transportation advances have that power.

COLIN G. CAMPBELL, president, CEO, and chairman of Colonial Williamsburg Foundation, 2003

HINDSIGHT CAN BE VERY CONVENIENT. With the ability to look backward it may be easier to understand how history repeats itself, and a case can be made that the explosive growth of high-tech dot-com and telecommunications companies in the late 1990s was quite similar to railroad growth and development in the 19th century. Both periods were marked by overbuilding, unconstrained greed, and eventual collapse of many, but it was also a time when great companies that started with little more than an entrepreneur's dream grew and extended their roots deep into the soil of U.S. business.

The financial excesses that marked railroad building were not unlike the tulip mania that beset Holland in the seventeenth century. In the Dutch tulip mania, during an era of very popular landscaped gardens, tulip bulbs were perceived more as investments than as beautiful decorations. Banks, newly minted capitalists, and even ordinary people had to get in on the new investment, the value of which seemed to go only one way—up—but soon collapsed, resulting in personal and corporate bankruptcies and the financial ruin of entire economies. Tulip mania was a classic example of the "greater fool" theory at work—the assumption that no matter how much an investor pays, there always will be a greater fool who will pay more.

Like tulip promoters, railroad promoters in the 19th century often relied on the greater fool theory when it came to raising capital. And in the crashes of 1873 and 1891, many people were wiped out financially, just as Dutch investors had been two centuries earlier.

In the years just before and just after the Civil War, developers rushed to build as much railroad infrastructure as they could, ignoring the fact that, cumulatively, they were building more capacity than could be absorbed either by the available business or by the business likely to be available. The rapid expansion and attempts to operate railroads that did not have enough traffic to support the infrastructure were followed by financial panic and sharp stock market decline—particularly in 1873. Railroads were such a significant sector of the economy in the latter half of the nineteenth century that a railroad collapse could trigger a national financial crisis.

The Civil War inadvertently provided an additional stimulus for construction of western railroads. Following the war's end, thousands of soldiers and officers flooded the western states and territories, looking for gainful employment. Many with engineering backgrounds became the builders and managers of railroads, and hundreds of them were memorialized in the names of towns and other locations.

The development of other methods of moving goods and people has lessened the impact of railroads on the U.S. economy in the 21st century, but the growing economy and the need to move even more goods than ever before mean that railroads still are essential to the health of the entire economy. And that is why the story of that interconnection is worth telling, from the earliest days of the railroad industry to the present time.

THE WEST IS NOT THE EAST

BNSF Railway Company is essentially a western railroad. Although railroad development in the eastern and western United States had some similarities, there was one significant difference. Railroads in the East connected existing centers of population, no matter how small they may have been. Economic activity and commercial opportunities existed before the railroad arrived. In fact, the railroads frequently supplanted existing canal and road transportation of people and goods.

Early eastern railroads were sponsored by ports along the eastern

General Herman Haupt: From Gettysburg to the Northern Pacific

The Civil War was the first conflict in which railroads played a significant role. General Herman Haupt, a West Point graduate known for being irascible, was in charge of the U.S. military railroads.

The Union had an interconnected railway system and was able to use railroads to great advantage, moving troops and supplies between various battles and removing the wounded to rear areas. The Confederacy, on the other hand, had less than 10,000 miles of railroad within its boundaries, and few of its lines were connected to one other.

Union commanders may have had rail resources, but they didn't necessarily appreciate what they had. Various generals "would stop trains and try to reassign them to specific units," writes Steven Ditmeyer, who holds the Department of Transportation faculty chair at the Industrial College of the Armed Forces. "Haupt accused them of causing train delays on the Orange and Alexandria Railroad that kept 10,000 Union troops out of the Second Battle of Bull Run in August 1862."

The Gettysburg battle in 1863 was about railroads. General Robert E. Lee led his army of northern Virginia into Maryland and Pennsylvania, intending to destroy rail facilities and to isolate the cities of Washington, Baltimore, Wilmington, and Philadelphia from agricultural and manufactured goods coming from the West.

Haupt, whose residence at Gettysburg was the site of one of General James Longstreet's artillery batteries on Seminary Ridge, played a major role in the battle. Knowing the area well, he sent messages to Union general George Meade, informing him of Lee's movements and that Lee was concentrating his troops at Gettysburg. Haupt commandeered locomotives, as well as freight, passenger, and baggage cars and crews, from the railroads serving Baltimore.

Haupt organized convoys of trains headed west from Baltimore to Westminster, Maryland, the rail-served point closest to Gettysburg. As soon as quartermaster troops unloaded the trains, they were backed down the single-track Western Maryland Railroad line to Baltimore. Another convoy of preloaded trains would proceed west while the original train was reloaded. Thus Haupt achieved a quantum increase in capacity. Meanwhile, General Adna Anderson and his 400-man Railroad Construction Corps—which consisted largely of former slaves—were ordered to move from Alexandria, Virginia, to Baltimore, where they began construction of the Northern Central Railroad and the Gettysburg Railroad so that trains could run directly to Gettysburg.

By July 3, the third day of fighting at Gettysburg, some 1,500 tons of cargo were moved to Westminster, and 2,000 wounded soldiers were brought out to hospitals in Baltimore. Haupt's plan worked perfectly, Ditmeyer writes. The first trains ran directly to Gettysburg on July 4, the day after the battle ended. Historian George Edgar Turner noted: "It is farther from Baltimore to Gettysburg than from Richmond to Fredericksburg, yet in four days during the heat of desperate battle, Haupt accomplished for Meade what the Confederate organization could not do for Lee in four months of quiet." Haupt urged Meade to pursue the retreating Lee, using the railroads to move blocking forces into the Shenandoah Valley, but the decision was made that the troops needed rest.

After the war, Haupt had a successful career in railroading and engineering. He became general manager of the Northern Pacific in the mid-1880s.

seaboard, each determined to protect its position as a trading center by making it easier for inland points to send and receive goods through the port. If one port gained a major economic edge, it was seen by others as a threat to their prosperity. Thus the Baltimore and Ohio Railroad (B&O) was financed by a public-private partnership of city bonds and private investment to connect growing communities beyond the Appalachian Mountains with the great port of Baltimore. Philadelphia interests sponsored the Pennsylvania Railroad in competition with the B&O. To connect their port with the Great Lakes to the west, New York financiers built several railroads that eventually became the New York Central.

Railroads in the West, however, had no indigenous population to serve. They were the driving force of economic development, and their construction is inextricably intertwined with western history. The West was a vast, undeveloped—and often uncharted—region. There were no cities that needed to protect their economic interests. Once travelers passed Chicago and St. Louis, there were no cities at all until they reached San Francisco on the Pacific coast.

But there was little money in the West. The unpopulated region had to rely on outside capital—frequently European—in developing its infrastructure. Would-be railroad developers became experts at convincing potential investors that western railroad projects would bring great riches to backers. Such developers became equally adept at securing public assistance—usually through grants of land from the federal government.

Prior to 1850, all federal assistance for transportation development had gone to roads and canals. With the exception of Illinois, Missouri, and Indiana, which then were considered western, the West consisted of territories under direct control of the federal government. Beginning in 1850, Congress sought to stimulate western railroad expansion by conveying public lands to the states as they were admitted to the Union, with the granted lands to be conveyed to railroad companies. Later the federal land grants were made directly to the railroad corporations. Once the land was certified— usually upon verification that the conditions of the grant had been met—the railroad was free to sell or mortgage the property. Proceeds could be used to repay loans taken to construct the railroad or to pay for further construction.

The government wasn't quite as generous as many history textbooks would have students believe. The United States doubled the usual price of $1.25 an acre on the alternate sections it retained within the grants, which meant that the U.S. Treasury broke even on the grants. Prior to the coming of the railroad, there were few if any takers at the $1.25 price, so the government proved itself a prudent investor by fostering a means of increasing the value of public lands.

The government also reserved the right to move mail, troops, and government property over the facilities built with land grants. Although the right originally was to be at no charge, in practice the government paid a reduced rate. According to railroad historian Frank N. Wilner in *Railroad Land Grants: Paid For in Full*, troops and government freight were to be moved at no more than 50 percent of established rates, and mail at 80 percent of established rates.

Railroads willingly accepted the tariff reduction requirement, which may suggest the extent of profit margins that existed. Two other aspects of the cost of land grants should be noted. Only about 8 percent of the rail system was built with the aid of land grants, and the competitive nature of the business meant that even railroads that received no land grants were effectively forced to extend the same discounts voluntarily if they wanted the business of carrying troops, mail, and other government property.

In 1940, Congress commissioned a study of the rate reductions that railroads provided in exchange for the land grants; the study determined that the value of the land grants had been paid 10 times over in reduced-price transportation the government had received. The requirement for reduced rates for freight and mail was rescinded by the Transportation Act of 1940. The requirement for reduced rates for troops and military supplies remained in place throughout World War II—when railroads accounted for more than 90 percent of war-related transportation—until 1946, when the railroads finally were relieved of the last of the obligation to supply reduced-price transportation.

MANIFEST DESTINY: PRESSURE FOR A TRANSCONTINENTAL RAILROAD

Railroads had first developed in the 1840s across the East; by the early 1850s, population in the midwestern territories was growing rapidly and people were clamoring for statehood. Texas had been annexed in 1845, and Oregon in 1846. Gold was discovered in California in 1848, triggering the great gold rush. The need for improved transportation across the vast continent was not in dispute.

The only way for easterners to join the search for gold near Sacramento was to make the long sea voyage around Cape Horn at the southern tip of South America. Or, after a dangerous, long journey by boat to Panama, it was necessary for the weary traveler to begin crossing the tropical disease-ridden isthmus and then sail up the Pacific coast. A third option was the equally long and dangerous trip by stagecoach or wagon across the prairies through Indian country and over the Rocky Mountains and then the Sierras. Pressure began to build for a railroad to connect the East with the West.

The demand for new transportation options was growing, and the railroad was seen as the solution, but the national debate over slavery intruded into the selection of the route. Would it go through slave or free territory? In an attempt to maintain the integrity of the surveys, U.S. secretary of war Jefferson Davis chose four Northerners and one Southern officer to lead the five teams dispatched to survey transcontinental rail routes. Congressmen lined up in geographic fashion, and the result was predictable—a stalemate that was not broken until the Civil War ended.

Even before the war was over, President Abraham Lincoln signed legislation in 1862 and 1864, chartering two transcontinental routes and providing land grants to help finance the construction of the Overland Route between Omaha, Nebraska, and Sacramento, California, and the northernmost route just south of the Canadian border between the Great Lakes and Puget Sound. Two companies, the Central Pacific (CP) and the Union Pacific (UP), began construction of the first transcontinental railroad over what became known as the Overland Route, connecting Omaha with Sacramento. As an inducement to build into the wilderness, each company was to be awarded cash and alternate sections of land on either side of the right-of-way. The railroad that progressed the fastest would end up with the most land. The backers would be repaid their initial investment by the proceeds of land sales. The UP and the CP met in 1869 at Promontory, Utah. It would be 14 years before the second transcontinental route was completed.

Less grandiose railroad ventures continued to spring up across the West. The humble start of construction of the railroads that were to become the BNSF Railway wasn't nearly as dramatic as the race between the Central Pacific and the Union Pacific to be the first across the country.

Few, if any, of the principal developers of the several railroads that eventually were joined into what today is the BNSF Railway believed they were embarking on the creation of a vast system that would stretch from the Great Lakes and Pensacola, Florida, in the East to Seattle and San Diego in the West. It took nearly a century and a half, numerous failures, and many mergers to accomplish that feat.

While a few railroad pioneers, like Cyrus K. Holliday of the Santa Fe, thought in terms of a transcontinental railroad, for the most part their ambitions were more limited. Most railroad promoters simply wanted to connect their people and goods to larger, dominant markets in order to make them and themselves more prosperous.

THE BURLINGTON ROUTE

The Aurora Branch, the first of today's BNSF railroads, was chartered in 1849 to connect the village of Aurora, Illinois, with the line of the Galena and Chicago Union Railroad so that people and goods from Aurora could more easily reach the already large and still-growing Chicago. Once in Chicago, people could travel and goods could be shipped to eastern points that already were connected to Chicago by rail.

The charter from the State of Illinois gave the Aurora Branch the right of eminent domain—the legal right to take private property from its owners for use by the railroad. The political midwife in the creation of the Aurora Branch was Lorenzo D. Brady, a resident of Aurora and an influential member of the Illinois legislature. His bill to charter the Aurora Branch Railroad Company became law in little more than two weeks early in 1849. Perhaps with prescience, the charter authorized the new railroad to unite with any other railroad and to construct any lines necessary to connect with other railroads.

And connect they did. The Aurora Branch began to merge with nearby railroads almost as soon as it began operations. Through the absorption of many small railroads, by the end of the 19th century the Aurora Branch morphed from a 12-mile farm-to-market railroad into the Chicago, Burlington, and Quincy Railroad, a major midwestern system that stretched from Chicago to Minnesota's Twin Cities, westward to Denver and as far as Billings, Montana, and south to Texas. Its operations covered 14 states.

Headed by president Stephen F. Gale, a well-known Chicago businessman and resident of Aurora, the Aurora Branch ran its first train on September 2, 1850. It traveled to Turner Junction on the Galena and Chicago Union, using a borrowed locomotive because neither the engine nor the cars purchased in the East had yet arrived.

Gale's first attempt to expand the little railroad failed when the directors of the Galena and Chicago Union narrowly rejected a proposal to combine the two companies. The Aurora Branch proceeded to expand on its own by laying more track. Unlike the management of so many railroads of the time, the Aurora Branch directors insisted that cash from stock subscriptions be in hand before construction occurred; from its earliest days, the Burlington Route was marked by fiscal prudence.

The arrival in Chicago of railroads from the East made it clear that railroad lines soon would stretch throughout Illinois, which produced huge quantities of agricultural and forest products to send east. By early 1851, the Illinois legislature had passed 28 bills authorizing or amending charters of railroads in the state. One that was to be significant for the future Burlington Route was the Chicago and Rock Island Railroad, which had authority to build between its two namesakes. Another was the Illinois Central, chartered to build a line from Cairo, at the junction of the Ohio and Mississippi Rivers, north to Galena and with a branch from Centralia to Chicago. Each was backed by the promoters of one of the two eastern systems then approaching Chicago.

The Aurora Branch grew through expanding connections with easterners building the Michigan Central Railroad. Its name changed as it grew. The Hannibal and St. Joseph Railroad, chartered in 1847, came under Aurora Branch control in 1854, and the railroad was renamed the Chicago and Aurora Railroad.

Rivalries played a significant role. A syndicate of wealthy Bostonians and other New Englanders, headed by Boston merchant John Murray Forbes, for example, provided the capital to buy out the state's interest in the Michigan Central and to complete a rail line between Detroit and Chicago. The Michigan Central was competing with the Michigan Southern, which also was building toward Chicago from eastern termini at Monroe, Michigan, and Toledo, Ohio. The two Michigan lines reached Chicago just one day apart in 1852. Railroad promoters already were lining up so-called friendly connections to ensure steady flows of freight and passengers for their companies.

The Forbes interests, as the New Englanders were known, anticipated a push west of Chicago and the need for friendly connections that would guarantee their railroad freight business to and from the West. They already had purchased some securities of the tiny Aurora Branch. With its rights over the Galena and Chicago Union, the Aurora Branch made a more attractive partner than its size otherwise would have dictated. The Forbes group elected two of its members to the Aurora Branch board of directors. The investor group was to dominate the railroad for many years, and the Burlington Route was led by groups rather than individuals for much of its early history.

The need for alliances and friendly connections was obvious to the early western railroad developers. By combining the Aurora Branch and the Central Military Tract Railroad Company, a railroad could be built from Chicago through Galesburg all the way across Illinois to Burlington on the Mississippi River, providing the Michigan Central interests with a guaranteed and steady flow of goods to their system from much of central Illinois. It also provided the Burlington Route with an early opportunity that it seized to extend its lines farther west beyond the Mississippi.

With interlocking investments, to say nothing of interlocking directors, other Illinois railroads were folded into the burgeoning system. In 1854 the Chicago and Aurora was renamed the Chicago, Burlington, and Quincy (CB&Q), signifying its passing through rich farmland and connecting the two largest cities in Illinois—Chicago and Aurora—with the principal Illinois community on the Mississippi. Meanwhile, the Forbes interests were financing construction of the Hannibal and St. Joseph across Missouri and the Burlington and Missouri River Railroad (B&M) across Iowa. Although separate corporations, they were viewed as sisters of the CB&Q. The Burlington and Missouri River had a planned terminus at Council Bluffs, Iowa. Unknown to the promoters at the time, this terminus would make the Burlington Route the principal connection to the East for the yet-to-be-started Union Pacific, which would build westward from Omaha, across the Missouri River from Council Bluffs.

Forbes persuaded Charles Russell Lowell—nephew of the distinguished poet James Russell Lowell and the person in charge of the B&M—to hire his 18-year-old cousin Charles Elliott Perkins as his assistant. Perkins, who was working in Cincinnati as an apprentice at a wholesale produce business, quickly took to the railroad business. He eventually would become president and one of the most important leaders of the Burlington Route in the late 19th century.

Even in the 19th century, one of the great truths of railroading was obvious: railroads needed large volumes of traffic to generate sufficient revenue to cover the fixed costs. That, perhaps more than any other factor, drove the surviving railroads continually to extend their lines into new territories and to acquire connecting railroads that could provide them with the needed volume.

As the railroads built westward, they acquired title to several hundred thousand acres of federal public land that had been transferred to the states. Railroads increased their wealth from the sale or mortgage of prime land. They also gained new shipping revenue as Iowa and Missouri settlers produced large crops of corn and grains that had to be moved back East.

Extensions came steadily in the years after the Civil War. The CB&Q or allies that eventually were included in its system reached Omaha in 1871, Denver in 1882, St. Paul in 1886, and St. Louis and Billings, Montana, in 1894. Expansion to the south came more slowly, but Burlington Route subsidiaries reached Texas and the Gulf of Mexico soon after the turn of the century.

Perkins was elected a vice president of the CB&Q in 1875, and although the company was headquartered in Chicago, he chose to remain in Burlington, where he had sunk family and personal roots. By remaining out of Chicago, Perkins managed to avoid getting bogged down in corporate minutiae and was able to focus on the truly significant issues that made it to his desk.

The Burlington Route and its principal competitors—the Rock Island and the North Western, which also stretched from Chicago to the Mississippi—formed a pool that was intended to protect all three railroads from the worst effects of unbridled competition. Earnings were to be divided according to a formula. Begun in 1870, the pool lasted until 1884. The Interstate Commerce Act—the first antitrust law—was passed by Congress in 1887 and, among other things, outlawed the by then common practice of pooling. Once one becomes ensnared in the tentacles of government, it is difficult to escape. Pooling still must be approved by federal regulators.

Perkins could take a hard-line when it came to attempts of workers to unionize. When a series of strikes threatened to paralyze railroads, Robert Harris, Burlington's Chicago-based president, kept the trains running and offered to discuss their grievances with the striking men. Out on the western end of the Burlington system, in an example of insubordination, Perkins shut down the Burlington and Missouri in Iowa, and the strike collapsed in three days. "We made no concession of any kind. . . . Anything like vacillation and unsteadiness in dealing with these men is fatal," Perkins later wrote in a letter to Forbes. Perkins opposed paternalism and believed that if an employer gave an employee something for nothing, the employee would come to view it as a right.

Reflecting the business standards of the late 19th century, Perkins opposed paying pensions to the men and viewed unions as a precursor to socialism. He believed in treating employees with basic fairness, and many of his management principles have become standards for railroads and other businesses a century later.

By the end of 1881, just three months after Perkins became president of the Burlington, the railroad had 2,924 miles of line in operation. The CB&Q was about to go through its greatest period of expansion. Although they had the same ownership, the CB&Q and the B&M had operated as separate though affiliated companies. When the B&M finally was acquired, it became the Burlington's Lines West. Perkins served as the operator, and Forbes was the capitalist who provided the money. When Perkins retired in 1901, the Burlington Route had 7,911 miles of railroad in operation.

Not long before his death in 1907, Perkins identified a fundamental problem with government regulation of railroads—rate-making based on capital values without regard to market realities. Richard C. Overton, in *Perkins/Budd: Railway Statesmen of the Burlington,* quotes Perkins:

> That shining light of Harvard University, Professor Ripley, who calls himself a political economist, has been lecturing to a convention of bankers on this subject (of overcapital-

ization) and . . . he thinks it important to determine the value, as he calls it, of the railroads, as a basis for rate-making. This is putting the cart before the horse with a vengeance, because the value of a railroad depends on the rates it can get, and not the rates on the value. I suppose what Professor Ripley had in mind was cost rather than value, but cost is no more a measure of rates than value, since a railroad over the Allegheny Mountains cannot collect higher rates between Chicago and New York than are charged and collected by a railroad running along the lake shore and through the valley of the Mohawk.

The issue would not be resolved until passage of the Staggers Rail Act in 1980.

THE GREAT NORTHERN RAILWAY

James J. Hill didn't even start the railroad that became the Great Northern Railway, but he was part of a syndicate that bought the nearly moribund St. Paul and Pacific Railroad in 1878, some 17 years after construction had begun. An impoverished but ambitious Canadian immigrant who moved to St. Paul, Minnesota, in 1856 at the age of 17, Hill quickly demonstrated an aptitude for business. He built a reputation for integrity and business acumen as a warehouseman and commission agent for the Mississippi River steamboats that served St. Paul and the merchants and grain growers to the west of St. Paul. Although Hill had a relatively short period of formal education at Rockwood Academy, a Quaker school in his hometown of Guelph, Upper Canada, he demonstrated great intelligence from the start of his business career. He credited his mentor, William Wetherald, for helping develop his ease of communication, his facility with numbers, and his discipline with facts. Before arriving in St. Paul, the teenage Hill had visited several eastern and southern cities, and his decision to settle at St. Paul was the result of methodical decision making.

His early involvement with railroads was as a customer when he relied on railroads to bring coal to St. Paul from Chicago for his new retail coal business. Hill planned to deal in volume by supplying the largest customer in St. Paul, the gas company. He pressed for lower prices for lesser-quality coal, figuring that if he expanded the customer

Charles Elliott Perkins

Charles Elliott Perkins provides considerable insight into his character and temperament through his writings. Considering that he was a 19th-century executive, some of his comments read as though they could have been written just yesterday. For example, on day-to-day management, he wrote: "Keep as much as possible out of petty everyday details. Let stated reports be made to your adjutants, if you choose, but do not take it upon yourself to see them all. So long as the machine works smoothly, you should be a looker-on."

Perkins was an outspoken advocate of laissez-faire economics but also had a streak of noblesse oblige that made him a mixture of consideration and firmness at the same time. While supporting the concept that business leaders should be free to run their enterprises in a manner that most rewarded the owners, he believed, on the other hand, that employees should be treated with respect. Employee loyalty and zeal could be engendered by paying a reasonable return for a man's labor and providing the prospect of future improvement. He believed that one way to obtain the loyalty of the men was through the proper selection of officers and supervisors who were to be in authority over others.

An example of the dichotomy in Perkins's approach to labor relations is his decision not to fund the YMCA when it wished to establish libraries and reading rooms for the men at various locations along the railroad. He indicated a willingness, though, to pay premiums to men who took extra risks or performed an extraordinary amount of work for the company. Perkins defended extending discounted or free transportation when it was clearly in the company's interest, but he disapproved doing so for charitable purposes. That, he believed, was giving away the owner's property without having been charged with determining the owner's charitable intent.

One of Perkins's principles of management was to maintain clear channels of responsibility in order to minimize the gap between decision making and execution. This proved to be a sound concept as the railroad grew in size. Organizationally, he created a system not unlike that of railroads today. Strategy was determined at headquarters, while tactics were carried out in the field. Broad grants of autonomy were given to officials in the field, but rates and motive power were to be the same throughout the system. Superintendents and general superintendents, the highest officers in the field, were expected to seek direction and advice from vice presidents and general managers at headquarters—and then to use their own judgment in carrying out the stated objectives.

Perkins also was an early believer in pushing decision making to the lowest practicable level. One of his "rules" was never to do yourself what can be done sufficiently well by a subordinate. Along with that rule, he enunciated that a supervisor should trust those under him and allow them to work out problems on their own; otherwise they would not learn to depend on themselves.

A prolific writer of memoranda, Perkins left a great legacy of his thinking not only about how employees should be treated but also about economic issues. He had little use or respect for academics and politicians who tried to impose their theories on the people who had the responsibility for running an enterprise, and he frequently wrote derisively about their efforts. Pooling of railroad earnings was made illegal "on the theory that without pools railroads will fight each other for the benefit of the shippers," he noted. He did not believe that would happen but instead believed that railroads would consolidate. "It is a fortunate circumstance," he wrote, "that the half-baked college professors and so-called political economists cannot change the laws of nature; at the present day they do not hesitate to meddle and interfere with them, and would, no doubt, in their superior wisdom, change them if they could."

base, he could grow the market that much faster. Prior to Hill's entry into coal merchandising, the retailers were generally passive, relying on producers to maintain inventory and assume market risks. Hill, on the other hand, offered to take larger quantities than the producers were used to selling and to accept entrepreneurial risk. He demanded lower prices and offered an expanded market in exchange. "We do not think it right that we should be obliged to pay the same rate on 500 or 1,000 tons as any blacksmith has to pay on three tons," he wrote the general superintendent of the Milwaukee Railroad.

When railroads began to penetrate the lands west of the Mississippi, Hill expanded his business to include grain dealing and shipping from the rich agricultural lands of the Red River Valley. Just as railroads were pushing westward across Iowa, Missouri, and Kansas to the south, there was a desire to extend the commercial reach of the Twin Cities and of Duluth, on Lake Superior, across Minnesota toward the Red River Valley on the eastern edge of Dakota Territory. Construction of the St. Paul and Pacific Railroad Company, which later was to become the foundation of Hill's railroad empire, began during the Civil War—in 1862—backed by a state charter and a land grant. Minnesota had granted charters for railroad construction as early as 1853, but no railroad had managed to survive financial weakness; the St. Paul and Pacific was the first to operate in the state.

Hill's earliest recorded involvement with the St. Paul and Pacific, which extended from St. Paul to Dakota Territory, was in 1866. At that time, the young commission agent and the railroad announced that they would transfer freight between riverboats and the railroad free of the usual transfer charge. Hill continued to learn about railroads during the years that he was building his grain merchant business and serving as agent for another early railroad. He finally became a railroad owner when he and three associates acquired the bankrupt St. Paul and Pacific in 1878. Hill and his associates—Donald Alexander Smith, Norman Wolfred Kittson, and George Stephen—initially intended to push the railroad's tracks across Minnesota and then north through the Red River Valley to Winnipeg, Manitoba. Over the next 15 years, "the associates," as his syndicate became known and liked to refer to itself, acquired or merged numerous small railroads throughout the region. Changing their ambitions, direction, and collective name to Great Northern Railway, the Hill group managed to complete a transcontinental line in 1893, with the final burst of construction across the northern plains taking just three years.

Hill's feat was all the more impressive because the Great Northern (GN) was built without the assistance of federal land grants that were available to help finance other western railroads, although several of its predecessors did receive valuable state-owned acreage. The lack of public assistance was a blessing in disguise. Hill needed to spend considerable time in the East, securing financing for each construction phase. Forced to advance methodically, the Great Northern Railway never was overbuilt, and it remained profitable throughout its history. Prudent management was instilled early as a way of life at the GN.

The St. Paul and Pacific and the Northern Pacific (NP), which was chartered to build a transcontinental railroad between Duluth and Puget Sound, were great rivals from their earliest days, each company doing everything in its power to dominate rail transportation in central Minnesota. They fought over land grants and property rights in the courts, and they battled over route alignments.

Financial weakness on the part of both companies dictated that they compromise. Rather than build a competing parallel line from St. Paul to St. Cloud and Sauk Rapids along the west bank of the Mississippi River as it had planned, the Northern Pacific agreed late in 1878 to accept trackage rights—the right to operate its trains over the St. Paul and Pacific tracks—for 99 years. The NP—as its president, Frederick Billings, insisted—needed every penny to build its line to the Pacific, and the compromise would save money while simultaneously providing it with the market access it sought.

The associates in 1879 formed the St. Paul, Minneapolis, and Manitoba Railway Company—known simply as the Manitoba—absorbing the former St. Paul and Pacific properties. Stephen was elected president, and Kittson vice president. Hill, the only one of the associates with any transportation experience, was named general manager. His interests, however, went beyond the Manitoba. He served on the board of directors of the Canadian Pacific Railway (CP), and his associate Stephen won the contract from the Canadian government to build the CP west from the Great Lakes to the Pacific Ocean. The railroad adopted the route Hill had recommended as shortest and best, and Hill reminded the engineers that the directors wanted the line to be no closer to the U.S. border than 100 miles.

In 1882, Hill was named president of the Manitoba. His ambition until then had been to build a railroad into Canada to gain access to the vast grain production of the prairie provinces and to connect with the Canadian Pacific. His earliest vision of a transcontinental empire involved connecting the Manitoba with the Canadian Pacific. Frictions between the interests of the Manitoba and the CP, however, led to Hill's resignation from the board of the Canadian company, and from that point on he devoted his energies to expanding the Manitoba.

With a foothold in Dakota Territory by the end of 1879, the Manitoba legally could expand westward on the U.S. side of the border with Canada. Despite the negotiated truce, the rivalry with the Northern Pacific continued. Each strategic move by one triggered a response by the other. When the NP backed a north-south venture on the west bank of the Red River of the North, the Manitoba built farther into Dakota Territory.

The Manitoba, however, wasn't focused only on the Northern Pacific. It also wanted to preclude expansion of the Milwaukee Road, which already was in southern Minnesota, into Dakota Territory. The early railroad pioneers thought nothing of being opponents one day or in one place and allies on another day and in another place.

Back in Minnesota, the Manitoba wanted stronger connections to Duluth, and Hill negotiated to acquire the St. Paul and Duluth

Russell Sage

A New Yorker Becomes a Western Robber Baron

The Minnesota and Pacific Railroad (M&P) was a predecessor of the St. Paul and Pacific, but its brief tenure—during which it never ran a train—was marked by scandal. One of its promoters was Russell Sage, a transplanted New Yorker who honed his skills at railroad promotion in Wisconsin, enriching himself with several railroads that were to become the Chicago, Milwaukee, St. Paul, and Pacific Railroad Company. Bribing state senators, assemblymen, state officers, newspaper editors, and other influentials, Sage had issued what later became known as "corruption bonds" in exchange for land grants and railroad charters. Although he was neither the first nor the only so-called robber baron, Sage certainly typified the breed.

There were no consumer or investor protection laws at the time. There was no Securities and Exchange Commission to protect investors from rapacious promoters, and no antitrust laws to moderate corporate behavior. Though today their business practices seem to have been reprehensible, the robber barons mostly reflected the standards of the time. Their behavior was not much different from that of their entrepreneurial counterparts in other industries.

Sage later became most famous—or infamous—for his involvement with the notorious Jay Gould in taking over and bankrupting the Union Pacific. His sojourn in Minnesota, however, didn't hurt him financially, although it contributed nothing to transportation in the state. The Minnesota and Pacific was touted as a road that would extend to the Pacific. A 14-million-acre state grant of prime timber- and farmland was made available.

The M&P plunged into bankruptcy even before it was built or ran its first train, and its assets were placed in a new Sage-organized company, the St. Paul and Pacific. Sage suffered not a bit. He severed 30,000 acres of the M&P land grant and treated them as personal holdings. It took the state until 1905 to retrieve the land, and only after Sage had forced the farmers to buy him out or leave the land.

(originally the Lake Superior and Mississippi, which had been owned by the NP). Hill's motivation in joining the partnership was to keep the Milwaukee from gaining complete control of the St. Paul–Duluth line.

The commercial warfare served neither railroad well. Construction of competing lines diluted the traffic base of each, and the NP was financially distressed by the expensive effort to complete its line to the Pacific coast, which was accomplished in 1883.

Like rail developers to the south, Hill too was constantly involved in maneuvers to preserve commercial territories for his railroad. When Minneapolis milling interests built a line from Minneapolis to Sault Ste. Marie, Michigan, to carry their flour to the East, Hill saw the Soo Line as the new railroad was known, as an annoyance if not a serious threat. He understood that it was more economical to ship wheat, and to ship it through Duluth, than to ship milled flour. Besides, the Minneapolis interests were putting themselves into direct competition with flour millers in Buffalo, New York. The millers were happy to purchase their wheat from Minnesota and have it shipped to Buffalo, where they could convert it to flour. The Manitoba had a more efficient route, and Hill was confident that with himself and economics on the same side, the Soo could not prevail.

The Burlington Route became an early ally of James J. Hill's Great Northern. Forced to compete with the Chicago, Milwaukee, and St. Paul (later to be the Chicago, Milwaukee, St. Paul, and Pacific) and the Chicago and North Western, which also ran between Chicago and the Twin Cities, Hill determined that the Manitoba needed the protection of a friendly connection to Chicago, especially if it was to fend off the expected westward movements of the two older Chicago-based railroads into territory that he considered his. The more he researched the possible alliances and looked into the managements involved, the more he determined that the Burlington would make an excellent connector. Hill also recognized that he would have to broaden the equity ownership of the Manitoba, but he wanted investors who would hold the stock and not dump it on the market every time it gained a few points. The Forbes syndicate, which had demonstrated that it was in railroading for the long haul, matched his criteria.

Hill and the Forbes interests were a natural fit. Both operated with higher levels of integrity than were common in those times. Hill had imposed rules on his growing company that strictly prohibited employees from using information gained through their employment for their own advantage. Each group could satisfy the other's needs. Forbes wanted an alliance that would carry his rail empire into the Northwest. Since 1882, Boston investors who controlled the CB&Q were interested in building a line between Chicago and St. Paul. They wanted more than the local traffic, however, and were seeking a friendly connection for long-haul traffic. CB&Q president Perkins inspected both the Manitoba and the NP in 1883, and pronounced the Manitoba to be the preferable connection. In *James J. Hill and the Opening of the Northwest,* the late Albro Martin quotes a Perkins memo to Forbes: "[The Manitoba road was] probably the snuggest and best of the properties lying beyond St. Paul, [with] every mile of it in the best kind of wheat country."

Hill saw the Boston investors as good allies. From his perspective, a relationship with the CB&Q provided a friendly connection to Chicago and strengthened the Manitoba in its rivalry with other, less friendly Chicago-based railroads like the Milwaukee, which already extended west of St. Paul, or the Chicago and North Western. The alliance was consummated by the Boston investors' acquisition of an equity interest in the Manitoba in 1885.

The Manitoba, reacting to continued inroads by the Northern Pacific into its Red River Valley territory, continued to expand westward. In 1885, Hill privately took a financial position in three related Montana companies with ventures in mining, land, and railroading. The Montana Central Railroad was to connect Great Falls with Helena and Butte.

Hill acted boldly to forestall the Northern Pacific and the Union Pacific, which already were operating in Montana Territory. The Manitoba began building west from Devil's Lake, Dakota Territory, toward a junction at Great Falls with the Montana Central, which had been acquired. By the end of 1887, Hill's construction gangs had built 643 miles of railroad in just seven and a half months and had connected Minot in Dakota Territory with Helena. The Manitoba at the same time continued to expand its system in Minnesota and Dakota Territory, generating more grain traffic as it completed branch lines and penetrated new growing areas.

Despite its vast land grants, the Northern Pacific never prospered as a railroad, and Hill couldn't comprehend why its management did some of the things it did. Albro Martin, in his biography of Hill, wrote:

> Hill could never understand the men who ran the Northern
> Pacific. They were constantly biting off more than they
> could chew, as their badly engineered, poorly managed line
> to the Coast demonstrated. Chronically short of funds,
> when they did get their hands on a substantial sum of

James J. Hill

The Empire Builder

A tribute to Hill exists today in the Chicago-Seattle passenger train known as the Empire Builder, which operates over the tracks of the BNSF. Within 10 years of migrating to the United States, Hill was a rising young businessman with varied business interests in transportation and fuel.

When he and his associates took over the bankrupt St. Paul and Pacific Railroad in 1878, Hill embarked on what he called his "great adventure." They first completed a connection north from the Red River Valley of eastern North Dakota and western Minnesota to Winnipeg in Manitoba, then a boomtown. By 1893, Hill had extended what had become the Great Northern across the Northwest to Seattle.

Hill's Great Northern was the first transcontinental railroad built entirely without land grants. Even though it was completed on the eve of the worst depression in the United States to that time, it had been conservatively financed, and because it never was overbuilt, it was the only northern transcontinental and one of the few railroads anywhere to avoid bankruptcy.

Proving that "empire builder" was an appropriate sobriquet, Hill bought the bankrupt Northern Pacific and then, in collaboration with New York financier J. P. Morgan, acquired the Burlington Railroad. In doing so, he simultaneously blocked the expansion plans of E. H. Harriman, who had taken over the bankrupt Union Pacific and, like Hill, considered the Pacific Northwest as "his" region.

Hill attempted to combine his railroad empire into a single entity but was thwarted by President Theodore Roosevelt and his famed trustbusters. It was to be another 70 years before the Great Northern, the Northern Pacific, the Chicago, Burlington, and Quincy, and two other railroads were merged into the Burlington Northern.

Though Hill, who admitted to having Napoleonic ambition, is memorialized not by his own name but as "Empire Builder," many of the men who built the western railroads are memorialized in numerous communities along the rail lines that today bear their names. Crookston, Minot, Billings—all were railroad financiers or engineers. Name-dropping occurred throughout the West.

When Hill retired from active involvement with the Great Northern in 1912, he sent a 23-page letter to stockholders that not only served as a valedictory on his 40-year career with the railroad but also provided insight into the values and thinking of one of the most important figures in the history of the American West. Foreseeing, for example, the shift from a focus on building the railroad to one of managing it and its related resources, Hill wrote that "the present is a favorable time for making the change" from an active part in the affairs of the company. He added, "It seems wise to begin the process of adjustment to other hands at this time, when all the outlook is fair and every change may be weighed with deliberation in the light of what is for the best interests of the property."

Hill's letter demonstrated the depths of his thinking and traced the history of the Great Northern and its influence on the development of the Northwest, describing briefly what he called the points of historic interest. Tracing his own record of positions held with Great Northern and its numerous sub-sidiaries, Hill pointed out, "At no time have I accepted any salary for my serv-ices as President or Chairman of the Board of Directors, since I have felt that I was sufficiently compensated by the increase in the value of the property in which my interest has always been large."

A key factor in the company's success, Hill said, was that the route had "grades so low and curves so moderate as to make possible cheaper over-land carriage than had ever been previously considered." Not one to dwell on his failures, he dismissed the saga of the ill-fated Northern Securities Company and his battle with President Theodore Roosevelt in a single para-graph. At greater length, Hill described how the Great Northern broke with business practices of the latter part of the 19th century and reinvested the railroad's earnings in further expansion. The custom of the time was to dis-tribute all profits to the stockholders, who were the owners of the assets, and to finance expansion with new bond sales. In just two pages, Hill explained how the Great Northern was soundly financed while other railroads were saddled with debt that in most cases would lead to collapse and reorganiza-tion. "The financial outlook of this Company is as well assured as that of most governments," he wrote, adding that there never had been a default on any Great Northern bonds and that dividends had been paid on the stock ever since 1882.

Hill concluded the dissertation with a statement that could resonate with successful entrepreneurs in any field: "Most men who have really lived have had, in some shape, their great adventure. This railway is mine. I feel that a labor and a service so called into being, touching at so many points the lives of so many millions with its ability to serve the country, and its firmly estab-lished credit and reputation, will be best evidence of its permanent value and that it no longer depends on the life or labor of any single individual."

money they often spent it in ways that made no sense to Hill. At the very moment when they were behind in their rentals to the Manitoba road they were planning their own "short line" between St. Paul and Minneapolis. Hill was dumbfounded. The Manitoba road had virtually rebuilt its own "short line"—the first railroad in Minnesota—and its four all-steel tracks stood ready to carry all the trains that would ever conceivably run between the Twin Cities. . . . [T]he Northern Pacific seemed willing to spend its last cent to prove that it was independent of Hill.

Hill gradually expanded the Manitoba's activities, adding non-railroad businesses that contributed to the railroad's success. To facilitate transfer of grain from train to ship for movement to the east, the Manitoba built a massive grain elevator at West Superior, Wisconsin, across the state line from Duluth. The elevator was leased to the Great Northern Elevator Company, the first related business to use the Great Northern name. In 1888, Hill formed the Northern Steamship Company with six ships designed to carry coal, iron ore, and other bulk freight through the Great Lakes system as far east as Buffalo. His empire now stretched from Butte to Buffalo.

The decision to extend all the way to the Pacific coast was made in 1889, and the Great Northern name was born. Aware of the excellent reputation of England's Great Northern Railway, Hill chose the name consciously, and he used the 1856 charter of the Minneapolis and St. Cloud Railroad as the vehicle for the name change.

The Great Northern then leased the properties of the Manitoba in January 1891, which—although it continued in existence and owned most of the Great Northern's property—ceased to be a railroad operating company. As the Manitoba built additional lines to the West, they immediately were leased for the Great Northern to operate.

Hill, the empire builder, moved quickly. He cut a deal with the Union Pacific to build a jointly owned Puget Sound and Portland Railroad between Seattle and Portland to compete with the Northern Pacific. He also managed to extend lines north of Seattle and entered Canada, reaching the Pacific port at Vancouver.

The final push west began in 1890, crossing the Rocky and the Cascade mountain ranges and connecting Washington, Idaho, and western Montana with the original Manitoba line. Hill dictated a northern route so that traffic would not have to be split between the Great Northern and the Northern Pacific to the south. Construction gangs worked from east to west and from west to east. The Great Northern transcontinental line was completed on January 6, 1893, when crews met at Madison, Washington, later renamed Scenic, on the western slope of the Cascades.

THE NORTHERN PACIFIC RAILROAD

Whereas the Great Northern had begun with modest ambitions but achieved great things because it had outstanding management, the Northern Pacific had great ambitions but was hampered by weak management and scarcity of capital. The NP was chartered by Congress in 1864 to construct a railroad across the northern tier of states, connecting the Great Lakes with the Pacific coast. In addition to its charter, the NP had a federal land grant of nearly 50 million acres. It also had the backing of some of the most prominent residents of Minnesota. The land grant was to prove to be the company's most valuable asset.

Despite a slow start and more than one bankruptcy, eventually the NP became the second transcontinental railroad after the Union Pacific/Central Pacific combination. It traversed the rich agricultural areas of Minnesota, Dakota Territory, and Montana before crossing both the Rockies and the Cascades to reach Washington and Puget Sound.

Early in the railroad's history, Northern Pacific's promoters allied themselves with Jay Cooke and Company, a Philadelphia investment bank that had made its reputation by successfully marketing federal bonds during the Civil War. Cooke assumed the task of selling NP bonds to pay for construction. He also acquired a majority interest in the railroad and took control of the entire venture.

Virtually from the start, the NP and the railroads that were to become the Great Northern found themselves in competition. It was a competition—marked by occasional periods of truce and collaboration—that was to continue for nearly a century. The rivalry didn't end until the 1970 merger of the two that created the Burlington Northern.

Although the NP had been chartered by Congress and had a land grant, its start was halting, for it and the St. Paul and Pacific had similar short-term goals in their early days. Each wanted to build west to the Red River of the North, which formed the border between

Minnesota and Dakota Territory. The St.P&P intended to reach Canada at St. Vincent. From the border, a line would be built north to Fort Garry, later to be known as Winnipeg, and then west across Canada. Construction on the NP began in early 1870, with an initial line to run between Duluth and Moorhead, also on the border of Dakota Territory.

Promoters of the NP were drawn early to the St.P&P, which together would give them access to lake and river navigation at Duluth, St. Paul, and Breckenridge, Minnesota. Almost from its very beginning, the NP wanted to link Duluth with St. Paul and Minneapolis, where the nascent system would connect with rail lines to Milwaukee, Chicago, and St. Louis. The initial flirtation between the NP and its rival to the south came to naught.

While Hill avoided dealing with those he called "speculators" and developed the Great Northern more conservatively, the Northern Pacific never was as well financed or strong as its rival and was unable to withstand economic downturns the way the GN was able to persevere. The collapse of its original financier set the NP back, and it never was able to demonstrate financial stability for the rest of its building phase. Even though Congress had conferred almost 50 million acres of public land on the Northern Pacific to help finance its construction, bankruptcy and reorganization preceded the August 23, 1883, completion of the NP transcontinental line. As with the UP/CP combination, construction had proceeded from each end to the final meeting point at Independence Gulch, near Deer Lodge, Montana. A golden spike ceremony to mark completion of the second transcontinental line was held September 8 at nearby Gold Creek, a more scenic location.

With a route through largely unsettled territory, the NP would have to develop its own traffic. In 1870 there were no whites in northern Minnesota, and not a single farm existed along the route in Dakota Territory. There may have been potential, but there was virtually no population in the Montana plains nor in eastern Washington and Idaho. NP officials recognized the need to attract population as quickly as possible. The federal land grant consisted of twenty 640-acre sections to the mile in states (Oregon and Minnesota) and 40 sections to the mile in territories (Washington, Idaho, Montana, and Dakota.) The necessity to stimulate migration was clear.

The NP established a Land Committee and a Bureau of Immigration, which worked closely with one another. The Bureau of Immigration organized a European sales operation based in London and with offices in Liverpool, Germany, Holland, and the Scandinavian countries. The appeal was clear. Young European farmers could not expect to acquire land in their native countries, and the ready availability of large expanses of land and cheap financing made the northern tier of the United States attractive to ambitious young people. Northern Pacific is credited with spurring population growth across the northern tier of states. To the south, the new Atchison, Topeka, and Santa Fe Railway was doing the same thing at the same time to market its land grant and to create a population base in Kansas.

The 1864 charter mentioned a branch down the West Coast into Oregon's Willamette Valley. Even before the western terminus was determined, the NP began construction on a line south from Puget Sound.

Northern Pacific's spending led to a crisis for the railroad in 1872 and triggered the Panic of 1873, which resulted in the liquidation of Jay Cooke and Company and the loss of financing. By that time the railroad had reached Bismarck on the Missouri River in Dakota Territory, leaving a 1,500-mile gap between the eastern and western sections. The railroad slipped into bankruptcy and receivership that led to an 1875 reorganization.

The original charter had time limits for completion of the main line. Several extensions already had been granted to the NP, and when another was sought in 1879, the Union Pacific worked strenuously but unsuccessfully to block the grant of additional time. Recognizing that further extensions might be difficult to obtain and that the railroad had to be built quickly, Frederick Billings, the NP's new president, turned to J. P. Morgan, a New York investment banker and one-time rival of Jay Cooke, to finance the completion of the railroad. Just as it earlier had come under Cooke's control, the NP now came under Morgan's control.

NP lines reached west of the Missouri River, which it crossed in Dakota Territory, and occasionally encountered threats from the Sioux Indians, whose territories it traversed. The company even advertised that it was the only route that had U.S. military protection. One of the assignments that brought the ill-fated Colonel George Armstrong Custer to the Little Bighorn River in Montana was to protect the crews building the Northern Pacific.

The Northern Pacific's line to the Pacific Ocean was completed under Henry Villard, who had assumed control of the railroad. An immigrant from Germany and a representative of European investors, Villard had come to the United States before the Civil War and had worked as a war correspondent for the *New York Herald*. As a representative of German bondholders, he had rebuffed attempts to bribe him into giving control of the bankrupt Kansas Pacific (KP), an early rival of the Union Pacific, to Jay Gould, who then controlled the UP. Gould needed the KP if he was to monopolize western railroading. Confounded by Villard's honesty, Gould eventually capitulated and agreed to acquisition terms that protected the German bondholders.

In a separate venture, Villard meanwhile began construction of a rail line along the south bank of the Columbia River. He saw the NP as a potential competitor to his Oregon Railway and Navigation Company (OR&N), especially if the NP decided to build a rail line along the north bank of the Columbia. Unable to persuade NP to enter a long-term arrangement for shared use of the south-bank line, Villard and a group of associates began buying up NP stock and eventually gained control in 1881, with Villard replacing Billings as president of the Northern Pacific Railroad.

Under Villard, construction proceeded at a feverish pace. The NP did not own its entire route, however, and was forced to operate between Wallula, Washington Territory, and Portland on Villard's still-separate OR&N tracks. The NP had a line from Kalama, across the Columbia from Portland, to Tacoma. A shortage of capital and the prospect of costly construction combined to keep the railroad from building across the Cascades from Wallula to Tacoma and Seattle, as originally planned.

Tacoma and Seattle could be reached from Portland, and there was no railroad competition. Thus there was little incentive to build the shorter mountain route, and Villard did not encourage construction of a route that would compete with his Oregon Railway and Navigation Company. So the NP continued with a 214-mile ownership gap separating its West Coast operation from the rest of the railroad.

Villard's financial empire collapsed suddenly in 1884, and in 1887 the south-bank line along the Columbia was leased to the Union Pacific, certainly no friend of the Northern Pacific's or of Villard's. Fortunately for the NP, though, shortly before the UP's intrusion into the Columbia Basin, the NP had started construction of a line over Stampede Pass primarily to meet the requirements of the federal charter and to retain the land grant. The Stampede Pass line would save the NP from being at the mercy of the Union Pacific.

The Northern Pacific became overextended and fell into bankruptcy again in the Depression of 1893, largely the result of too rapid expansion of main and branch lines that had insufficient traffic. As was the case with other railroads, some of the extensions were undertaken not because they were economically justified by traffic but because the company wished to preempt competitors in the expectation that traffic later would grow to justify the construction. This was a strategy that Hill and the Great Northern avoided.

The 1896 reorganization of the Northern Pacific was spurred by the efforts of New York financier J. P. Morgan. The reorganization was to haunt the railroad and its successor, Burlington Northern, for generations. To protect bondholders of the reorganized company and to ensure that the railroad's management would continue to invest in the railroad, the rich natural resources that came to the railroad with its land grant were pledged as collateral for two series of bonds. Bondholders feared that Northern Pacific management might be tempted to focus on exploiting the land grant at the expense of the railroad. For that reason the two series of bonds were structured to prevent milking of the natural resource assets. The two bond issues, one of 100 years and one of 150 years, had no sinking-fund requirement. In addition, they were not callable before their maturity in 1996 and 2046. Under the terms of the indenture, before the company could realize any revenue from timber, mining, or other resource sales, it had to certify to the trustee of the bond issues that an amount of money equal to the resource revenue had been expended on the railroad's property.

The forced investment in the railroad was not a serious issue for many years when it needed every cent of investment that its managers could obtain. The restrictive indenture was a requirement of emerging from bankruptcy reorganization, but Northern Pacific executives understood that a time might come when development of the resource properties might result in the railroad's being "gold plated" with more capital investment than would be prudent. The conditions of the bond issues also served to discourage the company's management from more aggressively developing the timber, mineral, and real estate assets. By the late 20th century, the NP was one of the largest private owners of timber, coal, oil, and mineral reserves in the United States, much of it undeveloped. In an effort to gain relief from the restrictions of the bonds, the managers of Northern Pacific and, later, of Burlington Northern tried unsuccessfully to get the bonds called in or otherwise paid off, including an ill-fated attempt to persuade the U.S. Treasury to issue very long-term bonds to replace the Northern Pacific bonds. Finally, in 1988 the bonds

Hill versus Harriman

Yesterday and Today

James J. Hill and E. H. Harriman were completely dissimilar men, and it is no surprise that they became archrivals. Each man sought economic dominance throughout the northwestern region in which their railroads operated. The clashes began as soon as the Union Pacific and the Great Northern began to compete for business. Hill and Harriman, for example, each perceived the need for friendly railroad connections to Chicago and saw the Burlington as the premier railroad to meet that need—serving Omaha-Chicago in Harriman's case and Minneapolis-Chicago in Hill's case.

Hill's maneuver of having the Great Northern and the Northern Pacific jointly purchase the Burlington and splitting the ownership 50-50 had thwarted Harriman's attempt to purchase outright control of the Chicago-based railroad. Harriman then tried to get Hill to sell him a one-third interest in the railroad, but Hill turned him down. Harriman was coldly furious at being outmaneuvered, calling Hill's refusal to let him share in the Burlington's ownership a hostile act for which Hill would take the consequences. For all his efforts, though, Harriman and his successors would not gain direct access to Chicago until the end of the 20th century.

Hill announced his purchase of the Burlington on April 20, 1901. From that

were eliminated, and the natural resource assets of the Northern Pacific were soon separated into Burlington Resources Inc., an unrelated company that was spun off to stockholders.

By the late 1880s the Great Northern had replaced the Union Pacific as the Northern Pacific's principal competitor. Hill took advantage of the Depression of 1893 to purchase Northern Pacific stock, eventually acquiring one-fifth of the company. Hill and J. P. Morgan, the man who bankrolled the 1896 NP reorganization, now were in position to jointly play a significant role in the development of the NP.

The bankrupt Union Pacific had meanwhile come under control of Edward H. Harriman, who had bought much of its stock for four cents a share. An accountant and son of a pastor, Harriman believed correctly that the most effective way of creating long-term value was to pour capital into his railroad and put it on the path to regional dominance. Originally squaring off in Oregon and Washington, with

day forward, Harriman devoted all his physical and financial energy to snatching control of the Northern Pacific away from Hill. Years later, Drew Lewis, a Harriman successor, similarly tried to keep the Santa Fe out of the hands of a Hill successor. In each case, the Union Pacific succeeded only in making the venture more costly for the Hill roads but ultimately failed to gain its own expansion.

Determined to fight for regional supremacy, Harriman began a frenetic drive to acquire as much NP stock as he could. Hill learned of the move when he saw NP's stock price climbing on the ticker, and he began his own buying spree. By May 3, only 30,000 shares of common stock separated Harriman from control of the NP. Harriman's investment banker was the house of Kuhn, Loeb, which had financed many railroad ventures.

On Monday and Tuesday, May 6 and 7, Hill, J. P. Morgan, and their allies began buying up every Northern Pacific share they could lay their hands on. The price per share shot up from $110 to nearly $150. Hill ended up with 150,000 shares, five times more than was needed to retain control of the Northern Pacific. A short-lived market panic followed when speculators tried to capitalize on the buying spree by offering shares they didn't own—selling short. In the frenzied bidding that followed, the price shot to $300, then $500, and finally to $1,000 a share. A framed piece of the ticker tape that transmitted stock activity in those days hung in the Burlington Northern executive offices for many years.

the UP approaching Washington from the south and Great Northern eyeing Oregon from the north, the Harriman and Hill interests developed a rivalry that has lasted for more than a century.

It was both predictable and inevitable that Hill and Harriman would become rivals, although they were quite dissimilar men. Harriman was a railroad financial genius, while Hill was a practical railroader. Harriman was a man with knowledge of balance sheets, while Hill was an unpolished builder who sometimes swung a pick with his construction gangs and who was said to know every curve and grade on the Great Northern.

The UP's system ran westward from Omaha, and just as Hill perceived the need for a friendly connection between the Twin Cities and Chicago, Harriman needed a friendly connection from Omaha to Chicago. Harriman initially sought to acquire the profitable Chicago, Burlington, and Quincy, which also would provide a Kansas City–Chicago line as well as entry to the Twin Cities. He was turned down and secretly began to acquire Burlington stock. Hill, learning of the Harriman threat to his friendly connection, out-flanked Harriman, allied with Morgan and the Vanderbilt interests of New York, and bought the Burlington, dividing its ownership between his Great Northern and the Morgan-controlled Northern Pacific in 1901. The dual ownership of the CB&Q continued until all three roads were combined in the Burlington Northern in 1970.

After the Hill-Harriman war for control of the Northern Pacific ended, Morgan was determined to maintain order in the market in the future. He persuaded Hill and Harriman to put their stock in the Northern Pacific, together with Hill's Great Northern, into a holding company to be called Northern Securities Company, effectively merging their interests. Had the NP and the GN merged successfully, it would have assured dominance throughout the Northwest for Hill and a share in the profits for Harriman, with the latter retaining his Union Pacific empire.

The Northern Securities Company case, however, became the first railroad merger to be rejected by the federal government. A new order was unfolding; the government had been granted antitrust authority. President Theodore Roosevelt would soon be known as "the trustbuster."

THE SANTA FE AND THE FRISCO

In the Southwest, the Atchison, Topeka, and Santa Fe Railway Company gradually spanned the West, connecting California and the Midwest generally along the lines of the historic Santa Fe Trail. Beginning as the Atchison and Topeka Railroad, the line was char-tered in 1859, shortly before the start of the Civil War. Actual construction did not begin until late 1868, however, and the first train did not run until June 28, 1869, more than a month after the Union Pacific and Central Pacific railroads had completed the first transcontinental railroad. Cyrus Kurtz Holliday, an antislavery Pennsylvania lawyer who migrated west to Kansas and allied himself with the Free Soil Party, was one of a group of pioneers who staked out Topeka and eventually made it the state capital. A colonel in the Kansas free militia, Holliday participated in the fighting between slavery and antislavery forces in Kansas in 1855 and 1856 and later was promoted to brigadier general.

Holliday caught railroad-building fever early and obtained a charter for the Atchison and Topeka Railroad Company. He was forced to watch as other railroads laid ballast, ties, and rail. He wasn't even the first to envision what became the Santa Fe Railroad. By 1857 a dozen railroads had been chartered for construction westward from the towns in eastern Kansas, and several specified Santa Fe as their western terminus. As did so many of the railroad pioneers, Holliday struggled to raise money to take his railroad west to Colorado so he could qualify to receive a federal land grant. His state charter provided a grant of some three million acres but contained a condition that the land would become the railroad's only if it was extended to Colorado within 10 years.

One of the Atchison and Topeka's original sponsors was S. C. Pomeroy of Atchison, who had become a U.S. senator when statehood for Kansas was rushed through by Republicans anxious to garner all the strength they could in the years leading to the Civil War. Pomeroy had been a strong supporter of the Pacific Railway Act of 1862, which chartered the Union Pacific and Central Pacific railroads, and Holliday saw Pomeroy as an ally in securing a federal land grant for his Atchison and Topeka. Holliday sent a draft bill to Pomeroy that would provide for the federal government to grant lands to the state to help build a railroad from Leavenworth south to the boundary with Indian Territory (now Oklahoma) and a line from Atchison to the western boundary of Kansas in the direction of Santa Fe. Pomeroy introduced the measure, which passed Congress and was signed into law by President Abraham Lincoln on March 3, 1863. Pomeroy served as Santa Fe president from 1864 until 1868, replacing Holliday. The Santa Fe founder remained a director of the railroad until his death in 1900 and even served as president again for four years following an 1895 bankruptcy reorganization.

The Santa Fe's backers were armed with a federal charter, and in a speech in Wakarusa, Kansas, Holliday enunciated in flowery prose his grand vision of what the small Kansas railroad could become. Nevertheless, the Santa Fe's beginning was quite modest. As other western railroad promoters had done, Holliday made numerous trips to Boston, New York, Philadelphia, and Washington, seeking investment capital. It wasn't until potential investors were reassured by the issuance of county bonds and the provision of county lands, though, that money was forthcoming to build the railroad.

The short trip to Wakarusa, where Holliday made his now famous speech, was made with locomotive No. 1, the Cyrus Kurtz

Holliday. The railroad's only other locomotive in its early days was the General Burnside, named for the Civil War general who became treasurer of the railroad.

Despite its late start, Holliday's Santa Fe soon became a competitor in the transcontinental stakes. Although some rail promoters dismissed the Santa Fe as two streaks of rust (numerous railroads were to share that title over the years), it reached Colorado in time to preserve its federal land grant and began heading through New Mexico and eventually to Los Angeles.

The railroad accessed the coal fields near Carbondale, Kansas, and began generating traffic and revenue from hauling coal to Topeka. It had a 15-year contract with its parallel rival, the Kansas Pacific Railroad, to provide coal for its locomotives. The Santa Fe received one of its biggest boosts when Texas cattlemen began sending their herds to Dodge City, Kansas, on the Santa Fe line in 1872. Long stock trains loaded with cattle headed east provided the railroad with a $500,000 windfall.

The railroad couldn't escape financial stress, however, when a number of members of the original Atchison Associates syndicate were unable to come up with the money they had pledged. This led to a change of financial control, and the new, financially stronger backers were allied with Kidder, Peabody, and Company, a Wall Street investment bank that was to remain a leading railroad financial institution until it was acquired late in the 20th century. Through the connections of Kidder, Peabody, the prestigious Baring Brothers of London became the European agent for the Santa Fe.

The new president, although he would serve only a short time, was Henry Keyes, who already controlled a railroad in Connecticut. Keyes moved the Santa Fe headquarters to Boston, and it was he who arranged for Kidder, Peabody to become the railroad's banker. For the Santa Fe, Keyes provided integrity and a keen business mind. Early Santa Fe financing had been in the form of deeply discounted bonds with a stock bonus to investors. This method raised considerably less cash than the purported capitalization of the railroad, and the stock was considered "watered," a not unusual method of financing new railroads. Kidder, Peabody reversed the process, selling stock and tossing in a bond bonus. This strategy reduced the discount and the amount of watering significantly, and the outstanding stock and bonds more nearly represented the value of the company's

Cyrus Kurtz Holliday

Cyrus Kurtz Holliday was known for his bold and perhaps naive vision for his railroad, which started construction in November 1868 in Topeka, Kansas. A few months into construction, in April 1869, after seven miles of track had been laid, Holliday led an excursion of distinguished citizens in two passenger coaches across this track, covering the seven-mile distance in 30 minutes. They traveled another five miles in carriages, to their destination at Wakarusa, Kansas, where he held a celebratory picnic.

There Holliday delivered his famous "Wakarusa speech," outlining his plans for this railroad company in an oratory style that rapidly built in enthusiasm and optimism. He first announced to his audience that someday the railroad would cross the Rockies and reach Santa Fe. This first prediction was stunning enough to the audience, but he followed with a prediction that reportedly was met with disbelief and even scorn: the railroad would extend to "Galveston, the city of Mexico, and San Francisco." He followed this with a description of the railroad's impact on the nation's growth: "The coming tides of immigration will flow along these lines of railway, and like an ocean wave will advance up the sides of the Rockies and dash their foaming crests down upon the Pacific slope."

Despite the audience's skepticism, Holliday remained true to his vision and inventive in its realization. He lived to see it accomplished by 1887, when his little seven-mile railroad had expanded to 7,373 miles of railroad, extending from Lake Michigan to the Pacific coast, from Denver to the Gulf of California, and from Kansas to the Gulf of Mexico.

assets. Like Hill's Great Northern to the north, the Santa Fe became known for its conservative financial practices.

Keyes died after less than two years as president of the Santa Fe and was succeeded by Ginery Twichell, who had experience running a stage line and the Boston and Worcester Railroad in the East. Twichell, who kept the headquarters in Boston, also was a member of Congress at the same time that he held the Santa Fe presidency, giving the railroad another voice to go along with Pomeroy's in the Senate.

Santa Fe construction gangs reached the Colorado-Kansas border at the end of December 1872, meeting the conditions for receiving the 3-million-acre land grant. By building the line across southern

Kansas, they also ensured that the Santa Fe would capture the Texas cattle trade. The Kansas Pacific had sought the same business, but the cattle drives would go no farther north than the nearest railroad's cattle pens. The cattle business also gave the railroad a west-to-east movement, balancing the predominantly east-to-west merchandise traffic flows of most western railroads.

Like the Northern Pacific, the Central Pacific, and the Union Pacific, and unlike the Great Northern, the Santa Fe was awarded a land grant by Congress, although it received no direct financial assistance as others had. Compared with the Union Pacific/Central Pacific total grant of 26 million acres and financial aid of $61.4 million, and the Northern Pacific's nearly 50 million acres, the Santa Fe's three million acres was minuscule. Even the Santa Fe's rival, the Texas and Pacific, got 23 million acres, and the Southern Pacific received 14 million acres for their proposed joint southern transcontinental route.

Much of the railroad land grants consisted of desert land that neither contained valuable mineral deposits nor was suitable for farming. Although the railroads sold millions of acres to settlers for agricultural use, much of the property remained unsold on the railroads' books until late in the 20th century. The creation of holding-company structures resulted, among other things, in the separation of the land grants from the railroad-operating companies. One of the largest early Santa Fe land sales occurred in 1874 when Santa Fe land commissioner A. E. Touzalin lured some 15,000 Russo-German Mennonites to farm the Kansas farmland. The Mennonites had established a colony in southern Russia and were about to lose the protection of the German kaiser who had been asserted for years. In a deal struck between Russia and Germany to keep Russia out of the Franco-German War, Germany agreed to give up its protector status over the Mennonites, who then were given a choice of accepting Russian citizenship—and service in the czar's army—or leaving the country. The Mennonites left Russia and bought Santa Fe land in Kansas.

Holliday's vision was realized during the eight years that William Barstow Strong was president of the Santa Fe. By the time Strong left in September 1889, the railroad had become a transcontinental system with 7,000 route miles of track. Terminals were in Chicago, San Diego, Los Angeles, Denver, Galveston, El Paso, and Guaymas, Mexico. Even before the drive to the west, the railroad achieved access to Kansas City, which was rapidly outstripping Atchison and other Missouri River towns as a center of commerce, by acquiring an existing railroad between Topeka and Kansas City. Barstow, California, where the BNSF main line splits—with one leg going to Los Angeles and the other north through the California agricultural region—is named for Strong.

Before he became president and while he was general manager, Strong commanded one of the most significant episodes in Santa Fe history. The railroad had reached Pueblo, Colorado, in 1876 and had plans to continue west to coal fields near Canon City, and also to turn south toward Trinidad, Colorado, and then cross over Raton Pass into New Mexico and on to Santa Fe, Albuquerque, and Mexico and the Pacific. Colorado interests, however, had founded the Denver and Rio Grande Railroad to connect Denver with El Paso, Texas, on the border with Mexico. Both companies coveted the same geography, but only one railroad would be able to get through the Royal Gorge of the Arkansas River to the coal fields or Raton Pass, the route of the original Santa Fe Trail. The winner of Raton Pass would have a clear path to the West. Although the Denver and Rio Grande triumphed in the Royal Gorge, that would be its last victory, because the Santa Fe was victorious in gaining the Raton Pass route. The Santa Fe went on to achieve Holliday's vision, but the Denver and Rio Grande never became more than a regional railroad and, after several mergers, now is part of the Union Pacific system.

The St. Louis–San Francisco Railway was as ambitious an undertaking as the Santa Fe, but ill-fated. It was, according to its sponsors, to be a transcontinental railroad, running roughly along the 35th parallel. Its initial route—beginning at Fort Smith, Arkansas, on the Arkansas River—was one surveyed by the U.S. Army in its 1853 mapping of potential rail routes in the West. The original 12-man survey team, led by Lieutenant Amiel Weeks Whipple, set out by river steamer from St. Louis, sailing down the Mississippi and then up the Arkansas to Fort Smith. Although it was the southernmost of the surveys conducted by the army, it was opposed by Southern politicians who feared federal and therefore Northern control of any railroad that might eventually be built.

St. Louis interests, headed by Senator Thomas Hart Benton of Missouri, had sought a 38th-parallel route for a railroad to the West beginning at St. Louis, but two disastrous expeditions led by John C. Fremont, Benton's son-in-law, convinced the St. Louis backers that their preferred route was impractical. Fremont found that the

The Battle for Raton Pass

The race between the Denver and Rio Grande Railroad (D&RG) and the Santa Fe to become the first railroad over Raton Pass stopped just short of being a war. Some of the maneuvering certainly had the attributes of a military campaign.

At the end of February 1878, Santa Fe president William Barstow Strong ordered his chief engineer, Albert Alonzo Robinson, to take possession of Raton Pass and to hold it at all costs. Meanwhile, General William J. Palmer, just as committed to expansion as Strong, was determined that his Denver and Rio Grande would control Raton Pass. He organized a construction gang and headed to the pass, but Robinson moved even faster.

In a strange twist of fate, both Robinson and J. A. McMurtrie, the Rio Grande chief engineer, rode the same D&RG train from Pueblo to El Moro, the southernmost rail point. When they arrived, McMurtrie and his men went to the local hotel for the night. Robinson, however, did not rest. By the time the D&RG crews arrived at daybreak, they found men in the pay of the Santa Fe already at work grading the right-of-way for the railroad.

Rocky Mountains of Colorado, due west of St. Louis, were virtually impenetrable.

The St. Louisans then agreed to a railroad beginning at St. Louis and running southwestward to Fort Smith and then west along the 35th parallel. The alignment held appeal in the southwestern corner of Missouri, where the price of corn was twice the price in St. Louis and where isolated communities had to haul wheat 250 miles to the nearest mill. The final persuasion that the 35th-parallel route should be the one built was word that John Gunnison, commanding a survey party along the 38th parallel, had been killed by Indians. Before his death, Gunnison had reported that the route was impractical.

Even before the army surveyors completed their westward trek and were barely inside California, Missouri interests began construction of the Frisco, as the railroad became known, in 1854, initially calling their new railroad the South-West Branch. The same backers had planned to build a railroad—the Pacific of Missouri—to Kansas City, but more public land was available for grants to the southwest, so the branch line was constructed first. Its sponsors ran out of money, and though the railroad entered Indian Territory, it never progressed any farther west than what now is Avard, Oklahoma.

In the middle of the 19th century, St. Louis saw itself in a competition with Chicago to be the gateway to the West. A railroad was seen by civic boosters as a necessity. The dream of a railroad to San Francisco originated four years before Jefferson Davis ordered the army to survey potential transcontinental rail routes. As historian H. Craig Miner noted, Senator Thomas Hart Benton stated in an 1849 speech that he had developed the idea some 30 years earlier. He believed that trade with Asia had "determined the seat of wealth and power in the world from Phoenician times onward" and that it was "imperative that the United States immediately tap this source of strength among nations." Benton suggested a publicly owned transcontinental railway because, in his opinion, private ownership would only make such a project "a great stock-jobbing business."

Construction on the new railroad proceeded apace but was marked by a disaster on November 1, 1855. To demonstrate to state legislators that the railroad was a reality, and to set the stage for a petition for funding of a new bridge over the Gasconade River, an excursion left St. Louis that day. Thomas Sullivan, the railroad's chief engineer, argued that the bridge was sound, but riding on the locomotive tender, he was the first person killed when the bridge collapsed, throwing the 13-car train into the icy river. The locomotive turned over backwards onto the following cars, killing 43 legislators, officers, and directors.

The South-West Branch's builders tried to continue construction during the Civil War but ran into problems that included guerrilla raids and a scarcity of labor. The Union sent troops down the railroad with the intent of occupying territory before Confederate sympathizers could organize. One significant engagement was fought, but it resulted in a stinging defeat for the federal troops, whose commander, General Nathaniel Lyon, was killed. The railroad carried his body back to St. Louis in a black-draped car while the retreating soldiers walked; their equipment was in wagons, because rail transportation was considered too expensive for general use.

The South-West Branch penetrated an area of Missouri where there was considerable support for secession from the state and the Union. After dealing with repeated raids on its bridges and tracks by the likes of irregulars led by "Bloody Bill" Anderson, William Quantrill, and George Todd, the railroad directors petitioned Washington, D.C., for security and aid. Bureaucrats back East were of two minds. To assist the railroad was to help the area where the raiders known as bushwhackers lived and operated, but to refuse aid would deny the Union the supply link in operations against the same guerrillas. President Lincoln broke the stalemate when he ordered

General William Rosecrans to contract with the railroad, accepting its offer of free transportation on the 56-mile section west of Rolla, Missouri, to Lebanon, Missouri, in exchange for iron for construction and for protection. The aid was justified on military grounds. Frisco historian H. Craig Miner wrote: "Lincoln could look with favor on a line into the slavers' domain; so could those with less principle at stake."

The South-West Branch owed so much money that by the end of the war it was taken over by the state and then sold to new owners. Renamed the Southwest Pacific, construction continued on to Springfield, Missouri, where the line would head west roughly along the 35th parallel.

In July 1866, Senator Benton's son-in-law Fremont, who had been the first Republican candidate for president and became a general in the Civil War, obtained a charter for what he called the Atlantic and Pacific Railroad Company (A&P), to run from Springfield to the Pacific. Fremont was a better promoter than he was a business executive; a multimillionaire before the war, he was reduced a dozen years later to dictating his memoirs to earn enough to support his family. Prior to his involvement with the Missouri railroad, he had been connected with three failed railroad projects in other areas of the West. The Atlantic and Pacific had few assets, but it had a charter.

The struggling Southwest Pacific went on the block and attracted several syndicates, including one headed by Jay Cooke, whose Philadelphia investment banking firm had financed most of the Civil War for the Union. Cooke, who later agreed to finance the Northern Pacific, decided the Missouri railroad was not a wise investment and dropped out of the bidding. Fremont, amid accusations that he was buying the railroad only as a town site and as land speculation, won the bidding at $1 million, agreeing to raise his offer to $1.3 million if his bid was accepted within two days. The Southwest Pacific passed into the control of Fremont and his Atlantic and Pacific. The A&P fell into receivership in 1875.

The Santa Fe and what became the Frisco developed a close relationship long before either was completed. Santa Fe management in 1879 negotiated with the St. Louis–San Francisco Railway for a half interest in the Atlantic and Pacific. Meanwhile, what was to become the St. Louis–San Francisco was undercapitalized, and its promoters struggled unsuccessfully to stay afloat while building westward toward Indian Territory. The line changed hands and names several times during its first 20 years. When the A&P failed, its property in Missouri was acquired by the St. Louis and San Francisco Railway Company in 1876. The company, renamed yet again as St. Louis and San Francisco Railroad Company, acquired property in Indian Territory in 1897. When railroads that had failed financially were reorganized, it was a common practice to rename a failed railroad as a "railway" and a failed railway as a "railroad." It was a difference important only to the old stockholders who were wiped out and to the new stockholders who owned the assets.

Caught geographically between the wealthier Santa Fe and the Southern Pacific, the Frisco was beset by financial weakness and endless fights over its ownership. Some of the names involved read like a who's who of the robber baron era. Collis P. Huntington, a member of the "Big Four" who founded the Southern Pacific, was allied with financier Jay Gould in efforts to gain control of the Frisco as a block to Santa Fe expansion. Proving that some things never changed in that era, Russell Sage—who first was heard from in Wisconsin and Minnesota in the 1850s and later was a Gould associate involved with looting the Union Pacific—was elected to the Frisco board as a representative of the Gould interests during one of the fights for control.

Gould's interest in the Frisco was clear. As principal owner of the Texas and Pacific, he had a pact with Huntington and Leland Stanford, another Southern Pacific founder, to create an alternate southern transcontinental route by connecting the Texas and Pacific with the Southern Pacific at El Paso. In contrast to Gould, and by the standards of the times, the Santa Fe promoters were considered relatively honest men.

The A&P, which had been consolidated with the South Pacific Railroad, for a short time even took control of what later became the Missouri Pacific, running across Missouri and connecting St. Louis with Kansas City. Both the Missouri Pacific and the A&P defaulted on their mortgages in 1875, and the two properties were separated, with the Missouri Pacific going on to an interesting history of its own.

The A&P assets were sold in foreclosure to the St. Louis–San Francisco in 1879, and later that year the Frisco and the Santa Fe agreed to cooperate in building a line over the 35th parallel to California under the original 1866 Atlantic and Pacific charter. The Frisco and the Santa Fe each was to own 50 percent of the Atlantic and Pacific, and though the A&P may have been the owner of the new line, the Santa Fe clearly was the driving force.

The alliance made sense for both companies. The Santa Fe lines had extended from Kansas through Colorado to Albuquerque, whereas the Frisco had reached only to Vinita in Indian Territory. The Frisco was about to complete its line from southwestern Missouri to Wichita, Kansas, and hoped to extend the final 37 miles from Pacific City, Oregon, into the St. Louis on its eastern end. By combining to close the gap between the Santa Fe at Albuquerque and the Frisco at Vinita and to build a joint line from Albuquerque to California, the two railroads would complete a southern through route from the Mississippi River to the Pacific Ocean.

Construction west of Albuquerque began in 1880, and the A&P venture was well into Arizona Territory by 1882. Construction was pushed by Lewis Kingman, one of the Santa Fe's best engineers. In another example of railroad builders leaving their names for posterity, today's BNSF main line runs through Kingman, Arizona. The A&P also was able to claim land grants that had been offered in the original 1866 charter for completed construction. On its eastern end, the A&P constructed a connection with the Frisco at Avard, Oklahoma. Typical of the rivalries that began in the nineteenth-century railroad-building era and continue to today, Jay Gould's Texas and Pacific and Collis Huntington's Southern Pacific (SP) by 1882 already had a southern transcontinental route in operation, stretching from San Francisco to New Orleans.

The A&P route was a competitive threat that led Huntington and Gould to buy enough shares of the Frisco that they were able to take seats on the A&P board of directors. Their intent was to keep the Santa Fe from building into California either through the A&P or on its own. For a while at least, the Santa Fe found itself in an alliance with its two greatest competitors. Without sacrificing the A&P's charter right, the Santa Fe agreed to Huntington's proposal that the Santa Fe abandon its plan to build into California and that the Southern Pacific build a line from its main line at Mojave to Needles, California, on the Colorado River, where it would connect with the A&P. The agreement was good for Santa Fe in that its freight was able to reach San Francisco, and at considerably lesser expense than if it were to build its own rail line west of the Colorado River.

The Santa Fe appeared to have sacrificed its plans to build a rail line into California, but, in an example of the kind of strategic thinking in which early railroad builders engaged, the Santa Fe figured a way to reach a saltwater port and the Pacific Ocean. Santa Fe tracks had reached Deming, New Mexico, where they linked with the Southern Pacific main line. Through a combination of trackage rights over the SP between Deming and Benson, Arizona, and the construction of a rail line north from the Mexican port of Guaymas on the Gulf of California through Nogales on the Arizona-Mexico border to the SP main line at Benson, the Santa Fe by 1882 had cobbled together access to salt water.

The Santa Fe line gave the U.S. interior a route to Australia that was 1,400 miles shorter than the route through San Francisco. It also made the Santa Fe the longest railroad in the world at the time. Despite the agreement with Huntington and the SP, Santa Fe president William B. Strong still was determined that the Santa Fe would have its own lines in Southern California. Another series of transactions gave the Santa Fe access to San Diego Bay and a line up the California coast almost to Los Angeles. That line, through San Bernardino, connected with the Santa Fe's line at Mojave.

In a process not nearly so dramatic as the westward expansion, the Santa Fe at the same time was extending its lines in the opposite direction and building a system that covered much of the rich Kansas farm territory. Through a series of branch line constructions and acquisitions, the Santa Fe system reached Kansas City by 1884. Combined with the Atlantic and Pacific acquisition of the SP line from Needles to Mojave and trackage rights over the SP to San Francisco, passenger trains with sleeper car service could operate without change or transfer between San Francisco and Kansas City. The Santa Fe entered Chicago in 1885.

Finally acquiring the Frisco in 1890, the Santa Fe gained complete ownership of the A&P. The Santa Fe system now stretched from Chicago and St. Louis to the Pacific, with branches throughout Kansas and south into Texas. The system may have looked good on a map, but unlike some of the other transcontinental routes, the Santa Fe system traversed long stretches of desert with little traffic or immediate likelihood of economic growth. The Frisco acquisition put a severe strain on the Santa Fe's finances, and both the Santa Fe and its Frisco subsidiary fell into receivership in the Panic of 1893.

Under the vigorous leadership of Edward Payson Ripley, its new president, the Santa Fe emerged from bankruptcy by 1897, although it was forced to divest the Frisco while retaining the western division of the A&P. Ripley came to the Santa Fe from the Chicago, Milwaukee, and St. Paul Railroad but previously had worked for the Chicago, Burlington, and Quincy, which ultimately was to become a key part of the Burlington Northern and Santa Fe system. The newly separated Frisco remained independent until it was acquired by the

Burlington Northern Railroad (BN) in 1980. The 1995 merger of the BN and the Santa Fe would reunite the Frisco with the Santa Fe in an even larger rail system. As an independent company, the Frisco was primarily a regional bridge carrier that originated and terminated relatively little of its own traffic on its lines. As part of the BNSF system, the Frisco strategically tied the former Santa Fe's east-west main line to the eastern rail connections at Memphis, Tennessee.

A COMPLETED SYSTEM

The railroad map in the western United States was pretty well determined by the end of the nineteenth century. Gaps remained to be filled and total railroad route miles would continue to increase for another two decades, but for all intents and purposes, the national rail system was much as it is today.

Although the basic route structure of the railroad industry was set, the problem of overcapacity continued to haunt railroads throughout the 20th century. Overcapacity is defined in simple terms as the possession of more assets than can be supported by the volume of business and the revenue it produces. Overcapacity was a principal driver of the industry consolidation that eventually created the BNSF Railway. Overcapacity also led to business behavior by many railroad leaders that contributed to the movement to bring railroads—the most powerful economic force in the nation—under government regulation.

During the post–Civil War years, when railroads had an effective monopoly on intercity transportation, agricultural interests protested that the railroads held unreasonable economic power over them. Following a series of state efforts to control railroad business practices and federal court decisions nullifying the state laws, Congress in 1887 passed the Interstate Commerce Act. The Interstate Commerce Commission was created to administer the nation's first venture into economic regulation. Although its significance was unrecognized at the time, the commission was to have a devastating impact on the fortunes of railroads throughout the country.

Railroad mergers had been occurring almost from the time that railroads first were built in the United States, but the biggest merger was about to be proposed. In 1901, James J. Hill, J. P. Morgan, and E. H. Harriman, who controlled the Union Pacific and owned a large share of the Northern Pacific, decided to combine the NP and Great Northern systems across the northern tier of states.

2

Roosevelt, War, Depression

Regulation Restrains Railroads

Most men who have really lived have had, in some shape, their great adventure. This railway is mine.

JAMES J. HILL, on his retirement in 1912

D ESPITE THE EFFORTS OF THE RAILROADS to bring farmers to the western lands and to provide them with land ownership at reasonable rates, there was no affection between the two economic interests. Railroads were the tools of, by the standards of the period, unspeakably rich and ruthless men who dined at Delmonico's and traveled on steamships to Europe. Much of their wealth was made at the expense of farmers in the Midwest and West.

By the latter part of the 19th century, as the railroads neared completion of a national network, farmers and farm-state legislators managed to pass a series of state regulatory laws designed to rein in the economic power of the railroads over farmers. It was a theme that would continue up to the present. Many farmers continue to believe they have lost control over their own fate to outside forces. In North Dakota, for example, one still can hear talk of "foreign banks," only to learn that the speaker is referring to banking companies based in St. Paul and Minneapolis.

Forgotten was the fact that the railroad had brought civilization to the Great Plains, selling the land that had been given by the government in exchange for building the lines into the wilderness. No, it was the railroad that set rates for moving grain to milling centers, and those rates were too high. The railroad—all railroads—became the object of farm-state anger. That many citizens of western states and territories had been harmed by the Panic of 1873 and wiped out by the many railroad promoters who took the money and ran no doubt contributed to the animosity toward the railroads.

Farmers were convinced they were at the mercy of the middlemen who sold their grain. In the farm states the railroads often owned or at least controlled the grain elevators. The railroad, then, became the enemy.

State efforts to regulate railroad rates met with little success. Most state laws were found to be unconstitutional by federal courts. But the Granger movement, which supported embattled farmers in their quest for fair (lower) shipping rates, would not die. The focus shifted to Washington, and in 1887, President Grover Cleveland signed the Interstate Commerce Act, the first instance of economic regulation of business in the United States.

The original Interstate Commerce Act (ICA) was hardly a burden on the railroads. Although all railroad rates were to be "just and reasonable," the new Interstate Commerce Commission (ICC) did not have the authority to set maximum rates. Rebates, revenue pooling, and rate discrimination were prohibited, and railroads were required to publish all rates and to file them with the ICC. Orders of the ICC were effective immediately, but only if the railroads voluntarily accepted them. Otherwise the orders would not take effect until an injured party took the order to court and the courts upheld it.

Although it is now an accepted theory by some railroad historians that the Interstate Commerce Act protected the railroads as much as it restricted them, the contemporaneous record does not support that thesis. The railroads certainly did not view the new law as something that worked to their benefit. What railroad leaders wanted, other than no regulation at all, was federal preemption of state regulation.

The railroads created an environment where shippers had the economic leverage. While traffic grew steadily between the depressions of 1873 and 1893, track mileage grew even faster, resulting in a lowering of density in an industry that required density to ensure profitable operations. Even though rate wars were suicidal in the long term, they had become a way of life for competing railroads as they sought to draw the traffic needed. In the short term, as long as the revenue received for any shipment covered direct operating expenses and made some contribution to fixed costs, it was considered good business. The bankers—particularly J. P. Morgan of Drexel, Morgan—saw the railroad rate wars as threatening the flow of capital from Europe. Although they did not openly favor government regulation, and they preferred that they themselves be the regulators, nevertheless the bankers saw the need to bring about some type of rate stability to the industry. The Interstate Commerce Act, whose primary purpose was the protection of shippers from the depredations of railroads, also saved railroads from some of their most egregious and self-destructive business practices.

The real impact of economic regulation on railroads would come in the future. The passage of the Hepburn Act in 1906 gave the ICC rate authority over the railroads that it had not been granted in the original ICA. Many observers trace the decline of the U.S. railroad industry to the period following 1906, when the ICC declined to grant general rate increases to the railroads. The rise of competing trucking companies in the 1930s exacerbated the railroad industry's decline that had begun three decades earlier.

It was not until the 1970s that a coalition of economists, railroad executives, government officials, and customers recognized that regulation no longer served the interests of anyone. Railroads were regulated as though they were a utility. In exchange for the monopoly franchise, the theory went, they had to accept regulation of their business practices and their earnings. The monopoly had long since vanished, but economic regulation continued as though the monopoly still existed.

Albro Martin, in *Enterprise Denied: Origins of the Decline of American Railroads, 1897–1917,* makes a case that government regulation that limited revenue was the biggest contributor to the industry's decline because it discouraged capital investment that might have made the railroads more efficient and better able to deal with the onslaught of new technologies and new competition. That theme is frequently heard today.

HILL AND MORGAN VERSUS ROOSEVELT

The United States at the turn of the twentieth century was experiencing unparalleled economic growth and prosperity and was rapidly making the transition from an agrarian to an industrial society marked by big railroads, big steel, and big oil. The development of an industrial base, the likes of which had not been seen anywhere else, required the carrying capacity of railroads. No other form of transportation could carry the steel, oil, and manufactured goods

Railroads Saw Regulation as a Threat

Although railroad moguls would have preferred no regulation at all, they much preferred federal regulation, considering it to be far less deleterious than what resulted when numerous states tried to regulate what the railroad owners knew was a national system. According to historian Gabriel Kolko, "The rise of state commissions may have prejudiced some railroad men against regulation, but more often than not, as we shall see, these agencies converted them to a belief in federal as opposed to state regulation."

Railroad executives believed that natural competition would not be controlled easily by a government agency, a view that they still hold today. As Burlington historian Richard C. Overton has pointed out, "Many different ways were found to give an advantage to a large shipper even without resorting to secret rate-cutting. A powerful customer, for example, could demand commissions or could insist on using his own cars, for which the railways had to pay rentals. By devices of this sort, established rates could be nominally maintained."

Charles E. Perkins, the Chicago, Burlington & Quincy president, expected that one result of regulation would be secret rate concessions and the attempts to restore rates to their former level. Railroad agents, Perkins said,

churned out by American industry. The railroads, which to a great extent had made all this possible, went about the business of moving people and goods and earning what the railroad titans considered a reasonable profit.

The Santa Fe is a good example of the rapid growth experienced by many railroads. Restored to financial health after its own 1893 bankruptcy, the Santa Fe was blessed by explosive economic growth in Texas and Southern California. By 1910, the Santa Fe was double-tracking almost 250 miles a year and had built the Abo Canyon line, which enabled freight trains to cross the Rocky Mountains 1,000 feet lower than the Raton Pass in New Mexico. The Raton Pass Route, once key to visions of expansion, now is a secondary route of the BNSF Railway.

Double tracking of the Santa Fe main line, well under way before 1910 and still not completed, was to stand the railroad and today's BNSF in good stead. The railroad continues to build the second main line, and in 2005 less than 5 percent of the 2,200-mile route

would meet and after much discussion would agree secretly to reestablish the old rates. All would also agree to be honest. Perkins observed:

> This would last for a little time, and then, as men are weak, somebody would fall, and the business of certain of the large shippers would begin to go over some one road. Then the whole thing would be done over again . . . and everyone would go round again in the old circle. . . . You should not make laws which put a premium on weakness and dishonesty. Is the honest railroad owner to lose all his traffic by conforming to the law, while the weak or dishonest ones make money by violating it in the spirit, if not in the letter, by giving secret advantages through evasions of the law?

In Perkins's view, the new law created an environment in which large shippers had all the advantages and were making money at the expense of the small shippers and the railroad stockholders.

These laws, though superseded by more broadly based acts, have become a part of the railroad fabric. Railroads and the unions representing their workers have developed a working relationship and, more often than not, are able to reach an accommodation, negotiate necessary changes, and then persuade Congress to codify the result of their negotiations.

remained to be completed. Modern signaling allows the railroad to operate trains both eastbound and westbound on each track, and because the line originally was designed to handle fast passenger trains, it can more easily handle the high-speed intermodal business involving trailers and containers on rail cars that developed late in the 20th century. BNSF today handles more of this intermodal business than any other railroad.

In the midst of the prosperity in the early twentieth century, though, the effort to combine the Hill railroads, as they became known, into a massive holding company proved to be a major event. Hill had won control of the Northern Pacific after a bitter takeover battle with E. H. Harriman in 1901, but when the fight was ended, Harriman still held a significant position in the Northern Pacific. Harriman's holding, however, was primarily in preferred stock, which was scheduled to be retired and converted into common stock. And Hill owned a majority of the common stock.

The Hill-Harriman rivalry was nearly constant, with each of the

Railroads Were Too Important to Be Left Alone

The railroad industry was the first to be forced to deal with government economic regulation, and eventually it came under four other federal laws, which exist today, in addition to the Interstate Commerce Act. The railroads were so important in American life and in the economy that the industry was singled out for special treatment time and time again. In each case, subsequent federal and state legislation brought most of the rest of the country under similar laws.

- The Federal Employers Liability Act (FELA), passed in 1908, created a tort-based system for compensating injured rail workers. Although all states now have workers' compensation systems that are designed both to compensate injured workers and to return them to productive employment, studies have shown that complying with FELA costs railroads some $200 million more each year than if they were under workers' compensation laws.

- The Railway Labor Act (RLA) of 1926 was intended to prevent economically disruptive railroad strikes by creating a process based on potentially lengthy mediation. It predated the National Labor Relations Act and the Taft-Hartley Act, which allow the government to try to mediate labor disputes in other industries. Airlines were added to the RLA in 1936. The

rail titans considering the Northwest to be his legitimate preserve. They reckoned without another formidable Edwardian titan who had made the West and its means of transportation a special study. Theodore Roosevelt had moved into the U.S. presidency, and he saw its pulpit as active chance to further his populist agenda.

Hill moved to protect his still precarious position in the GN/NP/CB&Q grouping. Late in 1901 he organized the Northern Securities Company with himself as president. Northern Securities was a holding company to control the northern lines and their joint ownership of the Burlington.

The capitalization of the Northern Securities Company was to be $400 million and would absorb the stock of all three Hill railroads. The holding company "would act as a conduit for profits, and protect the component roads," wrote Edmund Morris in *Theodore Rex*, a biography of Theodore Roosevelt. Morris explained that "Harriman would be rewarded with board seats proportionate to his Northern Pacific holdings, free access to the Burlington system, and a huge sum of cash." Northern Securities went on to earn $100 mil-

last nationwide railroad strike was in 1991 and, due to the economic and national security threat, was ended by Congress in just 17 hours. A defensive shutdown by rail management that affected most of the country a year later ended after three days.

- The Railroad Retirement Act preceded the broader Social Security Act. Railroads and rail workers each still pay a larger tax than do employers and employees in other industries—and retired rail workers receive a somewhat larger pension from the government agency.
- The federalized Railroad Unemployment Insurance Act provides compensation for laid-off railroad workers. All other industries are covered by state unemployment programs, although the federal government contributes significantly to state funds. Congress sets the unemployment compensation rate for railroad workers, usually slightly above the midpoint of the weekly amounts paid by the states.
- Federally imposed railroad job and income protection arrangements are unique in American industry. From the Emergency Railroad Transportation Act of 1933 and the creation of Amtrak in 1971 and Conrail in 1976 to today's federally mandated protection arrangements such as those for New York Dock, railroad employees are economically shielded from most railroad restructuring initiatives.

lion annually and become the second-largest business combination in the world, trailing only the U.S. Steel trust.

The Sherman Antitrust Act had been enacted, and there were concerns that because the Great Northern and the Northern Pacific were competitive roads, mutual operation might be seen as a restraint of interstate trade. Hill's lawyers had researched the issue and found no precedent to threaten the venture.

Despite a coterie of expensive lawyers, Hill misread public and government reaction to his plan. The 1901 stock market panic that involved the battle for control of NP stock drew unfavorable attention to Hill's plans. Formation of the Northern Securities Company was a poorly timed move on Hill's part. Newspapers across the country inflamed public opposition to the company, and the U.S. government developed an active interest in it.

Roosevelt's lawyer, Attorney General Philander C. Knox, saw the situation differently from the way Hill's lawyers saw it. Knox had made his reputation in Pennsylvania, where he had been instrumental in creating the steel trust. Yet, at the instruction of his client, the president, Knox determined that the Northern Securities Company had violated the provisions of the Sherman Act.

An arrogant J. P. Morgan called at the White House seeking to ameliorate the problem, asking Roosevelt and Knox why the administration had not asked him to fix the new trust's charter before announcing its opposition. In *Theodore Rex*, Morris quotes the following conversation:

ROOSEVELT: That [fixing the charter] is just what we did not want to do.

MORGAN: If we have done anything wrong, send your man to my man and they can fix it up.

ROOSEVELT: That can't be done.

KNOX: We don't want to fix it up, we want to stop it.

MORGAN: Are you going to attack my other interests, the Steel Trust and others?

ROOSEVELT: Certainly not—unless we find out that in any case they have done something that we regard as wrong.

Morris relates Roosevelt's musing after the meeting that Morgan considered the president of the United States to be "a big rival operator" with whom he could cut a deal.

Although Morgan and Harriman, concerned about protecting their other interests, urged a settlement of the government suit, Hill was adamant and determined to fight the suit all the way to the Supreme Court. The government suit named Hill and Morgan as defendants, while Harriman was granted technical anonymity as an "associate stockholder," although in a brief to the court he was named as one of "the great triumvirate."

In what may rank as one of the great misreads of reality and the government's zeal, Hill took the position that, after all, the Great Northern and the Northern Pacific had worked cooperatively for more than twenty years and, where they could have competed, the two railroads charged almost identical freight rates. He refused to recognize that such behavior was a restraint of trade. He also failed to grasp the depth of Roosevelt's feeling. Roosevelt had to overcome opposition from within his own cabinet, several of whose members had significant rail investments.

The Northern Securities Company was not the only rail combination that troubled the government. Harriman was believed to be building a true transcontinental system based on the Union Pacific, the Southern Pacific (which he controlled), and the Illinois Central. Morgan meanwhile was assembling a cohesive system in the South that eventually would become the Southern Railway.

Railroad tycoons, convinced they were masters of the universe, were blind to public opinion and helped create their own problems. While every student learns of William Vanderbilt's "the public be damned" statement, others of that time contributed equally to public distrust of railroad power. Harriman talked of a "community of interest" in discussing the alliances that were being formed throughout the industry.

Martin gives an example of the railroad titans' attitude in the 1906 colloquy between Harriman and then government lawyer and later secretary of state Frank B. Kellogg:

KELLOGG: Supposing that you got the Santa Fe?
HARRIMAN: You would not let us get it.
KELLOGG: How could we help it?
HARRIMAN: How could you help it? I think you would bring out your power to enforce the conditions of the Sherman anti-trust act pretty quick. If you will let us, I will go and take the Santa Fe tomorrow . . .
KELLOGG: Then it is only the restriction of the law that keeps you from taking it?
HARRIMAN: I would go on as long as I live.

After Roosevelt was upheld by the Eighth Circuit Court of Appeals, Hill appealed to the Supreme Court. Roosevelt said in regard to Hill, "He detests me, but I admire him. He will detest me much more before I have done with him."

The Northern Securities case came to a stunning close on March 14, 1904. Justice John Marshall Harlan read aloud a narrow 5–4 decision upholding the government. The decision was to stand for 66 years and was reversed only after economic circumstances of the involved railroads had radically changed.

The Roosevelt administration didn't treat Harriman any better than it had treated Hill. Harriman's effort to combine his Union Pacific with the Southern Pacific was denied in a similar Sherman Antitrust Act case that went to the Supreme Court a few years later. More than 80 years passed before Harriman's dream reached fruition, in 1996. Harriman's Union Pacific system and Hill's progeny, the BNSF Railway system, now are the two major rail carriers serving the western two-thirds of the nation.

The sparsely populated Pacific Northwest was an example of an area with railroad overcapacity. The Great Northern and the Northern Pacific were head-to-head competitors for long-haul freight, and both competed with the Union Pacific for transcontinental traffic to and from Portland and the Puget Sound area, even though the Harriman road was several hundred miles to the south for much of the distance.

The Chicago, Milwaukee, St. Paul, and Pacific, which had been a vigorous competitor between Chicago and the Twin Cities since the 1860s, had continued its own westward expansion with a line across southern Minnesota, South Dakota, North Dakota, and Montana. The Milwaukee finally completed its transcontinental route, reaching Seattle in 1906. As the third carrier in a market that already was served by two major railroads, the Milwaukee Railroad's western extension never was more than marginally profitable. When the Milwaukee filed for bankruptcy reorganization in 1977, the first thing its chief executive—Worthington Smith, a former GN executive—did was to halt all service west of Ortonville, Minnesota, near the South Dakota border.

In the years before World War I, the railroads that were to become today's BNSF Railway—like all railroads—devoted their energies to completing their systems, building branch lines, and filling in gaps. One of the most significant was the development of the iron ore lands and business by the Great Northern. Unlike the Northern Pacific, which had been forced to mortgage its natural resource properties as part of its 1896 bankruptcy reorganization, the Great Northern never faced such restrictions.

Spurred by the growth of the steel industry, iron ore transportation played an increasingly important role in the fortunes of the Great Northern. Even before the GN entered the business that was to prove so beneficial to it for many years, Hill in 1889 had purchased a property "consisting of a line of railroad, some logging road and a large quantity of ore lands," as he described it. The purchase was made by Hill individually for slightly more than $4 million. "My purpose was to secure the shipments of ore from these properties for the Great Northern; and the profits from the mines, if there were any profits, for the stockholders of the Company," Hill later wrote to the Great Northern stockholders. He turned the rail line over to the GN at cost, and the rest, also at cost, to the entity developing the ore properties. Along with acquisitions of smaller regional railroads—the Duluth, Superior, and Western and the Duluth, Mississippi River, and Northern—Hill had added some 35,000 acres of land on northern Minnesota's Mesabi Range. By 1912 the Great Northern holdings were 65,000 acres, about one-third of the Mesabi Range as it was then defined. About three-fourths of all the iron ore used to make steel in the United States came from the range.

In part because the GN charter did not authorize mining, Hill kept the mining properties separate from the railroad, although he structured the relationship so that the financial benefits accrued to the GN stockholders. The original vehicle for holding the mining properties—and other nonrailroad operations—was the Lake Superior Company Ltd.

By 1906, Hill changed his mind and separated the increasingly valuable mineral properties, turning them over to a new trust, Great Northern Iron Ore Properties. A large part was leased to the United States Steel Corporation until the steel company, concerned about possible antitrust action against it, canceled the lease at the beginning of 1915.

The ore business continues today but in considerably different form. As the richest iron deposits were consumed, the mining companies developed technology to concentrate lower-grade ores and process them near the mines into taconite pellets with high iron content that are shipped in much smaller volumes than raw iron ore was at the turn of the century. As the mines have been worked out, the traffic isn't as great as in the past, but the higher-grade taconite still provides steady, profitable business for BNSF. The total tonnage hauled may be less, but the value of the processed commodity—and the rate charged—is greater.

Ore always was appreciated by the Great Northern and later the Burlington Northern. Assignment to Kelly Lake, where iron ore operations were centered, was considered a plum operating post. Over the years, some of the best operating executives of the Great Northern gained valuable experience on the Iron Range.

HILL LEAVES THE SCENE

After nearly 40 years, Hill was nearing the end of his active involvement in the Great Northern Railway. He retired as chairman of the board of directors on July 1, 1912, months short of his 74th birthday. In his letter to the stockholders, the empire builder said his work "has been substantially accomplished; though its results have been extended far beyond the foresight of any one at that time."

Hill was succeeded as chairman of the board by his son, Louis W. Hill. Carl R. Gray, who had been president of the Spokane, Portland, and Seattle subsidiary, added the GN presidency to his list of responsibilities. The era of railroad entrepreneurship was over. James J. Hill died less than four years after his retirement. He was the last of the great western rail developers still active in the business. Professional managers replaced the legendary leaders.

The Great Northern and the Burlington Route were not the only railroads to be blessed by outstanding leaders. The Santa Fe came under the leadership of Edward Payson Ripley at the end of 1895, coincidental with the railroad's emergence from bankruptcy reorganization as the Atchison, Topeka, and Santa Fe Railway Company (ATSF).

Ripley, a descendant of one of the earliest families to settle in Massachusetts, was born in Dorchester, Massachusetts, on October 30, 1845. Despite his heritage, he was a man of modest means, and his formal education ended with graduation from high school in 1862. His first railroad job was with the Pennsylvania Railroad in 1868, as an agent in the freight department in Boston. In 1870, Ripley moved to the Chicago, Burlington, and Quincy Railroad, as a clerk in its general eastern agent office in Boston. In 1878, the same year that Hill and the associates acquired the St. Paul and Pacific, Ripley moved to the Burlington's Chicago general office as a general freight agent. Still in the traffic department—what today would be called marketing—he was appointed traffic manager in 1887 and was made general manager in the Burlington operating department a year later. Ripley moved to the Chicago, Milwaukee, and St. Paul Railway in 1890 as a vice president in charge of traffic operations and remained with that railroad until he was persuaded to take the presidency of the Santa Fe. While with the Milwaukee, the civic-minded Ripley took a leading role in developing the Columbian Exposition world's fair in Chicago in 1893.

Ripley's reputation for honesty and integrity, along with his executive skills, brought him to the attention of J. P. Morgan, who promoted Ripley's candidacy for president of the Santa Fe. Ripley is considered one of the four great early leaders of the Santa Fe, the others being Holliday, Strong, and Robinson. While the others carried out Holliday's vision and built the Santa Fe, Ripley was an administrator who ensured that the railroad was a properly financed coherent system. He served more than 24 years, retiring in January 1920, just short of his 75th birthday and only months before his death.

When Ripley took over, the Santa Fe had emerged from bankruptcy, although it still owned the Frisco and the Atlantic and Pacific. The properties were in need of extensive rehabilitation. Ripley determined that the financial integrity of the Santa Fe system would best be maintained if the Frisco were turned over to its creditors. Even though the A&P, the Santa Fe's route to the Pacific, was losing money and was jointly owned by the Frisco and the Santa Fe, Ripley foresaw the growth of long-haul traffic that would make the A&P valuable. He came up with a plan to acquire complete ownership of the A&P while letting go of the Frisco. Selling new bonds on its own credit, the Santa Fe acquired control of the A&P by buying the latter's first mortgage bonds for a little more than 50 cents on the dollar.

With the Santa Fe's route to California secure, Ripley acquired ownership of the Southern Pacific link from Needles to Mojave in California, over which Santa Fe had trackage rights. He traded the Sonora line to Guaymas, Mexico, for the California property, giving the Santa Fe full ownership of its line from Chicago to the Pacific Coast.

By 1906 the economy of the Southwest, through which the Santa Fe ran, was rapidly growing and providing huge traffic increases. At times, the railroad was hard-pressed to provide service, because the traffic was so great. With the traffic growth came an increase in the Santa Fe's profits, more than 50 percent in 1906. Physical expansion increased. Between June 1897 and June 1906 system mileage increased from 6,444 miles to 9,527 miles, a gain of nearly 48 percent, while revenue more than doubled, reaching $78 million.

The Santa Fe was known for its conservative fiscal and expansion policies, so much so that it was referred to as "the Pennsylvania of the West"—high praise indeed, for the Pennsylvania was known as "the standard railroad of the world." Much of the Santa Fe's expansion was financed by issuing new bonds, particularly convertible bonds. Bondholders tended to convert their bonds into common stock, particularly as the common stock rose steadily in value. This trend reduced the Santa Fe's debt obligations, although the increase in outstanding stock also increased the amount paid out in dividends. Bond interest was required to be paid, whereas dividends

55

were paid only when the board of directors approved payment out of earnings. Because of the company's conservative financial policies, the Santa Fe bonds were regarded as quite safe.

Nearly all reports on the Santa Fe emphasized the independence of the board and the diversity of stock ownership, considered a bulwark against hostile takeover. This was of more than academic interest, as representatives of E. H. Harriman and the Rockefellers were brought onto the Santa Fe board. Harriman, using Rockefeller money, acquired several hundred thousand shares of ATSF stock and placed allies on the board. But Ripley made it clear he had no desire for the Santa Fe to be acquired, and Harriman chose peaceful coexistence over conflict. The Santa Fe ended its expansion in Arizona south and east of Phoenix, ceding that territory to the Southern Pacific. It formed a partnership with the SP north of San Francisco and pooled California citrus traffic with the SP and the Union Pacific. Having achieved what they really wanted, Harriman and his allies sold their interests in the Santa Fe in 1906.

Ripley, like Perkins at the Burlington, saw before most other railroad executives the threat that government economic regulation was to become. His outspoken views brought the railroad into conflict with a number of state governments, particularly those in Kansas and Texas. Battles over state-mandated rates and other issues brought a spate of bad publicity, which Ripley tried to lessen through a public relations campaign. In the process, he contributed to railroad lore a term that many wish had never been used. When he was asked what he considered reasonable rates, he replied,

> There never was any better definition than that which was
> given many years ago by somebody and which has been
> used as a by-word and a reproach ever since, namely,
> "What the traffic will bear." That does not mean all the
> traffic will bear, it does not mean all that can be extorted or
> squeezed out of it, but what the traffic will bear having
> regard to the freest possible movement of commodities, the
> least possible burden on the producer and the consumer,
> [and] the middleman can take care of himself.

Ripley was succeeded in 1920 by William Benson Storey, who served as president until 1933. Storey became a Santa Fe employee through the 1901 acquisition of the San Francisco and San Joaquin Valley Railroad. An engineer by education, Storey rose through the ranks to become vice president in charge of the construction and operating departments in 1910. Born in San Francisco, he was the first executive who was a native westerner. While he was president, Storey emphasized the industrial department, with a focus on developing the economy of the regions served by the Santa Fe.

THE RAILROADS GO TO WAR: GOVERNMENT TAKEOVER

World War I—the Great War—had raged in Europe for three years before America's entry. It was another time of great stress for the railroad industry. Nearly one-sixth of industry mileage was in receivership. During this period, railroads increasingly had to deal with congestion, rapidly rising labor costs, and the effects of Interstate Commerce Commission rate orders.

The Interstate Commerce Commission, which had been granted the authority to set maximum rates by the Hepburn Act, not only refused to allow general rate increases but also ordered rate reductions. For the Great Northern, one of the commission's decisions in 1915 meant a reduction in iron ore rates from 60 cents to 55 cents a ton.

A recession in 1914 that was triggered by a decline in steel production cut into railroad traffic and profits. By 1916, however, flush with orders from the warring countries and beginning the build-up for U.S. entry into the war, business was booming throughout the country—and the railroads had more to carry than they ever anticipated.

Railroads, particularly those in the West, were created primarily to carry agricultural produce and forest products to the East and manufactured goods to the West, but the U.S. economy was changing, and the changes affected the railroads greatly. Where once steel was made in Pittsburgh and a few cities near the Great Lakes, technology dictated that steel increasingly was being poured at smaller, more geographically diverse mills.

Now the railroads were expected to carry raw materials, chemicals, textiles, and huge amounts of coal for a rapidly growing electric utility industry. They weren't prepared for the business at hand, and the industry's problems cascaded downward in a vicious cycle.

Nationwide congestion and a severe car shortage developed. By mid-October 1916, more than 19 percent of freight cars owned by the Great Northern were off-line, and the GN could not make use of

Edward Payson Ripley

Honest Accomplishments

Edward Payson Ripley was an example of probity that more-modern executives in other industries might emulate. At a time when the United States had no securities laws designed to protect public investors, the Santa Fe adopted bylaws calling for the stockholders annually to elect an independent auditor to audit the books and accounts of the railroad at the end of each fiscal year. Such an audit now is required of all public corporations.

Early in his tenure, Ripley ensured the financial integrity of the Santa Fe by relinquishing control of the Frisco, which was in need of more-extensive rehabilitation than he thought the Santa Fe could afford. He retained the Atlantic and Pacific, though, preserving the Santa Fe's route to California.

With the ownership and financial structure of the Santa Fe settled, Ripley turned to the physical improvement of the railroad, beginning a program of grade reduction, line relocations to reduce curves, replacement of wooden bridges with steel structures, and relaying the main lines with new and heavier steel rail. Freight cars were enlarged and fitted with automatic couplers.

other railroads' cars that were on its lines because of the poor condition of the cars. Half a million bushels of grain were piled on the ground at GN stations in Montana, and by late November the railroad was unable to fill 50 percent of requests for transporting coal.

Grain transportation, for which much of the western rail system was developed, always has been a point of contention between railroads on one side and growers and elevator operators on the other. Congestion originating hundreds or thousands of miles from grain-growing areas only compounded the difficult relations of railroads and agricultural interests. If boxcars—the standard vehicle for moving grain—were stuck at ports or otherwise commandeered by other railroads, the shortage quickly was felt in the grain areas where the Santa Fe, the Burlington, the Northern Pacific, and the Great Northern operated.

The problems were industry-wide. The Burlington reported lower traffic levels and revenue in 1914 and a further deterioration in 1915. When traffic surged in 1916, however, efficiency suffered and operating expenses rose even more rapidly than traffic or revenue. Coal demand increased in the West when users could not obtain coal from eastern sources.

With the price of coal climbing, the Santa Fe managers determined that oil could replace coal as fuel for locomotives, and the company acquired oil lands near Fullerton, California, in 1900. Oil became the principal fuel for Santa Fe locomotives operating in the west end of the system.

Although Ripley's focus was on rehabilitation, in the following years the Santa Fe also completed a number of relatively small line extensions to gain access to specific sources of traffic. The company also acquired the San Francisco and San Joaquin Valley Railroad in 1898, giving it a route between Stockton and Bakersfield through the agricultural heartland of California. The Santa Fe quickly pushed the Valley road through to San Francisco, thus coming into direct competition with the Southern Pacific. One of the most significant construction projects for the Santa Fe was the building of the Abo Canyon line in 1903, a more direct route through eastern New Mexico and the Texas Panhandle to lines in Oklahoma. The lower-graded line now is an integral part of BNSF's Transcontinental line, relegating the original Raton Pass line to secondary status. The Santa Fe also began double-tracking the Transcon, as the line now is known, a process that hadn't quite been completed by the end of 2004, when only about 150 miles remained to be double tracked.

Mills closed, perishables rotted, and prices rose because the rail system was clogged, according to an ICC statement on December 1, 1916. The car shortages in the West had resulted in severe congestion in the East, and "service had been thrown into unprecedented confusion," the ICC wrote.

The rail system had indeed reached a crisis in late 1916. Allied war purchases moving to East Coast ports placed a burden on eastern railroads. The railroads failed to coordinate either among themselves or with the ports. When the western grain crop and the fuel supply for the winter began to move into the Northeast, the railroads found themselves in an emergency. Terminals were congested, and there was widespread use of rail cars for storage, which resulted in near paralysis in the East. Western and southern railroads at the same time were drained of their cars. The western railroads were headed for the same crisis as those in the East.

At the urging of the ICC, the railroads tried to coordinate more-efficient return of empty cars. Certain railroads, though, refused to participate. It became increasingly clear that federal control was likely.

The railroads weren't the only institutions that failed to coordinate activities in the national interest. The federal government contributed to the problems. The ICC reported that many government agencies, each with power to set priorities for shipments of troops and materials, were not coordinated, forcing the railroads to deal with conflicting orders. In the chaos that followed, the government determined that the national interest required it to take over the railroads.

Labor difficulties affected most railroads. In the years before World War I, while traffic continued to grow, railroads had been reluctant to increase wages significantly without rate increases, which the ICC refused to grant. Against vigorous railroad opposition, Congress in 1916 passed the Adamson Act, which mandated an eight-hour workday. Workers were to be paid as much for an eight-hour day as they previously had been paid for a 10-hour day. For the railroads the federal action meant an increase in labor expenses, further cutting into operating income.

There was little public sympathy for the railroads when they demonstrated an inability to handle the demands on transportation brought about by the war. The railroads' failure to build a base of public support before the war came back to haunt them. They were seen as operated by greedy robber barons who had little concern for the public interest. It was not a difficult decision, then, for President Woodrow Wilson to order that as of January 1, 1918, the government would take possession and control of privately owned railroad properties—nationalization.

The industry was placed under control of a new agency, the U.S. Railroad Administration. It would be managed by a nonpartisan group of presidential appointees, who named regional directors to manage railroads in their territories through federal managers.

At the Northern Pacific, Jule M. Hannaford, a longtime employee who had been named NP president in 1913, resigned to become federal manager of the NP. He spent most of the war battling with Howard Elliott, NP's chairman of the board who again assumed the president's duties. Elliott had been NP president from 1903 until he resigned in 1913 to become president of the New York, New Haven, and Hartford Railroad. Elliott had given the Northern Pacific one of its relatively rare periods of stability until then, having earned James J. Hill's confidence.

After the railroads were returned to private ownership in 1920, it took more than 20 years and several court battles for the NP and the federal government to settle their differences. The Northern Pacific certainly wasn't the same railroad as before the war. Heavy traffic forced the railroad to press into service every available locomotive and car, while maintenance was reduced to levels that were below normal for the amount of traffic handled. Maintenance problems were compounded by the relatively small population of the Northwest and the effect of the military draft, which removed many skilled workers. Cars couldn't be repaired; roadbeds and track deteriorated at the NP. Major expenditures were required after the war to put the railroad and its equipment back in shape.

The CB&Q serendipitously was in better physical condition to deal with the traffic surge than a lot of other railroads were. A relatively large capital spending program had been undertaken in the years just before the war. In 1914 the company had completed a heavy-duty line between Laurel, Montana, west of Billings, and Orin Junction, Wyoming. An eight-mile link between Guernsey and Wendover, Wyoming, had been completed in 1915. A new Kansas City bridge went into service early in 1917, and late that year a new bridge over the Ohio River at Paducah, Kentucky, provided improved connections to the South. The Q—as the Chicago, Burlington, and Quincy was known—completed rebuilding the locomotive repair shops at West Burlington, Iowa, in 1917.

Hale Holden, president of the Burlington, anticipated employees would be drawn away to the war. He issued an order in June 1916 that "all employees who were or might become members of the National Guard in the various states, and who might therefore be called for army service, should be granted leaves of absence with the understanding that their regular positions will be held for them while absent and will be available for them upon return from service." Informed that 126 CB&Q employees already were in the National Guard, Holden ordered that a list be kept "in all cases where enlistment caused distress or privation resulting from lack of support of dependent relatives during enlistment period." The general chairmen of the operating brotherhoods agreed to protect the seniority of all employees called into service.

President Wilson's seizure of the railroads had been made possible by the Army Appropriation Act of 1916, which provided that "the President in time of war is empowered, through the Secretary of War, to take possession and assume control of any systems of transportation, or any part thereof, and to utilize the same, to the exclusion as far as may be necessary, of all other traffic thereon, for the transfer or transportation of troops, war material and equipment, and for such other purposes connected with the emergency as may be needful or desirable."

The Military Railway Service

The Military Railway Service (MRS), a unit of the Army Corps of Engineers, was active in France. The MRS initially consisted of the Thirteenth Engineers, which was commanded by a regular army colonel. The executive officer or second in command of each regiment was a lieutenant colonel drawn from a railroad. The rest of the regiment was made up of railroad men who were soldiers only temporarily. The Thirteenth had been organized in 1916 to support General John Pershing's incursion into Mexico to capture Pancho Villa but had not seen service. Each of its six companies was drawn from a different railroad headquartered in Chicago. By World War II the MRS had been expanded considerably and consisted of regiments drawn from different railroads.

Major General Carl Gray Jr., who served as director general of the Military Railway Service during World War II and was the son of a Great Northern president, relates in *Railroading in Eighteen Countries* that each MRS regiment in World War I (ultimately there were nine regiments) had a roster of 57 officers and 1,839 enlisted men. In addition to a regimental headquarters of seven officers and 41 enlisted men, there were two battalions. The first battalion had three light railway operating companies and a light railway shop. The second battalion consisted of two light railway maintenance-of-way companies and a light railway construction company. Some 20,000 rail workers saw active duty.

The railroad industry tried to avoid federal seizure. Even after war was declared, the American Railway Association—forerunner of today's Association of American Railroads—tried to organize a railroad coordinating group to improve operations. CB&Q's Hale Holden was elected chairman of the special committee of 50 railroad presidents that met in Washington, D.C., and called itself the Committee on National Defense. An executive committee, known as the Railroads' War Board, was chosen and given delegated authority to carry out the activities of the Committee on National Defense. Holden was one of five railroad presidents named to that board.

After he returned to Chicago, Holden persuaded the Q's board of directors to accept the pledge of cooperation of the Committee on National Defense. He also was granted authority by his own board to act on the Railroad's War Board. Despite the best efforts of the Railroads' War Board, the situation did not improve. The board tried to arrange unification and pooling but was blocked by Congress's refusal to suspend antitrust laws or the antipooling provisions of the Interstate Commerce Act. The situation was compounded by conflicting priorities ordered by the army, the navy, the Shipping Board, and other government agencies, each with its own set of priorities. Ports remained congested as a lack of ships—compounded by losses to German submarines—prevented timely unloading of rail cars. By the beginning of November 1917, there were 180,000 cars more than the normal number waiting to be unloaded on eastern lines.

The ICC early in December 1917 declared that unifying railroad operations was indispensable to "their fullest utilization for the National defense and welfare." The U.S. railroad industry was seized by the federal government on December 28. The U.S. Railroad Administration (USRA) would manage the railroads and control the flow of traffic until nearly 18 months after the end of World War I.

The USRA was headed by William G. McAdoo, President Wilson's secretary of the treasury, who became director general of the agency. His deputy as assistant director general was Walker D. Hines, former chairman of the Santa Fe board of directors. McAdoo retained his cabinet post, which meant that Hines essentially ran the railroad industry on a day-to-day basis. Late in the war, Hines succeeded McAdoo as director general. Ironically, although Hines had opposed numerous federal laws affecting railroad operations and management while a Santa Fe executive, he became a strong advocate of federal coordination of rail operations in the midst of the war.

As a rule, the former president of each railroad became its federal manager during the period of federal control. The Great Northern designated William P. Kenney to be its federal manager. At the same time, he was elected president of the railroad. When the USRA decided that separation between government and private corporate loyalties was desirable, Kenney resigned as the GN president and was succeeded by Louis W. Hill, who until then had served only as chairman of the board of directors. Executive vice president Ralph Budd acted as chief executive officer.

The period of government control was disastrous for the Great Northern and most other railroads. Each railroad was to be compensated by a "standard return" equal to the average net railway operating income for the three years that ended June 30, 1917. Because this included the recessionary period of 1914 and 1915, government compensation was considerably less than if a different base period had been selected. The USRA took over accountability for operating revenue and expenses, taxes other than war levies, and rents on equipment and joint facilities, while the railroads received nonoperating income and the standard return.

The contract with the USRA provided that the railroad was to be returned to the corporation "in substantially as good repair and in substantially as complete equipment" as on the day the railroad was seized. That simply didn't happen.

Rank-and-file employees benefited greatly from federal control. At the Great Northern, average employment rose 5.4 percent, but total compensation—approved by the USRA—increased 48 percent. Treasury Secretary McAdoo, who headed the USRA, justified government-mandated wage increases by pointing out that the cost of living rose more rapidly than increases in compensation for railroad workers and by insisting that wages were raised no more than conditions demanded.

More lasting changes were effected that still are being dealt with by railroads in the 21st century. Prior to the period of federal control, the railroads had not had common work rules and practices. Under federal control, however, rules and conditions of work that had been accepted only by some railroads were applied to all. Common work rules and conditions made it easier to institute industry-wide bargaining with the numerous craft unions that represented workers, a system that was codified in the Railway Labor Act of 1926 and largely continues today.

The USRA recognized the right of railroad employees to unionize and to have collective bargaining, something that the government did not impose on other industries for another 20 years. Seniority was accepted as the guide for pay and promotion. Piecework was abolished in the shops. Jobs were classified in minute detail, with the result that a worker could perform only one function. For any other task, no matter how closely allied, another worker had to be called in or the first worker would receive extra pay while the "other worker" also would be paid for doing nothing. This has since changed greatly, with work rule reforms achieved in the late 1980s and early 1990s; but the practice continues to this day and is known as time-slipping. It occurs when an employee believes that work to which he was entitled has been given to a member of a different union. He then submits a claim for payment for the time. Nonoperating employees clearly gained from federal control when five of their unions concluded national agreements with the USRA.

The USRA's favorable policy toward organized labor triggered a sharp increase in operating expenses. For the GN, operating expenses rose 46 percent in two years, while operating revenue increased only 20 percent. The GN's ratio of operating expenses to operating revenue, a key measure of operating efficiency, went from 66.9 in 1917 to 83.8 a year later. That meant that less than 17 cents of every dollar of revenue was available to pay down debt, to pay for capital expenditures, or to pay dividends to stockholders. The USRA authorized increased passenger and freight rates only once during the 26 months of federal control.

Similarly, the Santa Fe's transportation ratio—the percentage of transportation expenses to gross revenue—deteriorated under government control. Between 1913 and 1917 the annual ratio had ranged from a low of 28.62 percent in 1916 to a high of 31.37 percent in 1917. Following the government takeover, the transportation ratio was 35.48 percent in 1918, 36.05 percent in 1919, and 38.75 percent in 1920. There was steady improvement from 1921, when the railroad was returned to private management, and the ratio was down to 30.82 percent in 1923.

Payroll costs at the Burlington increased more than 50 percent from 1917 to 1918. The cost of materials and supplies climbed rapidly, and the price of fuel, which was fixed by the Fuel Administration, was 41 percent higher in 1918 than in 1917. The ratio of overall operating expenses to revenue for the CB&Q increased 13 percent.

The operating ratio of the railroad industry, 65.5 percent in 1916, rose to 94.3 percent by 1920. Putting these figures in context, it meant that where railroads once had 34.5 cents of every dollar of revenue available for capital spending, dividend payments, and reduction of debt, just four years later they had only 5.7 cents of each dollar of revenue available for those purposes. Inadequate revenue began the decline of what then was the largest sector of the American economy.

At a time when traffic was increasing exponentially, total expenditures on track and the buildings, bridges, and rail yards that are called fixed plant remained about the same in 1918 as in 1917. During this period, spending for equipment was slashed by 75 percent. A shortage of skilled employees contributed to the difficulty of maintaining the railroad. By the end of the war in late 1918, more than 5,500 Burlington workers were serving in the army and the navy.

The end of the war didn't end the railroads' tribulations. The national economy remained on a war footing through most of 1919, and the railroads, tied to the economy, did also, even though war-connected traffic fell off rapidly. Car shortages had been reduced from 144,000 in January 1918 to fewer than 40,000 by November. Business declined so rapidly, in fact, that by March 1919 there was a surplus of nearly 500,000 cars parked on just about every available piece of track. A surplus of cars was no better for a railroad's accounts than was a shortage. The cost of ownership continued whether the car was bringing in revenue or not. A coal strike in November 1919 only contributed further to the railroads' revenue decline.

Nor did the federal government honor its commitment to return the railroads to their owners "in substantially as good repair and in substantially as complete equipment" as on the day the railroad was seized. Congress was called upon to appropriate funds to meet the deficit run up by the director general of the USRA. It didn't respond until midyear, and when it did, it did so inadequately. The Santa Fe, for example, asserted that government control had cost it $98 million in damage and wear to rolling stock, track, equipment, and so on. The railroad received only an additional $21.5 million. The Great Northern eventually received the nearly $5 million it was owed for the period of government operation, money it used to purchase steel rails and new locomotives.

The dispute over government payment in part was a result of the additions-and-betterment (A&B) accounting system used by railroads until 1981. Unlike the accounting used by most industries, A&B accounting did not allow railroads to depreciate track and roadbed. Track work was charged as an operating expense that reduced earnings, but track improvements were accounted as capital spending, and improvements remained on the books with no depreciations charged until the next time the railroad performed track maintenance. The government took the position that much of the money sought by railroads was not for current operations, which would have been the government's responsibility, but represented expenditures for the capital account, which were the railroads' responsibility.

A precursor to key provisions of the Railway Labor Act could be seen in 1919. A Burlington shop worker strike was ended through arbitration by the director general, who took a middle ground and authorized a small pay increase for the workers. The workers had to return to work before negotiations even began. They did so reluctantly. The 1926 labor law was designed to make it extremely difficult for unions to strike or companies to shut down or lock out and have a loss of rail service.

3

The Transportation Act of 1920

More Regulation

You and I will be rich together, or we will be poor together—and I know what it means to be poor.

JAMES J. HILL in a speech to farmers, 1880s

D URING 1919, THE BASIS for the return of the railroads to their owners and the kind of regulatory system that should be established were debated. Some in government opposed the return altogether. There was consensus that the entire system was in need of revision, and most agreed that the government should not remain in control of the railroads. William G. McAdoo, who had been the first director general of the U.S. Railroad Administration, proposed a five-year extension on the government's control of the railroads, but his proposal was not accepted and the railroads were returned to their owners on March 1, 1920.

The Transportation Act of 1920, enacted only days before the return took place, set the shape of regulation for more than half a century. Reversing earlier policies that discouraged rail consolidation, the new law provided that one railroad might acquire another, provided that the Interstate Commerce Commission found the acquisition or merger to be in the public interest. Pooling of traffic and revenue again became legal, and railroads were exempted from the antitrust laws to the extent necessary to permit combinations or cooperative arrangements as long as they were sanctioned by the ICC. The ICC was to draw up a plan under which the railroads would be grouped into a limited number of systems. The commission was to preserve competition wherever possible and to group the individual companies so that the resulting systems could charge uniform rates and earn substantially the same rate of return. The idea behind the latter provision was to solve the problem of weak railroads by parceling them among stronger companies and merging them into systems of approximately equal size and strength. By accepting the concept that rail combination should be encouraged, the Transportation Act of 1920 put an end to the Teddy Roosevelt–era trust-busting. The ICC was granted the authority to set minimum as well as maximum rates. The agency also gained authority over line abandonment.

The Transportation Act of 1920 had the effect of slowly strangling the railroads through external government regulation. The ICC simultaneously protected shippers from high rates and rail competitors from low rates. Rate making, as prescribed by the act, however, still was intended to produce net railway operating income based on a government-determined fair return on rail property. It was classic public utility regulation, and it made no allowance for the value of the service provided. That concept would not change until passage of the Railroad Revitalization and Regulatory Reform (4R) Act of 1976. The government continued to ignore the 1906 admonition by the Burlington's Perkins that railroad rates could not properly be set based on the value of the assets.

THE GOLDEN ERA OF RAILROADS SHOWS TARNISH

Some historians considered the 1920s and 1930s to be the golden era of railroads. And it was—but only if bigger and faster locomotives were the criteria. Throughout the industry, railroads concentrated on developing and acquiring ever more-powerful locomotives that could pull passenger trains faster and could haul heavier freight loads than ever before. For those whose breath quickened and whose heart rate increased at the sight of a train, it was a golden era. But it was to be short-lived. The diesel electric locomotive made its commercial appearance in the 1930s—the first diesel-powered passenger train was the famous Burlington Zephyr in 1934—and within two decades the steam locomotive had made its last commercial run and would be remembered only in a few tourist excursion operations and occasional rail-fan trips.

U.S. railroads were in decline by the onset of the Great Depression, but the industry was so large and important in American society that few realized the extent of the deterioration. Like a giant ship's change of direction at sea, the turn away from leadership and growth in the rail industry initially was almost imperceptible. Even as the nation emerged from recession and traffic returned to pre–World War I levels, the railroads failed to earn prewar profits. In *Northern Pacific,* historians Frey and Schenk described the situation as it affected most railroads:

> Several reasons accounted for this condition. Although the amount of traffic tended to increase, the cost of labor and materials increased even more rapidly. It was extremely difficult for railroads to recover their increased costs by means of rate increases, on account of the ICC's preference toward shipper and public interests over those of the railroads. Finally, and perhaps most importantly, the competition of the highway carriers became a reality in the 1920's.

Operating revenue for the Northern Pacific had reached $113.1 million in 1920 but slumped to $97.9 million in 1925. Its net railway operating income, which had reached $23.8 million in 1915, fell to $7.9 million in 1920 and recovered only to $22.2 million in "prosperous" 1925. The prewar operating ratio of 58.7 percent climbed to 71.5 percent by 1925, although revenue ton-miles of freight handled (a ton-mile is one ton carried one mile) increased from the prewar level of 5.16 billion to 6.75 billion in 1925.

The Great Depression was to have an even more-devastating impact on the NP's financial performance. By 1938, operating revenue had fallen to $57 million, net railway operating income was only $4.3 million, the operating ratio had increased to 82.5 percent, and revenue ton-miles of freight dropped to just 4.72 billion. The Great Northern would not see its prewar operating ratio again. The ratio was 79.5 for 1921 and improved to 76.9 percent in 1922. It improved steadily through the 1920s but started rising with the advent of the Great Depression and reached 71.7 percent in 1931. Freight revenue, which had been $89.8 million in 1920, rose to $104 million in 1928, and plunged to $63.3 million in 1931.

Though owned jointly by the Great Northern and the Northern Pacific, the Chicago, Burlington, and Quincy operated quite independently from its owners and was considered one of the best-managed railroads in the nation. The proud Q in 1926 even ran full-page advertisements in newspapers and magazines trumpeting the fact that 10 presidents or chairmen of U.S. railroads had been trained on the Burlington. Of those 10, nine had left the Hill family of railroads, and Howard Elliott had gone on to be chief executive of the Northern

Pacific. Hale Holden, president of the Burlington and considered one of the ablest men to have held that position, would leave in 1929 to be chairman of the Southern Pacific, then considered the strongest railroad in the West. Despite its ownership, the Burlington was sufficiently large and profitable that it was able to lure Ralph Budd from his post as president of the GN in 1932. Serving during a critical period until 1949, Budd would take his place alongside Charles Elliott Perkins as one of the true statesmen of the Burlington and of the railroad industry.

For the Santa Fe in the early 1920s, rising expenses were sharply outrunning any gains in revenue. According to historian Keith L. Bryant Jr., for every $1.00 the Santa Fe had spent on labor in 1915, it was spending $2.15 eight years later, and for every $1.00 in taxes it paid in 1915, it was paying $3.69 by 1923. But for every $1.00 it had received in freight revenue in 1915, it received just $1.39 in 1923, not nearly enough to balance its higher costs. Nevertheless, spurred by economic growth primarily in Southern California, the Santa Fe increased its handling of industrial and forest products shipments relative to agriculture, which previously had been the dominant freight category. The railroad also concentrated on relaying rail, relocating track to reduce grades and curves, building new bridges, and constructing larger terminals. In 1924, the Santa Fe had 6,934 miles of 90-pound rail (each 3-foot section weighed 90 pounds) and 2,296 miles of 85-pound rail. In 1926, Santa Fe president William Benson Storey announced that 110-pound rail would be the standard for Santa Fe main lines.

THE DEPRESSION HITS

The decline of the railroads did not happen all at once or even at a steady pace. There was momentum within the industry, and the huge increase in the American economy after the end of World War I carried the railroads through to the Great Depression. The Burlington, for example, reported net railway operating income that was almost $2.5 million higher in 1929 than in 1928 and the highest for any year since 1916. The stock market crash, though, was a precursor to the collapse of the national economy. The Wall Street crash almost immediately led to a sharp decline in railroad traffic. For a number of months, Burlington president Frederick Williamson maintained optimism about the economy in his periodic reports to the board of directors. But by March 1930, revenue was less than in any comparable month since 1919, and the Burlington was cutting maintenance and transportation expenses wherever possible. Passenger traffic plunged as people stayed home. Manufacturing volume dwindled, and the only bright spot in mid-1930 was generated by continued heavy grain movements. The Q remained profitable through 1930, however, and paid dividends to shareholders in June and December.

By 1931 it was impossible to ignore the impact of the Depression. In January, employment was at levels that Williamson called "just about the minimum possible" and then was cut even further in April. A railroad tradition, called holding for tonnage, involved discarding schedules and ensuring that every train had the maximum freight the engines could pull and was the maximum length that would fit on sidings. Honored wherever possible, especially during the Depression, the tradition was designed to reduce expensive train starts and crew costs. Both passenger and freight train miles were reduced, and schedules changed and trains consolidated, but service reliability suffered.

By year-end 1931, the Burlington's revenue and car loadings had both fallen by approximately 21 percent. Average employment had fallen from 38,000 to 31,000. Rigorous economizing kept the Burlington profitable, though, and its operating ratio for 1931 was held to 69.65 percent.

The Santa Fe, which had grown steadily in the post–World War I years, also hit hard times in the 1930s. Following the stock market crash in 1929, the Santa Fe responded favorably to President Herbert Hoover's call for industry to maintain capital spending plans and employment levels. By June 1930 the optimistic plans had disappeared. The Santa Fe, it should be remembered, served much of the territory that was to become known as the dust bowl, where drought and recession combined to destroy the agricultural economy. The Santa Fe suffered the worst traffic losses in its history. By mid-1930 it ordered cuts in maintenance and shop crews as part of a retrenchment program. In 1931, branch-line freight and passenger operations were slashed. At the end of 1931 the quarterly dividend was cut in half, effective with the March 1932 payment. Even the reduced dividend was suspended in June 1932. Although its net income dropped by some 85 percent, the Santa Fe did manage to eke out profits throughout the Depression.

Overcapacity had become a problem even before the Depression, as railroads struggled with the reverse of the pre–World War I congestion. Railroad track in the United States reached its maximum in 1916, with about a quarter million miles. By the mid-1920s—after nearly a century of nonstop building—railroads had begun to abandon track. In 1929 the United States had 229,530 route miles of railroad, but when double and triple main lines, yard track, and sidings were included, total track miles were 381,417. A decade later, on the eve of World War II, route miles had dropped to 220,915 and track miles to 364,174. In 1929, U.S. railroads laid 2,281,316 tons of new rail and 81,964,000 crossties, figures that never again have been matched. The 57,559 locomotives in service in 1929 also were a high-water mark, almost treble the 20,000 units in service in 2000. Even though railroads have fewer locomotives today, their pulling power is greater than ever before. Rolling stock hit a high of 2.6 million freight cars in 1929, double the current 1,380,796, although increased operating efficiency allows today's railroads to provide more transportation service with half the cars. Cars are considerably larger, averaging 92.7 tons of capacity in 2000; the average capacity in 1929 was just 46.3 tons.

What has changed even more significantly is railroad ownership and employment. Class 1 railroads—a government designation based on revenue—owned 87 percent of the freight cars in 1929, but by 2000, major railroad ownership was down to 40.5 percent, with smaller railroads, shippers, and car leasing companies accounting for a majority of the fleet. There were many more rail workers in 1929, when 1,661,000 were employed in the industry. Steam locomotives required more maintenance than today's modern diesel engines, and passenger operations were much more labor-intensive. Employment on Class 1 railroads was down to 168,000 in 2000, the lowest since records have been kept. The reduction in employment was matched by a sharp increase in productivity. Whereas more than three workers were needed to produce 1 million revenue ton-miles in 1929, each employee could produce 8.7 million ton-miles by 2000, also a record level.

During the Depression, one-half of the locomotive fleet went into storage. Companies that accounted for one-third of railroad mileage were in bankruptcy proceedings, and a government agency, the Reconstruction Finance Corporation, loaned railroads almost $600 million to keep them afloat. Not only did railroads have to contend with economic depression in the 1930s, but also for the first time they faced competition from other modes of transportation. The trucking industry began to make its presence felt, and nothing would ever be the same again for railroads. New roads were needed for the thousands of Model A Fords, Chevrolets, Plymouths, and trucks delivering the groceries and manufactured goods America demanded even in a declining economy. America was rapidly becoming a society driven by the internal combustion engine. If imitation is the highest form of flattery, the engineers who laid out the modern highway system routes flattered the men who surveyed the rail routes in the nineteenth century. They paralleled the rail routes wherever possible because the rail routes had the easiest grades and required the least amount of grading, excavation, and fill work. The engineers who had selected the rail routes, however, had relied on even earlier "surveyors." In *Burlington Route: A History of the Burlington Lines,* Richard C. Overton pointed out that American Indians had established the most feasible routes:

> As transportation engineers, the red men [American Indians] had no peers. When they had a journey to make athwart the prevailing direction of navigable streams, they unerringly located trails along the easiest grades and the most direct routes. The pathway they trod across southern Iowa between the great rivers was well established as the most feasible east-west route in the region.

Throughout the West, railroad surveyors were smart enough to retrace those trails.

Railroads initially and ironically were among the most ardent supporters of highway construction, playing a key role in the Good Roads movement and believing they were acting in their own as well as the public's interest. After all, the reasoning went, it would be good for the rail business if farmers could more easily bring their crops to railheads. Some railroads even sponsored promotional Good Roads trains, with exhibits intended to stir support for rural roads as feeders to the rail system. Beginning in Iowa, the heart of CB&Q territory, the Good Roads movement rapidly expanded, and pressure increased for the federal government to play a greater role in road building. Although railroad leaders could not anticipate the truck competition that would be impelled by greatly improved roads and the wholesale switch of passengers from trains to private automobiles, they were not naive in their support of roads. If farmers could more easily bring their produce to main-line points, many branch lines and small agencies could be abandoned. The savings would far outweigh the costs of maintaining the lines.

The rapid growth of the automobile spurred the Good Roads

movement, as Americans increasingly wanted to be able to move about the country. From 3.4 million registered vehicles in 1916, the total exploded to 26.4 million by 1929. Annual production was at a rate of 5.3 million. The automobile and the industry that grew with it soon would supplant the railroad as the major force in the U.S. economy. Road building became a major pump-priming mechanism. It provided employment and inspired the country to get back on its feet during the Depression. The combination of this extensive road building and the rigid regulation of railroads would combine over time to cripple the railroads.

U.S. railroads are the only transportation mode that owns, maintains, and operates its own infrastructure—and pays ad valorem property taxes for the privilege. There is a tremendous competitive difference in public policy in the way competing forms of transportation are aided or not aided by government. Trucking companies, for example, pay for their publicly provided infrastructure—the roads—through user charges. When business is soft and motor carriers operate fewer vehicles, they also stop paying for infrastructure costs. The railroads, however, still must maintain their property and bear the ownership costs. User charges are an operating expense, and with few fixed costs to be covered, motor and water carriers can charge lower prices to their users and still make a profit. Railroads, on the other hand, must price their services to cover both operating expenses and the considerable fixed costs of their track and terminals. Improved roads also allowed trucking companies to carry heavier loads at higher average speeds. This enabled motor carriers to siphon some of the railroads' more highly rated freight, such as manufactured goods, forcing railroad companies to rely to an ever-greater extent on the lower-rated bulk commodities such as coal, grain, sand, and gravel that could not effectively be carried by truck, barge, or ship.

Burlington's Ralph Budd was one of the first railroad executives to recognize and articulate the threat that trucking represented to railroads. Addressing the Inland Daily Press Association in Chicago on February 16, 1932, Budd told the audience that until the Depression it had been assumed that railways had a virtual monopoly of transportation. In that earlier time, regulators could prescribe rates that would enable railroads to earn a fair return and manage improvements and expansion. The railroads, Budd said, had spent as much on capital in the 1920s as in all their history and had achieved their highest degree of efficiency. By the end of that decade railroads had the greatest capacity of all time. What was not commonly understood at the time, Budd said, was that a great deal of rail activity involved carrying car and truck parts and highway construction material. Railroading was becoming incidental to the building of new and improved highways and the development of the automotive industry. The net result was what Budd termed "an elemental change": railroads no longer possessed a monopoly of overland transportation. Under such circumstances, the Burlington chief asserted, "it should be very clear that the controlling ideas and policies of regulation which may have been entirely appropriate when railways enjoyed a practical monopoly of overland transportation have now become obsolete and should be modified."

It was to take nearly half a century and numerous railroad bankruptcies before the federal government would recognize the accuracy of Budd's insight. Ralph Budd, a graduate of what has been referred to as the James J. Hill school of railroad management, had risen to executive vice president of the Great Northern by early 1918, and after William P. Kenney left to become a federal manager during the period of federal control, Budd acted as chief executive officer while Louis W. Hill held the presidency. Budd was named the GN president in October 1919. During the recession that followed the end of the war and the return of the railroads to private control, he remained confident that the GN could help stimulate the recovery he was certain would occur, and he moved forward with capital plans. The company committed and spent $15 million in 1922 for rolling stock and roadway improvements. New powerful locomotives were built in GN shops, using parts of dismantled older locomotives, while other engines were rebuilt and more locomotives were converted from coal to oil. A nationwide strike by shop workers in 1922 resulted when management sought wage reductions that were approved by the Railroad Labor Board, which consisted of three union, three management, and three public representatives. While several unions accepted the cuts of two to nine cents an hour, shop employees did not, and they began a strike on July 1. Violence broke out on various railroads, including the Great Northern.

During this period, however, the men who handled the wrecking train at Whitefish, Montana, showed their loyalty to their industry by helping to restore service after a serious derailment, even though they were on strike. The company accepted their offer of help, and they came off strike long enough to help clean up the wreck but, as a matter of principle, refused to make a pay claim for their work.

Budd had learned well the philosophy of James J. Hill. He was determined to reduce operating costs by lowering grades and reducing curves. Small year-by-year expenditures were evidence of his "a little here, a little there" approach and over a period of years resulted in impressive savings in the costs of maintenance and operation. Budd considered the Great Northern to be in a competitive battle with the Northern Pacific, the Milwaukee Road, and, to a lesser extent, the Union Pacific. By upgrading the car fleet, locomotive power, and track structure, the Great Northern would assure shippers of fast, reliable service. The GN would thus strengthen its competitive position. But to generate satisfactory profits in the face of capital outlays and inexorably rising operating expenses, Budd knew—as he had been taught by Hill—that the GN had to relentlessly attack costs.

During Budd's presidency the locomotive fleet increasingly was converted from coal-burning to less expensive oil. Almost one-third of the fleet had been changed over by 1931. Under Budd, the GN also began to abandon little-used lines. Some 300 miles were removed, much of it in British Columbia, as the railroad gave up on the Hill desire to develop a direct route between Spokane, Washington, and Vancouver, British Columbia. The idea of running a line through Canada from Vancouver to Winnipeg, if it ever was more than a thought, was laid to rest. Budd initially misread the competitive threat from the highways. Once he recognized it, however, he joined other railroads in advocating that the trucking industry also be brought under economic regulation by the Interstate Commerce Commission.

When it came to the passenger business, however, Budd had no illusions that the railroad could fend off competition from the growing number of private automobiles and buses. There were those inside the Great Northern who pressed for reduced fares to bring passengers back to the railroad. Budd realistically recognized that there was a place for each form of transportation and that trying to deny that would be futile. As he put it, "the best way to make money in local passenger business is to get out of it as soon as local passenger trains fail to pay their way." He was more optimistic about long-distance trains, though, upgrading and improving the GN's transcontinental passenger service, including the 1924 start of the Oriental Limited, considered one of the finest passenger trains in the nation. The even more-luxurious Empire Builder followed in 1929. Budd devoted resources to the GN's long-distance trains both to increase revenue and to attract shippers and others to the Northwest. "The Passenger Department is the show window of the railroad," he asserted, "and contributes more to its successful operation than actual passenger revenue."

Despite the competitive challenges, the Great Northern managed to expand some lines and even invaded a new market under Budd. New construction and trackage rights over the Southern Pacific allowed the railroad to enter Klamath Falls, Oregon, some 400 miles south of Portland, and to participate in the growing lumber business of western Oregon. Even before the negotiations with SP were completed, Budd turned to the bigger California market. In 1930 the ICC granted approval for the Great Northern to build a line south from Klamath Falls to a connection with the Western Pacific at Bieber, California. When Budd left the Great Northern in 1932 to become president of the Burlington, he was succeeded by Kenney, who was able to make sharp reductions in maintenance expenditures during the Depression, in large part because the property had been left in such good shape by his predecessor.

The competitive battle between trucks and railroads that had begun in the 1920s was accentuated by the Depression. Differing approaches to rate making also favored the truckers in competition with railroads. Railroad rates were a complex matrix based on the value of the commodity and the distance it was carried. The Santa Fe's Ripley may have coined the expression "what the traffic will bear," but the actual rate structure was more complex. Truckers, on the other hand, set rates based on the cost of providing the service. With few fixed costs, the cost of providing service for most truckers was lower than the rail rate for the same commodity. Truckers, too, were affected by the Great Depression, but they were more flexible than railroads and were nimble in responding to the business crisis. The Burlington saw traffic diverted to truckers, who hauled small lots of feed to farmers who were buying on a hand-to-mouth basis. The unregulated truckers then carried small loads of cattle to points at which more feed was available. Truckers also carried coal and wood on back hauls. All this traffic once had been the exclusive business of the railroad.

Although the Great Northern's ore shipments were not threatened by truck competition, truckers did begin to cut into apple shipments from the Wenatchee Valley of Washington. Less-than-carload freight, or LCL, was hit especially hard. LCL then was a significant share of each railroad's traffic mix, because much merchandise was

Ralph and John Budd

Father and Son

Ralph Budd

Even though the Great Northern owned 50 percent of the Chicago, Burlington, and Quincy (CB&Q), the CB&Q was bigger than either the GN or the Northern Pacific, which owned the other 50 percent. Ralph Budd, who had worked his way up the managerial ladder, left the GN to assume the Burlington presidency in 1932. Budd was no stranger to the Burlington. He had represented the Great Northern on its board since 1916. At the Q, he had to cope with the effects of the Great Depression and then almost immediately moved the railroad into crisis mode for the duration of World War II. The postwar years were almost anticlimactic. Ralph Budd had been a voracious reader, particularly in history, ever since his childhood on a farm near Waterloo, Iowa. At the Burlington in 1933, he was reading Chaucer's *Canterbury Tales* one evening when he came across a reference to Zephyrus, the Greek god of the west wind who typified renaissance. Before long, Burlington's first streamlined passenger train that was under construction was named Zephyr.

Near the end of his active involvement in railroad management in 1949, Budd addressed the American Newcomen Society in Boston to mark the centennial of the Burlington Lines, now made up of some 206 once-separate properties. Budd's studies of Burlington history had given him an appreciation of the 49 years the railroad spent under the influence of Boston investors led by Forbes. In an era of reckless promoters, the Forbes interests had brought a businessman's approach to the construction and acquisition of railroads. The Burlington, he said, remained "singularly free" of dubious practices. He added:

> The Burlington was built and managed as an investment enterprise in which profits were to be made from that railroad itself through a consistent policy of building a solid and well-planned road, of reinvesting in the property a substantial portion of the earnings, of buying no other railroads unless they would fit into the growing system and would be remunerative, of developing the country through which the railroad operated, and of giving good service at the lowest rates consistent with continuous provision of such service.

John Budd

Although reserved in manner and known to shun publicity for its own sake, John Budd had an appreciation of the value of public communications. He sponsored the 30 years of research by husband-and-wife historians Ralph W. and Muriel E. Hidy that resulted in the publication of *The Great Northern Railway: A History*. The GN supported the research through the Business History Foundation and made its voluminous archives freely accessible to the researchers. Ralph Hidy's health broke before the manuscript was completed, and after his death his widow continued the project with the help of Mississippi State University professor Roy V. Scott, one of the original researchers. Eventually, rail historian Don Hofsommer edited and completed the Hidy manuscript.

Hofsommer credited John Budd with continuing the tradition of his father and James J. Hill that the Great Northern should be continuously maintained and improved. John Budd pushed for completion of dieselization; acquisition of specialized rolling stock that would meet customers' changing needs; continued attention to track, yards, and other facilities; and adoption of new technology such as computers. Under John Budd, the GN continued to promote regional economic development. He also was willing to consider the possibility of merger with another railroad. As normal as that may appear today, in the era of regulation Budd was like a Renaissance man before the Reformation. The conservative fiscal tradition of the GN from the time of James J. Hill came in good stead during this period and allowed Budd to carry out his plans. Like other railroad executives in the post–World War II period, John Budd believed that the government should consider transportation policy in a coordinated manner, rather than approaching each mode as though it operated in a vacuum and the actions of one neither affected nor was affected by other modes. Budd recognized that government could not induce Americans to reject airplanes and private automobiles and that railroads could not regain their near monopoly in moving freight. He believed, however, that railroads provided a needed service and that they could do it more economically than their competitors if only the government would allow the railroads to compete on an equal basis.

An example of the inequitable treatment that offended Budd was the airport at Cut Bank, Montana, where GN taxes for its support amounted to $2,241 in 1956, while Western Airlines, which used the field, paid only $22.92 in property taxes. Other examples are too numerous to mention, but it was not until 1976 that Congress, in the Railroad Revitalization and Regulatory Reform (4R) Act, outlawed discriminatory state taxation of railroads. A more serious inequity was that the GN "depended for one-third of its total freight revenues on the transportation of commodities which now moved by truck without regulation," Budd said in 1958.

transported in carload lots over long hauls to distribution centers where it was then shifted to LCL for local distribution. Because the Depression had hurt retailers and other consignees, orders became smaller and trucks could expedite the handling of the entire shipments. LCL shipments on the GN declined 43 percent for the five years ending on December 31, 1934, in relation to shipments for the previous five years.

The Good Roads movement had shifted. Now it was Great Northern workers who formed ship-by-rail clubs. The Citizens' Transportation League, even larger, sought regulation for highway carriers and water transport. The GN had no official connection with these groups but clearly welcomed their activities. Future rail efforts to control truck size and weight also relied on front groups that appeared to be independent of the industry.

The Motor Carrier Act was passed in 1935. It gave the ICC the authority to grant certificates of public convenience and necessity to common carriers, to control mergers, and to set maximum rates for motor carriers. The act was in part a result of the efforts of railroads to improve their own economic position by imposing regulation on competing truckers. William P. Kenney understood, as Budd did at the Burlington, the nature of the competition. "What I am trying to beat into the heads of our people," Kenney said, "is that we no longer have a monopoly." Sometimes his efforts went astray. In the mistaken belief that unionization would hurt highway carriers, he cheered efforts by the International Brotherhood of Teamsters to unionize truck drivers.

The Burlington was both financially strong and well run. It managed to remain profitable, if only barely, throughout the Depression. In 1940 the average mileage of the North Western, the Rock Island, and the Milwaukee—Burlington's principal competitors—was 8,997, or just 43 miles less than the average operated mileage of the Burlington. The revenue of the three competitor railways averaged only 5 percent less than those of the Burlington, and none of the competitors had any net income at all. All but one of the major components of today's BNSF Railway survived the Great Depression. While the Great Northern, the Northern Pacific, the Burlington, and the Santa Fe all scraped through and avoided bankruptcy, the Frisco fell into bankruptcy in 1933 and did not emerge from reorganization until 1947.

Water carrier competition was also affecting railroads in the period between the wars, but not all to the same degree. The Transportation Act of 1920 called for competition between rail and water carriers, but it also required that railroads set joint rail-water rates even on traffic that could be moved entirely by rail. The ICC's power to set minimum rail rates also deprived the railroads of their principal weapon for meeting water competition. Water carriers of bulk commodities—grain, petroleum, coal, and so on—were completely exempt from economic regulation. Railroads, on the other hand, had to go through the regulatory process. They were required to file tariffs that were subject to challenge and suspension whenever they wanted to change rates—either up or down. Of the railroads that eventually became BNSF Railway, the Burlington was the one most affected by river-borne competition. On the Mississippi, for instance, barge operators charged rates that were low enough to attract grain from growing areas a considerable distance from the river. This forced the Burlington into joint rate agreements in which it received only the revenue for the short haul to the river, while the barge operator took the long-haul revenue.

The railroads didn't merely fight with motor carriers. They also tried to embrace the competition, running their own motor vehicles on the roads. The Northern Pacific won permission from the Montana Railroad Commission in 1934 to put trucks and buses on several routes and to abandon rail service on four branches in the state. The Great Northern applied for and obtained similar authority and permission to replace rail service with trucks, including pickup and delivery, along stretches of its main line. The Santa Fe and others tried to protect their less-than-carload business by offering pickup and delivery service through their trucking subsidiaries. LCL carried higher rates than full carload shipments, and losing that business cut the railroads' profits more deeply than it cut revenue. It was a development that would be repeated when the Interstate Highway System was built in the 1950s and 1960s, because as trucks gained speed and service reliability, they increasingly captured business that had long belonged exclusively to railroads. Federal law and regulation, however, forbade the railroads from becoming true multimodal transportation companies. Although many railroads set up motor carrier subsidiaries, their operation was restricted to traffic that would be making part of its trip by rail. Railroads were not allowed ownership in the fledgling common carrier airline industry either. Some rail critics argued that the rail industry might kill off airline competitors if given the opportunity.

In addition to new competition, some of the railroads' problems before World War II were functions of geography. The Northern Pacific, for example, was considered a Granger road, heavily invested in moving agricultural commodities. Agriculture, though, was depressed for much of the 1920s, and tonnage available for the NP declined to the point that, by 1926, grain, cattle, and other agricultural product shipments trailed shipments of forest products, such as paper, timber, and pulp (38 percent of total traffic), and products from mines, mostly coal from southern Montana (26 percent). Manufactured products accounted for only 13 percent of NP volume that year, low even for a Granger road. Rates on manufactured products returned the highest profits, while rates on agricultural shipments were held down by the regulatory system. With Congress dominated by members from rural states, there was no chance of legislative relief. The Northern Pacific management recognized the need to secure more manufacturing businesses along its lines but was thwarted by the Great Depression.

ANOTHER ATTEMPT TO CONSOLIDATE IN THE NORTHWEST

Hill and Roosevelt were gone, but under the direction of J. P. Morgan's son, J. P. (Jack) Morgan Jr., the Northern Pacific and the Great Northern tried again in 1927 to merge, relying on the provisions of the Transportation Act of 1920 that called for consolidation of the nation's railroads. "The trouble with the Northwestern carriers is that there are too many," Ralph Budd wrote in 1925. By that time, of course, there was a third northern transcontinental. The Milwaukee Road had built its western extension in the belief that economic growth would make the investment pay out—an early example of "build it and they will come."

Stockholders of the Great Northern and the Northern Pacific overwhelmingly approved a merger, and an application was filed with the ICC. In 1930 the regulators authorized a merger between the GN and the NP but conditioned their approval on each railroad's disposing of its 50 percent ownership in the Chicago, Burlington, and Quincy. Forcing the Great Northern Pacific, as the merged railroad was to be called, to sever ties with the Burlington was an attempt to protect the Milwaukee, which had its own lines to Chicago. Executives at the GN and the NP remembered James J. Hill's advice that "a railroad without terminals is like a body without hands and feet" and quickly determined that the ICC condition was unacceptable. They were not about to relinquish their access to Chicago. The merger petition was withdrawn on February 19, 1931.

Congress may have indicated a predilection toward mergers in the Transportation Act of 1920, but the ICC interpreted the law differently. As the ill-fated effort to merge the northern lines showed, however, what Congress says and what Congress does frequently are two different things. Under pressure from rail labor, which wanted no rail consolidations, and politicians such as Senator Burton K. Wheeler of Montana, the Senate adopted an antimerger resolution and encouraged the ICC to reopen hearings into the merger. Withdrawal of the application made the issue moot.

Passenger service revenue fell rapidly during the period between the wars. Americans were buying their own cars and driving them over better roads or were riding on intercity bus lines instead of taking the train. The private automobile proved even more destructive of the rail passenger business than did the airliner. Some of the loss was attributed to improvement in long-distance telephone service, which did away with the need for travel across the miles.

"The ICC was reluctant to allow the NP to remove passenger trains from service, but state regulatory agencies were adamantly opposed to 'train off' requests," wrote Frey and Schrenk in *Northern Pacific*. "Thus the familiar sight of empty passenger trains began to replace what had been a modestly profitable business prior to World War I." The Great Northern also stumbled at the state level when it tried to cancel money-losing passenger trains. The Montana Railroad Commission, for example, bluntly rejected a GN request in July 1935 for authority to cancel three intrastate trains between Great Falls and Butte, Great Falls and Lewistown, and Shelby and Sweet Grass. One commissioner stated that he was going "to keep the railroad running those trains, even though they are empty." On appeal to a federal court, the railroad gained permission in 1936 to end one of the trains—a victory of sorts. For the Great Northern, 1932 was the low point. The government was priming the pump, generating traffic. The GN carried construction materials for highways, dams, bridges, and public buildings, and the railroad's freight volume increased in every year after 1932. GN executives exulted that the railroad's operating ratio was lower than those of the NP and the Milwaukee, and soon they were pointing out that that ratio was even lower than that of the Union Pacific. The rivalry with the UP had outlived both Hill and Harriman.

RAILROADS GO TO WAR—AGAIN

The struggle to find traffic and to keep the railroads running soon came to an end. Even before the U.S. entry into World War II in December 1941, the national economy and rail traffic picked up as war in Europe generated growing traffic. In contrast to the experience in World War I, however, the railroads managed to meet the demands that were placed on them, and government takeover was avoided. The industry rose to the challenge. Railroads carried 90 percent of the military freight and 98 percent of the troops to both the Atlantic and Pacific ports of embarkation as the nation fought a two-front war. Industry leaders, many of whom were holdovers from the First World War, knew they would be closely watched, particularly by those who wanted public ownership. A second government takeover might permanently end private ownership of railroads. Although the railroads had sharply reduced spending for new locomotives, freight cars, and investment in fixed plant, the industry still was better able to handle the demands of war because of the large capital programs of the 1920s.

Using powers granted by the Army Appropriation Act of 1916, President Franklin D. Roosevelt appointed a Council of National Defense, including an Advisory Commission, in May 1940. Ralph Budd was the commission member concerned with transport. In World War I, virtually all transport needs had fallen on the railroads, but this time Budd drew on representatives of many forms of commercial and private transport—truck, bus, automobile, pipeline, barge line, domestic water, air, and interurban transit—in addition to the railroads. When the duties of the Advisory Commission were transferred to the newly created Transportation Division in the Office of Emergency Management in January 1941, Budd was named director of the division, although he had no executive authority.

The government avoided many of the mistakes that had been committed nearly a quarter of a century earlier, and the railroads were able to respond effectively. The Car Service Division (CSD) of the Association of American Railroads (AAR) issued orders that prevented the use of rail cars for storage. In addition, it stipulated measures that kept the car fleet moving and returning rapidly for new loads once they were unloaded. In the national interest the CSD essentially managed the national rail car fleet as a pool even though the Interstate Commerce Act expressly forbade pooling. The railroads were able to move record volumes without commensurate increases in capacity.

World War II brought an unprecedented increase in freight and passenger traffic to the railroads. It did so in such a short period of time that the industry had no chance to increase either equipment or personnel to handle the burden that was placed on it. Shortages of material were such that the railroads were forced to make do with the infrastructure that had been available in peacetime. War distorted the normal traffic patterns, further complicating the railroads' burden. Military installations and defense plants were established virtually overnight and frequently in locations chosen for strategic reasons rather than for proximity to railroad tracks or major roads. By disregarding track ownership and using the most efficient routes, rail industry coordination allowed the carriers to handle far more traffic than they might have otherwise. Similar cooperation in peacetime enabled the railroad industry to continue operations during the Great Flood of 1993, when much of the Midwest was underwater.

There may have been no combat on continental U.S. soil, but the war nonetheless had an effect on transportation. German submarine attacks along the East Coast caused coal shipments to be switched to rail from the usual Hampton Roads, Virginia, to New England water routes, increasing the demand for coal hopper cars. Similarly, petroleum shipments from Gulf ports to the Northeast were shifted from coastal tankers to all-rail routes so they would not be vulnerable to attacks from submarine "wolf packs." It took a Herculean effort, but U.S. railroads managed to cope with the sharp increase in demand. Freight service increased 27 percent in 1941 over that in 1940. In 1942, railroads provided 70 percent more service than in 1940, and in 1943 the gain was 94 percent. From a low of 379.2 billion ton-miles of freight handled in 1940, the industry nearly doubled its production of transportation service to 746.9 billion ton-miles in 1944. Railroads also increased their share of total transportation provided during the war. The inroads of trucks, airlines, and barges had reduced the railroad share of intercity ton-miles to 64.26 percent by 1939. Yet by 1943 the railroad share had increased to 72.79 percent of a significantly larger transportation pie.

The demand surge handled by railroads was even greater for passengers. The demands of a two-front war meant that troop trains were moving from bases in the interior to ports of embarkation on both the Atlantic and Pacific Coasts. Railroads handled 24.8 billion passenger-miles in 1940. Passenger-miles increased 23 percent to

30.3 billion in 1941, then jumped to 55 billion in 1942, 89.9 billion in 1943, and 97.7 billion in 1944, when passenger volume was 295 percent higher than in 1940. Railroads accounted for almost all troop movements in World War II.

The magnitude of the challenge accepted by railroads was even more impressive when the decline in the fleet is taken into account. The industry owned 2.32 million freight cars with aggregate capacity of 96.8 million tons in 1918. By 1940 the fleet had fallen to 1.65 million cars with just 82.7 million tons of capacity. Railroad-owned and Pullman passenger cars had declined from 35,613 and 7,726, respectively, in 1918 to 22,576 and 7,059, respectively, in 1941. Club, observation, lounge, and parlor cars were converted into coaches and three-tier sleepers to augment the fleet, and retired equipment was overhauled and returned to service. Many men, obviously, had left the railroad industry during the Great Depression and for service in the war, and that meant that the industry handled the immensely heavier demands of World War II with fewer workers than in World War I. The situation became so dire that late in the war the military was persuaded to furlough 4,000 men to rejoin the railroads' workforce. Joseph R. Rose, who served as historical officer of the Office of Defense Transportation, wrote in *American Wartime Transportation,* "Despite the shortage of equipment and labor and the magnitude of the load the railroads successfully met the wartime demands made upon them." He also noted that, despite weather-related strains and port congestion, "there was never such a disruption of the railway system as to impede the continuous flow of traffic consigned to war theatres abroad or to war industries at home."

At individual railroads, the pressure of serving the nation's needs in time of war was all but overwhelming. The Great Northern, for example, still relied largely on steam power and had made no major additions to the locomotive fleet since 1930. More than three-fourths of its road engines were more than 15 years old, and its switch engines averaged 40 years of age. Only 2,500 freight cars had been placed in service in the seven years before 1939. The passenger fleet was a mix of 108 steel and 181 wooden cars. Track work on the GN had been reduced during the Depression, when rail steel purchases averaged 8,000 tons annually, far short of the 25,000 tons the engineering department believed was necessary. C. O. Jenks, newly named vice president of operations, proposed the acquisition of 7,800 new freight cars, 37 new locomotives, and work equipment of all kinds, as well as increased track work, yard expansions, new signaling, and electrification of the main line through the Cascades. Frank J. Gavin, who succeeded Kenney as president in 1939, committed the Great Northern to diesel power. The GN had managed to place 49 diesel locomotives in service by the time the United States entered the war. The new power was financed by conditional sales contracts with payment spread over a number of years. Gavin also authorized Jenks to acquire more freight cars and to increase expenditures for roadway. Demand for iron ore shipments increased sharply following the German invasion of Poland on September 1, 1939, and the GN improvement program turned out to be fortuitous; the railroad handled 53 percent more freight tonnage in 1941 than in 1939. In the face of improving revenue and income, conservative GN directors chose to apply cash to reducing the railroad's bonded debt rather than immediately restoring the dividend that had been discontinued in 1932. Even during the war, however, the Great Northern managed to make some permanent improvements. New shops were built at Havre and Great Falls, Montana, and construction began in 1945 on a 1.25 million–bushel grain elevator at Superior, Wisconsin. Line improvements included new and lengthened passing tracks, expanded yards, improved signaling, and continued work to lower grades and reduce curvature.

The Great Northern soldiered on despite the loss of 8,775 employees to active duty. Of those, 898—including future GN president John M. Budd, Ralph Budd's son—served in the 704th Railway Grand Division and the 732nd Railway Operating Battalion in campaigns from North Africa to Germany. The railroad recruited replacement workers, taking them where it could find them. The story is told that a switch tender hastily hired in 1945 in Minneapolis "spent most of his time during working hours cracking safes around the city"; although highly recommended by a local trucking firm, he had actually spent the preceding years in "three or four penitentiaries." The manpower shortage continued to be acute. Demand for workers was so great that the government authorized the hiring of Mexican nationals, and by the beginning of 1944 more than 200 Mexican nationals were on the payroll. Their work proved more satisfactory than an experiment with German prisoners of war. By September 1943 the GN had more than 1,500 women in its workforce, including coach cleaners and roundhouse laborers in addition to the traditional secretarial or clerical jobs. The GN actually managed to increase employment by 52 percent from 18,461 in 1939 to 27,995 in 1945.

Despite the best efforts of the GN and the AAR Car Service Division, car shortages disrupted traffic flows during the war. In 1943, with more than 20,000 of its boxcars off-line, many GN on-line grain elevators were full and grain was stored on the ground. The GN started 1944 with only 74 percent of its cars on-line, and the problems increased as the car supply for grain movement fell to 39 percent in March 1945. Shippers were not mollified. In cries similar to those heard in present times, grain elevator operators pleaded for relief that was beyond the railroad's ability to grant. Public criticism increased, and one Montana shipper wrote: "The Great Northern seems to make a practice of falling down."

The Great Northern, however, managed to set records for freight volume handled throughout the war. In 1942 it handled 59.7 million tons, 82 percent more than the 32.8 million tons handled in 1939. Records were set for mine products in 1942; for wheat, animal products, and other agricultural commodities in 1944; and for manufactured and miscellaneous goods in 1945. Records were also set during the war for measures of operating efficiency—gross ton-miles per train hour, trainload in net tons, ton-miles per car per day, and gross miles per ton of fuel consumed.

The war years were marked by more than revenue gains. Despite government programs to constrain costs, labor rates increased, and the average hourly wage rose 32 percent between 1939 and 1945. At the same time, the ICC granted relatively small rate increases that proved less than compensatory. During wage negotiations in 1943, the industry came very close to a strike, a situation that would have forced the government to seize the railroads as it had in World War I. President Roosevelt made himself the mediator between the unions and the railroads and persuaded the engineers and trainmen to accept an increase of nine cents an hour. It was four cents more than had been recommended by an emergency board. Other unions rejected the settlement and resolved to strike. At that point the government stepped in and on December 27 took control of the railroads. Ralph Budd of the Burlington was appointed colonel in charge of the Central Western District and served in uniform until the railroads were returned to civilian control. Realizing they would not be permitted to use their economic weapon of a strike, the other unions soon accepted the same terms as the engineers and trainmen, and government control of the railroads ended on January 18, 1944. Under Gavin's prodding, the operating ratio, which was 65.9 percent in 1939, improved to 56.5 in 1942, the lowest since 1916. The ratio increased to the low 60s in 1943 and 1944, but shot to 79.9 in 1945 as rising costs outdistanced revenue gains and efficiency improvements. The Great Northern used its growing revenue to refund numerous series of debt, many of them before they were due, during the war. Much of the refunded debt was at lower interest rates. The ratio of debt to equity shifted from 57.04/42.96 in 1938 to 47.62/52.39 in 1945, and the annual charge for interest payments was cut by 30 percent between 1938 and 1945.

Ironically, for the Northern Pacific, which had lurched from crisis to crisis throughout its history, the war years were financially its most successful. Unlike the GN and other major railroads that were unable to continue major capital spending programs during the Depression, the NP continued to buy locomotives and rolling stock and entered the World War II period with a modern fleet. Under Charles Donnelly, NP president from 1920 to 1939, the railroad had begun its conversion to diesel-electric power. Following the death of Donnelly in September 1939, the Northern Pacific board chose "outsider" Charles E. Denny, president of the Erie Railroad. Highly regarded by the operating department, Denny served through the war years and later, retiring in 1951 at age 72. He is probably best remembered for track and roadbed improvements made during his tenure.

NP traffic surged even more than at other railroads as a result of the war. A series of outstanding harvests would have accounted for growth even if other commodity movements had not increased. As a land grant railroad, however, the Northern Pacific was required to move troops and government property at 50 percent of the tariff and to move mail at 80 percent of the tariff. The Transportation Act of 1940 had narrowed the discount so that only troops and military equipment still moved at deep discounts, but the result was that the NP saw more troop trains than the parallel Great Northern. Traffic and volumes of tonnage handled on the Northern Pacific increased steadily in 1942, 1943, and 1944, peaking finally with the highest freight tonnage and passenger volume in the NP's history. Even though almost 50 percent of traffic was moving at the reduced land-grant rates, net operating income increased sharply. In 1944, net operating income was 48 percent higher than in record-breaking 1943, which in turn was up 56 percent over 1942, also a record year, and 110 percent higher than a solid 1941. The 40 new locomotives purchased during the Depression contributed to the NP's ability to handle 75 percent more ton-miles per train in 1942 than in 1929. The NP continued to acquire new steam locomotives as well as diesels during the war. According to Northern Pacific historians Frey and Schrenk, the railroad continued its reliance on steam in part because coal from its extensive and inexpensive coal reserves could be delivered to locomotive tenders for 80 cents per ton, while wartime prices of diesel fuel were high.

Like other railroads, the NP saw many of its employees— 5,500—volunteer for military duty even though most skilled railroad positions were made draft exempt. Recruiting replacement workers was even more difficult because so much of the NP territory was lightly populated. The government finally allowed interregional recruitment for the NP and the GN, among others. To the south, the Atchison, Topeka, and Santa Fe also was forced to grapple with the loss of certain land-grant claims and the continued deep discounts it was required to give for the movement of troops and military cargo under provisions of the Transportation Act of 1940. According to Keith L. Bryant Jr., in *History of the Atchison, Topeka and Santa Fe Railway,* "Between 1942 and 1946 the Santa Fe discounted $151,243,773 in freight charges and $38,252,191 in passenger fares for a revenue loss of $189,295,964. Even raw materials moving to federally leased plants received the discount."

Even though much of its traffic moved at discount, Santa Fe earnings soared, and as at the Great Northern, much of the gain went to reduce debt. Management also warned that while profits were excellent, locomotives, cars, and trackage were taking a heavy beating. The Santa Fe had the key line between Chicago and the West Coast, much of it double-tracked, and it was used to capacity. Ton-miles of freight nearly doubled between 1941 and 1942, and passenger volume increased by 88 percent. In addition to recruiting new and replacement workers, Santa Fe also welcomed retirees back to the job. New freight diesels could move 60 cars from Kansas City to Los Angeles, some 3,150 tons, in 53 hours. Steam passenger engines ran through from Argentine, Kansas, to Los Angeles, a distance of 1,788 miles. The Santa Fe put its locomotive shops on two shifts and then three shifts daily to keep the power serviced.

Although all railroads strained to meet wartime demand, the Santa Fe had an extra burden because so many military installations were along its lines. Both Los Angeles and San Diego, for example, became major military centers with aircraft plants, naval installations, and nearby army and marine bases. Moving one army division required 55 trains totaling some 22 miles of cars. Some 12,000 Santa

Fe employees joined military units, many serving in railroad battalions in India, Burma, Italy, France, and North Africa. Santa Fe men filled three railway battalions, the 710th, 713th, and 758th. In 1943, of Santa Fe's 58,767 employees, 4,250 were Mexicans.

A wartime line expansion turned out to be vital for today's BNSF Railway. During the war, the Santa Fe asked for permission to reach the harbor at Long Beach, something it had sought for forty years. Wartime traffic made the connection mandatory, and an ICC hearing examiner (the equivalent of an administrative law judge today) recommended approval to give the Santa Fe equal access with the Southern Pacific and the Union Pacific. The full commission concurred in June 1945, following which the Southern Pacific allowed the Santa Fe to have trackage rights over the SP line to the harbor, eliminating the need for costly construction. The twin ports of Los Angeles and Long Beach today are the busiest ports in North America, and following industry consolidation the merged BNSF carries more intermodal traffic—containers and trailers on flat cars—than any other railroad.

The railroads paid much of their rising earnings to the government in war taxes, income taxes, and excess profits taxes. Still, enough was retained that the Santa Fe was able to retire $100 million in debt, and by 1945 all callable bonds had been paid, with reductions in annual interest charges. The Santa Fe also began installing centralized traffic control in 1944. This innovation reduced train running times by one-third and added as much as 80 percent to the capacity of a single-track line.

The Chicago, Burlington, and Quincy contributed mightily to satisfying wartime demand. While it produced nearly 49.5 billion ton-miles and three billion passenger-miles of service in the six years from 1934 through 1939, the Q accounted for more than 93 billion ton-miles and nearly 8.5 billion passenger-miles, reflecting increases of 88 percent and 179 percent, respectively, in the six years 1940 through 1945. As Ralph Budd said later: "During the war years we at the Burlington did twice as well as we thought we could."

The traffic statistics are astounding. During 1942 through 1945, plants located on the CB&Q lines originated 370,685 cars of shells and bombs. At the same time, the Burlington participated in moving the largest grain crops ever produced up to that time. From the attack on Pearl Harbor through the end of 1945, the Burlington operated 10,117 special trains carrying 3,075,643 men

Wartime Rivalries

Despite the focus on serving the country, cooperation between railroads was not always smooth, as they fought for scarce allocations of equipment.

In 1942 the War Production Board (WPB) took control of allocating not only completed locomotives in manufacturers' hands but also all future production. The Great Northern (GN) had 20 diesels on order, including 13 four-unit, 5,400-horsepower Titans for service in the Rocky Mountains. They were diverted to other railroads, leading Frank J. Gavin to complain: "There is not much change of chance to get anything. The Pennsylvania, Southern, and a few other lines run the show." In November 1942, when the WPB gave no diesels to the GN but allowed the Northern Pacific to acquire 22, C. O. Jenks was forced to recommend that steam locomotives be purchased.

Gavin rejected the suggestion. Even during the war, he recognized that the future success and even survival of the GN would require that the railroad be operated efficiently. "One thing we will have to do if we are going to stay in business . . . is to operate the railroad efficiently," he said.

Railroads also fought over scarce supplies of rail steel. The GN contracted in 1941 for 23,000 tons for delivery in 1942 but received only 16,100 tons. When the company asked for 23,000 gross tons for 1943, the WPB allotment was 22,000 net tons, half the amount granted the Northern Pacific. Gavin was furious: "We tried to play fair . . . and asked for only what we thought was absolutely necessary. . . . [W]e played the game wrong because if we asked for twice as much as we needed we would have gotten what we wanted." He, too, would play the game. In 1944 the GN reported its need as 50,000 net tons and obtained 37,326 tons.

and handled 1,479,698 additional military personnel in extra cars on regular trains, an average of nearly 3,000 a day. The figures do not include the millions of servicemen who traveled individually.

The Burlington experienced the same critical shortages in wartime personnel as other railroads did. Budd turned to women and Mexican nationals to supplement the workforce as well as having regulars work harder and for longer hours. Burlington employees staffed the 745th Railway Operating Battalion for the Military Railway Service (MRS) and saw service in the far northeast of India, where the battalion helped operate the Bengal and Assam Railway, which carried supplies to Ledo on the Burma border. From Ledo,

The Ledo Road

The Military Railway Service (MRS), as Carl R. Gray Jr. wrote, played a significant and different role in the China-Burma-India (CBI) theater of the war. All previous MRS missions had involved logistical support of Allied forces fighting Germany. In the CBI theater the MRS was to haul supplies from Calcutta to Ledo over some 800 miles of the Bengal and Assam Railway. From Ledo, supplies were flown over "the hump"—the Himalaya Mountain range—to Chinese troops trying to block the Japanese advance in China. Supplies also were trucked over the famous Ledo and Burma roads. First, however, the railway troops had to bring the supplies needed to build the Ledo Road and the airfield for the airlift.

The Bengal and Assam Railway (B&A) was operated by the 705th Railway Grand Division, sponsored by the Southern Pacific, with five railway operating battalions (ROB) and one railway shop battalion (RSB) assigned to it. The units were made up of men from the New York Central (721st ROB); the Chicago, Rock Island, and Pacific (725th ROB); the Wabash (726th ROB); the Chicago, Burlington, and Quincy (745th ROB); the Texas and Pacific (748th ROB); and the Santa Fe (758th RSB). After the U.S. railway men constructed double track over more than 100 miles of the B&A and put the Indian railway shops on a 24-hour schedule, they were able to increase the tonnage they hauled from an average of 15,000 to 20,000 tons a month to a minimum of 25,000 tons, with a target of 30,000 tons.

The MRS troops faced real war conditions. In early 1944, Japanese forces penetrated to within four and a half miles of the rail yard at Mariana, but British and American troops were brought to the front by rail in just 24 hours. They repulsed the Japanese. Even though the Japanese had been pushed back, roving bands continued to try to disrupt and destroy the railroad, the trains, and their cargo. Rail motorcars with mounted machine guns were sent ahead of the trains both to watch for damage to track and structures and to draw and reply to any Japanese fire.

Troops and freight movements on the B&A increased almost immediately upon the arrival of the MRS troops. In their first 26 days in control, the U.S. railway men increased tonnage handled by 46 percent. In the 20 months that they operated the B&A, it handled 6,217,143 tons. In 19 months of passenger operations, the MRS handled 5,559 passenger trains, an average of 310 per month, or 10 trains a day.

they were ferried by air over "the hump" of the Himalayas or by the Ledo and Burma roads to China.

The demands and problems of the war made for creative solutions. The Burlington leased a chicken ranch near Lincoln, Nebraska, in early 1945 so that, despite the shortage of meat, passengers on Burlington diners would be well fed. The ranch provided 30,000 birds a year. Although many skilled railroad occupations were draft exempt, the War Department had arranged even before the war for the staffing and training of units that would be assigned to the Military Railway Service. Major General Carl R. Gray, who served as director general from 1942 to 1945, said the MRS was "simply an American railroad in uniform." Individual railroads were asked and agreed to sponsor various units of the MRS. Railway operating battalions and railway shop battalions were staffed by men from a single railroad where the railroad was large enough; men from other railroads filled those battalions where one carrier could not provide a full complement. Railroad officers were given commissioned and noncommissioned officer status.

The railroaders-turned-citizen-soldiers spent their active duty time repairing damaged and sabotaged rail facilities in each of the countries the Allies liberated. They operated thousands of locomotives built expressly for the war effort, shuttling troops, munitions, food, and other supplies from ports to the front lines. One train even had a Red Cross doughnut car, the Yankee Dipper, attached. The car was a rebuilt Italian coach, and the Red Cross ladies handed out doughnuts and coffee to any soldier who rapped on the car at any hour of the day or night. U.S. railroads served the country well during World War II. Their managers and employees performed heroically in providing essential transportation service both in the United States and abroad while on active duty. They would have little time to bask in the satisfaction of a job well done, however, as the railroads would move on to more than three decades of decline.

4

The Aftermath of War

*Railway investors cannot be expected to continue putting
up risk capital unless there is evidence of fair treatment in a
way of permitting them to earn a reasonable return. Inability to obtain new money for the business inevitably would
tend to a deterioration of plant that would be far more costly to the country as a whole than the cost of adequate rates
and charges, which would insure the best of transportation.*

RALPH BUDD in a speech to Burlington stockholders, 1948

The war changed America in many ways, and some of those
changes affected the railroads in ways that could not have been
foreseen.

Nearly 12 million returning servicemen created a tremendous
demand for housing, education, and transportation. The nation had
added little to its store of housing during the decade before the war
or during the nearly four years of hostilities. Private automobile production had been halted during the war as defense production took
precedence. Scarce steel, rubber, and gas had been devoted to building tanks, aircraft, and other military equipment instead of Fords
and Pontiacs. The high rate of production following so quickly on
the Depression years meant that industrial America was in need of
huge replacement programs. Almost immediately the country
engaged in a capital spending boom, much of it focused on infrastructure investments.

Returning veterans were not about to resume their prewar lives,
and a grateful nation took steps to help its returning servicemen reen-
ter civilian life. The GI Bill provided education benefits for a still-
youthful workforce that had been unable to find good jobs during the

95

Depression. Housing assistance made it possible for war veterans to acquire houses and start families of their own.

These postwar measures were monumental. They also produced unanticipated consequences. As new families expanded, for example, the supply of available and desirable housing in the central cities and close-in suburbs was quickly exhausted. Real estate developers were quick to recognize the demand and moved to satisfy it. Vast tracts of GI housing began appearing within a year of the war's end, and entire communities sprang up virtually overnight.

As manufacturers returned to producing civilian goods, veterans rushed to buy new automobiles, and easy financing quickly put them behind the wheel. The combination of new housing and improved mobility contributed to a huge population migration. Where prewar America consisted of rural areas and cities, postwar America had growing suburbs and exurbs around the cities, with lower population density.

Demographically, population shifted to the west and the south as young families gravitated toward what became known as the Sun Belt. Hundreds of thousands of veterans elected not to return to the lives they lived before they went to war. Many who had left home for the first time when they entered the service chose to settle in parts of the country they had seen while in the military. The population expanded rapidly in California, which had been home to many military posts and had numerous ports of embarkation and disembarkation. Rapidly growing communities created a demand for new infrastructure.

Industry also began to shift geographically, both to fill customer demand and to tap a growing labor force. The automobile industry, which had assembled cars almost entirely in the Midwest before the war, provided an example of industry relocation. Assembly plants sprang up in California, Georgia, and Texas, among other locations. In the early postwar years, new manufacturing plants added to supply, augmenting the production from older plants because there was demand for more goods than the prewar industrial base could produce. Once that demand was satisfied, however, manufacturers found that their new plants were more efficient, and when it became necessary to adjust capacity, they reduced production at older plants, gaining even more efficiency in the process.

The railroads were changed too. Metropolitan New York, for example, had a well-structured rail network, and commuter trains continued to be filled with workers traveling to city jobs from burgeoning suburbs in Long Island, New Jersey, in Westchester, and even in Connecticut. Chicago also relied on railroads to provide commuter service between the city and its suburbs. Lack of population density made rail commuter service impractical except in the eastern megalopolises. Southern California, for example, never had an extensive commuter system, and as the area grew with few controls, jobs were spread farther and farther from central Los Angeles. The San Francisco Bay Area, however, had a rail commuter service, and new communities developed along existing rail lines.

These factors alone would have affected much of the railroad industry. But the dispersal of population and industrial production created increased pressure for new and improved roads. Where there was a lack of commuter transportation, workers demanded the opportunity to drive their new cars to their jobs. The new focus was on intercity highways in contrast to the former thirst for farm-to-market roads.

Economically, the United States avoided a postwar depression like the one experienced in 1921. After nearly 15 years of depression and war, there was huge pent-up demand for civilian goods, and industry converted from war production as quickly as possible. The economy was also stimulated by relief efforts to help rebuild the war-ravaged countries. The economy hardly missed a beat as it moved into the second half of the 1940s.

The railroads, however, did not come close to sharing fully in the postwar prosperity. If the railroads could have retained the share of the transportation business that they had during the war, they might have prospered. But they were hamstrung by regulation and forced to contend with less-regulated competitors. The railroads, before long, were in economic difficulty.

Had the railroads not paid down debt and reduced their fixed charges during the war period and invested heavily in labor-saving and cost-cutting devices in the postwar years, the industry "might well have experienced a plague of bankruptcies similar to that of the mid-1930's," as Richard C. Overton wrote.

On the surface, the actuality doesn't appear so grim. While the relative share of the railroads' freight and passenger markets declined, national economic prosperity was such that more freight was carried in each of the first four postwar years than in any of the prewar years. Even in 1949, when traffic had slipped to its lowest level since the end of the war, the railroad industry produced 17.8 percent more ton-miles than in 1929, a boom year before the Depression.

Despite the loss of market share in both freight and passenger traffic, many railroads, particularly in the South and the West saw continued opportunities to grow. There was considerable maneuvering by a number of railroads in the early postwar years to fill gaps in their systems. Budd had established a policy of concentrating the Burlington's efforts annually on what then seemed to be the weakest portion of its main-line system. The railroad, for example, sought to improve its routes between St. Louis and Kansas City and between Chicago and Kansas City. The railroad's own line across northern Missouri was circuitous and not competitive with those of other railroads, and there was a need to shorten the through route between Chicago and Kansas City. The Santa Fe, meanwhile, long had sought entry into St. Louis, which ranked second only to Chicago as a gateway to eastern and southern railroads.

Budd came up with a plan that would serve the needs of the Burlington, the Santa Fe, the Alton Railroad, and the Gulf, Mobile, and Ohio (GM&O), and the four-way agreement was presented to the ICC in 1945. Under the Budd plan, the GM&O would acquire the Alton, which had lines from Alton, Illinois, just up the Mississippi from St. Louis, to both Chicago and Kansas City, giving the GM&O its long-desired independent entry to Chicago. The Burlington would help finance the GM&O's acquisition in exchange for the Alton's line from Francis, Missouri, to Kansas City (the GM&O would retain trackage rights), and the Burlington would share the acquired line with another railroad. The other railroad was to be the Santa Fe, which would help modernize the line and provide both railroads with an efficient St. Louis–Kansas City route. A large volume of traffic moved between St. Louis and the West Coast, and the only way the Santa Fe could participate in it was through connecting railroads at Kansas City. Also, in exchange for enabling it to reach St. Louis, the Santa Fe was to allow the Q to have trackage rights from Kansas City to Bucklin on its Chicago main line. The latter would provide Burlington with a fast Chicago–Kansas City through route.

Budd's plan was logical, and he was joined enthusiastically by Fred G. Gurley, who formerly had worked for Budd at the Burlington and was now president of the Santa Fe. Not a single foot of new railroad would be built under the plan, but all four companies would achieve strategic goals, and the shipping public would benefit from the existence of a second high-speed service between Chicago and Kansas City. It was all perfectly logical. At the time, it appeared that logic never met the ICC, and though the agency approved the

GM&O acquisition of the Alton in 1945, it rejected the rest of the plan in 1948 on the grounds that there was no pressing need for additional St. Louis–Kansas City service and that the entry of the Santa Fe into St. Louis would divert traffic from those roads that vigorously opposed the plan. These were the Missouri Pacific, the Frisco, the Rock Island, and the Cotton Belt—all then in receivership—and the Texas and Pacific.

The ICC decision was not unanimous. Speaking for the three dissenters, Commissioner Charles D. Mahaffie said: "Competition, unless clearly shown to be destructive, still has advantages as a spur to progress. I would approve the applications and permit improvement to continue." Thirty years later, that concept was to be at the heart of railroad deregulation.

Budd may have been thwarted in his grand plan, but the Burlington was able to gain ICC approval of freight trackage rights over the GM&O from Francis to Kansas City, eliminating the interline at Mexico, Missouri, and—coupled with the Q's own line between St. Louis and Francis—providing an efficient route. Service over that route began in September 1949.

The era of railroad construction was not entirely over. The Burlington managed to gain approval from both its board of directors and the ICC to build a new line, known as the Centennial Cutoff, running 45 miles between Missouri Junction, Missouri, on the Wabash Railroad and Tina, Missouri, on the existing CB&Q Carrollton branch. This would provide a shorter, high-speed link between Chicago and Kansas City. The new line, which was completed in 1952, featured 112-pound rail, grades of no more than 0.8 percent, and curves that did not exceed 1 degree.

The Burlington poured money into yard expansion, new rail, ties, and ballast. Capital spending on its roadway alone from 1946 to 1949 exceeded the average net income of the three years 1946–1948. This also was a harbinger of general railroad financial malaise some years later when most railroads were found to be consistently spending more on their capital programs than could be justified by earnings.

The Burlington also spent millions on new freight and passenger equipment. Popular mythology says the railroads conspired among themselves to eliminate their passenger services after the war, but this simply was not so. The Q committed millions of dollars to new passenger equipment, adding to its fleet of Zephyr high-speed passenger trains and contributing its share for five new Great Northern Empire Builder trains, the orders coming even before the war ended.

Other railroads also invested in passenger trains. Quite apart from the contribution of passenger service to revenue, the Q believed that passenger service was a show window to the success of the railroad business, one that would lure freight business.

This was the same philosophy that Budd had articulated when he was president of the Great Northern. Budd also persuaded the board of directors to approve $8 million to revamp the Burlington's Chicago-area commuter service, investing in rebuilding existing cars, adding new stainless steel gallery cars, and converting to all-diesel operations as quickly as possible. Knowing that there was no chance that regulators would allow the Burlington to exit the commuter business, Budd figured the logical thing to do was to provide a service that would at least produce contented passengers. The railroad's commuters included some important shippers.

Dieselization accelerated with a series of new locomotive orders. By the end of 1948 the CB&Q operated 55 percent of all of its freight train miles, 85 percent of its regularly scheduled freight train miles, 65 percent of its passenger train miles, and 75 percent of its switch engine hours with diesel locomotives. Freight cars of all types were purchased from car builders, and more were built in the railroad's own shops. The oldest and least efficient equipment was retired. So the total carrying capacity of the CB&Q system increased, although the fleet expanded only slightly in numbers.

The decline of passenger markets, noticed before the war, continued despite the initial success of the new equipment on the long-distance, high-speed trains. Numerous main-line secondary trains and branch-line locals failed to bring in enough revenue to pay out-of-pocket costs, Budd wrote in the CB&Q's annual report for 1948. Calling them "passenger-abandoned," the Q stepped up its efforts to gain regulatory approval to eliminate the losers.

State commissions varied in their reaction to the applications. Sometimes they even varied within a state on separate but similar applications. In early 1949 a federal district court overruled the Illinois Commerce Commission, finding that enforced continuation of a train that consistently lost money was not justified. Such action constituted dissipation of the company's assets and was a deprivation of property without due process. Going further, the court said the prolonged continuance of cases on the part of the state agency violated the equal protection provision of the Fourteenth Amendment to the Constitution. Some reason was entering the process.

Almost all traffic promotion efforts had been suspended during the war, as the railroads already had all the traffic they could handle without worrying about finding new business. With the war's end and the return of truck and water competition, Burlington traffic executives, along with their counterparts at other railroads, resumed the marketing campaigns that had been suspended for the duration of the war.

Railroads tried a number of approaches to deal with the competitive challenges. The Burlington sold its intercity bus operations to a new company organized to compete with Greyhound Lines, remaining in the trucking business through its Burlington Truck Lines. The Santa Fe organized Santa Fe Skyway in 1946 as a contract air carrier in the territory served by the railroad. It also sought common carrier authority from the Civil Aeronautics Board (CAB). The Santa Fe also acquired a fleet of war surplus DC-3 aircraft and hired veterans to pilot them. The new line specialized in hauling perishable commodities between California and midwestern markets. When the CAB refused to allow the railroad to operate a common carrier airline, the attempt at coordinated air-rail service was ended in late 1947.

The Santa Fe, like the Burlington and others, tried to deal with competition in the only way railroad executives knew. They sought to retain and grow traffic by offering more-frequent and faster freight trains, by providing specialized equipment for specific customer needs, and by encouraging industrial and agricultural development along their lines. Nearly all branches received at least daily service, and running times were reduced where dictated by competition.

Unlike many roads, the Santa Fe benefited from the phenomenal growth of the southwestern economy. The populations of California, Texas, and Arizona skyrocketed, and the Santa Fe's traffic kept pace. Like others, the Santa Fe spent money to improve key routes and to acquire new passenger and freight equipment following the heavy usage of the war years. A new direct access route to Dallas shaved 72 hours off the Dallas-Chicago transit time. The Santa Fe also gained improved access to Chicago when it joined with three other railroads (one was the Burlington) to buy the Illinois Northern Railway from International Harvester Company in 1947.

Conservative but progressive management won recognition for the Santa Fe when *Fortune* magazine called it the nation's number one railroad. Employee morale was high, and the railroad's performance consistently improved. In a harbinger of the future, *Fortune* also pointed out that in 1946–1948 the Santa Fe earned more than the New York Central, the Pennsylvania, and the Southern Pacific combined.

Financially, the Santa Fe's management focus on reducing debt and lowering interest charges freed cash for dividends and other capital purposes. Following the expected traffic dip at the end of the war, Santa Fe revenue reached $522.7 million, with record net income of $82.1 million by 1950.

The Great Northern passed from Hill family control and influence with the death of Louis W. Hill, the empire builder's son, in 1948. GN management faced the same issues as other railroads but had considerable cause for optimism about the future. Although several key executives were nearing retirement, the company had replacements trained and ready to succeed them. One of the new generation of leaders was Ralph Budd's son, John, who resigned as president of the Chicago and Eastern Illinois to return to his home railroad as vice president of operations. He would be named president in 1951.

John M. Budd was the first 20th-century-born president of the Great Northern, having been born in 1907 in Des Moines, Iowa. He also spent most of his professional life on the GN, after earning a civil engineering degree from Yale. Like so many sons of railroad executive fathers, he spent college summers working on the railroad. The younger Budd worked his way up through the operating department, putting in time as a trainmaster, and by the early 1940s he had been named a division superintendent, where he was responsible for all aspects of the operation of his division. During the war, Budd served in the Military Railroad Service, commanding the 704th Railway Grand Division overseas. His first postwar assignment was as general manager of the lines east of Williston, North Dakota. He left the Great Northern in 1947, when, at age 39, he was elected president of the Chicago and Eastern Illinois Railroad, the youngest president of a Class 1 railroad in the United States. Four years later, he was back at the GN.

Budd was one of the first railroad executives anywhere to see himself as a transportation man rather than a railroader. He viewed the company's task as moving goods and people first, and figuring out how the railroad could handle the job second. He continued the tradition of steady, prudent management for which the GN had become known, and he soon became an industry leader, even to those outside the railroad community. In a history of the Great

Northern, Budd was described thusly: "Those who knew him considered John Budd extremely ethical, thoughtful, sound of judgment, loyal, reserved in manner, fair-minded, perhaps even a little on the soft side. He was a good man to work for, asking associates their viewpoints and not afraid to learn from anybody. Not a publicity seeker, Budd avoided drama simply for effect, but his positions reflected careful analysis."

The Great Northern had geography in its favor as the railroads faced the postwar competitive issues. The resumption of housing and commercial construction after 15 years of depression and war assured the company of strong lumber traffic between the Northwest and the Midwest. Iron ore could not be moved practicably other than by rail. The GN's iron ore deposits had been heavily worked during the war, but there was every expectation that steelmakers would continue to draw much of their raw materials from the Iron Range of Minnesota.

While traffic held up well for some railroads in the postwar years, profitability suffered, as they were caught between uncontrolled cost increases and government-controlled limits on their own ability to recover higher costs through rate increases. Labor cost increases were notable. The head count on the Burlington declined by 13 percent from 1945 to 1949, but total payroll costs rose by 16 percent. The average annual compensation on the CB&Q increased nearly 35 percent from 1945 to 1949.

Caught in a cost-price squeeze, the railroads sought to maintain profitability through operating efficiency. Dieselization occurred rapidly throughout the industry. Great Northern diesels, which produced 17 percent of train miles at the end of 1945, reached 63 percent just six years later. The steam locomotives that remained in service all were converted from coal to less costly oil for economy. Railroads installed heavier rail that required less maintenance. They undertook projects to reduce grade and curvature, which allowed higher-speed operations in both freight and passenger service.

Cost-cutting measures on the GN included curtailed passenger operations on branch lines, elimination of Sunday services, and replacement of lightly used passenger trains with mixed freight and passenger trains. Closing stations on weekends and at other times when there was little demand became a standard practice. By substituting coffee-shop cars for dining cars, the passenger department was able to reduce employee head count, although it did nothing for the gustatory gratification of passengers.

In a continuation of the competitive battle that began well before the war, the Great Northern fought for greater regulation of commercial truckers. Its traffic department was constantly watching truck rates and schedules. A half century later, with economic regulation largely ended, the railroad-truck rivalry continues over the size and weight of trucks that are permitted on the public highways.

Wages were a particularly burdensome issue for all the railroads. Rail rates were controlled and increases limited by the ICC, but rail workers received general wage increases in 1941 and 1943. Even before the war ended, unions were seeking work rule changes and even higher wage rates. Formal demands under the Railway Labor Act of 1926 were filed in July 1945, and mediators came in December of that year. Anticipating—correctly—that workers would be granted significant wage increases, the railroads asked the ICC for rate increases ranging from 20 to 25 percent, depending on the commodity. That made it very clear that the requested rate increases were specifically to offset wage increases.

Although the unions had agreed to the arbitration process, they declined to accept the increases awarded by arbitration boards. Despite the intervention of President Harry S. Truman, labor peace was not achieved, and on May 17, 1946, Truman seized the railroads, placing them under the control of the Office of Defense Transportation. Six days later, the engineers and trainmen struck, bringing the U.S. rail system to a standstill.

In a nationwide radio address the next evening, Truman called on employees to return to service by 4 P.M. on May 25 and said he would appear before a joint session of Congress at that time. Minutes before the president's speech, the carriers and the striking unions reached a settlement that later was extended to all the unions. In his speech, Truman asked for authority to draft the engineers and trainmen into the armed forces. With settlement of the dispute, however, nothing came of the proposal, and the railroads were returned to their owners on the afternoon of May 26.

Not everything that happened to the railroad industry at the hands of government in the immediate postwar period was negative. Railroads, and particularly the Northern Pacific and the Santa Fe, benefited from Congress's passing legislation that finally relieved them of the discounted rate requirements that went with their acceptance of federal land grants. Though only land-grant railroads were required to discount government traffic, most non-land-grant railroads that competed with land-grant carriers felt forced to extend the same discounts in order to retain the traffic. The Great Northern, for example, discounted traffic in order to keep the Northern Pacific from having an effective monopoly on government business, particularly during the Depression.

Ironically, most of the textbooks used by American secondary and college students continue to perpetuate the land-grant myth, failing to point out that only about 8 percent of the U.S. rail system was built with land grants or that the land granted was virtually unsellable at the time. When the grants were made, public land carried a price of $1 to $1.25 per acre with no takers. With the coming of transportation to the American wilderness, the government immediately raised the price of the remaining public land to $2 and $2.25. The textbooks ignore the finding that, aside from creating value where none had existed, the railroads had paid for the land grants several times over through discounted carriage of troops, mail, and government freight.

5

Decline Accelerates

Markets Shrink, but Not Assets

I've never seen a Greyhound snowplow out on the highway during the winter.

GRAHAM CLAYTOR, president of Amtrak, commenting on complaints that Amtrak received government subsidies that its bus competitors did not

Competitive threats to the economic dominance of U.S. railroads accelerated in the 1950s. The industry had been facing increased competition since the 1920s and 1930s. At that time government public works projects stimulated expansion of highway and navigable inland waterway systems, and now the competing barge and truck operators went beyond nibbling at the margins of rail business. They took large bites out of the core.

The decade of the 1950s saw a continued slide in the railroad market share of freight and passenger business. The industry's share of the intercity freight market fell below 50 percent for the first time, and as of 2005 it still has not recovered to that level. The passenger business virtually disappeared as travelers began to rely only on the automobile or the airplane.

The deleterious effect of competition was compounded by restrictive economic regulation. For more than five decades from the time of Teddy Roosevelt's presidency, the federal government prevented the railroads from recovering inflationary cost increases through higher rates and from trying to keep valuable traffic through lower rates. When they did receive permission to raise rates, market conditions increasingly prevented railroads from taking the full amount authorized. They feared losing more traffic to trucks and barges and ending up with even less revenue. The steady shift of freight markets away from railroads and to competing forms of transportation is shown the following tables.

COMPETITIVE BALANCE SHIFTS—U.S. RAIL INDUSTRY

	1929	1944	1947	1955
Originated carloads	36,821,868	36,540,944	36,966,971	32,761,707
Ton-miles (in billions)[a]	447.3	737.2	654.7	623.6

[a] A ton-mile equals one ton carried one mile.

INTERCITY FREIGHT MARKET SHARE (PERCENT) BY MODE

	1929	1944	1950	1955
Rail	75.0	67.8	56.2	49.4
Truck	3.3	5.3	16.3	17.7
Great Lakes/rivers	17.5	13.7	15.4	17.0
Oil pipelines	4.4	12.2	12.1	15.9

Source: Association of American Railroads.

After the war, when truckers no longer were limited by fuel and tire rationing, they were able to take advantage of more and better roads and their own operating flexibility. Most of the increase in water transportation came on rivers and canals as government-financed and -built improvements allowed bigger towboats to push more and heavier barges, while the declining iron ore business led to a drop in Great Lakes volume.

More pipelines were built throughout the country, to the extent that railroads today are essentially out of the oil transportation business except for a few specialized unit tank train movements and carriage of their own fuel supplies to refueling depots. BNSF Railway does have an expanding fuel-by-rail program and moves unit trains of ethanol fuel additive from midwestern grain processing facilities to West Coast refineries.

One measurement of the impact of the growing trucking industry on railroads can be seen in the average length of haul. From 334.1 miles in 1929, the average rail haul distance increased to 479.5 miles in 1947, slipped to 446.6 miles in 1955, and increased again to 462.3 miles in 1960. Stimulated by increasing amounts of low-sulfur western coal moving to eastern electricity-generating stations, the average length of haul continued to increase until 2001, when it hit 858.1 miles. Data for 2003 show a slight increase to 862.4 miles, reflecting the longer hauls of low-sulfur western coal and the growth of intermodal traffic. According to transportation economists, the increasing length of haul reflects the railroads' focus on intermodal business where they can compete effectively with trucks, as well as an inability to compete with trucks over shorter distances.

Perhaps the most striking example of the shift in the rail-truck competitive battle is in the revenue that each mode receives from carrying freight for customers. From a vitally profitable, virtual monopoly that brought railroads under rigid and restrictive government regulation, they now have only about 10 percent of total domestic intercity freight revenue, taking in about $38 billion annually. Motor carriers, with an estimated $360 billion in annual revenue, account for 80 percent of the transportation revenue pie. Air freight, pipelines, and barges all have a piece of the remaining 10 percent. Even if traffic that is not really competitive between trucking and rail is factored out (local drayage, local pickup and delivery, and short haul, for which railroads aren't suited), the railroads come up short, with perhaps one-third of the market by revenue.

The railroads that today are incorporated in the BNSF Railway system were affected by these trends along with the rest of the industry, but not always to the same degree. Because of the greater distances in the western United States, the economics of transportation meant that western railroads were more resistant to the inroads of truckers than were their brethren in the East.

Railroad failures (more about this subject later) tended to be in the East, and later spread to the Midwest. In the East, industrial relocation—the Rust Belt revolution that closed thousands of industrial plants or moved them elsewhere—accelerated in the postwar years. It left railroads with far more physical plant than they needed. Further, the railroads were left serving empty factories and warehouses following the loss of many once-significant customers, and the relatively short hauls in the region made them more susceptible to truck competition for the traffic that remained. The Midwest simply had more railroads operating in head-to-head competition in major markets than the available traffic could support. When the venerable Chicago, Rock Island, and Pacific Railroad filed for bankruptcy protection from creditors on March 17, 1975, John Ingram, its chief executive, said, "The Northeast rail crisis just reached Tucumcari." Tucumcari, New Mexico, was the westernmost point on the Rock Island system. Railroad difficulties in the West and the Midwest were not so much related to industrial dislocation. There were instead too many light-density lines operating within a changing economic structure that made it unprofitable to continue those lines in service.

The competitive impact of truckers was twofold. Just as they had during the Depression, motor carriers continued to savage the railroads' less-than-carload (LCL) business and increasingly siphoned off the service-sensitive traffic that moved at higher rates under the railroads' pricing system. By the end of the 20th century, the railroads effectively were out of the LCL market, as customers that had smaller quantities to move steadily shifted to the more flexible trucks and semis that sought their business. The Association of American Railroads stopped keeping data on LCL in 1987, when average weekly volume was measured in single digits for the entire industry. More recently, intermodal has recaptured some of that traffic as less-than-truckload carriers have increased their use of rail intermodal service.

In the 1950s, large rail systems relied heavily on connecting railroads to complete most shipments. With more than a hundred Class 1 railroads, there were few opportunities for even the largest railroads to carry freight all the way from origin to destination. A railroad with as little as $3 million in revenue in 1950 was considered Class 1. The designation rose to $5 million in the early 1960s, then to $50 million in the 1970s, and finally to $250 million in 1991, with annual increases to reflect inflation. Even into the 1980s, more than two-thirds of rail traffic relied on more than one railroad, a built-in inefficiency with which truckers did not have to contend. With industry consolidation to today's seven Class 1 railroads, only about 35 percent of freight is interlined.

As it had in the prewar years, the Atchison, Topeka, and Santa Fe in the postwar years still originated and terminated a larger proportion of its traffic than other railroads—more than two-thirds of the traffic it handled—thanks to the rapid economic development of the Southwest. Its interchange traffic was mostly with eastern carriers. Not being forced to rely for interchange on railroads with which it also competed on other routes, the Santa Fe had more "friendly connections" than did most other railroads.

More important was that only about one-third of trucking was economically regulated. Many ICC-regulated carriers held certificates of public convenience and necessity—the authority to engage in for-hire transportation—to serve specific routes or commodities. Those certificates were so restrictive that many truckers had no authority to fill their trucks for the return trip—that is, back-hauling. Agricultural commodities, however, were not regulated, and many truckers saw an opportunity to generate revenue from their otherwise empty return trips by carrying vegetables, fruit, or grain. Because their regulated rates were set to provide a profit even if there were no back-haul revenue, they were in a position to accept very low rates for unregulated commodities, often charging only for the cost of fuel to get their rigs back to their origin. The effect was twofold. On the one hand, they took traffic that railroads traditionally viewed as their own, and on the other hand, they drove average rates down, putting even more pressure on railroad profitability.

Because auto manufacturers were producing tanks, trucks, jeeps, and other military vehicles in 1942–1945, an enormous backlog of consumer demand for automobiles and the highway capacity to accommodate them accompanied the end of the war. Cars became more than a utilitarian means of moving about the community. They created a tourist economy as Americans took family vacations and drove about the country. Motels and motor inns that offered inexpensive but increasingly comfortable accommodations began to replace prewar tourist courts of small cabins. Congress acknowledged the new paradigm by shifting federal emphasis from rural roads to metropolitan needs by authorizing a 40,000-mile interstate network.

The Interstate and Defense Highway System was one of the major accomplishments of the 1953–1961 Eisenhower presidency. Clearly, the interstate system has been a blessing to most Americans. It has increased their mobility and spurred the economies of communities and businesses that benefited from tourism. But under the law of unintended consequences, it also accelerated the collapse of a number of railroads. As primary road mileage increased from 217,000 miles in 1945 to more than 500,000 miles in 1955, it became easier for shippers to use trucks. Trucks, after all, had the ability to drive right up to a loading dock. The sudden outbreak of the Korean War in June 1950 slowed the development of new limited-access, multilane, divided highways, although the pressure resumed once the war ended in 1953.

Large-scale federal financial assistance for road building was slow in coming, as the highway program still relied on the Good Roads movement of the 1930s. Highway promoters focused on the states, although they began seeking increased federal funding. Initially, the demand for major new highways was met by states, which had limited financial resources. Many resorted to construction of toll roads. By 1955, states had completed 1,239 miles of toll roads and had another 3,314 miles under study. A motorist—or trucker—could travel from the East Coast cities of Philadelphia, New York, and Boston all the way to Chicago on modern toll roads and never encounter a traffic light. Another significant benefit of the toll roads for truckers was that they tended to bypass major cities, allowing long-haul trucks to avoid costly urban congestion.

To the extent that users paid for toll roads, the railroads had little to complain about. The trucker on a toll road was at least paying for the right-of-way it used, just as railroads paid for theirs, and the trucks seemed to attract traffic for which they had a natural advantage. That did not stop the railroads from using their considerable political power to try to block development of new toll roads, but the demand for them was so great that the railroads were overwhelmed.

Transportation economists discovered an interesting phenomenon. Highway improvements created even greater demand for more highway capacity. Many new roads carried their designed capacity almost as soon as they were opened, and they frequently created congestion as much as they relieved it. This, of course, generated additional demand for more highway improvements.

The mid-1950s were the height of the cold war. The Soviet Union had developed its own atomic and thermonuclear weapons, and the United States was in the midst of a huge peacetime military program. As a young army captain, Eisenhower had been assigned to a convoy of 20 U.S. Army trucks ordered from Washington, D.C., to the West Coast in 1919. The trip took two months to reach the Presidio in San Francisco. He never forgot it. It was one incident in a series that played into the demand for better roads. Later, as supreme commander of the Allied Expeditionary Forces in Europe during World

War II, Eisenhower was impressed with the limited-access, high-speed German autobahn despite the destruction of the war. As president of the United States, Eisenhower strongly supported a larger federal role in building an expanded highway system. Eisenhower's Interstate Highway System was sold to Congress and the public—which did not need much selling—on the basis that military needs required wider roads with thicker pavements and greater clearances for the movement of tanks and other heavy and outsized equipment.

Congress passed the Federal Aid Highway and Highway Revenue Act of 1956, adopting pay-as-you-go financing of a 40,000-mile system of new highways. New federal user taxes, mostly on gasoline and diesel fuel, were dedicated to a Highway Trust Fund. The act increased federal highway spending from $175 million to $2.2 billion for the first fiscal year and set a goal of finishing the Interstate system in 16 years. The new program was the most massive public works project ever seen.

There was some similarity, at least in concept, between the twentieth-century highway program and the 19th-century federal involvement in railroad construction. The Pacific Railroad Act had been as wide in scope, and its results were just as far-reaching. Before the Interstate Highway System was developed, the typical intercity truck averaged a speed of about 30 miles per hour with a total gross vehicle weight (truck, trailer, and cargo) of 50,000 pounds. On the new highways that soon were to crisscross the nation from east to west and north to south, trucks were allowed a gross vehicle weight of 73,280 pounds—which has since been increased to 80,000 pounds. With greatly improved roads they reached an average speed of 50 miles an hour. The economics of trucking were changed radically, and unit costs plunged. Lower costs of operation were translated into lower rates and a marketing drive to serve customers that never before had used trucks to move goods. Although many truck rates remained higher than rail rates for the same commodities, with their greater flexibility and higher level of service truckers were able to take more business away from railroads. The railroads, already converted to diesel locomotives, did not have an offsetting cost reduction and were no match for the truckers when it came to providing service.

During this period, the trucking industry also benefited from the creation of an extremely powerful political coalition. Trucking companies by themselves could not have obtained the federal highway program that they sought, but they were joined by the American

Automobile Association, which represented ordinary motorists and a budding tourism industry, road builders, and companies that sold everything from asphalt and concrete to guardrails. The trucking industry also had one of the strongest lobbies, the International Brotherhood of Teamsters, which had close to a million jobs in the industry and saw highway improvements as a way to expand its membership. The teamsters were able to persuade many members of Congress to accept the argument for more spending on federal-aid highways, while the public was persuaded that the program would benefit ordinary Americans and that the new user charges would not benefit only commercial interests.

Railroads, on the other hand, were in a contentious period of labor relations. They could not muster the energy or clout to respond to the highway interests with a countercoalition. The shrinkage in the railroad industry that had begun after World War I was continuing. Thousands of jobs were vanishing. This was particularly so as passenger trains disappeared and as diesel locomotives replaced steam, which required more maintenance. The loss of labor-intensive passenger operations and the conversion from steam contributed to a decline from more than one million railroad workers to fewer than half a million in just 25 years. The railroad industry was in a drive to lower costs, and unions were on the receiving end of that campaign; antagonisms were strong.

The only good thing that the highway program did for railroads was that railroads got to carry the construction equipment and the raw materials for the highways that would benefit their competitors. It has been said that the last profitable year for the New York, New Haven, and Hartford Railroad was the year it carried the construction material for Interstate 95, the road that paralleled its main line between New York and Boston and eventually contributed to its bankruptcy.

Waterways were being improved, expanded, and dredged to enhance commercial traffic, and this trend affected the coal and grain business of railroads that operated near the Mississippi, Illinois, Missouri, and Ohio Rivers. Coal and grain were basic commodities for the railroads. They moved in large volumes, and the steady revenue they produced provided a disproportionate support for the rail infrastructure. Railroads that had a good business carrying grain for export were particularly hard hit as lower-priced water carriers took their traffic and carried it to export terminals at the mouth of the Mississippi. Even railroads that did not compete with barges all the way to the Gulf Coast saw their business erode as they got the short haul from country elevators to barge transfer terminals on the nearest waterway. Coal also was diverted to barge lines that served utility plants that were built near the rivers, often just to take advantage of low-priced water service.

Those railroads with primarily east-west routes were less affected, but they too faced competition from barge operators. Although most grain was not grown adjacent to the waterways, unregulated barge rates were so much lower than rail rates that many landlocked farmers and grain elevator operators found it economical to truck grain to river transfer points, cutting the railroad out entirely. The Burlington, for example, could carry Kansas and Nebraska grain by a somewhat circuitous route through Colorado to the ports of Houston and Galveston, Texas, on the Gulf of Mexico. Grain from Missouri and Iowa origins either had to be interlined with another railroad with tracks to the Gulf or could be carried the relatively short distance to barge transfer facilities on the Missouri and the Mississippi.

The railroads faced two choices, neither appealing. They could accept that barges could draw grain from greater distances from the rivers and that much of it would be shipped to barge transfer facilities by trucks, or they could reduce rates and keep the shorter haul to the river points. Even the northerns—the Great Northern and the Northern Pacific—faced water competition. Eastern Montana grain growers could use a combination of trucks over the Rocky Mountains to the Snake River and barges on the Snake and Columbia Rivers to Portland, while their North Dakota and Minnesota customers could use trucks to the Missouri and Mississippi Rivers. These options put an effective cap on the rates the railroads could charge.

While barge operators were regulated by the ICC for the carriage of many commodities such as steel and manufactured goods, they were unregulated for bulk commodities, and only about 10 percent of the commerce on the inland waterways actually was regulated. Water carriers learned, just as motor carriers had earlier, to "sharp-shoot" the huge volumes of grain, coal, and chemicals that were the base-load business that many railroads relied on.

The Army Corps of Engineers first performed the economic analyses required to justify new waterway projects and then supervised the construction once Congress approved. The corps joined forces with water carriers that held out their lower rates as a benefit to shippers, while ignoring the cost of displaced rail workers and the loss of business by their regulated competitors.

Competition wasn't the only force that capped railroad rates during this period. The ICC and state regulatory agencies continued to treat railroads as though they still had the monopoly that led to regulation in 1887, limiting the industry's ability to raise rates quickly in the face of continually increasing wage and material costs. Cumbersome procedures for "general increases" had railroads struggling to recover rising costs. Maximum rate regulation may not have been as harmful to the railroads in dealing with truck and barge competition, however, as was minimum rate regulation. In a number of instances the ICC refused to allow railroads to reduce their rates even though they had lower costs, and the traffic went by barge or truck. It would take the financial collapse of as much as 25 percent of the U.S. railroads before the federal government would consider putting the industry on a level competitive field with barge and truck operators.

Other efforts by railroads to help themselves were thwarted also by the Civil Aeronautics Board, which regulated air service in much the way that the ICC regulated surface transportation. Airlines were authorized to fly only specific routes, and rates had to be approved by the CAB before they could go into effect. After the war, the Santa Fe created Santa Fe Skyway, using war surplus Douglas C-47 Skytrain aircraft. Santa Fe Skyway specialized in carrying perishables and made the trip between Los Angeles and Chicago in less than 21 hours and 30 minutes. The contract service proved popular, and the company then bought four Douglas C-54 aircraft, each capable of carrying more than 10 tons.

As related in chapter four, Santa Fe Skyway operated under a temporary restricted license from the CAB while its application for a permanent common carriage license was under consideration. Despite steady growth in business, the application was rejected in 1947—as was a similar petition by the Missouri Pacific—and the Santa Fe exited the air transport business once and for all in January 1948. The CAB simply did not approve of airlines controlled by surface carriers. It was, of course, supported or goaded in this opinion by such carriers as Eastern Airlines and American Airlines. When an eastern railroad was found to have secretly acquired control of an airline in the late 1960s, the embarrassing scandal resulted in a CAB order that the railroad turn the airline over to a bank trustee until it could be sold.

Not only did railroads have to deal with more-restrictive regulation than their competitors did, but they also were forced to contend with public policy that favored other modes of transportation, often at the expense of railroads. While public agencies provided and managed the infrastructure—highways, airports, and waterways—for truckers, barge operators, and airlines, railroads paid property and user taxes on their property. The navigable waterways during this period were completely free for water carriers. No tolls or other user fees were levied, and a strong lobby of the Army Corps of Engineers, the water carriers, key members of Congress, and key coal, grain, and chemical shippers that benefited greatly from low-priced transportation made sure that public money continued to flow to waterway projects and that no offsetting tolls or other fees were imposed. This was, after all, a century-old system.

But there was more to come. In 1927 the corps had presented plans for the multipurpose improvement of navigable streams and began work on a series of locks and dams along the Mississippi. By 1929 the corps had completed dredging a nine-foot-deep channel on the Ohio River, and a decade later a nine-foot channel was completed between St. Louis and St. Paul on the Mississippi. The Mississippi below St. Louis is a wide and deep waterway that requires only relatively inexpensive channelization to maintain the congressionally authorized 11-foot channel. In that channel, tows of as many as 40 barges can be pushed by a single 10,000-horsepower towboat. Above St. Louis, though, the Mississippi is open to commercial navigation only with the help of a series of 27 locks and dams.

Similarly, the Ohio and the Missouri Rivers are open to Pittsburgh and Omaha, respectively, only as a result of improvements paid for by taxpayers and sponsored by the Corps of Engineers. Shippers of bulk commodities, such as coal, grain, and chemicals that do not require the speed of rail service, are drawn to low freight rates. These projects benefited shippers as well as barge companies, but they did nothing for the railroads.

The waterway lobby had a long list of desired projects. Maps do not show Tulsa, Oklahoma, as an international seaport, but it is, thanks to the Arkansas-Verdigris project. It allows barges to move from Tulsa to the Mississippi and on to the Gulf of Mexico. This project diverted thousands of carloads and millions of dollars of revenue from the Santa Fe, the Frisco, and, to a lesser extent, the Burlington. The Arkansas-Verdigris even affected eastern railroads, as it became less expensive to ship oil-field pipe from steel mills in Pennsylvania and Ohio by barge down the Ohio and the Mississippi and then up the Arkansas to Tulsa.

Although economic deregulation did not really take hold until the 1970s, railroads achieved their first regulatory freedom in the Transportation Act of 1958. Shifting authority over abandonment of passenger service from state regulatory agencies to the ICC, Congress made it clear that railroads should be allowed to close parts of their businesses if they were not profitable. After lengthy proceedings, the change resulted in the termination of many passenger trains that state regulatory agencies had ordered railroads to continue operating. The ICC had also forced the railroads to cross-subsidize these losers with profits from freight operations, though the passenger rail issues were not really addressed until the creation of Amtrak in 1971. The antimerger climate finally was changing. The 1958 act encouraged combinations that would reduce costs. For the first time Congress suggested that mergers might be approved among parallel railroads where duplicate facilities could be eliminated.

The men who ran the railroads believed in their industry. They were not quitters, and they did everything they could to reverse, delay, or stave off decline. Freight service was improved and expanded with faster scheduled transit times in major markets. Railroads met with customers to try to find ways of providing the services they wanted. Fleets of specialized freight cars were purchased in the hope of retaining business.

The net result of these efforts was that debt represented by equipment trust certificates skyrocketed at the same time that revenues began to slide. Equipment trust certificates were a creative way to finance railcars and locomotives at a time when railroad credit was insufficient to carry the debt. With trust certificates, a third-party trustee retained ownership of the equipment until the railroad fully paid for it through regular installments. Between 1945 and 1955, new equipment obligations amounted to at least 40 percent of all railroad capital expenditures, and the vast bulk of new rolling stock was financed in this way. Only after the countermeasures failed to slow the loss of business did railroad executives turn to full-scale cost cutting. But the deep cuts did not lead to prosperity, and they also affected service levels and drove even more customers to take their business to trucking companies.

Even in passenger service, the railroads refused to give up. Frank Gavin, president of the Great Northern, had determined in 1943 that an entirely new Empire Builder should be constructed as soon as the war ended. Rapid amortization of the investment under Internal Revenue Service rules encouraged the GN to invest large amounts to acquire modern passenger equipment. The new Empire Builder, with a 45-hour schedule between Chicago and Seattle, was a surprising 13 hours faster than the train it replaced.

Under Fred Gurley, the Santa Fe continued to fight back against airline and passenger car competition. It became one of the three biggest users of diesel power, with cleaner, more reliable, all-diesel passenger service by 1959. In 1956 the railroad instituted service with high-level Vista Dome passenger cars that allowed customers to have an unobstructed view of the countryside while their baggage and restroom facilities were on the lower level.

Not only did the Santa Fe stick with passenger service longer than did many other railroads, but it also continued to try to be the best at it. The Super Chief, which replaced the steam-powered deluxe liner the Chief, was an all-Pullman Chicago–Los Angeles service. It was followed by the El Capitan, an all-coach offering that ran on a similar high-speed schedule. Even more luxurious was the California Limited, an all-Pullman train on which every passenger was required to purchase a ticket, even the president of the railroad. The Santa Fe, with much of its route double-tracked, offered 39-hour, 45-minute passage between Chicago and Los Angeles, a level of service never matched by Amtrak, today's nationalized rail passenger service.

All of these and other main-line trains were reequipped in the 1950s with new-technology, lightweight cars that cost less to pull and allowed the Santa Fe to maintain the demanding schedules. A pricing official at the Santa Fe warned against investing so much in passenger equipment. More-senior executives rejected his advice, saying that under avoidable cost accounting the railroad would be able to recover the investment.

The Burlington had begun Vista Dome service between Chicago and Minneapolis in 1945. It introduced "slumbercoaches" in 1956, providing less opulent sleeping quarters than standard Pullman accommodations for little more than the cost of a coach ticket. It continued to offer premium service with its family of Zephyr trains between major cities on its system. The California Zephyr was started in conjunction with the Denver and Rio Grande Western and Western Pacific railroads on a Chicago–Denver–Salt Lake City–Oakland routing.

Despite efforts like these and the purchase of stainless steel and lightweight passenger equipment that was less costly to operate and maintain, the railroads continued to lose money on passenger service. In fact, they lost money on it in every year after the start of the

Great Depression except for four war years. In addition to direct losses from train operations, the railroads carried the cost burden of stations, many far larger and more costly to maintain than the business could justify, because they had been built in Victorian days. From a $500 million loss in 1948, the industry passenger deficit reached $723 million in 1957. John Stover, the author of *American Railroads* and considered the dean of American railroad historians, points out that losses approached 50 percent of net railway operating income from freight service, an intolerable burden, especially when the freight operating income was itself declining.

The rapid growth of the airline industry, which was safer and faster than ever before, contributed to the public's abandonment of rail passenger service, but the real culprit was the modern highway. Millions of people who had ridden trains found that they could travel about the country in relative safety and comfort at their own schedules.

The ICC slowly came to understand that it could not force the railroads to lose money indefinitely, and it grudgingly began to look more favorably on abandonment, or "train-off," cases.

By 1959 eleven of the 112 Class 1 railroads (any railroad with at least $3 million annual revenue was considered Class 1 in 1959) had no passenger service at all, and in 1965 no passenger service was available on more than half the national rail network. In a message to Congress in 1961, President John F. Kennedy said, "If it is in the public interest to maintain an industry, it is clearly not in the public interest by the impact of regulatory authority to destroy its otherwise viable way of life."

The exit from the passenger business was accelerated by the U.S. Post Office Department's shift to air and truck for the movement of most mail. Railway Post Offices (RPO), special railroad-owned cars where postal clerks sorted mail en route, were part of many passenger trains, along with baggage cars filled with bulk mail. The revenue from them kept many railroads from abandoning otherwise money-losing passenger services. Once the RPO and bulk mail cars were removed from service, more trains became uneconomical and were quickly eliminated. Much of the investment required for handling mail had been made by the railroads and became stranded capital.

Gaining regulatory approval for train-offs still was not easy, despite pressure on the ICC from President Kennedy and even if there was no demand for the service. The Milwaukee Road, for example, had been required to continue a train in Indiana until the

Powerful People Don't Ride Trains—Do They?

A vignette in Frank Wilner's book about the workings of the Interstate Commerce Commission (ICC)—titled "Powerful People Don't Ride Trains—Do They?"—detailed the misadventure the Chicago, Burlington, and Quincy Railroad and one of its executives had in removing from service a lightly used train running from Omaha, Nebraska, to Billings, Montana:

> A Chicago, Burlington & Quincy operating official became so frustrated at legal maneuvering in passenger-train abandonment proceedings in August 1969 that he took matters into his own hands. He learned to regret his action.
>
> Upon receiving word that a three-judge federal district court in Cheyenne, Wyoming, had upheld an ICC discontinuance order, CB&Q Vice President Ivan Ethington ordered the affected train—already en route from Omaha to Billings, Montana—halted immediately. And so the train was halted—in the dead of night, on August 13, 1969, near a corn-patch named Hemingford, Nebraska.
>
> Only twenty passengers and probably fewer sacks of mail were aboard, and they were transferred to motor coaches that had been ordered by Mr. Ethington. Only because tens of thousands of restless, non-conformist and often disobedient rock-music fans were clustered in Woodstock, New York, that week did Mr. Ethington and his railroad avoid front-page attention in major daily newspapers.
>
> For it turned out one of the annulled train's unappreciated passengers—at least unappreciated by Mr. Ethington—was U.S. Congressman Glenn C. Cunningham of Nebraska, who just happened also to sit on the House Commerce Committee. For a reason quite alien to Mr. Ethington—an operating man with an infantry sergeant's opinion of public relations—Congressman Cunningham was not pleased, and the solon managed a telephone call to Washington before grudgingly boarding the alternate conveyance.

average daily revenue was less than the wages of the crew. Crew wages were considerable because even the best and fastest trains stopped every few hours to change engine crews. In most cases, 100 miles was considered a day's work (or 140 miles for passenger service personnel), no matter how few hours it took to cover that distance. This rule was a residual effect of the government takeover of the railroads in World War I.

Almost precisely as the bus—its sleepy and unwashed congressman aboard—arrived in Billings, a press officer at the Interstate Commerce Commission was distributing to news reporters a hastily drawn official statement:

> Yesterday's action [by Mr. Ethington] . . . was taken without the knowledge of the Interstate Commerce Commission. The Commission will not condone such treatment of the traveling public.

The ICC then ordered all railroads—where the pendency of court proceedings is uncertain—to give at least forty-eight hours notice to the public before discontinuing any train. The Commission's press officer was not the only government official arriving at work early that day. Before most in Washington had finished breakfast, Supreme Court Justice Hugo L. Black had signed an order restoring the annulled service pending outcome of further litigation.

Limply, the railroad, through a chagrined spokesperson, told *Traffic World* it would not contest the order, but asserted that the Supreme Court's action in restoring a discontinued train was 'unique'—but perhaps no more so than rousing a United States congressman from his sleep and ordering him into the chill night air.

The railroad paid a $2,500 fine, but criminal charges against Mr. Ethington were dropped at the request of a federal prosecutor.

The congressman had been accompanied by his son and the two were on their way to a fishing trip during a congressional recess, facts that made the story all the more appealing to the Washington press corps. The Supreme Court eventually affirmed the district court's decision. The train was gone forever, and Mr. Ethington recovered from the embarrassment and his brush with the criminal justice system later to become an executive vice president of the Burlington Northern.

Dining car service was another economic drag. Industry-wide, dining service cost $1.44 for every $1 of revenue by 1954. Various railroads tried to stem the losses. The Santa Fe sold five-meal tickets for $10 on its El Capitan streamliner, which only slowed the rate of increase in the losses. The Northern Pacific considered the dining service loss as good public relations, proving that few in the industry had learned much about public relations since the "robber baron" days of the late 19th century.

Ironically, the decade from 1950 to 1960 was marked simultaneously by a decline in the fortunes of railroads and by significant investments in modernization and efficiency. The Santa Fe—under Ernest S. Marsh, who succeeded Fred Gurley as president in 1957—committed capital to counter rising labor costs. It also began to replace jointed rail with welded rail, which required less maintenance. Initially installed as a cost-cutting move, welded rail later was determined to provide a better-quality ride and was a contributor to lower customer loss and damage claims along with less wheel wear. Virtually all main-line track in the United States now is welded rail.

Marsh was the Santa Fe's first 20th-century leader, having been born in Virginia in 1903. He was moved as a child to Clovis, New Mexico, on the Santa Fe main line and joined the railroad as a teenager in 1918. A graduate of the advanced management program at the Harvard School of Business Administration, Marsh rose through the executive ranks and was named vice president of finance in 1948 and a member of the board of directors in 1956. He was well suited to deal with the efforts to battle cost increases and to stem the decline in earnings. As other railroads did, most notably the Southern Railway in the Southeast, Marsh persuaded the board to increase capital spending for labor-saving mechanization. In 1961 alone, the Santa Fe reduced employment by 4,000. The inexorable decline in fortunes of the railroad could be slowed but not stopped. The operating ratio, which was 71.9 in 1953, had climbed to 77.6 in 1957, the year Marsh took over. By 1963 it had climbed further, to 80.6, before improving to 76.9 in 1966.

The Santa Fe began to experiment with the transport of truck trailers on flatcars—called piggyback but known now as intermodal—in 1952. The Burlington began its first piggyback service in 1954. Two highway trailers could fit on one flatcar. Initially, piggyback was a railroad marketing response to the inroads of truckers. The flatcars were already owned by the railroad and were a wasting asset if business continued to decline. The trailers tended to be owned by railroad motor carrier subsidiaries. Little business was provided by truckers, who faced union and regulatory obstacles to working with railroads even if they had been inclined to do so.

Piggyback was met with varying degrees of opposition and wariness by traditional railroad operating and marketing executives. Because it was designed to compete directly with truckers, the railroads had to provide reliable service, which was a problem for the operating departments. And because the traffic moved at low rates, marketing officials didn't embrace it either. At many railroads, piggyback was managed by younger, more aggressive officers who had been "exiled"—often for being too aggressive in seeking change in an industry slow to change—to the new niche after running afoul of their more traditional seniors in the marketing and operating departments.

The Great Northern was not immune to industry economic problems, but it was blessed with management in depth. When Frank J. Gavin retired as president in May 1951, he was succeeded by John M. Budd, although he had "wandered off" in 1947 for two years to be president of the Chicago and Eastern Illinois. As historian Don Hofsommer said, Budd "grew up at the knee of his father," Ralph, who had been president of the GN and subsequently became president of the Burlington.

Budd was forced to face the issue of rapidly declining passenger service and demanded that the GN's passenger service reduce losses without sacrificing the service quality for which the railroad was known. He set a policy for the GN that walked a middle course between industry activists who believed in promoting passenger service and those who energetically discouraged it. While seeking to reduce losses by eliminating the railroad's worst performers, Budd also demanded that remaining GN trains be run in a manner that the company could be proud of.

One of the most contentious issues of the 1950s was the railroad industry's campaign to gain managerial flexibility at the same time that rail unions were seeking new and more-restrictive work rules and even greater job security in the face of company efforts to control costs. Dieselization, for example, eliminated the work of the locomotive fireman, but union work rules continued to require that every train have a fireman in the cab, and the Brotherhood of Locomotive Firemen and Enginemen refused to negotiate a change. Various states, stimulated by union lobbyists, enacted "full crew" laws that required extra brakemen regardless of the work to be performed en route. The five-man crew was standard. Rail unions often saw technology as leading to job losses rather than a means of making the job safer and easier, as management claimed. Thus, when radios made it possible for conductors in the caboose to communicate more efficiently with engineers in the locomotive than they could signal with a lantern, the unions demanded and got an extra payment—known as an arbitrary—for using the radio. Early radios were bulky and heavy, like the radios used during the war, which was part of the union's argument for an extra payment.

In 1959, through the Association of American Railroads, the industry sought a thorough revision and modernization of the wage structure and work rules. Daniel P. Loomis, AAR president, said that unproductive labor policies were a form of "featherbedding"—"an economic albatross around the neck of American progress" and the "handmaiden of the ruinous inflationary spiral."

With the industry hamstrung by restrictions on its ability to manage its workforce and to adapt to changing conditions, the term "featherbedding" backfired. It implied that all rank-and-file workers were lazy and sought to gouge their employers, when in reality the railroad workers were incredibly loyal to their crafts and merely were abiding by contracts negotiated with the companies by their unions. The men believed management had attacked them unfairly. Budd was one executive who disapproved of the term, seeing it as inflammatory and counterproductive. Although Budd enthusiastically supported the industry campaign to reform work rules, he quietly made it known that GN officers were not to use the word "featherbedding."

Railroad jobs were among the best in industrial America, though many employees worked long hours. Pay was significantly higher than in most industries. In addition, the Railroad Retirement system provided better pensions than workers in other industries could anticipate, and over many years railroad workers had assumed a position among the industrial elite. Even after the featherbedding battle, railroad workers continued to perform their jobs with pride and enthusiasm. Railroading had a tough culture, though, as most front-line managers had been promoted from the ranks they now supervised with no formal management training. They considered it normal to impose the same kind of discipline on their subordinates that had been successfully applied to them. Even while many American businesses had adopted a friendlier and more equality-based labor-management philosophy, railroads still managed their people through a command and control system. The result was a workforce that liked its work but didn't particularly like the people who managed it.

The still-profitable and well-managed Burlington performed just as other railroads, investing capital to gain greater efficiency and cutting costs wherever possible. It began to abandon little-used lines in the 1950s. At the same time, it improved grades, upgraded ballast, increased protection against floods, and steadily increased the weight of its rails on the lines it intended to retain. By the end of the decade, the CB&Q adopted 136-pound rail as the standard weight for future main-line installations.

The Centennial Cutoff, described in chapter four, was the largest single new railroad built in the United States since World War II. The $16 million project shortened the Chicago–Kansas City route by 22.25 miles. In another major investment, the railroad replaced the 92-year-old bridge across the Mississippi at Quincy in 1960. The original bridge was worn out and had to be opened several times a day, delaying trains in favor of barges. The new bridge was high enough to eliminate the draw span—and the need for a bridge tender to operate the draw. The government provided $2.4 million of the $10 million cost of the project to reimburse the railroad for changes required to benefit navigation, one of the few instances of federal financial assistance for a railroad since the land grants of the mid-nineteenth century.

The Burlington, which had been one of the first railroads to install centralized traffic control (CTC), equipped all single-track sections of the Chicago-Denver line with CTC by 1955. This effectively increased capacity, allowing the railroad to run trains in both directions more safely, and it allowed dispatchers to plan train "meets" and "passes" more efficiently. The railroad began to install cab signals beginning in 1951 and later in the decade began installing two-way radios in engine cabs and cabooses and on passenger trains so engineers and conductors could communicate with each other as well as with dispatchers.

Recognizing that—no matter how well freight moved over the road—terminal operations determined efficient on-time delivery, the Burlington invested millions in terminal facilities and freight houses, particularly in Chicago, Minneapolis, and Kansas City. The Kansas City freight house—a building where railroad cars could be loaded or unloaded and cargo held until the consignee came for it or it was loaded into outbound railcars—opened in 1960. It was 709 feet long, with more than 100,000 square feet under one roof, and in recognition of the growing importance of piggyback, it was designed for piggyback operations, with 116 docks for trailers.

Burlington continued to invest heavily, including making improvements of passenger stations through the 1950s. In fact, in the 14 years between 1949 and 1963, the company spent more than $430 million to improve land and equipment. The Q also invested millions in new passenger train sets as it expanded its Zephyr offerings, refusing to abandon the passenger business altogether.

Much of the investment was designed to counteract the inexorably rising cost of labor. By handling longer trains with greater tonnage more efficiently, the railroad was able to reduce the amount of labor per unit of transportation service produced. That was one of the few ways of holding down costs. By the end of 1962, for example, gross ton-miles handled per train-hour on the Burlington had increased 55.9 percent over the 1947–1949 average.

Piggyback grew slowly at first, but by the second half of the decade it had become a significant line of business for the Burlington. In the 1959 annual report to stockholders, the railroad proclaimed that the future of TOFC (trailer on flat car) service was almost unlimited. It predicted that piggyback not only could prevent further erosion of traffic but also could help regain business previously lost to truckers.

Burlington Truck Lines (BTL) was a significant factor in the railroad's growing piggyback business. Because the railroad had started BTL in 1935, prior to the effective date of the Motor Carrier Act, the truck operation had valuable "grandfather" rights and could compete for freight business that other railroad and their trucking affiliates were denied. BTL was one of the few railroad-owned highway operators to offer an independent service in competition with other motor carriers. It could handle traffic that did not have a prior or subsequent move by rail.

The decade of the 1950s ended with railroads grappling with continued competitive pressure. They were still overregulated by federal and state agencies and still focused on reducing costs because their ability to increase revenue was limited. Even before the decade began, some railroad executives understood better than others the problems they faced. The Budds—father and son—were in the forefront of those who realized that they were not in control of their companies' fate. Speaking before the Chicago Association of Commerce and Industry in 1945, the Burlington's Ralph Budd said:

> Should the financial future of the railroads become so unfavorable that private ownership cannot be continued, it will not be because railway management has failed, but because government has created a situation making it impossible for the major, and most efficient, transportation agency of the

country to survive the inroads of subsidized carriers, the
burdens of social experimentation, and the assumption of
managerial functions by the government. In other words,
the financial outlook for the railroads is a political question,
rather than one of finance or operation.

It would take another 30 years, and the bankruptcy of companies
that owned 25 percent of railroad mileage, before a majority of railroad presidents would form an alliance with the unions that represented their workers and with many of their customers to undertake
a concerted political campaign to deregulate the railroad industry.

6

A Third Try to Combine the Northerns Succeeds

I let Uncle Sam subsidize me.

ALFRED PERLMAN, New York Central Railroad president, explaining that he had traveled from New York to Washington by air rather than cost the Pennsylvania Railroad the loss associated with carrying another passenger

The Transportation Act of 1958 didn't really help the railroad industry. Railroaders really needed relief from discriminatory public and regulatory policy that limited their ability to earn a reasonable return on investment and affected efforts to stem the loss of traffic to trucks and barges.

The act was helpful, though, in that it did make it clear that Congress intended that the Interstate Commerce Commission should shift to a more merger-friendly stance. The ICC, in fact, responded to the new law by approving a number of mergers. It particularly encouraged mergers of parallel railroads where significant cost savings could be realized by eliminating redundant facilities and assets.

The railroad industry clearly had more assets than the business could support, a factor in rail mergers ever since the first mergers had occurred in the early 19th century. The 43 Class 1 carriers in the East had seen return on investment drop from an anemic 3.3 percent in 1956 to 2.4 percent in the 1960s (the Class 1 designation then applied to railroads with $5 million or more of annual revenue; today the criterion is $287 million). Southern district railroads had a similar decline over the same period from 5 percent to 2.9 percent, while western carriers declined by one-third, from 3.5 percent to 2.4 percent.

Overcapacity was a particular problem in the Midwest. The Santa Fe and the Burlington, among railroads that now are part of the BNSF Railway, fought aggressively to survive. Not all would.

Both the Rock Island and the Milwaukee Road would pass into bankruptcy in the 1970s. Much of the Milwaukee was abandoned, and its core lines were absorbed by the Canadian Pacific. The Rock Island finally shut down in 1980 during a strike of train service workers. The Rock attained the dubious distinction of being the only Class 1 railroad ever to be liquidated in bankruptcy, many of its lines being torn up for scrap.

While a number of mergers followed the ICC change in policy—more than a dozen, according to Frank N. Wilner in his definitive work on rail mergers, *Railroad Mergers: History, Analysis, Insight*—three major combinations over the next decade began to change the shape of the railroad industry and led to the further consolidation that today has the United States covered by four huge systems, one very large regional system, and several hundred smaller railroads. These three major combinations were the Penn Central, formed by the combination of the New York Central (NYC) and the Pennsylvania; the Seaboard Coast Line, formed by the merger of the Seaboard Airline and the Atlantic Coast Line; and the Burlington Northern. The Burlington was formed by combining the Chicago, Burlington, and Quincy; the Northern Pacific; the Great Northern; the Spokane, Portland, and Seattle; and the Oregon Electric.

Railroad mergers didn't just happen when applications were filed. Each of the mergers took the better part of a decade to work its way through the cumbersome regulatory process. Every competitor, union, community served by the merging carriers, and community served by competing carriers, as well as numerous shippers, seemed to think it had a right to intervene in the mergers—and did. Numerous government agencies also participated in the merger cases, further complicating the ICC's task of filtering many views and determining what the public interest was. A judicial review of any ICC approval of a combination, brought by one of the unhappy parties, invariably followed. The Penn Central, the Seaboard Coast Line, and the Burlington Northern mergers that were approved were not the only combinations during the 1960s, but they were the largest and affected more of the industry and the country than did others.

The railroads that now make up BNSF Railway were active early in the merger movement—or at least tried to be. The Santa Fe first tried unsuccessfully to acquire the Missouri Pacific, then sought also without success to acquire the Western Pacific, which would have given it access to the Pacific Northwest. Another possibility that never materialized was a courtship by Santa Fe of the Frisco, which it had controlled in the nineteenth century, but the two could not reach financial terms and never presented a case to the ICC. The Frisco also had a flirtation with the Southern Railway, which coveted its access to Texas, Oklahoma, and Kansas, but nothing came of those talks either.

Rail mergers, then as in the past, were based on two strategies. One was increasing volume and revenue by extending the franchise into new geography. Another was increasing line density and reducing unit costs by eliminating competing rail lines. Some mergers featured both strategies.

Arguably, of the three huge regional combinations, only the BN merger was successful. The Penn Central never earned a penny and, after only a thousand days, fell into what was then the largest corporate bankruptcy in the United States. Ironically, the Penn Central's collapse occurred only weeks after the BN merger was completed. The Seaboard Coast Line, which also included the Louisville and Nashville Railroad, was short of capital to fully implement its merger and never achieved great prosperity. The railroad limped along until it was acquired by the Chessie System in the 1982 merger that created CSX Transportation.

The Penn Central in the East and the Seaboard Coast Line in the South faced more-severe competition from trucks than did the western railroads. Operating in a geographically more compact region of the country, they had a shorter average length of haul, and their traf-

---

Examples of Overcapacity in Major Midwest Markets (Railroads Competing by Market, 1970s)

Chicago–Kansas City	Chicago–Omaha
Atchison, Topeka, & Santa Fe	Chicago, Burlington, and Quincy
Chicago, Burlington, & Quincy	Chicago, Milwaukee, St. Paul, & Pacific
Chicago, Milwaukee, St. Paul, & Pacific	Chicago and North Western
Chicago and North Western	Chicago, Rock Island, & Pacific
Chicago, Rock Island, & Pacific	Illinois Central

fic was more susceptible to diversion to trucks. That difference alone accounted for their lack of success relative to that of the Burlington Northern. Penn Central also had to contend not only with slow economic growth in the northeastern region where it operated but also with a shift of much of its industrial base to the South and the West.

Penn Central, in particular, was an ill-fated combination. Both major partners already were losing money and traffic when they combined. The Pennsylvania once was known as the "standard railroad" of the world, an arrogance that offended executives of railroads like the Santa Fe, the Great Northern, the Union Pacific, the Southern Pacific, and others. The Pennsy, as it was known, and the NYC began merger talks in 1957, when they still were in reasonably good financial and physical condition. Still, it took until 1968 to accomplish the merger, by which time both were showing signs of significant deterioration.

The courtship was anything but smooth, and the honeymoon was nonexistent. The Penn Central was the largest consolidation in U.S. business history up to that point, and less than three years later it became the largest bankruptcy. The difficulty of merging two systems that had been bitterly competitive for more than a century was borne out by the term "red team–green team" in recognition of the principal colors of the Pennsylvania and the New York Central and the cultural enmity that existed between them. The merged company never developed any cohesiveness.

The Penn Central merger was further complicated by having to run the full gauntlet of federal regulatory approval, including a trip to the Supreme Court after the ICC finally gave its consent. The applicants faced opposition and demands for concessions from organized labor. Other parties weighed in, including competing eastern railroads and communities that feared the combination would negatively affect their economies. The proceeding amounted to virtually full employment for commerce lawyers and consultants, as everyone—from individual citizens to governors of states—presented arguments for and against the merger. The Burlington Northern, on the other hand, while it had to work its way through the same process, did not face the same degree of opposition.

To buy off labor opposition to the Penn Central merger, the now infamous Luna-Saunders Agreement was negotiated in 1964. The agreement was named for its principal negotiators: Charles Luna, president of the Brotherhood of Railroad Trainmen, and Stuart Saunders, chairman of the Pennsylvania Railroad. In the agreement, the merging railroads agreed to recall furloughed workers, retain five-person crews on freight trains, and provide lifetime income protection to 98 percent of their unionized workers, who were represented by the 24 unions that signed the agreement. The settlement worked insofar as organized labor dropped its opposition to the merger. It also guaranteed, however, that the new railroad would be financially crippled from its first day of existence.

Organizers of the Burlington Northern merger were similarly forced to offer lifetime job protection that included a right to refuse relocation to some union workers and to make concessions to competing railroads. However, as discussed later, BN executives believed they would obtain productivity and voluntary retirements that, if not offsetting the cost of the agreement, certainly would ameliorate it. Because the new railroad had other strengths and did not have the fundamental problems of the Penn Central, the BN wasn't brought down by the costly conditions it accepted. Future executives, though, would have to deal with the cost and cultural consequences of the concessions.

Mergers helped, but they were not the salvation of railroads that engaged in them. The railroad industry—and the railroads that today are part of the BNSF system along with it—continued to struggle. They fought to survive in a regulatory and public policy environment more suited to an earlier age—the time when railroads had an effective monopoly on freight transportation between cities. In numerous rate cases, the ICC continued to use its maximum-rate authority to protect rail customers from the railroads and its minimum-rate authority to protect rail competitors that had higher variable cost structures. Without reflecting on the railroads' higher fixed costs, the commission in several cases ordered rail rates to be maintained at higher levels than the railroads wanted. The ICC reasoned that, with their lower variable costs, railroads possibly could behave in a predatory manner when competing with truck and barge operators.

Perhaps the most notorious example of such rate making—and a particularly flagrant example of the regulatory process run amok—was the so-called Big John case. The Southern Railway sought to put a new jumbo covered hopper car into service, hauling grain from the Midwest to the Southeast. The new car, with a capacity of 100 tons, could carry twice as much as traditional grain-carrying cars. It was easier to load and unload, and because of its greater capacity, there was a smaller switching and storage charge in the cost assigned to each bushel of grain it carried. Southern executives saw an opportu-

nity to compete with trucks that were taking the grain free of regulation under the agricultural exemption. The railroad proposed a rate
that was 60 percent below conventional single-car rates.

Students of regulation and economics still study the Big John case
as an example of the worst of government economic regulation.
Frank N. Wilner wrote:

> Few cases to come before—and be decided by—the Inter-
> state Commerce Commission were quite as loony as the so-
> called Big John Case.
>
> Parties to the proceeding included no fewer than the
> Southern Governors' Association; the Southeastern Associa-
> tion of Railroad and Utilities Commissioners; the states of
> Alabama, Georgia, Kansas, Kentucky, Mississippi, North
> Carolina, South Carolina and Virginia; the U.S. Department
> of Agriculture; the U.S. Department of Justice; the Ameri-
> can Farm Bureau; the National Grange; the National Farm-
> ers' Union; the Southeastern Association of Local Grain
> Producers; the Waterways Freight Bureau; the American
> Waterways Operators; the Tennessee Valley Authority;
> more than 100 millers, farmer cooperatives, grain mer-
> chants, grain exchanges, trucking companies, and grain ele-
> vator operators; seven railroads, 420 chambers of com-
> merce; and 747 towns and cities.

It took five years from the time the Southern Railway filed its rate
until the case was completed. The aggressive rate initially was
opposed by competing barge lines, truckers, port interests, and grain
elevator operators—all fearful of new competition, as economist and
historian Frank Wilner points out. Some elevator operators that had
only water access to their facilities objected that the new rail rate—in
which they could not participate without making considerable capital
investment in rail loading and unloading facilities—would put them
at a competitive disadvantage to those elevators that already had
access to the Southern's tracks. Water carriers argued that the Southern was creating a "Chinese wall" to block them from participating
in the grain business. They insisted that the combined truck or short-
haul rail rate from the grower to the river and the water rate would
not be competitive with Southern's proposed lower all-rail tariff.

The ICC agreed with opponents that the Southern was creating a
Chinese wall against competitors. The commissioners ordered the

proposed rate canceled and subject to refiling a higher rate. On appeal by the railroad, however, a federal district court set aside the commission's order, citing a lack of substantial evidence. The Supreme Court then vacated the lower court order and sent the case back to the ICC to give it an opportunity to justify its original order.

The agency finally ruled in the railroad's favor, finding that the rate was not so much aimed at barge traffic as it was to compete with unregulated trucks, which made it lawful. Under ICC procedural rules, however, the Southern's originally proposed rate had remained in effect the entire time that the case was litigated. During the time the case was before regulators and courts, the Southern's annual movement of grain soared from 700,000 tons to more than 72 million. The more efficient covered hoppers allowed the railroad to charge lower prices to haul grain, and the lower prices stimulated the growth of the broiler chicken industry in the Southeast. A relatively small number of cars carried far more grain at lower cost than the cars they replaced. Southern Railway's director of cost and price analysis, John Ingram—who later would become federal railroad administrator and then president of the Chicago, Rock Island, and Pacific Railroad—noted that the Big John cars had carried more tonnage in three years than grain boxcars carried in a lifetime. Jumbo covered hopper cars, pioneered by the Southern Railway, now are the standard vehicle used by all railroads to carry grain.

Many states continued to exercise regulatory authority as though each were a separate country, with no concern for the national ramifications of their decisions. States continued to levy ad valorem and other taxes on railroads in a discriminatory fashion, as though the railroads could provide an endless stream of revenue to state and local governments. That railroads had brought much of the regulatory system on themselves by their market behavior more than seventy years earlier was no longer a valid reason for punitive regulation, if it ever had been. What really was at stake by the 1960s was that railroads could be made to pay. Unlike other businesses that could choose to expand or even relocate where the business climate was more favorable, railroads literally were anchored in the ground. This made them inviting targets for local politicians. Congress finally banned discriminatory state taxation of railroad property in the landmark Railroad Revitalization and Regulatory Reform (4R) Act of 1976.

Finding themselves unable to achieve meaningful regulatory change, railroad executives focused on reducing costs as a way to retain profitability. They sought to eliminate jobs and to increase the productivity of those workers who were retained. Managers were particularly frustrated that they had been unable to achieve the full benefits of new technology such as dieselization in the 1950s. The railroad industry embarked on a campaign to gain increased productivity from its workers. Following a failed labor-management conference over work rules in mid-1960, President Eisenhower named a special commission to study the dispute. Thomas A. Jerrow, Great Northern's vice president of operations, was one of 15 people named to the panel.

In early 1962, following extensive hearings and by which time John F. Kennedy had succeeded Eisenhower, the commission issued its report, largely upholding the railroads' position. Fortunately for the country, transportation tends not to be subject to partisan politics. Typically, neither Democrats nor Republicans have a transportation agenda, and most presidential campaign platforms are silent on transportation issues except to say that the party supports more and improved transportation. Though it was begun under Republican Eisenhower and completed its work under Democrat Kennedy, the commission determined that railroads should be allowed to eliminate firemen from freight and yard service by attrition. In addition, the companies should be allowed to adopt technological advances in operating trains, and the so-called dual system of pay (time and mileage) for operating personnel should be changed. In addition, the report stated, crew change practices should be updated to reflect modern high-speed operations.

Train crews now operate across two or more divisions at a time today, reducing the number of expensive crew changes and increasing the standard for a basic day's work from 100 miles to 130. Nevertheless, the dual system of pay still prevails at BNSF and most of the railroad industry. To minimize the effect of the proposed changes on workers, the retirement age was to be lowered and severance pay was to be offered to workers who would lose their jobs. For workers who were released, there was to be job retraining. Preferential hiring of workers displaced by technology was a final goal. Outraged union leaders immediately rejected the recommendations.

Bargaining talks that followed the release of the 1962 report were unsuccessful. The National Mediation Board could not get either side to budge, and under provisions of the Railway Labor Act of 1926, the agency finally offered binding arbitration, which the carriers accepted and labor rejected. Although the companies then were legally free to implement the commission recommendations, doing so undoubtedly would have resulted in a calamitous nationwide railroad strike.

President Kennedy's public appeal accomplished nothing, so Kennedy turned to Congress, which passed legislation creating a new arbitration board and empowered it to make a binding decision on the issues of firemen elimination and crew size—known as crew consist. Late in 1963, the board ruled that railroads could terminate firemen with less than two years' service, of which there were relatively few; those with two to nine years' service could be moved to other work with no reduction in pay or be offered severance; and those with ten or more years' service would retain their jobs until they retired and would not be replaced when they did. The unions refused to accept the decision and appealed to the Supreme Court, but they lost.

The next year, mediators achieved success when the railroads and unions reached agreement on a number of issues. Union employees got seven paid holidays annually, a 3.5 percent pay increase for yard workers, and a lodging and meal allowance for road crews that had to lay over four or more hours away from their home terminal. The unions abandoned their demand for overtime and premium pay for night shifts, and the railroads yielded on their demand that train crews accept a change in the dual system of pay issue.

As the nation became mired in the Vietnam War, inflation took its toll on the railroads, with wages and fringe benefits spiraling upward. The clerks gained a 5 percent wage increase on January 1, 1967, another 6 percent in 1968, and another 5 percent in 1969. By 1968, employee compensation at the Great Northern was 125 percent of the 1950 level, while employment had fallen to 56 percent of 1950 levels. The Great Northern extended the gains won by unions to its nonunion employees. Many other railroads did the same.

Despite the rancorous relationship of the railroad industry with the unions that represented most of its workers, individual railroads tried to heal the wounds that had been opened by the productivity campaign. The Great Northern, under John Budd, was a leader in trying to create an environment that encouraged loyalty toward the company and productivity among employees. New hires received indoctrination and help in preparing them for advancement. The railroad adopted a policy of promotion from within and gave clerical and other employees incentives and opportunities for new positions. Such progressive approaches were not limited to the ranks of organized labor. The GN had begun student officer training in the 1920s and expanded it in the 1960s. Mid- and upper-level managers were sent to advanced management programs at Harvard and other universities. The GN, like many other major railroads, also actively recruited management trainees among the graduates of major universities and graduate business schools. A problem that continues to the present, though, was getting veteran engineers and conductors to accept promotion to supervisory positions, because senior operating employees generally earned more than first- and second-level supervisors.

Throughout this difficult time, the Great Northern continued to upgrade its locomotive fleet, buying fewer but more powerful diesel units. The railroad acquired specialized freight cars, particularly jumbo covered hoppers, to handle grain and bulk and granular commodities such as flour, sugar, and chemicals. The GN purchased 14,000 cars during the Budd years, and many others were rebuilt. Passenger equipment also was added. As has been said, though, Budd simultaneously supported the elimination of money-losing passenger service while pushing the premium long-distance trains. He did this because losses on shorter-distance trains were escalating rapidly, while he believed the long-distance trains presented the railroad in its most favorable light, even if they were losing money.

Efforts to serve shippers by tailoring services to their specific needs were hampered, however, by the regulatory system and the ICC's imposition of general tariffs. Railroads were not allowed to sign contracts with customers, because all rates had to be published as tariffs. In the vernacular, as *Business Week* magazine once observed, a tariff means you say what you charge and you charge what you say. But because a tariff, often called public pricing, had to be available to all like-situated shippers, and carriers had to treat those shippers without discrimination, railroads were prevented from offering a truly total transportation package tailored to specific customers. The tariff covered movements of specific commodities between specified stations, and even additional services were required to be spelled out in great detail. Railroads understood what they were dealing with and tried to battle the unregulated or less regulated competitors, but they entered the ring with their hands tied by regulation.

Senior Great Northern executives became convinced that the future of the company did not appear very bright, because higher costs and keener competition restricted its earning capacity. The railroad remained profitable, but the return on investment was so minuscule as to make it exceedingly difficult to sell new securities to fund capital programs. Terms like deferred maintenance and delayed capital became common throughout the industry as the railroads gradually were consuming themselves and were unable to replace capital as it became worn out.

In 1967 the GN became one of the first railroads to replace its traffic department with a marketing department, to become more customer focused. Consultants had recommended that the railroad concentrate on meeting individual customers' specific needs, with special attention to the place of transportation expense in total distribution costs. Today that is considered logistics.

Robert Downing Jr., who worked his way up in the Great Northern from an assistant trainmaster to retire from the Burlington Northern as vice chairman, was interviewed for this book. He believed that the GN had a progressive culture that differed from that of many other railroads, and that the GN benefited because of it. "John Budd had a very forward look," Downing said. "I think maybe the culture on the Great Northern was more favorable than it was in other places. That, I think, was partly due to his leadership. He really believed in it, and if you believe in it at the top it works its way down through the ranks much faster than if you do it with an order."

Despite the best efforts of Great Northern managers and fairly stable volumes of freight as measured by tonnage, financial performance was lackluster at best. The operating ratio, which for a long time had been in the mid-70s, went above 80 in the late 1960s. During this period of declining railroad earnings, the GN was buoyed by nonoperating income, mostly from dividends and interest in other companies. The Great Northern owned shares in pipeline companies, the Western Pacific Railroad Company, and the Trailer Train Company, the railroad-owned leasing company that provided much of the growing intermodal car fleet. And, of course, the GN held its interest in the Chicago, Burlington, and Quincy Railroad, which continued to pay dividends.

The decline in the passenger business accelerated. Individual carriers responded by increasing the rate at which they filed to eliminate the largest money losers. Passenger "train-offs" involved long, arduous regulatory processes. They also often involved a dash to the courthouse, as interests that wanted to retain trains whether the public used them or not, could be counted on to appeal to federal courts. More than once a railroad was required to operate a money-losing passenger train while a federal court reviewed the ICC decision. The commission's decision invariably was upheld, but there was no mechanism to reimburse the railroad for the cost of delay.

Occasionally, it became a race between railroad operating executives and lawyers for opponents to see if railroad officials could eliminate the train before protestors could obtain a restraining order. The railroads relied on the concept that the courts wouldn't try to "unscramble an egg."

While the railroads were battling the unions that represented their employees, the competition from unregulated and less regulated truck and barge operators, and the vagaries of government policy, the Great Northern, the Northern Pacific, and the Chicago, Burlington, and Quincy were pursuing another attempt to merge at the same time that each of them was struggling to adapt to the changes affecting all railroads.

The Northerns, as the NP and the GN were known, long had recognized that they could prosper if they operated as a single rail system. James J. Hill had understood it late in the 19th century, which was why he first tried to merge the two systems in 1896 and then formed the Northern Securities Company in 1901 to operate as a holding company for the competing carriers. Hill failed both times.

In fact, the Great Northern and the Northern Pacific occupied a single office building in downtown St. Paul, with the NP on the Fifth Avenue side and the GN on the Fourth Avenue side. Although the structure had a common heating plant, each company occupied half the building with no passage permitted between the two halves.

Leaders of the Northerns and the Burlington had tried for a second time to merge in the early 1930s—and seemingly won approval from the ICC—but the conditions imposed for approval were so draconian and economically onerous that the combination was scuttled by its proponents. On July 16, 1960, the three railroads jointly announced that they would seek federal approval to join in a new railroad to be known as the Great Northern Pacific and Burlington Lines Incorporated. It was the third attempt in 60 years to unite the Northerns. Stockholders of all three railroads approved the proposal early in 1961, the application was filed with the ICC, and hearings began later that year.

Downing was assistant to the president and the principal GN officer involved in planning and implementing the merger. Downing, who began his railroad career on the Pennsylvania Railroad in 1935 after graduating from Yale University with a degree in civil engineering, took his first Great Northern job in the mechanical department in Whitefish, Montana, and worked his way up, with time out for military service during World War II. He retired from the Burlington Northern as vice chairman and a member of the board of directors.

Downing noted that the merger was not just a revival of earlier failed efforts. "The chain of events goes back to Mr. Hill, but I really think the last merger, the BN merger, took off from a fresh start," he said. "Sure, we studied the history of the previous attempts, but the situation was so completely different that I think it's only fair to say that we started off fresh with the BN merger. We looked back at what had been done, but we didn't use that as a basis for planning." Downing said the merger was planned and implemented in the context of the times:

> When John [Budd] and Bob [Macfarlane] became presidents of the Great Northern and Northern Pacific, it was about the same time, around 1952. The railroads were having kind of a long decline from the very high level of traffic during World War II. The properties had somewhat deteriorated due to heavy traffic and not spending enough money, and good manpower wasn't available. So the immediate postwar period was a time of decline in traffic, and the competition from other forms of transportation was rapidly increasing. John and Bob both felt that something needed to be done to reduce the number of companies and reduce the overhead [and to] run the combined properties more efficiently. This was not an end-to-end type of merger, where you tried to expand geographically. Instead, it was—as between the Northern Pacific and the Great Northern, and to some extent the Burlington—a side-by-side merger.

The greatest potential for a merger of essentially parallel lines was in the ability to reduce expenses and eliminate redundant facilities and people. The merger process actually had begun five years earlier, in 1955, when each railroad appointed members of a committee to study the potential of consolidation. The steering committee took a year studying the various aspects. Downing explained: "[The study] was a rather thorough thing, because we realized that if we were going to merge, we would have to make a case before the ICC. Therefore, this study would be the basis for our eventual application." There had been so few major rail mergers in the previous quarter century that the planners essentially began from scratch. "That was all brand-new to them," Downing said. "They didn't really know how to handle it."

Even before the merger application could be prepared, though, the railroads had to determine the relative valuations of the properties so that owners could be fairly compensated with stock in the new railroad, and they had to develop a theory of the case that they hoped would receive a favorable reaction from the ICC. "In other words," Downing said, "you've got to know how the finances would work out, and in particular that led to what would be the exchange ratio of the shares in the new company. They didn't want to touch that until they had to, so that took a while. Then, the second thing was to get the lawyers to decide how to get the thing approved by the commission, because previous attempts, of course, had failed. In the absence of other mergers, none of the commissioners or even the staff at the commission had ever dealt with anything quite like this."

No other railroad flatly opposed the merger, although the Milwaukee Road and the North Western both sought protective conditions if the combination were to be approved. Fearing job losses, organized labor opposed the merger. The unions were not persuaded by the companies' argument that "the best prospect for stable employment lies in approval of the proposed merger." The Milwaukee Road, which essentially paralleled the roads that would become the Burlington Northern from Chicago to Seattle, initially opposed the merger. According to Downing, "[The Milwaukee Road managers] could have asked to be included, but they chose not to. They said, 'We want to remain independent, but in order to survive in the merged company environment we need to have some gateways opened.' The way the tariffs were all arranged, the Milwaukee was not able to get a haul west of the Twin Cities to points on the NP or GN that the Milwaukee handled into the Twin Cities." Downing was referring to the time-honored system of keeping the longest haul possible for one's self.

The Milwaukee managers sought protection that would allow the railroad to serve points between the Twin Cities and the West Coast, which would give it longer hauls. "They said, 'We'd do all right if gateways at common points between St. Paul and the coast were named as open gateways and rates would be applied,'" Downing recalled. "They asked for, I think, 13 different places. That was their major request. They thought that they could by solicitation get those longer hauls and thereby increase their revenue. They also wanted access to two local points, which they couldn't reach, those being Billings, Montana, and Portland, Oregon."

Downing explained that the managers of the Milwaukee Road thought it could coexist with the merged railroad if it could reach new markets without having to turn cars over to the BN. "They thought there was enough business at Billings and more particularly at Portland, Oregon, that they wanted to run their own trains in there. You don't just voluntarily give another railroad the right to run on your railroad, but they wanted that." The North Western wanted similar market protections. Both railroads eventually reached negotiated agreements with the merging carriers, and the ICC imposed the agreements as conditions of its merger approval.

The Burlington Northern merger effectively doomed the Milwaukee, which probably should have sought to be included in the combination. By the time its management realized that, however, it was too late. Asked if the BN would have accepted the Milwaukee had it sought inclusion, Downing responded: "I don't know. We never really were asked, so we didn't decide." In the 1970s, as the Milwaukee slipped toward bankruptcy, it petitioned the ICC on more than one occasion to order that the BN take it into its system, but it was turned down each time. The Milwaukee filed for bankruptcy protection from creditors in 1977.

Leaving the Milwaukee out of the combination was just as well for the BN. As Downing observed, "It would have made it a lot more problematic from an antitrust standpoint. . . . We were having tough sledding with the Department of Justice to get just two parallel railroads merged. . . . The Justice Department did its very best to derail the merger." The U.S. Department of Justice was the principal party that objected to the BN merger, and even though it didn't have the legal authority to block the transaction, its views carried weight with the ICC. "Had we gone in and said, 'Here's three parallel railroads we want to merge,' I think we would have been turned down," said Downing. "Because at least at that time the Milwaukee didn't consider itself as failing. Had [its managers] been able to make the case that 'if you don't let us in, we're going to go broke anyhow,' it might have turned the tide with the Justice Department. But [the Milwaukee] didn't feel that way then, although it became evident not too much later."

The Milwaukee Road and the North Western may not have sought extensive conditions or inclusion in the Northern Lines case because they were contemplating their own merger at the same time.

The two Chicago-based railroads had flirted with merger in 1955 but ended the relationship even before becoming engaged. A Milwaukee–North Western combination would have created a 22,000-mile system stretching through 15 states from Indiana to the Pacific Coast. It would have been second in length only to the Northern Lines. The Justice Department, consistent when it came to railroad mergers, opposed the Chicago and North Western–Milwaukee Road consolidation as anticompetitive. Approval of that merger was recommended by an ICC administrative law judge (the current term for ICC officials previously known as examiners). The judge cited growing truck and barge competition but amazingly ignored the concurrent Northern Lines case. For reasons of their own, the Milwaukee and the North Western dropped their merger request.

On August 24, 1964, after nearly three years of hearings, filings of written testimony, rebuttals, responses to rebuttals, and depositions, ICC examiner Robert H. Murphy approved the plan subject to certain conditions. But Murphy's decision was not the end of the process. It would be nearly six more years before the new and renamed Burlington Northern would begin operating. On April 27, 1966, in a 6–5 vote, the ICC rejected the proposed merger on the grounds that consolidation was not essential to protect the GN, the NP, and the CB&Q from truck and barge competition. The commissioners found that the three railroads were "large, strong and prosperous." They also expressed alarm that employment would be cut by more than five thousand and that competitors would be harmed. In an ironic historical footnote, the ICC rejection came on the same day that it unanimously approved the ill-fated merger that created the Penn Central Transportation Company.

When word of the decision came from Washington, D.C., to his Chicago office, Louis W. Menk, president of the Chicago, Burlington, and Quincy, lowered his head into his hands and said: "Well, that's the ol' ball game." He was wrong. Menk, a career railroad operating executive who had started out as a telegrapher on the Frisco and worked his way up to chief executive, had moved to the Burlington just a year earlier and was being groomed to take over the combined railroads once the merger was approved. At six feet six inches in height, Menk was an imposing and courtly man. He also had the distinction, along with John W. Barriger, of having been president of four different Class 1 railroads during his long career. Others had headed two or even three railroads, but none had led railroads of the magnitude that Menk had. He started with the St.

Louis–San Francisco Railway, moved to the Burlington, then was president of the Northern Pacific, and ended his career as chairman, president, and chief executive of the Burlington Northern. The ICC's majority opinion cited the old, worn, and no longer operative reasons for not allowing the merger.

The five-commissioner minority criticized the majority for having a mind-set that maintained the status quo and ignored the intent of Congress that the commission look with favor on rail mergers and consolidations. Dissenting commissioner Kenneth H. Tuggle accused the majority of talking with "demagogic overtones," of imposing an "extreme evidentiary burden heretofore imposed only in criminal cases," and of "misapply[ing] the law and fumbl[ing] the facts." Murphy, in his written opinion, dealt with the objections to the merger from the Justice Department, labor unions, and competing railroads. His views would be incorporated in the concept that competition—not competitors—should be protected, a concept that would be adopted in the broader deregulation of railroads that would follow a decade and a half later. As Murphy put it,

> [The duty of a railroad] is to provide adequate and efficient transportation service to all of the public it serves, not to guarantee a certain level of employment at particular locations or to underwrite the taxing structure of particular states, or counties or communities.
>
> The criterion for authority to unify is whether it will in fact promote adequate and efficient transportation, not whether it will freeze the existing pattern of employment across the system.
>
> The record is replete with strong evidence that the proposed unification will promote adequate and efficient transportation, produce sound and proper economies and efficiencies and result in an improved rail transport system.

Murphy also made a case that although the GN and the NP served a number of common points—such as Seattle and St. Paul—their lines between served "entirely different geographical areas." In their application, the merging railroads pointed out that the combined railroad would serve 4,700 rail stations, but only 140, or 3 percent, were served by more than one of the merging railroads and by no other railroad. Further, the applicants claimed those 140 stations accounted for less than 5 percent of total station revenues and

The Civil War was the first conflict in which railroads played a significant role. General Herman Haupt was in charge of the U.S. military railroads. After the war he became the general manager for the Northern Pacific.

Charles Elliott Perkins, president and one of the most important leaders of the Burlington Route in the late 19th century.

General George Custer and some of his scouts were assigned the duty of protecting railroad building operations on the Northern Pacific Railroad.

James J. Hill, known as the "Empire Builder," and his associates created the railroad that was eventually to become the Great Northern Railway, through a series of acquisitions, mergers and the eventual construction of lines across the Northern Plains.

A scenic poster advertising the Great Northern Railway, designed to encourage travelers to explore the West.

Advertisement encouraging immigrants to settle some of the land owned by the Great Northern, which ran in The Farmer's Opportunity *in St. Paul, Minnesota in 1891.*

Workers on the cut at Oregon, Illinois, 100 miles west of Chicago on the Chicago, Burlington, and Quincy Railroad.

Cyrus Kurtz Holliday was known for his bold vision to create a railroad that would span from Chicago, cross the Rockies and reach the Pacific Coast. By 1887, Holliday saw this vision fulfilled in the 7,373-mile railroad that became the Atchison, Topeka & Santa Fe Railway (Santa Fe).

Construction of the Santa Fe at Fort Madison, Iowa circa 1886.

Great Northern's Oriental Limited was inaugurated in 1904. This photo is believed to be from that period.

An early locomotive from the Frisco.

A Frisco track gang with their lunch buckets going to work on a Salem Branch work train in Missouri, circa 1912.

After nearly 40 years with the Great Northern, James Hill (left) retired as chairman of the board of directors on July 1, 1912. Hill was succeeded as chairman of the board by his son, Louis W. Hill (right).

The famous "Harvey Girls" not only helped make Fred Harvey's chain of hotels and restaurants along the Santa Fe line a success, they also helped Santa Fe to develop a reputation for some of the best passenger service in the nation.

Spurred by the growth of the steel industry, transporting iron ore played an important role in the fortunes of the Great Northern.

The Great Northern president and his party, circa 1921. From left to right: H.K. Dougan, executive assistant; Ralph Budd, president; John M. Budd, son of Mr. Budd and an engineer; W.R. Wood, mechanical engineer; and H.B. Bassett, Mr. Budd's secretary.

The luxurious passenger train, the Empire Builder, was introduced in 1929 and the service continued to evolve in the decades that followed. Ralph Budd devoted resources to the GN's long-distance trains, both to increase revenue and to attract shippers and others to the Northwest.

Serving Burlington during a critical period from 1932 until 1949, Ralph Budd takes his place alongside Charles Elliott Perkins as one of the true statesmen of the Burlington and of the railroad industry. Budd was one of the first to recognize the importance of trucking as a rail competitor in the transportation marketplace.

The Burlington's exhibit at "A Century of Progress," the 1934 World's Fair in Chicago, included the Burlington Zephyr, the first diesel-powered passenger train.

Frank J. Gavin committed the Great Northern to diesel power. GN had managed to place 49 diesel locomotives in service by the time the United States entered World War II.

During World War II, railroads carried 90 percent of the military freight and 98 percent of the troops to both the Atlantic and Pacific ports as the nation fought a two-front war. Pictured above are marines disembarking at Los Angeles's Union Station after arriving on a Santa Fe Railway train.

The Chicago, Burlington, and Quincy contributed to satisfying wartime demand, even though they experienced the same critical shortages in wartime personnel as other railroads did. Many women were hired to supplement the workforce. Shown here are Havelock shop employees William Bourke and Mrs. Bruce Kimes, April 1945.

Several rail lines shared the philosophy of the Chicago, Burlington, and Quincy, known as "The Q," which believed passenger service was a show window to the success of the railroad business, one that would lure freight business. After World War II railroads invested heavily in their passenger trains in an effort to produce contented passengers.

Railroads tried a number of approaches to deal with the competitive challenges posed by other modes of transportation. The Burlington sold its intercity bus operations to a new company organized to compete with Greyhound Lines, and remained in the trucking business through its Burlington Truck Lines.

Be carefree, be comfortable and enjoy a
New World

The Santa Fe continued its passenger service longer than many other railroads and was one of the best at it. The Super Chief was an all-Pullman Chicago–Los Angeles service.

Standard in Travel
The new Santa Fe
Super Chief

Advanced ideas for your travel luxury... new cradled smoothness in the ride... daily between Chicago and Los Angeles

From the flanges on the wheels to the tip of the restful Pleasure Dome, the Super Chief is new — entirely new.

To give you the smoothest ride of your life on rails, this new Super Chief glides on cushioned springs . . . revises any ideas you ever had about any train.

The keynote is comfort.

You find it in the distinctive Turquoise Room in the lounge car—a delightful place to relax, enjoy a cocktail or entertain your friends at dinner—the first time such a room has been provided on any train.

You find it in the Pleasure Dome—"top of the Super, next to the stars"—that brings you an unobstructed view of southwestern scenery.

You find it in the new dining cars where Fred Harvey chefs present new and exciting menus.

Accommodations in this beautiful all-room train pamper you every mile of the way . . . "push-button" radio or music in your room when you *want* it . . . beds you just can't help sleeping in . . . charming apartments by day.

For your next trip between Chicago and Los Angeles say "Super Chief." Now, more than ever, it is America's train of trains. Just consult your local ticket or travel agent.

SANTA FE SYSTEM LINES
Serving the West and Southwest

Santa Fe

The Super Chief offered 39-hour, 45-minute passage between Chicago and Los Angeles, a level of passenger service that has not been matched since.

In 1952, the Santa Fe began to experiment with the transport of truck trailers on flat-cars—called piggyback, but known now as intermodal. The Burlington began its first intermodal service in 1954, and by the end of the decade, proclaimed that the future of intermodal service was almost unlimited, and would help regain business previously lost to truckers.

that alternative forms of transportation still would assure competition. In other words, the would-be merging railroads were not all that competitive within their territories, and they would continue to have competitors for the long-haul traffic.

This time, though, the Great Northern and the Northern Pacific—the principal parties—didn't take no for an answer. They petitioned for reconsideration, saying they would address each of the concerns of those opposed to the consolidation. The ICC granted a rehearing in January 1967, giving the merging railroads an opportunity to deal with some of the opponents. First, as discussed earlier, the railroads followed the precedent of the New York Central and Pennsylvania Railroad, buying off union labor by guaranteeing lifetime income protection. Wilner points out that the cost of income protection for union workers raised labor costs to 60 percent of revenue; that figure was about 45 percent at other solvent railroads.

Though the settlement may have been costly, labor withdrew its objections to the merger. Then the merging railroads bought off the North Western and the Milwaukee Road, offering to take care of their competitive concerns. The North Western was promised improved interchange privileges and trackage rights. The Milwaukee was offered access to the Northerns at 11 new points in North Dakota, Montana, and Washington State. The Milwaukee also was offered access to Portland, Oregon, its key demand, which would give it a direct connection to the Southern Pacific and the Union Pacific and the ability to solicit freight to and from Northern California. The two competitors dropped their objections to the merger.

The gains to be obtained from the merger far outweighed the costs of the concessions to labor and competitors. All but 309 miles of the Northern Pacific main line were to be reduced to secondary main-line status, which would relieve the new railroad of a huge amount of maintenance-of-way expense and future capital spending needs. The consolidation of nine separate yards in the Minneapolis and St. Paul area into one modern facility would enable the new company to handle freight in one-seventh the time previously required—and at a huge saving in operating expenses.

Fritz R. Kahn, a former general counsel of the ICC, recalled the scramble by the applicants to get opponents to drop their opposition. The Milwaukee Road wanted "gateways, which no one had any confidence in," he said, adding, "so this was all the Milwaukee wanted." In the year following the initial ICC rejection, the applicants "caved in to or reached an agreement with labor," remembered

The First Northern Lines Rejection

The initial ICC rejection of the merger of the Great Northern, the Northern Pacific, and the Chicago, Burlington, and Quincy, along with two smaller roads, was based on the damage that the commission thought the merger would do to competitors. The commission concluded that those factors outweighed the benefits offered by the applicants:

> The applicants have failed to show that their proposed consolidation would result in transportation service to the public that is superior to that which can be provided without merger.
> Benefits are not as great as . . . the damage [that the consolidation] would do to employees and competition.

Much of America seemed to have a better understanding than did the ICC that railroads were in greater danger of collapse than of monopolistic behavior. An editorial in the *Helena* (Montana) *Independent Record* read:

> [The unifying railroads] expect to be able to attract new business and a lot more of it by reason of increased efficiency and increased territory. We could kill the goose that lays the golden egg by fighting [mergers and consolidations] and forcing the railroads to maintain their old service. But we might gain a lot more by permitting them to grow and to discard obsolete practices.

The Chicago Tribune editorialized: "Railroads are no longer either powerful or monopolies; they are fighting for their lives against the competition of trucks and airplanes." Stating what had become obvious, Business Week magazine pointed out that "railroads have not had a practical monopoly of the transportation business for more than 30 years." Others, ranging from the Grand Forks (North Dakota) Herald and the Des Moines Register to Trains magazine, also weighed in with comments critical of the merger rejection.

Kahn, who still practices transportation law in Washington, D.C. Kahn continued: "They reached an agreement with C&NW. They accepted everything the Milwaukee wanted—trackage rights into Bismarck and trackage rights into Portland. So the Milwaukee withdrew its opposition. In the meantime . . . there was an interesting change in the lineup of the ICC." Three commissioners who voted on the merger in 1966 no longer were at the ICC. Two of the three had favored it, and one had voted against it. "So it was a relatively new agency" that voted a second time in 1967, Kahn noted.

Although the Department of Justice continued to fight the merger, most of the earlier opposition was out of the case, so it was easier for the ICC to reconsider its earlier rejection. This time, by an 8–2 vote on November 30, 1967, the ICC decided that the Northern Lines merger would serve the public interest. The concessions offered to labor and the competing railroads were formally adopted as conditions of the approval. Additionally, for a five-year period the door was held open for other railroads to join the consolidation. Only the Milwaukee later sought inclusion, but its request was turned down.

The commission explained its change of heart in its written opinion:

> Upon reexamination of legislative history and relevant authorities, we conclude that the policy of [Congress] is clearly to facilitate and thereby foster and encourage consolidations that can be shown to be consistent with the public interest.
>
> Broadening the focus of our appraisal to the area relevant to transcontinental traffic and other interterritory considerations, and reweighing the facts pertaining to the ever-increasing intermodal competition, have made it apparent that this merger can lead to the creation of meaningful rail competition through strengthening [rail competitors], as well as making the combined applicants a more proficient transport agency.

But the case still wasn't over. Senate majority leader Mike Mansfield of Montana and Commerce Committee chairman Warren Magnuson of Washington, both Democrats with populist leanings, threatened to introduce legislation to strip the ICC of its authority over rail mergers. That argument would be made again thirty years later when the Interstate Commerce Commission Termination Act was under debate, with the same outcome. The Surface Transportation Board, successor to the ICC, still has jurisdiction over rail mergers. The furor on Capitol Hill, where the ICC budget awaited approval, caused the commission to vacillate. It again decided to reconsider its decision, but several months later it reiterated its approval of the merger.

With the Congress more or less pacified, the case moved from the ICC to the courts. Fritz Kahn remembered the reaction to the final approval by the ICC: "It was absolutely fascinating once the decision came out. There was this race to the courthouse. There were at least four different lawsuits brought across the country. [The ICC general counsel's] office dispatched its attorneys to try to oppose temporary restraining orders, not with uniform success. One of the cases was brought by the Department of Justice here in Washington in the District of Columbia, and a stay of the ICC's decision was granted."

At that time, judicial review of ICC decisions began at the district court level before a special three-judge panel. (Appeals of regulatory decisions now go directly to circuit courts of appeal.) Eventually, under legislation dealing with multidistrict cases, all the cases were consolidated in Washington, D.C., where the three judges would hear arguments. The District of Columbia court entered the stay. "I don't know whether the applicants would go ahead and consummate the transaction in the absence of a stay," said Kahn. "Certainly, recent mergers were consummated even while the litigation was in progress."

The Department of Justice led the charge in opposition to the merger. Comparing DOJ reaction in other merger cases, Kahn said: "The [more] recent [merger] transactions weren't opposed on such a large scale as was the Northern Lines case. Justice just didn't want it to take place, period." Because the Justice Department was appealing a decision by another federal agency, the case took the name *United States of America v. United States of America*. The solicitor general of the United States, a Justice Department official, would normally have represented the government before the Supreme Court, but because two agencies were in opposition, the solicitor general represented the Department of Justice, and Kahn ended up arguing the case for the ICC. "At the start of case, it was U.S. versus U.S. in the district court," Kahn recalled. "When it went to the Supreme Court, it was U.S. versus ICC."

Chief Justice Earl Warren signed a 10-day stay of the ICC merger approval, which was followed by an injunction by the district court, pending a hearing on the merits of the appeal. In November 1968, after reviewing the evidence, the three-judge court concluded that the ICC had acted properly and that the unification should proceed. Kahn recalled that the Supreme Court had summarily reversed the same three-judge panel when the lower court earlier had ruled against the Seaboard Coast Line merger, and it had approved the

Penn Central merger, so the lower court perhaps saw the handwriting on the wall.

The Department of Justice fought on, seeking—and obtaining—a Supreme Court review. At that time, appeals from regulatory agencies could be taken directly to the Supreme Court, bypassing the circuit court of appeals, and Kahn recalled that it was by direct appeal, not by certiorari, where the appellant first must persuade the court to take the case. The Supreme Court was not interested in the merits of the merger, only in whether the ICC had properly applied the law. In court the issue that was argued was whether the ICC had provided due process to all parties and had followed the strictures of the Administrative Procedures Act. The substance of its decision was not at issue.

Only a couple of years earlier, the Seaboard Coast Line merger also had gone to the Supreme Court, which had upheld the ICC. In that case, the ICC believed that it had an extremely strong case. "We decided to go for summary reversal of the lower court decision, which had set aside the ICC's approval of the merger," said Kahn. "No argument. I'll be darned if we didn't get away with it. The Supreme Court said that the Interstate Commerce Act was the standard by which the ICC has adjudged mergers. [The commissioners] had to take the antitrust laws into account, but they did not have to go through the analyses of the markets." The ICC believed that the same principle of law would prevail in the Northern Lines case.

The Supreme Court had ruled twice previously against merger plans for the Great Northern and the Northern Pacific, once in 1896 and again in 1904; the third failed merger plan never got beyond the ICC. But the third trip to the Supreme Court would prove to be the charm. This time there was no equivocation. In February 1970, nearly ten years after the joint announcement that the Northern Pacific, the Great Northern, and the Chicago, Burlington, and Quincy, plus two smaller railroads, would seek to merge, the Supreme Court ruled 7–0 that the merger could proceed.

Writing for the unanimous court, new chief justice Warren E. Burger emphasized that the ICC—not the Justice Department's Antitrust Division—is best able to determine the public interest in rail merger cases. Burger wrote: "We do not enquire whether the merger satisfied our own conception of the public interest. Determination of the factors relevant to the public interest is entrusted by the law [to the Interstate Commerce Commission]. . . . In our view, the Commission . . . exhibited a concern and sensitivity to the difficult task of accommodating the regulatory policy based on competition with the long-range policy of achieving carrier consolidations. . . . [O]ur review, like that of the district court, reveals substantial evidence to support the Commission's determination that the [benefits] . . . outweigh the loss of competition between the Northern Lines."

The Northern Lines case was seminal, a true landmark. The Justice Department has opposed mergers since, but not with the ferocity with which it opposed creation of the Burlington Northern. "I don't think Justice has gone to court to oppose an ICC action since the Northern Lines case," said Kahn. "It really is a landmark case."

The extended process wasn't helpful to the Northern Lines from a financial standpoint, but "as a matter of getting the thing to work, long planning certainly was helpful," said Downing. Officials of each railroad had more than enough opportunity to get to know each other, and Downing added: "They also didn't know who was going to be boss, so they had to be nice to each other." Unlike the cases with some of the other mergers between longtime competitors, the Great Northern and the Northern Pacific executives had a lot of respect for each other, even though they had been fierce competitors for nearly a century.

Some of that professional regard may have been a function of proximity. As noted previously, the NP and the GN had separate but equal headquarters in the same downtown St. Paul building. John Budd, chief executive of a railroad that had never gone through bankruptcy and had prospered more than many of its peers, kept a large, pleasant, but not opulent corner office on the 10th floor. On the day the merger was consummated, Budd and Lou Menk, who had succeeded Macfarlane as president of the Northern Pacific, ceremonially unlocked the door that separated the executive departments of the two companies on the 10th floor.

Downing thought that the lack of enmity stemmed from the earlier attempts to combine the NP and the GN. Going back to Hill's Northern Securities Company plan, executives of both companies believed that they eventually should be a single railroad. There certainly were exceptions, and the executives of the merging railroads, if not enemies, were not necessarily buddies. "In fact, one of my friends who was close to retirement retired about a year early, because he said he'd be damned if he would work for a Northern Pacific man," said Downing. "But that was exceptional. I will say that when it came time to merge we really made an all-out effort—and this is something that John [Budd] and Lou Menk fully agreed with and, in fact, insisted on—that everybody be treated as fairly as possible."

The long merger approval process probably was a blessing in disguise. In Downing's opinion, it allowed those involved to undertake a more thorough implementation planning process than was common in most railroad mergers. "There was a joint planning committee of the operating officers of both companies," Downing noted. "They planned how this thing would work, realizing that they might well be the ones who had to do it after merger."

Thorough planning involved more than the people in charge. The BN had time to complete negotiations with unions on implementing agreements. As Downing pointed out, "One of the rocks in the channel that the Penn Central ran into was that they didn't have implementing labor agreements to start out with. We didn't either until about 1967, when finally the unions came around." Having come to regard the merger as inevitable, Downing recalled, the unions thought "maybe we ought to get these things straightened out."

Although the income protection promised to union employees was costly, it was a much better agreement than that hammered out by the Penn Central. Penn Central employees could refuse a transfer and receive a separation allowance, while BN workers were rewarded for accepting a transfer but received no severance if they declined. When it came to integrating operations, the Penn Central labor agreements provided for future negotiations and arbitration of each change, while the BN completed the job before the merger took place. Menk agreed that the labor agreements were costly, but he always contended that the BN got something in return, which the Penn Central had not done.

While other mergers have gone aground on the shoals of incomplete planning and lack of labor-implementing agreements, the 1995 Burlington Northern–Santa Fe combination avoided most of the same pitfalls that the BN had experienced 25 years earlier.

On March 2, 1970, a new company began operations as the longest railroad in the United States. The name "Great Northern Pacific and Burlington Lines" was found to be too cumbersome and was changed to "Burlington Northern." Great Northern's John Budd, the son of a Great Northern chief executive, was elected BN chairman and chief executive officer, and Menk, a relative newcomer to the Hill empire, was elected the BN's first president.

Fewer than four months later, the Penn Central would collapse in what was then the largest bankruptcy in U.S. history.

7

Coal, Bankruptcies, Railroad Deregulation, and Another Merger

How are you going to pay for it?

UNIDENTIFIED BURLINGTON NORTHERN DIRECTOR, when informed of management's plan to invest $2 billion in the then nascent coal transportation business

THE BURLINGTON NORTHERN RAILROAD came into existence at an inauspicious time for the railroad industry. The loss of market share to other modes of transportation was accelerating, passenger deficits were growing, profits were shrinking, and few in or out of the industry had any real idea of how to fix the problems.

Frank Wilner summed up the situation in his definitive history of railroad mergers:

This was the plight of America's railroads in the 1970s:

- Rail tonnage had grown by 16 percent since World War II, but truck tonnage had soared by 290 percent.
- Grain traffic was being diverted to truck in every significant crop-growing region.
- An increase in maximum lawful truck weights and lengths had enabled motor carriers to increase payloads by 43 percent since 1956.
- The railroads' deficit from passenger operations was exceeding $2 billion annually (as expressed in 1994 dollars).
- The railroads' operating income had tumbled from almost $1 billion in 1966 to $227 million in 1970.
- Class 1 railroads, exclusive of the Northeast bankrupts, had

deferred more than $4 billion in maintenance and capital improvements.

- Cash dividends paid [to] railroad investors—as measured in 1972 dollars—had declined by 78 percent over the previous four decades.
- Between 1966 and 1976, the train accident rate doubled; and where track defects were the cause, the accident rate more than quadrupled.
- Two-thirds of the freight transported by Class 1 railroads was concentrated on 20 percent of its track; one-third of the rail network produced only 1 percent of the traffic.
- Eleven major rail corridors contained more than two competing mainlines.
- Eight railroads competed between Chicago and Kansas City [before mergers]—Santa Fe, Burlington Northern, Chicago & North Western, Milwaukee, Rock Island, Illinois Central, Missouri Pacific and the Norfolk & Western.
- Six railroads competed between St. Louis and Kansas City—Burlington Northern, Rock Island, Missouri-Kansas-Texas, Missouri Pacific, Norfolk & Western and St. Louis–San Francisco.
- Six railroads competed between Chicago and Omaha—Burlington Northern, Chicago & North Western, Milwaukee, Rock Island, Illinois Central and Norfolk & Western.
- Five railroads competed between Chicago and the Twin Cities—Burlington Northern, Chicago & North Western, Milwaukee, Rock Island and Soo Line.
- Five railroads competed between Dallas and Houston—Burlington Northern, Rock Island, Missouri-Kansas-Texas, Missouri Pacific and Southern Pacific.

Although the Burlington Northern was a participant in each of the highly competitive markets identified by Wilner, the Santa Fe was present in only one—the Chicago–Kansas City market—where it had a superior, high-speed route. Even though the Santa Fe had tried to enter several of the highly competitive markets, its absence proved to be beneficial.

Clearly, there were more railroads and more railroad plants in the Midwest than could be supported by the available business. The stage was set for further consolidation of the railroad industry—in much the same way as in the previous century. Farsighted executives moved to ensure that their companies would have the density of traffic required to sustain their capital-intensive railroads. Rail customers, tired of poor service and inexorably rising rates, already were abandoning railroads where they could. Shippers would not use railroads if they could avoid it, but they continued to demand the market protection afforded by multiple rail competitors. As Wilner pointed out in his history of rail mergers, "A *Railway Age* poll of shippers revealed that 80 percent of respondents favored 'regional systems with two-railroad competition,' while 58 percent supported 'three or four coast-to-coast railroads.'"

Railroad industry executives and spokesmen began referring to the "balkanization" of the industry to describe the weakness of a system in which customers were required to deal with numerous railroads to get their freight from origin to destination. Even the largest railroads were no more than regional systems at that time.

Continued financial difficulties that resulted in deteriorating service finally became obvious to the political leadership of the country. The march toward economic deregulation began and gathered steam through the decade. In the first of several legislative acts intended to help the railroads attain at least a modicum of financial stability, the passenger deficit problem was alleviated. It was solved by the effective nationalization of rail passenger service when Congress created a government-owned corporation to operate a national rail passenger system.

The problems facing railroads were not confined to the Midwest. In the East the not-so-mighty Penn Central Transportation Company was headed rapidly toward bankruptcy. A number of eastern railroads had predicted that the merger of the Pennsylvania and New York Central railroads would lead to bankruptcy, but the collapse of the company occurred for different reasons. The Central Railroad of New Jersey went into bankruptcy in 1967, the Reading Railroad in 1971, and the Lehigh Valley, the Penn Central, and the Boston and Maine in 1970. During the summer of 1972, a hurricane named Agnes swept up the East Coast. Tracks and bridges were washed out. In its wake the already financially weakened Erie Lackawanna Railroad also went into bankruptcy. With the exception of the Boston and Maine, all major "bankrupts" eventually would join the Penn Central in a federally designed Consolidated Rail Corporation (Conrail).

Even in the West, things could have been better as the decade began. As the Interstate Highway System approached completion, motor carriers were able to handle bigger loads more efficiently. In addition, these truck companies continued to make inroads on the railroads' highest-margin traffic, which also was the most service sensitive. Trucks also were cutting into grain hauling, long a mainstay of the railroads. The competitive situation was made worse for railroads when Congress, in its rush to adjourn so members could campaign in 1974 midterm elections, increased the maximum allowable gross weight for vehicles on federal-aid highways from 73,280 pounds to 80,000 pounds. Neither house had voted for the change, but when Senate and House conferees inserted it, both houses adopted the conference report with no debate.

Trucks were not the only competitors the railroads had to face. The Arkansas-Verdigris waterway project soon would come onstream, opening a navigable channel from Tulsa, Oklahoma, to the Gulf of Mexico. This competition resulted in not only a loss of significant grain volumes by the Frisco, Santa Fe, and Burlington Northern railroads, but also a lowering of rates on much of the traffic they retained. Inland waterway interests, allied closely with the U.S. Army Corps of Engineers and a number of senior members of Congress from states that had or wanted waterways, turned to their next great goal: the Tennessee-Tombigbee project. This project would connect the Tennessee River at its southerly dip into northern Alabama with the Tombigbee River and would create a new water route to the Gulf of Mexico at Mobile, Alabama.

One railroad president referred to the TennTom, as it was known, as "double-tracking the Mississippi," because it would parallel the Big Muddy. TennTom cost $2 billion. Its backers argued that it would more than pay for itself by lowering the cost of coal and other bulk commodity transportation to the point where new traffic would be stimulated and new jobs would be created. The promise of economic development long had been a siren song for local business interests and governments and especially members of Congress. In a move suggesting that even its supporters had doubts about the data they used to sell the project in Congress, the rate of return used in the cost-benefit studies to justify Corps projects was reduced to half the rate used to justify other waterway projects, and the period of repayment was increased. Even these adjustments couldn't make the TennTom a viable project, although that did not stop Congress from authorizing and funding it.

Railroads fought the TennTom vigorously, but their objections fell on deaf ears. Railroads pointed out that the amount of coal that would have to be shipped down the waterway was greater than all the coal that was mined in the watershed, and that much of the coal would continue to move on the Mississippi because the larger tows possible there made it cheaper to do so even if the Mississippi route were longer.

The TennTom waterway eventually was opened, and, to no one's surprise, the traffic flows never have reached forecast levels. The waterway mostly is used for recreational boating and fishing.

Increasingly, railroads were being relegated to carrying bulk commodities and other freight that was impracticable to move by other modes. Many railroad executives, seeing little viable future for their heavily regulated industry, moved to protect the interests of their shareholders by forming holding companies. This was the era of the "conglomerate" in American business. With holding companies, the executives could isolate the unregulated assets from the railroad assets and create shareholder value by growing the unregulated businesses. The holding company structure allowed them to manage nontransportation ventures, such as their real estate holdings, out of the control of the Interstate Commerce Commission.

Most major rail systems ended up with holding-company structures, although the Burlington Northern did not adopt the mechanism until 1981. The Santa Fe, one of the first to create a holding company, formed Santa Fe Industries in 1968, and at one time had interests in coal and gold mining, logging and timber production, oil production, and real estate. Its transportation interests included rail, truck, and pipeline activities. Other major systems that formed holding companies included the Union Pacific, the Southern Pacific, the Western Pacific, the Penn Central, the Chicago and North Western, the Bangor and Aroostook, the Boston and Maine, the Missouri-Kansas-Texas, the Missouri Pacific, the Illinois Central Gulf, the Seaboard Coast Line, and the Denver and Rio Grande Western.

In addition to business based on natural resources and real estate, some railroad holding companies ranged far afield into ventures such as ownership of luxury resorts, newspaper publishing, chocolate candy manufacturing, and franchised automotive muffler and brake repair shops. All were seen as investments that would provide a higher rate of return than the original railroad business.

Real estate development, as the Penn Central was to prove, tended to require large capital investments on much the same cycle as did the original railroad. Thus an economic downturn could be particularly damaging for a holding company because the real estate development company would face cash demands at the same time as the railroad. Penn Central bankruptcy investigators determined that much of the railroad's financial collapse could be blamed on the shift of capital from the railroad to its real estate operations.

For other railroads, however, real estate development contributed to overall financial stability. Keith Bryant, in *History of the Atchison, Topeka, and Santa Fe Railway,* observed that real estate was one of the bright spots for Santa Fe Industries, the holding company that owned the railroad. The railroad's industrial development group sold large parcels of land for new plants. By 1968 the holding company and its subsidiaries held 22,000 acres of industrial land in 70 locations. It continued to acquire land throughout the Santa Fe's territory. The Santa Fe, unlike the Penn Central and others, used real estate it owned as its contribution to joint-venture developments, conserving its cash.

If new plants produced new rail traffic, well, that was all right too. In fact, the railroads' traditional reluctance to relinquish land that eventually could generate traffic was one reason they formed holding companies. Once the real estate was transferred to the holding company or a separate real estate subsidiary, it could be sold for uses that the railroad probably would have resisted. In the 1980s, the Burlington Northern management categorized the railroad's real estate assets into three classes: land that was needed for railroad operations; land that could directly produce new traffic and therefore would only be leased for relatively short terms; and land that had no clear rail use and could be made available for sale or real estate development.

The Santa Fe was aggressive in converting unused real estate into commercial development and joint ventures, using the land as its share of an investment. Keith Bryant wrote:

> Some sites, such as the Red Bird Industrial District in Dallas, grew very rapidly. Santa Fe Land Improvement Company also began to convert some of the railway's land holdings in the East Bay area of San Francisco into commercial and residential property. A $25 million waterfront village project on 30 acres of ATSF land in Oakland was initiated in 1971. In this project the Santa Fe Land Improvement Company became an equity partner. The real estate hold-

ings of Santa Fe Industries prompted another substantial acquisition.

In 1972, Santa Fe Industries bought Robert E. McKee Inc., a general contractor and real estate developer, for $19,650,000 in common stock and debentures. With the McKee purchase came Zia Company, a maintenance contractor that held the contract for the Atomic Energy Commission's Los Alamos project.

Ernest Marsh and John Shedd Reed, who succeeded Marsh as Santa Fe president in 1967, were career railroaders. Both men understood the changes their industry faced and realized that they had to improve the profitability of the total venture. Real estate and land operations were increasingly profitable. From 22 percent of Santa Fe Industries profits in 1966, nonrail earnings increased to 33 percent in 1967 even before adopting the holding-company structure.

The diversification efforts of Marsh and Reed broadened the base of Santa Fe Industries. The two men emphasized development of the nonrail subsidiaries, without ignoring the railroad. These men, and executives at most of the other railroad holding companies, were focused on using their holding companies to save their railroads, not as a way out of the railroad business. When Reed succeeded Marsh in 1973 as chairman and chief executive of Santa Fe Industries, he also continued as president of the holding company and the railroad subsidiary.

Under Reed and at his prodding, Santa Fe rail service continued to improve. Santa Fe executives avoided the worst aspects of traffic preservation through rate cutting, and Reed has said with a certain amount of pride that the railroad demonstrated pricing discipline that helped it remain profitable where other railroads operated at a deficit. The Santa Fe faced competition from other railroads, but its territory did not include the most overbuilt and competitive markets, a circumstance that provided a buffer from the worst aspects of competition.

The Santa Fe was more aggressive than many railroads at growing the new intermodal business, and not just as a way of stemming losses of traffic to truck competitors. Reed approved establishment of the Super C, an all-trailer/container on flatcar "hot shot" train that made the trip between Chicago and Los Angeles in just 34 hours and 30 minutes, at an average speed of 63.7 miles per hour. When the Super C began operation on January 17, 1968, the Santa Fe charged $1,400 per trailer, and the train proved popular with shippers. In conjunction with a fast Penn Central expedited train from the East Coast, trailers could move from New York City to Los Angeles in 54 hours and 20 minutes. Nearly four decades later, the best transcontinental intermodal train schedule still has not beaten that record.

The railroad also instituted a direct daily freight train between Richmond, Virginia, and Richmond, California, that ran over the Seaboard Coast Line and the Frisco, connecting with the Santa Fe at Avard, Oklahoma. The train covered the 3,494-mile route in four days.

Capital spending on the Santa Fe's rail and nonrail assets remained high, with a budget of $190 million in 1969. Although capital spending dropped to $119 million in 1972 following completion of major pipeline construction projects, in 1973 it climbed to $200 million, half of which was committed to the railroad. Projects included new piggyback terminals, grade separations, and installation of hundreds of miles of welded rail, in addition to new and rebuilt locomotives and freight cars.

The Burlington Northern had not yet adopted a formal holding-company structure, but it had separate transportation and resource divisions. Each had a separate management and budget, although the resource division still existed primarily to provide funds for the railroad's capital program. The BN recruited Robert Binger, a native of Minneapolis, from natural resource–oriented Boise Cascade Company, to manage the seven nonrail businesses that were placed in the resources division. When the holding company was formed in 1981, the new management group that succeeded Menk and his associates insisted that the railroad support its own capital budget and refused to cross-subsidize the railroad with revenue from resources.

Although railroads were increasingly seen as movers of bulk commodities, the growth of intermodal and the advent of what was then called land-bridge enabled railroads, particularly the Santa Fe, to grow the volume of service-sensitive traffic, albeit at lower average unit rates. Rail executives responded to critics of intermodal—then called piggyback—by pointing out that average costs were lower, but the trains made a contribution to overhead and fixed costs. Land-bridge initially involved taking containers off ships from Europe, moving them across the United States, and reloading them on ships at the West Coast bound for Pacific ports, or vice versa. International intermodal traffic that originated or terminated in the United States was known as minibridge.

Improved interline land-bridge operations reduced overall shipping times and stimulated further growth of the service. The Norfolk and Western Railway (N&W) gained ICC approval to operate over 30 miles of Santa Fe track between Camden, Missouri, and the Santa Fe's Argentine Yard at Kansas City, Kansas. Thus the two railroads created an expedited service from the West Coast to the East, particularly in automotive parts destined for Detroit, a major N&W point that was beyond the reach of the Santa Fe. A joint operation through Pueblo, Colorado, with the Denver and Rio Grande Western and the Western Pacific improved service to and from central California. The rise of globalization over the last 30 years has made intermodal into the fastest-growing segment of rail business. Where piggyback once was a defense against the loss of traffic from boxcars to trucks, it grew into a highly efficient, service-sensitive business that by 2002 accounted for more than 40 percent of the volume of the BNSF Railway.

Proving that there are no permanent friends or enemies, but only permanent interests, the Santa Fe built a branch line to the barge facility at Tulsa's Port of Catoosa on the Arkansas River, enabling it to participate in the rail-barge movement of bulk commodities. In 1972 and 1973, the Santa Fe had record revenues from massive export grain shipments, much of this activity in conjunction with barge operators. But for the regulatory regime in place at the time, financial results would have been much better.

The Santa Fe and other "Granger" railroads, including the Burlington Northern, faced a tremendous demand for grain transportation in 1972 when the Soviet Union made huge, unanticipated purchases of 19 million metric tons of U.S. wheat and corn, producing a significant run-up in U.S. food prices and depleting U.S. reserve grain stocks. The Soviet purchases accounted for one-fourth of the U.S. wheat crop. The plus from a national standpoint was a boost for the U.S. balance of payments and access to a vast new market that previously had been closed to U.S. producers and traders because of the ongoing cold war.

The purchase was dictated in large part by a massive failure of the Soviet crop due to poor weather and equally poor communal farm management. It was aided by a U.S. government policy decision to allow the Soviet government to finance the huge purchase and to lift shipping restrictions that required U.S.-financed commodities to be shipped only on U.S.-flag vessels. The grain deal was made more attractive by knowledge that the Soviet government intended to expand its grain-fed cattle market by 25 percent over five years, suggesting future sales. The USSR would become a regular purchaser of U.S. grain and at the same time agreed to make its oil reserves available for U.S. purchase.

Access to Soviet oil became particularly important within a year, when the Organization of Petroleum Exporting Countries (OPEC) shut off the oil tap in the winter of 1973–1974, following massive U.S. support of Israel during the 1973 Yom Kippur War. Munitions and weapons had been airlifted from U.S. stocks directly to the beleaguered Israeli forces. From $2.59 a barrel in 1973, the price of crude oil increased to $12 a barrel in 1976 and to more than $35 a barrel by 1980. The price of all energy in the United States skyrocketed by 50 percent in the span of a year. As will be seen, this situation also created a huge opportunity for the new Burlington Northern Railroad, which had access to a more-than-400-year supply of low-sulfur coal reserves in the Powder River Basin of Montana and Wyoming.

Dependent on imports for more than 50 percent of its oil, the United States was vulnerable to the effect of the oil embargo, and the national economy slipped into recession in 1974. Railroads were affected by the recession along with the rest of the economy, but although there was less freight to be moved, they suffered less damage in the ongoing competition with trucks because railroads consumed as little as one-fourth the fuel that truckers consumed per unit of transportation. Truck operators were forced to add surcharges to their rates to cover sharply higher fuel costs, while railroads were less affected because diesel fuel accounted for less than 10 percent of their operating costs on average.

An example of the effect of distorted public policy on the railroads, however, was that once the huge Soviet purchase of grain became known, the rates for unregulated barge transportation of grain to export terminals soared by as much as 400 percent virtually overnight. The water carriers ended up carrying only slightly more grain than normal, but their revenue and profit were measured in multiples as they took advantage of the high demand for and low supply of transportation. Railroads, on the other hand, were unable to increase their rates yet were required by their common carrier obligation to take all the grain that was offered. Grain-carrying railroads ended up moving the bulk of the Soviet purchase but failed to profit from it, as did their water carrier competitors and the grain dealers and elevator operators that saw the price of grain skyrocket.

The railroads were further penalized by a chaotic ocean-shipping situation. Irregular and sporadic arrival of freighters made it impossible for terminal elevators to maintain a steady flow of grain from their silos to ships. A lack of modern unloading facilities at Soviet Black Sea ports slowed unloading and delayed the movement of empty freighters back to the United States for reloading. Grain trains began to clog terminal facilities and rail yards near ports, and the railroads were unable to embargo shipments fast enough to avoid severe congestion. Increased rail operating costs hit the industry at the same time that revenue was effectively capped by the inability to obtain quick rate increases.

The ICC, faced with demands by grain dealers to do something about the congestion-induced shortage of grain-hauling equipment, ordered the railroads to break up their solid grain trains. The commission mandated spreading the existing car supply to more shippers to prevent discrimination by railroads against smaller shippers and in favor of big shippers, regardless of their inherent efficiency. Richard E. Briggs, an official of the Association of American Railroads, referred to the ICC service order as a "share the agony policy" that only exacerbated economic distortions while doing nothing to increase the flow of grain to ports.

RAIL BANKRUPTCIES AND CALLS FOR NATIONALIZATION

The Penn Central Transportation Company filed for protection from its creditors under what was then section 77 of the Bankruptcy Act on Sunday afternoon, June 21, 1970. Within a year, the Reading, the Lehigh Valley, the Lehigh and Hudson, and the Ann Arbor Railroads joined the Penn Central in bankruptcy. The Central of New Jersey and the Boston and Maine preceded it into bankruptcy, while the Erie Lackawanna held out for two years, filing its bankruptcy petition in 1972.

The disaster in the Northeast brought the specter of nationalization to the fore. In its desperate efforts to avoid bankruptcy, the Penn Central had cut spending to the absolute minimum and beyond. Track became so deteriorated from lack of maintenance that some main lines had slow orders, holding trains to top speeds of no more than ten miles per hour. So-called "standing derailments," where the track collapses under a standing train, were not uncommon. By the time the company filed for protection from creditors, the Penn Central was paying 8 to 10 percent for financing but was earning no more than 1 percent on capital, and that figure required putting the best possible face on the grim facts.

Politicians and rail executives were on the verge of panic, although many had little knowledge of the reasons for the largest bankruptcy in American history to that time. The Penn Central had been dysfunctional from the beginning, with a forced combination of different cultures and operating executives who had developed an intense dislike for each other over the years. In addition to its own managerial flaws, the railroad also faced the problems that beset other railroads—too much track for the available business, heavy and growing losses from commuter and passenger operations, and burdensome union agreements.

The management problems alone would have been sufficient to destroy most companies. Robert E. Bedingfield of the *New York Times* wrote that Penn Central president Alfred Perlman, former chief executive of the New York Central, was "pretty much ignored" by former Pennsylvania executives. Just a week after the June 20, 1970, bankruptcy filing, Bedingfield wrote:

> Not only did many Pennsylvania-trained operating employ-
> ees belittle many of Mr. Perlman's ideas so long as their
> overall "chief" was their old boss, but also Mr. Saunders
> [former chief executive of the Pennsylvania who held the
> same title at Penn Central] turned his attention more to an
> aggressive diversification program than to reviewing Mr.
> Perlman's suggestions for spending large sums to upgrade
> the consolidated company's transportation plant and
> expanding the railroad's marketing activities.

Suggestions that the railroads might have to be nationalized came from politicians and, surprisingly, from railroad executives. E. Spencer Miller, president of the Maine Central Railroad, was quoted in the *New York Times* as calling for legislation that would force all railroads to merge into a single American Railroad Corporation. He did not rule out the idea that such a corporation might be national-ized. Tennessee governor Ray Blanton and Massachusetts senator Edward M. Kennedy urged that railroad rights-of-way be national-ized, although railroad operating companies would have remained in private hands. Rail unions supported nationalization of the North-east bankrupts.

Those who supported nationalization or a variation of it did so on the assumption that rail service was absolutely essential to the national economy but that railroad companies could not generate sufficient revenue and income to support and regenerate their capital structures. Most railroads and the Nixon administration, which had taken office in 1969, adamantly opposed such solutions.

Congress passed a series of measures designed to deal with the railroad crisis. One of the first "solutions" undertaken by the government was to relieve railroads of the burden of intercity passenger deficits by effectively nationalizing passenger service. Congress passed the National Railroad Passenger Service Act in 1970, creating a government-sponsored company to take over passenger operations. The National Railroad Passenger Corporation adopted the trade name "Amtrak." Railroads still had to deal with commuter service problems that particularly affected the railroads serving eastern metropolises such as Boston, New York, and Philadelphia, as well as those serving Chicago, which included the Burlington Northern and the Atchison, Topeka, and Santa Fe.

Faced with a need to intervene, the government had three options for dealing with the passenger crisis. The least costly and most efficient would have been to subsidize the railroad companies that already were operating the trains. This was politically unfeasible, however, because the railroads had been identified in the public's mind as being the "bad guys" who were trying to kill the passenger trains. The "do nothing" option was considered briefly and discarded because government planners knew that doing nothing eventually would result in the demise of almost all intercity passenger trains in the United States. Outright nationalization was out of the question, and Congress was persuaded to adopt the third option, quasi nationalization through the creation of Amtrak.

Railroads could escape their losing passenger operations by paying the equivalent of two years of passenger losses into the new entity, either in cash or equipment. In return, the participating railroads received preferred stock in Amtrak, which they immediately wrote down to zero on their books. Amtrak began operations in 1971, and more than half of the remaining intercity passenger service was immediately discontinued.

Only three major railroads—the Southern, the Denver and Rio Grande Western, and the Rock Island—chose not to join Amtrak. The proud and profitable Southern was willing to absorb losses on its successful Southern Crescent service between Washington, D.C.,

John Shedd Reed

John Shedd Reed, whose father had died when he was a teenager, came from an old Chicago family. An admitted rail fan, he traced his interest in railroads back to when he was ten years old. He was sent east to the exclusive Hotchkiss School and graduated from Yale University before joining the Santa Fe in 1939. Reed's Yale degree is in industrial administration, which he referred to as "a junior MBA." Long after the 1989 relocation of Santa Fe headquarters to a suburban location from its Chicago Loop building, the retired Reed continued to keep an office in the Railway Exchange Building that the Santa Fe had called home for generations. He went to the office almost daily into the first decade of the 21st century to take care of his continuing civic and personal activities. One of the pictures on the wall of his mezzanine office was of the navy destroyer on which he had served as a lieutenant commander during World War II.

Like so many railroaders of his generation, Reed returned to the railroad after the war and worked his way up through the operating department ranks, serving as a train master and superintendent before becoming assistant to the vice president in the executive offices in 1954. After a five-year stint as vice president of finance, he became vice president of the executive department in 1964 and was named president of the railroad in 1967. Reed remained at the helm of the Santa Fe through the 1970s and well into the 1980s.

In an industry known for moving officers around the system frequently, Reed had his share of relocations early in his career. "The first part of my career is very easy to demarcate," he said in an interview for this book. "Every time you move from Podunk to someplace else, everything has a time frame to it. Then, when I came back [to Chicago], it was in December of 1954, and I never moved more than 35 feet from one office to another."

and New Orleans, at least until it faced the capital cost of replacing the fleet, and then it too joined Amtrak. The Rio Grande similarly chose to continue operating its segment of the famed Zephyr between Denver and Salt Lake City, and the Rock Island, which was awaiting ICC approval for a merger with the Union Pacific, determined that its out-of-pocket passenger service losses were less than it would have had to pay into Amtrak.

Amtrak inherited a polyglot fleet of passenger cars. As it gradually rebuilt old equipment and acquired new, it adopted a color scheme of its own. Santa Fe's John Reed, proud of the Santa Fe's former passenger service and offended by what he was quoted in *Time* magazine as calling a 19th-century French bordello look, refused to allow the use of the Super Chief name on Amtrak's Chicago–Los Angeles train.

The second of four major acts dealing with the railroad problem was the Regional Rail Reorganization (3R) Act, passed in 1973. Recognizing that traditional bankruptcy reorganization would not be possible in the case of the Penn Central and other bankrupt railroads, Congress passed this act, which was designed to help restructure the failed railroads in seventeen northeastern and midwestern states. Section 77 of the Bankruptcy Act, which then applied to railroads, had no provision for liquidation, but that made no difference, because the Nixon administration had determined that liquidation was an unacceptable solution.

The 3R Act imposed a mandatory restructuring process on most of the railroads in reorganization at the time of its enactment. A new federal agency—the U.S. Railway Association (USRA)—was created to design a new rail network for the region. Congress authorized the USRA to operate independently of existing federal agencies and statutes and to bypass civil service, budgetary, environmental, and other bureaucratic restrictions. It was a move that enabled the new agency to act expeditiously and efficiently.

The new organization hired some of the best transportation planners in the country to design the restructured rail system. Many of them later became senior executives of railroads. One, Jim Hagen, became chief executive officer of Conrail, the company that replaced the Penn Central and five other bankrupts. Paul Cruikshank, a former Great Northern and Burlington operating officer and a future head of operations at the Milwaukee Road, was a USRA vice president.

While the 3R Act bypassed the established regulatory mechanisms of the ICC, it created a new Rail Services Planning Office (RSPO) within the ICC. The RSPO was to serve as a policy office for the ICC, which until then had viewed itself as a quasi-judicial agency that considered each case before it without having an overarching policy. The RSPO became an outlet for the volatile and conflicting political views surrounding the massive rail reorganization. It was also an alternative to the usual ICC opportunity for the public, rail labor, and other constituencies to be heard on all rail matters. Unlike the ICC, which had delays built into the ICC procedures, the RSPO was not permitted to affect the USRA schedule. Congress also authorized public funding of more than $2 billion for rebuilding and modernizing the track and equipment of Conrail, the new, government-sponsored entity that would replace the six participating bankrupt companies. Another $250 million was authorized to pay for the continuing lifetime income protection that had been granted to Penn Central workers by the Luna-Saunders Agreement. Non–Penn Central employees were also included under this "Title U" protection, which was named after the applicable part of the 3R Act.

The planners studied virtually every inch of track in the area from the Mississippi River east to the Atlantic Coast and from the Potomac and Ohio Rivers north to Canada. Their experience told them this was their opportunity to eliminate thousands of miles of light-density lines without having to withstand the usual challenges to line abandonment at the ICC. Beginning with a Federal Railroad Administration study that identified lines that were candidates for abandonment, they produced a preliminary system plan for the Northeast and the Midwest. It covered both solvent and insolvent railroads and delineated lines to be abandoned and those to be retained.

USRA planners initially proposed a restructuring that would create three competitive rail systems in the region. One would be based on an extended Norfolk and Western Railway (C&O), one based on an extended Chesapeake and Ohio Railway, and one on a reborn Penn Central. They also expected the Southern Railway to acquire some lines, primarily on the Delmarva Peninsula of Delaware, Maryland, and Virginia.

The ambitious plan failed, however, when a number of the interests that were supposed to participate chose not to do so. The relatively rich N&W, which controlled the Erie Lackawanna (EL), was not about to take the risk that it might have to commit funding to the EL and declined to participate. The Southern and the C&O tried to help, the C&O negotiating a deal to take over the Reading and the EL, and the Southern taking over the former Pennsylvania Railroad Delmarva lines south of Wilmington, Delaware. Neither company was able to get labor to make the concessions the plan had demanded, and both companies dropped out of the restructuring. USRA planners didn't have time to revise their plan, and as a result the Erie Lackawanna and the Reading were made part of the new Consolidated Rail Corporation. Conrail began life with a virtual monopoly on rail service in the Northeast. As a last-minute antidote to this monopoly, the USRA granted to the Delaware and Hudson Railway (D&H), a regional bridge line carrier, trackage rights into northern New Jersey, Philadelphia, Buffalo, and Potomac Yard outside of Washington, D.C. The D&H, however, could never effectively compete with the titanic Conrail.

The 3R Act helped accomplish the restructuring of railroads and the continuation of service in the Northeast and the Midwest, but it did not deal with economic regulation. The new Conrail and all other U.S. railroads remained regulated. Conrail was to have a virtual monopoly on rail service in its region. Still, it became apparent even before the 1976 activation of the new company that, despite the financial assistance provided by the 3R Act, Conrail was unlikely to succeed financially. Congress again was forced to intervene.

Meanwhile, in the West, the new Burlington Northern was busy integrating the three major and two smaller railroads that had been merged to create it. As discussed earlier, the lengthy merger approval process enabled the railroads to plan the merger implementation in greater detail than in other mergers. The Budd-Menk influence was felt right from the beginning. Downing, who spent more than a decade of his career planning for and implementing the Northern Lines merger, believed that the long delay in creating Burlington Northern was operationally advantageous, although it was costly. "Financially it probably wasn't [good], but as a matter of getting the thing to work, long planning certainly was helpful," he noted.

A. Scheffer Lang was appointed by President Lyndon B. Johnson to serve as the first administrator of the Federal Railroad Administration while the Northern Lines case was wending its way through the regulatory process. His father had been a longtime director of the Northern Pacific and the BN. The younger Lang credited the success of the Burlington Northern merger in large part to the integrity that was embedded in the cultures of the involved railroads.

"While certainly there were internal politics in each of the organizations, they projected an image," Lang said. "I think this is particularly true of the Great Northern, and I'd put the Burlington second, and the NP third. They had a longstanding pride in the integrity of their organizations. It showed; it showed through. I think it suffused the long process of accomplishing the merger during the 1960s, which dragged out well beyond what they had anticipated." Lang agreed that having the labor implementing agreements in place was a significant factor: "I think in retrospect the Burlington Northern merger probably went as smoothly as or more smoothly than any other major merger in the last 40 years, certainly of companies of that size."

Downing, looking back 30 years, had a similar view but referred to leadership and integrity as pluses in getting the BN off to a good start. "John Budd had a very forward look," Downing recalled. "I think maybe the culture on the Great Northern was more favorable than it was in others. That, I think, was partly due to his leadership. He really believed in [the GN culture], and if you believe in it at the top, it works its way down through the ranks much faster than if you do it with an order."

Operationally, the new Burlington Northern was able to implement a premerger study that determined the most economic and efficient routes to be used once the railroads were combined. This plan affected primarily the former Great Northern and Northern Pacific, which essentially were parallel railroads. "We set up preferred routings on which we would concentrate freight traffic, especially transcontinentally," Downing said. "The Northern Pacific as a railroad was considerably less profitable than the Great Northern. The reason for that was that their route structure was not as efficient. They crossed the Rocky Mountains twice. You cross the Continental Divide west of Helena, Montana, but before you get there, you've already gone out of Livingston and up over Bozeman Pass west of there. You come down the other side, and then you go back up again at Helena. It was longer. Their costs to get a train from St. Paul to Seattle were simply higher. [The NP was] longer, and it had less favorable grades. So when the time came to merge the two companies, we used the Northern Pacific from St. Paul or Minneapolis to Fargo, North Dakota; the Great Northern (from Fargo) to Sandpoint, Idaho; and then the Northern Pacific to Spokane and the Great Northern from Spokane to Seattle. In each case, those segments were the most efficient. So we pieced the best parts of each company, and the Great Northern was about 75 percent of the total."

All large institutions have their own cultures. Downing compared the culture of the Great Northern to that of the Pennsylvania, where his father had spent his career. Downing's first boss on the Great Northern, the late Ira Manion, was "a mentor and not a general in command." Downing added, "Sometimes you would get some pretty direct orders. But whatever he said was for your own good, and he was on your side. In other words, you weren't fighting with him." Downing contrasted the GN approach to management with that of the Pennsylvania, where he worked briefly before joining the Great Northern in Montana before World War II. "The Pennsylvania had some dillies as officers. If you heard they were coming, you found work to do somewhere else and kept out of sight," he said with a chuckle.

The Great Northern managed to hire, train, and develop generations of outstanding executives. In fact, it produced more than it could retain, and many of its executives, seeing only limited opportunities for promotion on the GN, moved to other railroads. At one time, it almost appeared that the GN was a training ground for Milwaukee Road senior executives. So many GN executives moved to the Milwaukee that some observers believed there was a GN plot to infiltrate and destroy the Milwaukee. A former Milwaukee lawyer even wrote a book about the alleged plot, although no one who knew the people involved gave the plot theory any credibility. The finest management in the world couldn't have saved the Milwaukee Road.

Bill Quinn was president of the Burlington in 1966, having succeeded Menk, and was slated to become vice chairman of the Burlington Northern. Then, at BN merger time in 1970, he took the chairmanship of the Milwaukee even before the Northern Lines merger was completed. A lawyer by training, he needed an operating executive to handle the day-to-day management. Downing recalled: "Worth Smith's name came up several years after the BN merger, and he went to the Milwaukee. If anybody could have straightened the Milwaukee out from an operational standpoint, Worth could have done it. I felt very badly that he left, but we didn't have any clear line of succession that would advance him to anything like what the Milwaukee was offering as president. Worth came to me and said, 'What'll I do?' I said, 'Well, I can't promise you anything, and I'd hate to see you go. But if you want to take on a challenging job, this is it.'" Typical of so many in the railroad industry, which traditionally was a father-son business and almost a way of life, Worthington D. Smith's father had been a division superintendent on the Northern Pacific. Smith was able to attract Paul Cruikshank, who started his career on the GN, became a vice president at the BN, and then, after a stint as one of the planners at the USRA in Washington, D.C., went to join him at the Milwaukee as vice president of operations.

Lang, who never worked for any of the BNSF predecessor railroads, credited the Great Northern's "training program and recruitment program for officers that populated a lot of the western railroad industry." In addition to those who went to the Milwaukee, other GN-trained executives included Downing Jenks, who became chairman, president, and chief executive of the Missouri Pacific, and John German, a GN mechanical officer who became a senior executive at the Missouri Pacific. "That was the Great Northern," Lang recalled. "They had a very well-developed program for training and taking guys out of college and running them through the hoops as officers, as well as training them up. These guys were constantly going off to other railroads."

The Great Northern had understood, more so than most other railroads did, the importance of cultivating leadership from within the organization. Leaders are sometimes born. Many other times they're grown.

Great Northern was not the only railroad that recruited and trained officers. Others saw the need also. The Santa Fe, the Southern Pacific, and the New York Central, among others, had highly regarded management training programs. All recruited at the finest colleges and universities. The Santa Fe, under Fred G. Gurley's leadership, began a program to provide advanced business skills to rising managers. In 1952 it established a six-week summer training program for junior and senior executives that was run by the University of Southern California School of Commerce. As many as 40 men between the ages of 28 and 54 attended the program on the USC campus in Los Angeles, participating in classes and seminars eight hours a day, five days a week. The Santa Fe not only paid the men's expenses but also authorized spouses to accompany them. It was "understood" that the graduates of the summer program were the Santa Fe's future leaders.

Over the long span of railroad history, different railroads developed different institutional personalities and cultures. While all railroads had rigid command-and-control management systems, the Santa Fe, for example, became known for its tight top-down, militaristic management style, and the Southern Pacific had a reputation for managerial arrogance. The Great Northern, though, had a reputation of being—as railroads went—reasonably caring for the people who worked for it.

Downing related an anecdote that provides some insight into the culture of the Great Northern:

> I had been trainmaster [one of the lowest officer positions in
> a railroad] for about a year and half, and I got word
> through the grapevine, which was very much faster than
> any electronic device, that I was to be moved. They sent me
> to Kelly Lake, Minnesota. That's part of the Mesabi Iron
> Range. I had never been there in my life, but I knew it was a
> hot spot because of the iron ore business. The superintend-

ent there, who I worked for—I was trainmaster of the range—was C. O. Hooker. I can't think of any way to describe him except that he was of the old school. He was gruff. He knew exactly how trains should be run, and he had been a conductor. He was very confident. You really wanted to know what you were talking about when you talked to C.O., because he knew. Anyhow, the part that I came to realize not too long after I had been there was that this curmudgeon really had a concern for your well-being.

There was a delay in Downing's deployment. He later learned why his move had been delayed:

Years later, I was told that the reason for the delay between when I heard I was going and when I was told to go was because the Mesabi Division was kind of a closed corporation in many ways. Some of the other trainmasters there didn't want the job in Kelly Lake, but they had complained [to Hooker] that I had no experience in iron ore. They thought that was too important a job to have an outsider come in and be in charge. . . . The reason the logjam broke, I'm told, was that Hooker had gone to Manion, who was general manager in Seattle, and asked, "What kind of fellow is this Downing? Is he competent?" Apparently, Ira Manion gave me a good recommendation, because Hooker's response to his assistants was "If Ira Manion says he's OK, he's good enough for me, and you better treat him right." They did treat me right. So I use Manion and Hooker as typical of the culture of Great Northern, which most of the people really believed in.

"Then, of course, my great mentor was John Budd," Downing added. "I can't say enough good about him. Of course, his father, Ralph Budd, was famous in the railroad industry. He, too, was a wonderful leader. In personality, John was not very much like his father. His father was outgoing, and John was quite a bit more retiring. Nonetheless, people who knew him respected him highly."

Great Northern was like most railroads when it came to moving people around its system. Division superintendents had a lot of responsibility and were under intense pressure to operate their piece of the railroad with as much reliability and as little cost as possible. Division superintendent still is the last level of management where one individual has control of all aspects of the operation. Specialization begins at the next level, and some of the hands-on nature of railroading that makes the work so dynamic and satisfying is lost. Success as a division superintendent traditionally was a requirement for movement into the ranks of senior management, and even perceived failure can be a one-way ticket to early retirement.

The pressure led many new superintendents to surround themselves with supervisors with whom they had worked elsewhere and in whom they had confidence. The result was a seemingly constant lateral movement of trainmasters, mechanical officers, and maintenance officials around the railroad, with few of the moves involving greater responsibility. Years later, during a period when the BN was focused on reducing operating expenses, a chief executive would issue orders that transfers would not be approved unless they involved a promotion.

The Burlington Northern, blending the disparate cultures of the Great Northern, the Northern Pacific, and the Chicago, Burlington, and Quincy, began to develop its own culture almost as soon as it was created. That was helped along by the presence of Louis Wilson Menk, a native Coloradoan, who had spent some 20 years working on the Frisco before moving to the Burlington in 1965. A tall, courtly son of a railroad brakeman, Menk started his career on the Union Pacific in Denver. Laid off in 1940, he learned through the grapevine that the Frisco was hiring telegraphers in Tulsa, Oklahoma. Using employee passes, he traveled from Denver to Kansas and then to Tulsa, where he got the job. It helped that he had learned Morse code while working for the UP in Denver.

Menk spent countless hours in the late 1970s battling legislation that would have granted federal eminent domain authority to private developers of a proposed pipeline that would carry coal mixed with water from the Powder River Basin to a utility complex at White Bluff, Arkansas. The pipeline, which would not be a common carrier, was to be financed with "take-or-pay" contracts in which the utility customer either would take the 25 million tons of coal or pay the equivalent transportation charge.

The BN had considered joining the consortium that proposed to build the pipeline, allowing the pipe to be laid along the railroad's right-of-way. The railroad determined that it would not gain sufficient benefit to justify participating, however, and Menk became the

point man for the industry in fighting the pipeline, testifying numerous times before congressional committees considering the legislation. The coal slurry pipeline campaign, which eventually included
almost the entire railroad industry—the Southern Pacific owned the
only operating coal pipeline in the United States and remained out of
the fight—was successful, but at a cost of millions to the BN and
other railroads in antitrust fines and settlements.

The defining event for the Burlington Northern in the decade,
and one that is felt even today, was the energy crisis that hit the United States in late 1973. Intrastate prices of natural gas were deregulated in Texas, and the price of fuel for utility boilers shot up. The
OPEC oil embargo caused the price of residual oil—used for boiler
fuel at many coastal electric-generating stations—to skyrocket. At
the same time, the environmental movement was pressuring utilities
either to burn fuels with low sulfur content or to remove the sulfur
from their exhaust gases.

It had been known for many years that there were huge deposits
of low-sulfur coal near the Chicago, Burlington, and Quincy main
line to Billings, Montana, in the Powder River Basin of northeastern
Wyoming and southern Montana, but there was virtually no commercial demand for the coal. The Northern Pacific also had coal
reserves in roughly the same area, most of it lying under the land
grant. The NP had mined coal at Colstrip, Montana, for years for its
own use as fuel for steam locomotives.

That operation finally was closed in the late 1950s, "when the
Northern Pacific belatedly decided that maybe steam locomotives
weren't here to stay after all," Schef Lang recounted. The NP was
one of the last railroads to make the transition to diesel power. The
coal was so inexpensive to mine that the NP operated one of the first
unit coal trains in the industry, long before deregulation, in a short-
haul move of coal to a Montana Power Company generating station.

Until the energy crisis, coal traditionally had been a short-haul
commodity. In the Midwest and the East, coal was burned near
where it was mined, because industrial and population density
allowed utilities to site generating stations relatively near the coal
mines and close to the places where it would be consumed. There
was little opportunity, though, either to burn Powder River Basin
coal in the lightly populated area where it was mined or to use the
electricity without sending it over great distances. The fundamental
economics of coal and electricity generation changed rapidly, and the
new Burlington Northern Railroad quickly became a major coal-

hauling railroad.

Utilities in the Southwest simultaneously faced an expanding population, rising industrial demand, and increasing cost of fuel. In the search for alternatives to natural gas, one of the most attractive was Powder River Basin coal. Although it burned cleanly from an environmental standpoint, its principal negative was that it had low BTU content. It took about three tons of Powder River Basin coal to equal the heat content of two tons of eastern coal, but the cost of the coal at the mine was so low that customers could justify shipping large volumes over great distances.

Burlington Northern management saw the potential to add millions of tons of traffic, but knew they would have to make a huge capital investment if they were to realize the potential of the nascent coal business. Initially, when utilities inquired what it would cost to move coal to plants as distant as Texas, Arkansas, Missouri, Minnesota, and Wisconsin, the railroad costed the business as though it were incremental tonnage to be moved over an existing line, and it responded to the utility queries with a price. Critics referred to that method of rate making as setting "missionary rates," designed to attract the business and then to have later customers pay a rate that more accurately reflected market conditions and costs. Pretty soon, though, it became clear that the railroad would have to rebuild much of the original Burlington lines, upgrade former NP and GN routes, and add hundreds of new locomotives and thousands of coal cars. The estimated capital investment reached $2 billion, a huge amount in mid-1970s dollars. With that kind of investment, little of which had been factored into the earlier rate quotes, it was obvious that actual rates would have to be higher if the railroad were to profit from the business.

Downing described a board meeting at which the management presented its capital budget: "I don't remember who said it, but there was a pause and then a voice said, 'How are you going to pay for it?' Some of those board members asked some pretty pointed questions, but in the end they approved." From that point on, however, the BN quoted rates to recover its full costs, rather than simply making a contribution above variable costs, as most rates were set at the time. Downing recalled, "After the meeting, Lou and I were breathing our sighs of relief. He said, 'You know, Bob, I hope this works, because if it doesn't, you and I are both going to be looking for a job.'"

Once the BN began to factor in the recovery of its huge capital investment, the rates to carry coal became considerably higher, leading to one of the railroad's darker periods. The utility customers filed suit, charging that the railroad had been guilty of bait-and-switch tactics—quoting a low rate to get the business and then charging a higher rate once the utility was irrevocably committed to long-term coal supply contracts. Initially, the BN tried to defend itself by pointing out not only that it never had contracts—the ICC at that time did not allow railroads to have contracts with customers—but also that the utilities certainly should have known that. The utilities, the railroad said, were sophisticated customers and, as regulated businesses themselves, should have understood that rate quotes were not binding, that the railroad had to file a tariff, and that the tariff was the only binding rate. The utilities rejected the legalistic defense out of hand, and the ensuing publicity was embarrassing to the Burlington Northern and its leaders.

Even other railroads that had carried large amounts of coal far longer thought the BN was mishandling its battle with its utility customers. The late Brenton Welling Jr., a longtime transportation writer for *Business Week,* was riding in a business car on an inspection trip with John P. Fishwick, chief executive officer of the Norfolk and Western Railway, when Fishwick made some comments that were critical of the BN's coal pricing policy. Welling produced a story about the N&W that included Fishwick's remarks. An angry Menk responded with a note to Fishwick, suggesting that if, in the future, he had thoughts on how the BN should price coal, Menk would appreciate it if Fishwick would tell him first.

Getting into the coal business involved considerable risk, for the railroad would be the only party not protected by contracts. As Downing explained, "There were three parties to a deal. One was the utility company that was buying the coal, one was the mining company that was opening the mine, and the railroad was the third party in the middle. The utility companies were buying their coal on long-term contracts. The mining companies were protected because they had the contracts. We were sitting there in the middle with freight rates that were, in the final analysis, set by somebody else, the ICC. We really felt dangerously at risk."

Regardless of the pricing environment, the railroad still had to generate sufficient revenue to cover the debt it was issuing and to pay for the improvements. Downing cites the coal pricing issue and the need for huge capital expenditures as "an example of why deregulation was so necessary." The rail industry drive for deregulation still was several years in the future, however, and the BN had to deal with the problem then. With the ICC as the regulator, it seemed appropriate that the BN turned to the ICC looking for a solution. Downing described the events leading up to that decision:

> Lou [Menk] and I talked about this, and I said, "We've got to get something out of the ICC that gives us some protection." There already had been a number of rate cases that the commission . . . rather summarily turned down, including contract rates even if they were lower [than published tariffs]. They just didn't like contract rates. All the precedents they had set for 20 years wouldn't permit them. Anyhow, Lou and I decided we had to go to the commission, not officially but informally, and tell them what the problem was. So I made an appointment with Commissioner Hardin, who seemed like the most likely one to talk to.

Commissioner Dale Hardin headed the ICC division that dealt with rates. "He had two of his rate bureau people," Downing said, "and they were old-timers. They were looking aghast at anybody who would even talk about rates off the record." The ICC, as a quasi-judicial agency, had strict rules against ex parte communication. It required that all communication about issues before it be in open, recorded proceedings where all parties would be on equal footing. Downing said he nevertheless explained to Hardin and his associates "this matter of being terribly at risk because the other two parties to the deal had contracts between themselves and we in the middle were making enormous investments greater than either of the other parties were making."

As Downing recalled, "Mr. Hardin listened to the story and said, 'You fellows have a point. But you know, this flies in the face of all the precedents.' He looked at his two subordinates, who were gray-headed guys who had come up in the regulatory business all their lives, and said, 'Now you two fellows get together and figure out a way to do what these folks need to have done, but make it look like a tariff so it will pass muster.' He gave them those instructions."

Nothing happened for several months, and then Downing received a summons from Hardin to send BN rate experts to Washington to negotiate a solution to the problem the railroad had identified. "It never was called a contract rate, but we were in a position to offer rates that would move the traffic," Downing said. "That was in 1975, so the seeds [for deregulation] were being planted around the industry."

After several years of bad publicity and increasingly rancorous relations with key customers, the Burlington Northern was able to settle the suits filed against it. None went to court, and one—the suit by the San Antonio, Texas, public power company—was settled in the utility's favor by a provision that was inserted into the Staggers Rail Act of 1980. Initially the settlements involved the BN's agreeing to lower rates. Later, when rail competition was on the horizon and utilities saw new competitive options, some of the settlements were to shorten the duration of contracts.

To serve the new mines, the Burlington Northern needed to construct a new line that would cut through the Wyoming portion of the Powder River Basin between Orin Junction and Gillette. The hundred-mile line would be the longest new rail construction in half a century. Under regulatory law, however, the railroad needed permission from the ICC to build a new line. The Chicago and North Western, which had a line across northern Nebraska that ended not far from the coal fields, saw an opportunity to gain some of the coming coal business, and it also applied for permission to build into the mines. Although the ICC eventually allowed the BN to start construction, it ordered that the new line was to be jointly owned by the BN and the C&NW, ensuring competition for the new coal business.

The line was to cost approximately $100 million, but the C&NW did not have the money and was unable to get financing for its share. The BN went ahead and built the line, on several occasions extending the deadline for the C&NW to pay its share. Finally, the BN declared that the C&NW had forfeited its right to own half the line and to operate over it. The C&NW appealed to the ICC, which sided with the North Western, making it clear that the ICC got to say who could operate over a line, not the BN. The BN appealed that decision to the Supreme Court, which followed established doctrine of upholding decisions by regulatory agencies as long as the agency had complied with the Administrative Procedures Act provisions and was not acting arbitrarily or capriciously.

By now it was 1983, and the BN was moving about 100 million tons of coal a year out of the Powder River Basin. In desperation the C&NW sought financial assistance from the Union Pacific. Seizing an opportunity that had seemingly dropped into its lap, the UP advanced $50 million to the C&NW and drove a bargain that served the former's long-term strategic interests. In the deal a new C&NW subsidiary, Western Rail Properties Inc., would own half the coal line into the Powder River Basin. It would build a line from Shawnee, Wyoming, to a junction with the UP main line at South Morrill, Nebraska, where it would turn over its coal to the UP. Midwest-bound coal would be returned to the C&NW at Council Bluffs, Iowa, and the UP would handle any of the coal destined to areas not already served by the C&NW. The C&NW would defer plans—it eventually dropped them—to rebuild its long, light-density "Cowboy" main line across northern Nebraska. The UP also gained track-age rights for 999 years over the C&NW main line between Council Bluffs and Chicago, achieving a goal that had eluded the Union Pacific ever since E. H. Harriman tried to acquire the CB&Q in the nineteenth-century control battle with James J. Hill.

The deal sealed the C&NW's doom as an independent railroad and led in several steps to the 1995 acquisition of the North Western by the Union Pacific. The UP initially took two nonvoting director-ships and later asked the ICC to allow them to become voting posi-tions at the same time that it sought permission to acquire 30 percent of the C&NW. Still later, the UP sought permission to acquire the rest of the shares that it didn't already own. The UP understood the ICC's proclivity to consider each case before it on its merits and not as part of a broader set of issues. Two comments bear noting. A C&NW executive said later, "We knew we had lost our independ-ence when we went to UP for the money." And a former ICC com-missioner who voted on the UP's petitions told the *Journal of Commerce*: "If we had understood that it was part of broader strategy, we might have asked different questions and perhaps would have dealt with the cases differently."

Actually, it was the ICC's demonstrated rigidity of thinking, bor-dering on an inability to change its approach to regulation, that led finally to Congress's passing legislation that largely freed the rail-roads from what they called "the dead hand of government regula-tion." A young reporter for *Business Week* asked an ICC official in 1969 what the agency's regulatory policy was. The official looked aghast and responded: "We don't have a policy. We're a quasi-judi-cial agency, and we deal with each case before us on the legal merits of that case, not to fit a policy."

In any event, the BN did not have a monopoly on the Powder River Basin coal business for long. C&NW trains first rolled over the coal line in 1984, and with the Union Pacific in the background, the

C&NW proved an effective competitor, driving coal rates lower whenever there was a competitive bid to serve a utility. Today, with more than 400 million tons of coal rolling out of the Powder River Basin (PRB) annually, the BNSF and the Union Pacific continue to be the principle providers of transportation to utilities that use PRB coal.

In 1975, a railroad bankruptcy spurred the deregulation movement as nothing had since the Penn Central bankruptcy in 1970. The venerable Chicago, Rock Island, and Pacific Railroad entered bankruptcy proceedings on March 17, 1975. John Ingram, its president and chief executive at the time—the former Southern Railway pricing official who had developed the Big John grain rates—announced, "The Northeast rail crisis just reached Tucumcari." Tucumcari, New Mexico, was the westernmost point of the Rock Island system.

Living up to the folk song's declaration that "the Rock Island line is a mighty fine line," the Rock, as it was known, had been a solid competitor in the Midwest, reaching from Chicago to Omaha, Denver, and Tucumcari in the west, to New Orleans and Texas in the south, and to the Twin Cities in the north. At Tucumcari it connected with the Southern Pacific to form an alternate through route to the Santa Fe between Chicago and Southern California. The Rock Island, however, epitomized the problems that railroads faced. It had more competition and lighter traffic density than most railroads, and it exclusively served fewer points than any of the major railroads. Against an industry average of 7,657 ton-miles per mile of road per day in 1962, the Rock could generate an average of only 4,637. The Milwaukee was in even worse shape, with only an average of 3,718. Density is a proxy for measuring a railroad's ability to generate revenue, and in the cases of the Rock Island and the Milwaukee Road, both trailed the railroads with which they had to compete.

The Rock had been peripherally involved with the BN or other railroads that today are part of the BNSF system for more than half a century. In the 1930s the ICC had rejected a Rock Island proposal that it be consolidated with the St. Louis–San Francisco and the Chicago and Eastern Illinois. All three were in bankruptcy reorganization, and the Rock had proposed the plan without first having proposed to the would-be brides. The commission called the proposal "impracticable." The Rock also had joined with the Great Northern, the Burlington, and five other railroads in a failed 1938 attempt to dismantle the Minneapolis and St. Louis (M&StL), which then had been in receivership for 14 years. The would-be acquirers intended to abandon 25 percent of the M&StL and then absorb remaining portions into their various systems. In 1957, after 35 years in reorganization, the M&StL was merged into the Chicago and North Western. In a continuing relationship, the Rock and the former CB&Q shared ownership of a line in Texas between Dallas and Houston known on the BN as the Joint Texas Division.

John D. Farrington, a former CB&Q operating officer, became chairman of the Rock in a post–World War II reorganization that led to one of its brief periods of seeming prosperity, though with its light density it could not sustain itself indefinitely. The Rock reported net income of $18.7 million in 1956 but soon fell victim to truck competition that was devastating rail earnings. Income fell to $6 million by 1960 and disappeared by 1965, never to return.

The Rock also became the poster child for regulatory ills during a 10-year merger process that, had it taken place in a reasonable time frame, would have seen the Rock become part of another railroad, with its shareowners receiving payment for their interest. Instead, regulators consumed an inordinate amount of time handling the merger, the railroad continued to deteriorate physically and financially, and the would-be acquiring company finally walked away even though in the end the ICC approved the merger. The Rock Island stockholders received nothing.

The Rock was an attractive merger partner for a number of railroads. With a good line between Omaha and Chicago and no competition between the two elsewhere, the Rock was the Union Pacific's preferred partner to reach Chicago, its Holy Grail since E. H. Harriman had failed to gain control of the Burlington. The Southern Pacific had an interest in the Rock, particularly its southern lines. The two interchanged 100,000 cars annually at Tucumcari, and the SP coveted single-line service to Chicago as well as a shorter route from the West Coast to St. Louis than the SP's own Cotton Belt subsidiary provided. It could get both by acquiring all or part of the Rock Island. The Union Pacific, with the same goals as the SP—access to St. Louis and Chicago—persuaded the Rock that it would make a better partner, and the two railroads announced merger plans in May 1963, promising to sell to the SP the line from Tucumcari to Kansas City.

A manifestation of the excess capacity in the Midwest was that no railroad in the region could stand to see another solidify its traffic base. Even though previously rejecting merger overtures from the Rock Island, the Chicago and North Western, which itself was planning to acquire the Milwaukee Road, feared that a UP–Rock Island combination would divert from both the C&NW and the Milwaukee traffic that each interchanged with the UP at Omaha. The C&NW responded by proposing a three-way combination of the Rock, the Milwaukee, and the C&NW, freezing out the UP.

The Chicago and North Western moved first, filing to acquire the Rock Island in July 1963. The Union Pacific filed its merger application with the Rock a year later. Then, after the C&NW filed and withdrew its application to acquire the Milwaukee, the latter filed a petition asking to be bought out by either the SP or the UP. All this merger activity was too much for the ICC. It rejected the Milwaukee petition, saying it should remain an independent competitor to the Burlington Northern.

The ICC consolidated the competing UP and C&NW petitions to acquire the Rock. Hearings began in March 1966 with 23 separate railroads appearing, most asking for protective conditions if the merger were to be approved. The SP asked not only that the Tucumcari line be sold to it but also that it be granted the Rock Island line connecting Amarillo, Little Rock, and Memphis, which would give the SP improved connections to railroads in the Southeast. Just as in other merger cases, everyone with a real or imagined stake in the proceeding decided to participate, including 17 states, 13 separate state regulatory commissions, 47 chambers of commerce and port authorities, and the U.S. Department of Justice, plus numerous shippers and labor unions. As Frank N. Wilner noted, with some 500 attorneys appearing for the various parties, one was heard to say, "This is the closest thing our profession has to guaranteed lifetime employment." It may not have been lifetime employment, but it was long enough to destroy the Rock Island.

The UP promised to invest $200 million to upgrade Rock Island track and equipment if its application were approved. The C&NW didn't try to match the UP's offer—it didn't have the cash—but it tried to stress the public interest benefits of its proposal. The Department of Justice opposed the C&NW application on the grounds that much of the C&NW and Rock Island systems were parallel, but it had no objection to the UP–Rock Island combination if competing carriers were able to acquire some key Rock Island routes. Statistically, it was a record-setting proceeding. Wilner pointed out that the hearings lasted 279 days and filled 200,000 pages, "while the Rock Island hemorrhaged $1 million per month." In the end, the Union Pacific would not accept the conditions the ICC wanted to impose on its acquisition of the Rock Island. It abandoned the merger at the end of 1974.

The Rock Island slipped into bankruptcy less than three months later, on March 17, 1975. It limped along in reorganization until it was shut down by a 1979 strike of union clerks, brakemen, and conductors who were demanding industry-pattern wage increases that Rock Island management said it could not afford. Under a provision of the 3R Act, the ICC issued a "directed service order" to the Kansas City Terminal Railway—which was owned by 12 railroads, including the Rock—to operate the Rock temporarily. It also ordered a pay raise for the striking clerks. The cost to taxpayers of eight months of directed service exceeded $70 million. Once it was determined that the Rock could not be reorganized, a federal judge in 1980 ordered that it be liquidated, the only major railroad in U.S. history to suffer such a fate. The railroad's bankruptcy trustee sought buyers for the remaining assets, with some track pulled up and sold for scrap.

The demise of the Rock Island resulted in the SP's finally getting a line from Tucumcari to Kansas City and St. Louis. But in an indication that all was not well at One Market Street—the Southern Pacific's San Francisco headquarters—the SP had to arrange the financing of the purchase through its profitable Cotton Belt subsidiary (officially the St. Louis Southwestern Railway), using the subsidiary's assets to secure the debt.

The Chicago and North Western beat the Soo in a bidding war for the Rock's "Spine Line" between Minneapolis and Kansas City. The Burlington Northern and the Missouri-Kansas-Texas (Katy) each bought portions of the Rock Island line between Herington, Kansas, and Houston, the Katy taking the segment from Herington to Dallas and the BN buying sole ownership of the line between Dallas and Houston that it previously had shared with the Rock Island.

The impact of the Rock Island fiasco was a further stimulus to the movement to deregulate railroads and to place a limit on the time the ICC could take to resolve merger cases.

Burlington Northern, meanwhile, was continuing to implement its 1970 merger and investing millions into its physical plant so it could handle the now rapidly growing coal business. Merger implementation was made easier because the BN inherited an outstanding group of executives from its constituent railroads.

William Greenwood, who later served as BN chief operating officer, said:

> Burlington Northern had a tremendously strong management group. . . . Burlington Northern was hiring up to 50

Pie in the Sky

The Rock Island merger case usually is accompanied by the word "infamous." It was so convoluted that it led to legislation limiting the length of time the Interstate Commerce Commission (ICC) could consider railroad merger cases.

After seven years, ICC hearing examiner Nathan Klitenic recommended against the C&NW and in favor of the UP. His detailed recommendations—termed by *Railway Age* magazine "a Messianic restructuring" of the western railroad map—rivaled the restructuring plans of 1920. No party to the proceeding had sought his broad proposal, but considering the competing applications and the numerous requests for protective provisions, the examiner felt justified in going far beyond the original merger applications.

He proposed that four dominant rail systems be created in the West. They would be built around the Santa Fe, Burlington Northern, Southern Pacific (SP), and Union Pacific systems. Without the formality of the Klitenic proposal, these would end up as the last four major systems surviving in the West before the 1995 and 1996 consolidations that resulted in the BNSF and the UP.

The Santa Fe, under this ambitious plan, would acquire the Rock Island Amarillo-Memphis line, as well as the SP's line from Klamath Falls, Oregon, to Flanigan, Nevada, and trackage rights over the UP's line (originally the Rock Island's) between Kansas City and St. Louis. In addition, the Missouri Pacific and its Texas and Pacific subsidiary, the Denver and Rio Grande Western, and the Western Pacific all would be merged into the Santa Fe, giving it direct access to Memphis and St. Louis, a central corridor route to Northern California and direct access to the Pacific Northwest. The BN was to acquire all Rock Island track in Texas.

The SP, in addition to the Tucumcari line, would acquire a line between El Paso and Fort Worth from the Texas and Pacific. The SP also would acquire the Kansas City Southern, its Louisiana and Arkansas subsidiary, and the Missouri-Kansas-Texas.

college graduates a year for its management training program year after year. The Great Northern did it. The Burlington did it. That's how I came onto the Burlington. I was in their management training program. It wasn't very [sophisticated]. I know it was only sort of an on-the-job program, but [it] was a [program]. But if you have some-

The Union Pacific finally would gain access to Chicago by acquiring the Rock Island line between Omaha and Chicago and all other Rock Island lines not assigned to other railroads. The UP also was to acquire the SP's line over the Cascades, linking San Francisco and Ogden, Utah. The C&NW, which started the whole process in an attempt to acquire the Rock Island, was to be merged into the UP.

Although the hearing examiner endeavored to remake the western rail map, he couldn't quite manage the task. Three midwestern regional railroads—the Milwaukee Road, the St. Louis–San Francisco Railway, and the Soo Line subsidiary of the Canadian Pacific—were each to be given a five-year period to petition for inclusion in one of the four dominant systems.

Just about everyone rejected the proposals, and the words "arrogant," "cynical," and "unlawful" were used. In late December 1974 the ICC released its formal decision. It rejected the C&NW proposal and approved the UP's application to acquire the Rock, but it imposed conditions considerably different from those recommended by the hearing examiner.

As proposed by the UP, the Rock Island line between Tucumcari and Kansas City was to be sold to the SP. The UP was to sell the Rock's Amarillo-Memphis line to the Santa Fe, which in turn had its request for trackage rights between Kansas City and St. Louis rejected on the grounds that additional rail service between the two cities was not necessary, perhaps one of the few indisputable determinations by the commission. The UP also was to sell the Rock Island line between Denver and Omaha to the Denver and Rio Grande Western. The Santa Fe still would get its route to St. Louis, because the ICC would have it acquire the Katy—a recommendation consistent with the finding that additional rail service between Kansas City and St. Louis was not needed, because it would substitute one railroad for another. Finally, the UP was to commit for five years not to divert to its newly acquired Rock Island Omaha-Chicago line any freight the UP previously interchanged with either the C&NW or the Milwaukee.

The Union Pacific found the conditions unacceptable and withdrew from the merger. With no merger partner, the Rock Island slipped into bankruptcy.

thing in place for 30 or 40 years, you are going to stand a better chance of having better management than the people who don't have something like that in place, which most railroads didn't. Most railroads hired an entire five people in a good year.

Greenwood, a 1960 graduate of Marquette University, joined the Burlington Route in 1966 after a few years in banking and insurance. He rose through the CB&Q and BN operating department ranks to a division superintendent position with a brief stint as director of corporate planning. Following a successful assignment in the Alliance (Nebraska) Division, where the BN's coal business was managed, he moved into the railroad's marketing department in 1981.

The talent pool paid off when it came to financing the coal expansion, as Greenwood pointed out:

> We had the luck to have some people like [BN treasurer] Ray Burton. Nominally, our [chief financial officer] was Frank Coyne, but the real strength was Ray Burton. Ray is the guy who did the deals that allowed us to finance the coal buildup. He just did this imaginative financing. . . . Ray did that at a time when we had no cash. We had no financing ability, because we're now talking about the mid-1970s. It was a project [about which] Bob Downing said, "I don't care what the numbers say. I want this done." It was a time of high inflation; the costs were going up and everything else was too. We needed new assumptions. Bob Downing provided them. So those were the conditions under which Ray had to do it, but I've had people in the banking business tell me it's just a masterpiece what he was able to do—to be able to get it done and get so much of it off-balance sheet. So we were blessed to have those kinds of people in place at that time.

A key feature of the financing was that the utilities were persuaded to buy or lease the thousands of coal cars necessary to move millions of tons of coal. Historically, railroads owned and provided most freight cars, and their costs of ownership and maintenance were factored into tariffs, but the BN didn't have the balance-sheet strength to acquire cars. The utilities, on the other hand, were able to take advantage of investment tax credits that made it less costly for them to own the cars.

Despite the growth of coal and intermodal volume for the BN and some other railroads, the railroad industry continued to struggle. Congress had created a loan guarantee program, administered by the ICC, that enabled some of the financially weaker railroads to undertake minimal capital and maintenance programs. At best, the loan guarantees only staved off the time when fundamental changes would be required. They did nothing to correct the structural ills the railroads faced: tremendous intra-industry competition and overcapacity, plus increasing competition from less regulated trucking and barge companies.

Said Schef Lang, the former federal railroad administrator who became an economic planner at the Association of American Railroads:

> I argued unsuccessfully against the loan guarantee programs that were put in place and the branch line subsidy programs put in place as programs that would do relatively little good for the core of the industry—those companies that had sufficient strength in terms of their assets and operating capabilities, on the one hand, and their markets, on the other hand—to survive ultimately.
>
> Preserving a lot of branch lines and preserving even for a few more years a bunch of what were essentially feeder Class 1s that were no longer on their feet on their own—the Milwaukee, the Rock Island, the North Western, and a bunch of others—wasn't going to do anything for the industry in the long run, but they were going to pay a political price [for the loan programs]. I think they did. I think among other things, those programs may have delayed deregulation.

To friend and foe alike, Lang was known as outspoken when it came to railroads and public policy issues.

THE BEGINNING OF REAL DEREGULATION

At the beginning of the 1970s, deregulation was not uniformly favored by many of the top executives in the railroad industry. "There were a bunch of guys who really felt that the nature of the railroad business was such, the common carrier obligation was such, that deregulation was . . . inappropriate and was ultimately going to be damaging," Schef Lang observed.

Some railroads clearly were going to survive. The Burlington Northern, the Union Pacific, the Norfolk and Western, and a few others had traffic bases—coal, grain, ore, bulk chemicals, and other commodities that could not be moved effectively other than by rail—that assured they would have sufficient business to sustain them regardless of the regulatory constraints with which they dealt. After more than three-quarters of a century under the Interstate Commerce Act, railroad managers had learned to exist and even make the system work for them on occasion. The ICC protected railroads from the most ruinous competition almost as much as it protected rail shippers from the worst behavior of railroads.

It also was obvious by the mid-1970s that many railroads were doomed. Lang was one of a group of officials at the Association of American Railroads who worked with railroad executives to develop an industry strategy on deregulation. Essentially, key railroad leaders had to be brought around to the proposition that unless the industry was willing to abandon the weakest members, eventually even the strong would be weakened to the point of collapse. There was an understanding that, regulated or deregulated, some railroads just would not survive. "United we stand" would not work for the railroad industry. Of the BN lines, Lang said: "I think they would have been one of the survivors under any circumstances. I think they had enough traffic base and a good enough set of railroad assets."

Following the Rock Island bankruptcy and liquidation, even Congress began to accept that there was a serious national railroad problem and that ignoring it would not make it go away. Major corporations that relied on rail service began to make their views known: the rail crisis was becoming costly to the economy in the form of higher costs for those who suffered poor service or were forced to switch to other modes. Congress began work on an omnibus rail bill that combined numerous features: the Railroad Revitalization and Regulatory Reform (4R) Act of 1976.

The 4R Act began the process of relieving railroads of some of the worst aspects of government regulation. Most important, it gave railroads some relief by granting them a modicum of rate-making freedom. A "zone of reasonableness" was established; railroads were forbidden to set rates below or above the zone without ICC approval but could adjust rates within the zone more easily. A key section provided for the activation of Conrail—the Consolidated Rail Corporation—to complete the process begun by the 3R Act for the resolution of the rail crisis in the Northeast and the Midwest. This part—or title, as it is called in omnibus legislation—was absolutely essential if the government was not to be an open financial spigot for the bankrupts. The other parts of the bill, with numerous controversial provisions, were hung on the core like baubles and lights on a Christmas tree.

Another important provision of the 4R Act established the principle that if, in the future, rail service was mandated in the public interest, the public would pay for that rail service. Under this provision, while ICC approval still was required for rail line abandonments, railroads finally could hope to eliminate lines throughout the country that had outlived their economic usefulness. The 4R Act also provided for offers of subsidy from communities or customers to keep such lines in operation. There was little belief that opponents of line abandonment would come up with financial assistance, but the act moved them into a "put up or shut up" situation. Clearly, railroads now could eliminate unprofitable operations or begin to shift the economic burden to those benefiting most from them.

The 4R Act language on rail mergers made it clear that Congress wanted the ICC to lean toward approval of rail combinations that would particularly "tend to rationalize and improve the Nation's rail system." Congress also acted to prevent the ICC from killing, through inaction and delay, transactions that it might not like. Reacting to the Rock Island merger fiasco, Congress put a strict deadline of 31 months—since reduced to 15 months—on ICC rail merger proceedings.

Another section of the 4R Act barred discriminatory state taxation of railroads, a common practice that cost railroads an estimated $400 million annually. The new law required that railroad property be valued for tax purposes and assessed on the same basis as other commercial and industrial property. Another provision—since repealed—allowed the U.S. secretary of transportation to grant antitrust immunity to railroads in situations like that of the Rock Island, where cooperative action among railroads might provide a private-sector resolution.

Following the Rock Island's 1975 bankruptcy, rail chief executives had met secretly at Washington D.C.'s swank Madison Hotel to devise a plan to divide the Rock Island's lines among themselves. Eventually, the rail leaders met informally with the ICC staff to discuss the concept, recognizing that any formal move would be subject to ICC review and approval. Although the ICC reaction was slow and cool and the railroads failed to reach agreement, transportation planners thought the approach might prove useful in the future. Explaining the 4R Act provision to a railroad group, the head of the ICC's Rail Services Planning Office said, "This saves you guys the cost of renting the room at the Madison." Because of the antitrust concerns of conservative railroad lawyers, the imposition by the

Department of Transportation of onerous requirements and delays, and the railroads' suspicions of each other, the provision never was used to save a railroad.

The new law came too late to prevent another bankruptcy. The long-struggling Milwaukee Road, having been turned down by the ICC on its 1973 and 1976 requests to be included in the Burlington Northern system, finally succumbed in 1977. The ICC had rejected the last attempt by the Milwaukee to find a home by pointing out that when the BN consolidation was approved, it was intended that the Milwaukee continue to provide competition in the northern tier. The commission and its staff seemed oblivious to the notion that if the Milwaukee had been able to provide such competition, it would not have filed for bankruptcy. In rejecting the Milwaukee's last petition for inclusion in the BN system, the ICC said: "The Milwaukee, in its various pleadings and in its application, has failed to show that any financial or operational difficulties it may be facing stem from the Northern Lines merger." Within 10 months of the ICC rejection, the Milwaukee entered bankruptcy, never to reemerge as an independent railroad.

Recognizing that his railroad had far more track than the available or prospective business could support, the Milwaukee's Worthington D. Smith moved quickly to cut the steady losses by trying to end service on the Pacific Coast Extension—everything west of Miles City, Montana. The federal bankruptcy judge and the ICC, however, resisted the move, with the ICC commissioners observing that it was "the longest proposed rail abandonment ever entertained by us."

The bankruptcy trustee's first reorganization plan presented to the bankruptcy court called for sale or abandonment of everything west of Miles City. This plan also was blocked, but when it became clear that the Milwaukee was rapidly running out of cash, an embargo of lines west of Miles City was authorized on November 1, 1979. Some public officials, however, thought they could dictate an outcome more to their liking. Senate Commerce Committee chairman Warren Magnuson of Washington State complained loudly, and the bankruptcy judge delayed his embargo order to give Congress an opportunity to pass the Milwaukee Road Restructuring Act. The act would authorize emergency federal loans and loan guarantees to keep the entire railroad in operation while Milwaukee employees tried to raise the money to purchase and reorganize the railroad.

Once the ICC determined that such a plan was unrealistic and likely to fail, Senator Magnuson and others in Congress dropped their opposition to embargoes and asset sales. Interestingly, in 1978 the Union Pacific appeared to have a rescue plan for the Milwaukee. The rivalry created by James J. Hill and E. H. Harriman continued as the UP sought to break the BN dominance of northern-tier markets. The UP thought it might like to own the Milwaukee's western extension; it already connected with the Milwaukee at Butte, Montana; Coeur d'Alene, Idaho; and Portland and Seattle. But after inspecting its proposed purchase and realizing that the track was in such poor condition that the cost of rehabilitation would be prohibitive, the UP abandoned the idea.

Now the trustee moved quickly to cut the Milwaukee's losses, halting all operations west of Ortonville, Minnesota, and putting two-thirds of the entire system up for sale. Initially, the UP and the BN bought about 500 miles of Milwaukee track, and the BN subsequently ended up with much more. The balance in the northern tier wasn't disrupted, though, as both railroads bought only pieces that would fill gaps in their systems.

The state of South Dakota, which relied on the Milwaukee's western lines to move much of its grain to market, increased its sales tax by a penny to raise money to acquire the line that crossed that state's northern tier. The BN eventually bought the line from the state as part of what became known as the Iowa corn strategy. The BN had long owned a main line across southern Iowa and some gathering lines in the western part of the state. Only rarely was the ocean freight rate differential sufficiently high to drive Iowa corn westward to the Pacific Northwest ports served by the BN. In most years, the harvest in the western and southern parts of the state moved to Gulf of Mexico ports for export or moved relatively short distances to domestic millers and processors. The BN made relatively little money in either case. By acquiring the Milwaukee line across South Dakota and extreme southwestern North Dakota, the BN hoped to be able to reduce the cost of shipping Iowa and South Dakota grain for export through Pacific Coast ports.

The BN's purchase of the Milwaukee line almost became a political football and served as a good example of the way many politicians believed they had a right to be involved in what clearly were business decisions. Senator David Durenberger of Minnesota contacted BN officials and demanded that the BN make the same grain rates available to shippers located on the Milwaukee line in southern Minnesota that it already offered to shippers on its own parallel line. Richard C. Grayson, then chief executive of the BN, responded that the margin on the grain rates was so thin that if any politician tried to tell him what he could charge, he would simply walk away from the agreement to buy some of the Milwaukee lines, and the trustee and the politicians could try to find new buyers. The senator quickly dropped his demand, and the BN went ahead with its purchase. A BN executive who had been involved in the exchanges between Grayson and the senator commented, "I don't know whether Grayson was bluffing or not, but I know that I don't ever want to play poker with him."

The state of Montana, fearing a virtual monopoly of rail service by the BN, initially objected to the BN's acquiring any of the Milwaukee lines in that state. BN lawyers made a commitment to keep operating the lines that were to be acquired, and the state dropped its opposition to the line transfers before the ICC. Within a short time, however, railroads would be further deregulated and the grain transportation business would undergo significant changes that made some of the newly acquired lines uneconomic to operate or to upgrade, and despite its pledge, the BN filed to abandon them.

One of the more notorious was the Geraldine line, a former Milwaukee line that ran from Lewistown and Moccasin northwest to Geraldine. Key to the line was a high bridge that would have had to be rebuilt to enable the line to accept the new 263,000-pound-gross-weight grain cars that were rapidly becoming the industry standard. The BN determined that there wasn't enough grain available on the Geraldine side of the bridge to justify the cost of rebuilding the bridge, and without the grain available over the entire route, the remainder of the line was uneconomic and should be abandoned.

Knowing that it had little chance of prevailing if it fought the abandonment at the ICC, Montana sued the BN in state court, claiming that the commitment the railroad gave the state was in effect a contract and that the railroad therefore was guilty of breach of contract under tort law. After several years of negotiations, the railroad and the state reached a settlement and avoided a court trial. In the settlement, the BN transferred the disputed line to a short-line operator and agreed to offer shippers on the line the same unit train rates available to elevator operators that were actually loading unit trains at main-line points. This allowed the new short line to gather numerous smaller shipments and build unit trains that were turned over to the BN at the junction. The BN also provided several million dollars in capital to upgrade the line, which still is in operation.

The bankruptcy trustee for the Milwaukee meanwhile used the

proceeds of the various line sales to keep the remainder of the railroad operating while he tried to devise a successful reorganization. In 1981 the C&NW and two Canadian railroads, through their U.S. subsidiaries—the Soo Line and the Grand Trunk Western—looked closely at what was left of the Milwaukee. The two Canadian roads first joined forces to oppose the North Western, but the Grand Trunk unexpectedly dropped out. The ICC preferred the Soo Line plan because it had fewer competitive problems than did the C&NW, which had numerous lines parallel to Milwaukee tracks. Despite the ICC's opinion, the final decision lay with the bankruptcy judge. The C&NW raised its bid, and the Milwaukee trustee recommended it be accepted. To the surprise of many, the judge sided with the ICC and accepted the Soo Line bid, putting greater weight on the public interest aspects of the law than on the creditors' rights. The Milwaukee sale to the Soo Line closed on February 19, 1985, more than seven years after the railroad had entered bankruptcy. Rationalization of excess rail plant in the Midwest was a slow process indeed.

The Burlington Northern, the product of one of the largest mergers in rail history, wasn't finished yet. In February 1977 the BN and the St. Louis–San Francisco Railway announced they had begun feasibility studies for a merger, and by December of that year the two filed their merger application at the ICC. The BN-Frisco combination would be handled under the 4R Act limit of 31 months, the first rail merger to be handled so quickly. In fact the ICC took just 28 months, approving the consolidation on April 17, 1980. Court challenges delayed the merger until November.

The Frisco was one of those railroads that was destined to be absorbed by a larger system. Throughout is history, it never had been prosperous, and it had gone through several bankruptcies. Its name even connoted its historic financial weakness. Although it was intended to be one of the principal transcontinental railroads, and construction started along the 35th parallel, it ran out of money and never built west of Avard, Oklahoma, although its Atlantic and Pacific subsidiary participated with the Santa Fe in cobbling together a southern transcontinental route. More significantly for the latter part of the 20th century, the Frisco was a bridge carrier, one that relied more on traffic connecting to or from other railroads than on traffic it originated or terminated itself. As the industry consolidated into fewer and larger systems, most railroad experts were convinced that the bridge carriers would disappear.

Dick Grayson, who had been chief executive of the Frisco and was interviewed for this book shortly before his death, acknowledged that the Frisco management knew it would need to find a merger partner. The BN was not the first the Frisco considered. "I knew we were a likely merger candidate, and we had talked to the Santa Fe in 1965 about a merger and we never could get together with them," Grayson said. "We coasted along and had some informal talks with Southern Railway, and nothing came of that." Over the years, the Frisco also had flirtations of various degrees of seriousness with the Central of Georgia; the Illinois Central; the Gulf, Mobile, and Ohio; and the Chicago Great Western.

The Frisco route structure made it an attractive partner for other railroads, as has been noted previously. In the West it began at Avard, Oklahoma, where it exchanged traffic with the Santa Fe and provided that carrier with an efficient route to the Memphis gateway to eastern railroads. An attraction for the Santa Fe, aside from the line to Memphis, was that the Frisco ran into the economically growing Southeast through Birmingham, Alabama, and on to the ports of Mobile, Alabama, and Pensacola, Florida. The Frisco was attractive to the Southern for its direct access to Texas, Oklahoma, and Kansas. The Frisco also served St. Louis with a main line from the Southwest.

Grayson explained why the Frisco was willing to be merged out of existence: "[Missouri Pacific] was our bridge connection at Kansas City. We knew we'd lose a lot of traffic when they would eventually merge with Union Pacific—about 30 percent of traffic we didn't originate or terminate. I knew we had to merge with somebody. I saw a great future with BN and having a coast-to-coast route. The coal was coming along also."

The BN came calling in the mid-1970s. "[John] Budd and Lou Menk came to see me in St. Louis one day and said, 'We want to talk to you about merger,'" Grayson recalled. "I said, 'Well, I can't promise you we'll do anything, but we're prepared to talk anytime it's appropriate.'" Menk, of course, had begun his railroad career on the Frisco, having been its chief executive before moving to the Burlington in 1965. "Lou knew all of our people, and he and I had been friends since 1944," Grayson noted. "We decided to do a study. We put [Frisco vice president of administration] Jim Brown in charge of our team. He was a very knowledgeable guy—he was good for that study."

By early 1977 the BN and the Frisco were considering the financial aspects of a merger. Grayson said, "Finally, in 1977, Lou and I and our advisers [Frank Coyne, the BN chief financial officer; Elliot

Stein, a St. Louis investment banker; and investment banks Morgan Stanley and Lehman Brothers] had a meeting in New York. They made us an offer, and I said, 'If that's the best you can do, I'm going back to St. Louis.' They said, 'Wait a minute. Let's meet tomorrow.' We met again the next morning, and they made us an offer that we accepted, and we began the 31-month [merger] process."

Not everyone at the BN thought the Frisco was the right merger partner. As Bill Greenwood recalled, "One of the things that Menk had done that was a mistake was that he wanted to buy the Frisco." Menk seemed to have an emotional tie to the railroad where he had spent more than 20 years of his illustrious career.

Greenwood, who had been at the Chicago, Burlington, and Quincy before the Northern Lines merger, said, "Back when I was on the Burlington before we had the merger, he had the Burlington buying the Frisco. We got 10 percent [of the stock] accumulated on the market, and the ICC said, 'Bad, bad, bad, nope. You're not buying the Frisco Railroad. You must sell that stock.' So Burlington had to turn around and sell." The Burlington's interest in the Frisco occurred while the Northern Lines merger case was before the ICC. "Menk was bound and determined that Frisco was going to get included in this company," Greenwood said. "Everybody in the company—the strategic planning people, when I was in strategic planning—knew that it should have been the Missouri Pacific we should be going after, not the Frisco. But every manager does emotional things as well as rational things. That was not rational."

The Missouri Pacific (MP) had an excellent strategic route system from Chicago through St. Louis that cut diagonally across Arkansas, ran down to the Gulf of Mexico, and accessed the chemical plants along the coast, with their rich and growing traffic. The MP reached Mexico at the Laredo, Texas, border crossing, the busiest rail interchange point between the two countries. Its Texas and Pacific subsidiary connected with the Southern Pacific at El Paso, Texas. It also ran west to Pueblo, Colorado, where it connected with the Denver and Rio Grande Western, the Santa Fe, and the BN. Additionally, the Missouri Pacific had spent 25 years in bankruptcy reorganization, not emerging until 1957. When it did, it had a divided ownership structure that made a merger very difficult and scared off potential suitors. The long period in receivership served the railroad well because management was able to devote resources to maintenance and improvement of the MP physical plant, while delaying payment on its debt. Once the ownership disputes were settled, the Union Pacific moved quickly to acquire the MP.

When the BN-Frisco merger process began, 14 other railroads protested. Unlike the ill-fated Rock Island case, though, the ICC was under time constraints to process the application quickly, and settlements were negotiated with several of the protesting railroads that agreed to drop their opposition. Agreements were reached with the Southern Pacific in December 1978 and with the Union Pacific in January 1979. Five others dropped out of the case by July 1979. The Milwaukee Road, the North Western, the Katy, the Soo Line, the Santa Fe, the Illinois Central Gulf, and the Rock Island remained in opposition. There was little overlap, and the promise of more-efficient single-line service was enough to cause most shippers to support the BN-Frisco combination. The Department of Justice did not oppose it. For rail labor, the merging railroads offered income protection that the ICC called "significantly more protective of railroad labor than any previously imposed single set of employee protective conditions."

The Katy, by the BN's estimates, would suffer the most in traffic diversion to the larger BN as a result of its proposed acquisition of the Frisco. The Katy sought and failed to obtain financial indemnification if the merger were approved, and the ICC limited its traffic-protective conditions to just twenty-four months. This was intolerable for the financially weak Katy, and as soon as the ICC approved the merger, the Katy rushed to the Fifth Circuit Court of Appeals in New Orleans, which issued a stay on May 13, 1980. The stay was lifted in November, and the merger became effective November 21, 1980. Another of the famous lawyer footraces marked the end of the BN-Frisco merger case. This time it was between Katy's lawyers, who raced to the Supreme Court to seek a stay while they appealed further, and the BN's lawyers in Delaware, who rushed to file the merger documents, again on the theory that the courts would not try to unscramble an egg. The BN's lawyers won.

At 30,000 route miles and serving 25 states and two Canadian provinces, the Burlington Northern was now the longest railroad in the United States. CSX Transportation in the East had more track miles, reflecting the fact that more of its railroad was double tracked. The BN began advertising a Seattle-Birmingham train as the longest single train in the country. There was little Seattle-Birmingham traffic, but there was a reasonable amount of traffic to intermediate points as the train moved across the northern tier to the Twin Cities, down through Galesburg, Illinois, to St. Louis and Memphis, then on to Birmingham under a single number.

The BN-Frisco combination, as was usual following rail mergers, triggered a responsive move by the Union Pacific, which soon after agreed to acquire both the Missouri Pacific and Western Pacific railroads, effectively reducing the rail industry in the West to four major systems and a handful of smaller roads.

MORE DEREGULATION, AND THIS TIME
THEY MEAN IT

The disasters of the Rock Island and the Milwaukee and the obvious disconnect of the ICC from economic reality became another stimulus for continuing the deregulation of the railroad industry. As could be seen by any but the most myopic observers, the railroads would not prosper—and perhaps would not survive in the private sector—under federal regulation. They had engaged in mergers and consolidations that eliminated redundant lines and facilities. They had adopted new technology wherever possible, and they had invested in facilities and equipment that enabled them to take advantage of new business opportunities. But prosperity still eluded even the financially strongest railroads. None was earning its cost of new capital.

Railroads sought, or at least acquiesced in, federal regulation in the late 19th century, seeking protection from the effects of over-building, unbridled competition among themselves, and the chilling prospect of conflicting state regulations. Although rail executives were able to live with the original rules from the Interstate Commerce Commission, they were not nearly so sanguine about maximum- and minimum-rate regulation and the commission's reaction to changed market and competitive conditions. A popular theory that turns out to be a myth is that, until the 1970s, few industry leaders questioned the continuing need for the "protection" of regulation. As has been covered previously, executives like Ralph Budd of the Burlington and other farsighted industry leaders saw as early as the 1930s that government regulation was more of a hindrance than a help.

Finally, though, by the late 1970s even those who somehow believed they benefited from regulation reluctantly accepted that they eventually would join their bankrupt colleagues unless the regulatory landscape was radically changed. The rail chiefs in effect decided that while they could not save the weak, they might be able to save the strong if they were free to compete and to adapt more quickly to changing business conditions. The majority of the industry embarked on a drive for deregulation. The Staggers Rail Act of 1980 was the result.

By themselves the railroads could not have prevailed in any effort to obtain regulatory relief. Perhaps most important was that economic deregulation was a political favorite of the Carter administration. It persuaded Congress first to deregulate the airline industry in 1978, then the trucking industry in early 1980, and finally the railroads. Rail deregulation did not come easily, and it took a coalition of interests to overcome opposition. Major rail customers hoped that, freed from the worst aspects of regulation, railroads would be able to provide better, more consistent service. Customers even claimed to be willing to pay more for improved service, especially with high inflation driving up regulated rail rates anyway. Wall Street joined the drive, recognizing that moribund railroads not only provided little or no investment banking and underwriting business but also were a threat to the safety of billions of dollars of outstanding debt and equity securities. Rail labor eventually joined the deregulation coalition on the grounds that it was increasingly difficult to extract favorable wage and work rule agreements from an industry that was failing financially and competitively. Rail union leaders also did not want to negotiate the wage and work rule contracts with Congress, as they had, in part, in the legislation creating Conrail.

Deregulation still faced powerful opposition. Those railroads that had traffic bases did not like the idea of giving up industry-wide collective rate making, one of the trade-offs demanded by shippers. These were primarily railroads in the Southeast that had the benefit of historically high divisions of revenue on interregional freight movements. Customers that saw themselves as captive to the railroads also did not like the idea of giving railroads any greater freedom. Memories and fears of early rail practices and abuses died hard.

After months of hearings and negotiations between the parties and key members of Congress, a deregulation bill was set to pass a key House committee in June 1980. A surprising rejection of the proposed deregulation bill by the House Interstate and Foreign Commerce Committee shocked the railroads and their supporters. The deregulation coalition was restructured and persuaded the committee to reconsider the proposal. The Staggers Rail Act—named for Harley O. Staggers of West Virginia, the longtime chairman of the House Commerce Committee—finally was passed during the waning days of the congressional session and was signed into law by President Jimmy Carter on October 14, 1980.

The most significant feature of the Staggers Act was the new freedom that railroads gained to set rates based on their own considerations of costs and market realities rather than on their ability to persuade bureaucrats of their needs. Frank Wilner wrote that the Staggers Act had "legalized capitalistic acts among consenting adults."

For the first time in nearly a century, railroads could file tariffs and set rates without having to worry that they might be suspended for investigation and that they would be forced to undergo an arduous and expensive defense of their actions. While retaining a common carrier obligation, the railroads also were free to negotiate contracts with customers regarding rates and service. The Staggers Act led to more change in just a few years than the railroad industry had experienced in the previous century.

In his book about rail mergers, Wilner wrote of the impact the Staggers Act had on the railroads:

> Railroads used their new economic freedoms to improve productivity, lower costs and slash prices. A 1988 study by ICC and Federal Trade Commission economists concluded that the Staggers Act saved the nation's shippers and consumers as much as $15 billion annually through lower railroad rates and improved rail efficiency. Competitive pressures "force everyone in the transportation chain to seek the cheapest means to move goods," observed Conrail marketing officer Richard H. Steiner.
>
> Freed from the in-box of bureaucrats, railroad managers began thinking and acting more like rational business people. Innovations were introduced into pricing and marketing and greater effort was expended to improve asset and employee utilization—often through mergers and consolidations.

Because contract rates were agreed to mutually, they were completely free of regulation, and railroads only had to file minimal information that did little more than inform the ICC and others that a contract existed. Confidentiality extended even to information that could reveal the identity of a customer or information about the specific movement. This was key to large-volume movements of coal, grain, bulk chemicals, and other commodities and especially affected the Burlington Northern, which had become the largest grain hauler and one of the leading coal carriers.

Other rates were deregulated by formula. If a rate provided revenue that was less than 180 percent of a railroad's variable cost of handling the business, it also was freed from any regulation. The concept embodied in the Staggers Act was that railroads on average would need revenue equal to 140 percent of their variable cost on all traffic to generate sufficient revenue to provide a reasonable rate of return, assuming prudent management. Some truck- or barge-competitive traffic couldn't be priced that high without losing the traffic, so Congress was persuaded to raise the deregulation standard to 180 percent to allow for the fact that not all rates could be at the average. By definition, then, any rate that was less than 180 percent of variable cost was deemed to be at that level because there was competition and it didn't need government regulation.

For rates above 180 percent of variable cost, a series of thresholds was to be applied before the ICC could even consider a rate complaint. The shipper had to prove first that the rate was above 180 percent before it even had a right to complain to the commission. The shipper then had to prove to the ICC that the railroad had "market dominance" on the movement. This was rebuttable, and railroads had the opportunity to demonstrate that the shipper had geographic competition (eastern versus western coal, for example), product competition (metal versus glass for beverage containers), modal competition (another railroad could handle the traffic), and intermodal competition (trucks, pipelines, or barges offered competition). Absent a finding of market dominance, the rate was free from review or regulation, regardless of how much it contributed to the railroad's revenue. If a shipper satisfied the ICC on all counts, it then had the burden of proving that the rate in dispute was unreasonably high. The ICC could determine that a railroad had market dominance but that a rate still was not unreasonably high.

Railroads gained considerable freedom to abandon uneconomic lines. The freedoms went beyond those in the 4R Act. Each railroad was required to file a system map with the ICC that showed lines that were candidates for abandonment within three years, lines that were pending abandonment, and lines that might be considered for abandonment in the future. This provision was to enable shippers to make facility investment decisions with less risk. It also effectively hastened the end of lines that were identified as candidates for abandonment, because few potential shippers would build a plant or facility on one of those lines. Again, the burden was transferred from the railroad's having to prove that a line was losing money to the shipper's having to prove that it wasn't.

Although there was a reduction of 30,000 route miles, or 14 percent, of the U.S. rail system during the 1970s, the pace of abandonment accelerated after Staggers became law. In the 1980s, U.S. railroads shed themselves of 60,000 miles, or 33 percent, of the national system. Prior to the deregulation movement of the 1970s, no more than 15,000 miles had been abandoned in any decade since 1930.

Rail merger approval remained with the ICC. This was important because the Justice Department's Antitrust Division, to which rail merger authority might have been transferred, had a public interest mind-set that minimized the impact of intermodal competition and that assumed that more railroads, rather than fewer, would produce the best service for the public. In the capital-intensive railroad industry this could have been disastrous. The ICC, to the surprise of many railroaders and economists, has administered the act aggressively, even determining that in some cases a lessening of competition outweighed the benefits to the public interest.

The Staggers Act required that state regulation of railroads not be inconsistent with or stricter than federal laws and regulations. One result was the end of state regulation of interstate rail rates, and railroads gradually began to eliminate the freight agencies that they had maintained in just about every small town in America, usually to satisfy state regulators. Instead, railroads consolidated car ordering, customer service, and eventually marketing and sales in more-efficient, centralized service centers. As a result, thousands of clerical jobs were eliminated, while thousands of other positions were reduced by the spread of computer technology.

Before the Staggers Act, all rail rates and conditions of service were required to be published as tariffs that were open to all for inspection, and it was illegal for a railroad and a customer to agree privately upon specific rates or services. Any change in rates, either up or down, required notice and was subject to delay and action by the ICC or a state regulatory agency. Railroads, especially the Burlington Northern, readily embraced their new ability to enter into transportation contracts with customers. Such contracts were confidential and governed rates as well as other terms of service. Railroads now could guarantee rate and service levels in exchange for customer guarantees of freight volume.

Within two decades, almost 90 percent of rail freight was moving under transportation contracts. Unfortunately for railroad earnings, the average rates were lower than those under the old tariff system, and so were actual inflation-adjusted revenues, but the railroads were satisfied with the volume guarantees.

The greater regulatory freedom forced and allowed railroads to shed costs rapidly, something not really foreseen by the drafters of the Staggers Act. In particular, the decline in employment accelerated. As well as railroads have done, however, the industry still was unable to increase revenue to a level necessary to ensure long-term financial stability. Ironically, Congress believed that by deregulating railroads it would be giving them the opportunity to increase revenue by raising rates. But Congress also deregulated trucking a few months before the Staggers Act was passed, which negated the opportunity to raise truck-competitive rates.

Although deregulation of the several transportation modes occurred at roughly the same time, there were significant differences among the approaches to deregulation. In the case of the airlines and trucking, the idea was to help consumers by stimulating greater competition and lower prices by removing the barriers to entry. In the case of the railroads, the idea was to assist railroads to achieve economic health by allowing them to charge higher rates and to remove unduly stultifying and costly state and federal regulation, while retaining just enough federal regulation to protect rail customers, rail-served communities, and rail labor from the worst effects of unfettered commercial behavior. While a fundamental concept of reduced railroad regulation was to return the industry to financial health, the virtually simultaneous and almost total economic deregulation of the trucking industry deprived the railroads of the ability to increase rates and price their way to prosperity.

The Staggers Rail Act worked, however, in other ways that were not foreseen by its drafters or advocates. Almost as soon as the ink was dry on President Carter's signature, the railroads began to shed thousands of miles of low-density branch lines that did not generate enough traffic to pay their way and that the railroads were convinced never would. Freed of some of the worst aspects of regulation that had stifled or delayed many prior attempts at innovation and self-help, railroads began to offer new services that reduced operating costs, drew new business, or did both. One of the best examples was the unit grain train. Prior to the Staggers Rail Act, when harvest conditions resulted in shortages of grain cars, the ICC routinely ordered railroads to break up efficient solid grain trains and to allocate scarce cars to a wide spectrum of customers on a nondiscriminatory allocation formula. Most of the time, ICC grain-car service orders came too late to be effective and proved to be even less efficient than the railroads' own car allocation systems. After the Staggers Rail Act, unit grain trains remained intact, and although car shortages still occur at the peak of the harvest, grain transportation has been handled more smoothly than it was for nearly a century.

The industry rapidly adopted the 100-ton covered hopper for grain movement, retiring old boxcars that previously carried much of the crops. Most grain branch lines could not handle the 263,000-pound loaded weight of the new hopper cars, and, at first, few customers had storage tracks or elevator capacity to fill a unit grain train. With their new pricing freedom, though, railroads offered lower rates to grain shippers that used larger elevators with unit-grain-train loading and track capacity, usually along main lines. For most grain shippers, the railroads' unit-train discounts more than made up for the higher cost of trucking grain to main-line elevators.

The Burlington Northern, as the largest grain-carrying railroad, was one of the most aggressive at adopting the freedoms the Staggers Act allowed. This approach also led to some rancorous relations with agricultural interests and public agencies in part of the territory served by the railroad.

The 1980s would be a period of great change for all railroads and particularly for the railroads that today form the BNSF Railway.

8

A New Golden Age?

Not Quite

This was a whole different world. In so many ways, it's like stepping back into the 19th century.

RICHARD M. BRESSLER, commenting on his introduction to the railroad world in 1980

THE 1980 BURLINGTON NORTHERN–FRISCO MERGER created the largest rail system in North America. It also triggered a competitive response by rival Union Pacific that set both railroad giants on the path to becoming the final two survivors among major western railroads.

Even before the BN and the Frisco gained final approval for their merger, the UP moved in January 1980 to combine simultaneously with the Missouri Pacific and the Western Pacific, extending its market reach on both ends of its system. The UP, which traveled the Overland Route that it pioneered in 1869, would have direct access to all major Mississippi River gateways to the East (more than half of all freight shipments traveled over the tracks of more than one railroad in 1980). It also allowed the UP to join its western competitors—Burlington Northern, Southern Pacific, and Santa Fe—in providing single-line service between the Mississippi gateways and the West Coast.

Before its move to acquire the Missouri Pacific and the Western Pacific, the Union Pacific essentially was a big bridge line that relied on other railroads to originate and terminate much of its traffic. A number of rail economists believe that had the UP not jumped into the merger game when it did, it eventually would have been absorbed by one of the other emerging megasystems—huge railroads that blanket entire regions of the country, as the BN-Frisco did. Without the extended reach of its merger, the UP would not have been in a position over the long term to compete with the Southern Pacific, the Santa Fe, or the BN system, each with its superior franchises and single-line capability between the West Coast and eastern gateways.

The MP operated from Chicago and St. Louis to the Mexican border at Brownsville and Laredo, Texas, the latter the busiest border crossing to Mexico, and west from Kansas City to Pueblo, Colorado. Through its Texas and Pacific subsidiary, it crossed Texas from Dallas to El Paso, where it connected with both the Southern Pacific and the Santa Fe. It brought to the UP a franchise in the growing and lucrative chemicals industry that had developed along the Texas and Louisiana Gulf coasts.

The addition of the WP extended UP tracks into the San Francisco Bay markets and gave it further access to the Pacific Northwest through a connection with the BN at Bieber, California. The UP thus became a competitor to Southern Pacific and its north-south I-5 Corridor, named for the Interstate highway that paralleled it, and its line extended all the way to Seattle, while the SP went no farther north than Portland, Oregon. Through a connection with the WP at Ogden, Utah, the UP was able to route traffic through to California on its own line, depriving the SP of its traditional Overland Route interchange business, even though the SP had a superior route. The Southern Pacific was damaged more by the UP-MP-WP combination than were other railroads, and its ultimate demise as an independent rail system probably was sealed by that merger.

The UP—which never had reached Chicago or St. Louis, had a difficult route to Portland and Seattle, and was unknown in Texas— suddenly became a colossus. The application for an end-to-end merger sailed through the ICC, which seemed to have taken to heart the congressional admonition that it favor rail consolidations, particularly of the end-to-end variety. The Justice Department did not oppose the merger.

Part of the UP's justification for its merger was that the BN and the Frisco were in the process of combining and that the UP should be given the opportunity to compete on more equal terms with its longtime and larger rival. The merger was dubbed the "Mop-Up" as both a play on the involved railroads' initials and the tongue-in-cheek comment of an observer that the UP was "mopping up" all the

Lou Menk
A Big Man—and He Was Tall Too

Louis Wilson Menk became a railroader because a family tragedy prevented him from going to college and taking up a different career. Discussing his early start in the working world, Menk said years later, "I learned that making money could be fun, and I decided to make all the money I could, honestly. I learned, too, that you do get joy from achievement, from doing useful and productive things." His first job on the St. Louis–San Francisco Railway was as a telegrapher in Tulsa, Oklahoma.

Clark Hungerford, the Frisco president, became acquainted with and befriended Menk one night in a chance meeting in the Tulsa rail yard while the former was on an inspection of the railroad. Menk's advancement through the operating department was rapid after that, and in 1956 he was named general manager. Executive rank came with promotion to vice president and general manager in 1958, vice president of operations in 1960, and president in 1962. At 44 years of age, he was the youngest president in the history of the Frisco, and one of the youngest in the railroad industry.

Named chairman and chief executive in 1964, he remained less than a year at the Frisco. Harry Murphy was scheduled to retire from the presidency of the Burlington, which was owned jointly by the GN and the NP, and John Budd of the Great Northern and Bob Macfarlane of the Northern Pacific came looking for a successor for him. Menk made the move on October 1, 1965, and moved again just one year later to succeed Macfarlane at the Northern Pacific.

Menk took a number of college courses while working, but his frequent moves prevented him from earning a degree. He never lost his interest in education, though, and even served as an executive-in-residence at the Uni-

business. The Santa Fe's hopes of moving north into the Pacific Northwest were dashed. The BN was least affected, although the value of its acquisition of the Frisco was diminished considerably.

As each combination strengthened the surviving merged railroad and weakened competitors, it was increasingly obvious that even with just four major rail systems blanketing the West, there would be other combinations that would reduce that number. The Santa Fe soon would be involved in the consolidation movement, but more than a decade was to pass, and a merger to fail, before it would join with the BN.

Lou Menk, meanwhile, had put in 43 years in the railroad indus-

versity of Colorado School of Business in Boulder while he was chief executive of the BN. Years later, after retiring from the Burlington Northern, he became an adjunct lecturer at the Boulder school.

Menk had been active in civic affairs everywhere he had worked, including service on the Springfield, Missouri, school board and a member of the Missouri State Board of Education. At the BN he continued an active civic role and became an outspoken supporter of business causes. He also became a leading spokesman for the railroad industry, calling for deregulation several years before the industry even decided to support the movement.

He was outspoken in his belief that businesses must be good corporate citizens. In a 1973 speech before the Federal Bar Association, Menk said, "We all know there are companies that have not learned that no organization can pretend to be something it isn't and get away with it for long." He backed up his rhetoric by initiating a plan for Northern Pacific employees to acquire company stock through payroll deduction. Once the Northern Lines merger was accomplished, Menk created a scholarship program for the children of employees, declared that salaried employees should have annual performance reviews, and made sure that the BN provided employees with an improved health insurance plan, an improved pension plan for nonunion employees, and a tuition reimbursement program. Considered standard at most large corporations today, these were radical programs in 1970.

Menk also established a community relations department within the railroad, saying, "No man or woman in business can allow the pressures of their daily affairs to blot out their responsibilities in the community. Our nation is a collection of neighborhoods and communities, and the way you live in your community and the way I live in mine determines the way of the entire nation." The BN provided considerable financial support and encouragement for employees to participate actively in their communities.

try by the time the Staggers Act was signed, and he was approaching retirement. The Burlington Northern's board of directors determined that, with the coming of deregulation and Menk's approaching retirement, it was time to deal with both. The decision was made, while board members were on an inspection trip across the railroad in late spring 1980, that Menk would remain as chairman of the board until he was closer to the normal retirement age of 65 in 1983, that the BN would form a holding company so it could realize a greater return on its nonrail assets, and that a new chief executive would be brought in from outside the company.

The structural change was driven in part by the long-held views of former Northern Pacific directors that their company had never been fully valued in the Northern Lines merger and that a holding company would focus more on developing the company's natural resource assets.

When the terms of exchange between the Northern Pacific and the Great Northern were being negotiated in the 1950s, several Northern Pacific directors believed that the value of the NP was not so much in its railroad as in its land grant properties, particularly in oil and gas, which were just being developed when reserves of both were discovered in western North Dakota. The Northern Pacific held the mineral rights to millions of acres of land, and there was great hope that North Dakota might be another Texas—there had to be lots of oil. The price of Northern Pacific stock had gone up rapidly, and some believed that the natural resources of the Northern Pacific were extremely valuable if more oil was discovered, which was believed probable, and that other resources such as timber, coal, and real estate could be managed better.

Interestingly, the valuation of natural resource assets continued to be an issue well into the 1980s. At that time, executives at Burlington Northern Incorporated (BNI), the holding company that was established in 1981, strove successfully to devise a way to separate the railroad from the resource assets, and finally spun them off as a completely new company, Burlington Resources.

Norton Simon, a prominent investor and NP director, and his allies had demanded a more favorable exchange rate, reflecting what they were certain was the value of the mineral assets under the NP land grant if they were to approve the merger. It long had been an article of faith, however, that there was no way to separate the land grant properties from the railway, particularly with the two highly restrictive 1893 Northern Pacific bond issues outstanding. Simon and his allies eventually acquiesced, but there remained a feeling among some former NP directors that they did not really get their just share of the BN. As it turned out, there really wasn't very much oil.

The financial stress of investing for the rapidly growing coal business, and the impending retirement of Menk, gave the pro-resource faction of the BN board their opportunity. They made the case that the resource properties were not being properly managed by railroad people. There also was a perception on the board that despite the management training program and steady recruitment of new people, the BN didn't have the right executives in place or coming along for the changing environment of deregulation in which railroads would have to operate. Menk was a highly regarded operating executive who had become an industry leader, but there was a sense that the culture of the railroad was going to have to change if it were to prosper under deregulation, and that Menk and traditional railroad managers were not the correct executives to have in place.

The two themes—that resources needed to be managed separately from the railroad and that the railroad needed a different type of manager—came together in the summer of 1980. Despite a cadre of very good railroad officers coming along, the board decided to go outside the organization for Menk's successor. The search settled on Richard M. Bressler, a highly regarded executive at energy giant Atlantic Richfield Company (ARCO). Bressler, in an interview for this book, pointed out that he and Menk knew each other from their membership on the board of directors of the Minneapolis-based food conglomerate General Mills Incorporated.

Bressler was not received with open arms by the BN management. Because he came from outside the clannish railroad industry, there was an immediate suspicion that he had been given the task of separating the natural resources from the railroad. There also was the realization that his presence meant the end of promotions for a number of longtime BN executives.

The new BN chief executive had been executive vice president and chief financial officer of Southern California–based ARCO. His arrival in the conservative Twin Cities created a stir. Bressler's contract, although quite modest by today's standards, was huge by the standards of 1980 and of the railroad industry. He received a package of stock grants, options for BN stock at 10 cents a share, a loan with which to exercise the options, a loan to acquire housing, and guaranteed salary and bonuses.

Responding to media inquiries, railroad spokesmen explained that, in leaving ARCO, Bressler sacrificed a large compensation plan and unvested benefits and that the BN had to make up what he was leaving behind if he were to take the BN position. Although it appeared at first that every reporter who talked to the BN wanted to know about Bressler's compensation arrangement, the curiosity soon died.

Bressler's arrival at the BN was a bit of a shock to the railroad executives who had not known that the board was looking outside the company for Menk's successor. "I was in St. Paul for the board meeting that elected me," Bressler recalled. "I was waiting in Lou's [Menk] office. Unbeknownst to me, he had assembled all the top officers. So Lou came in and said, 'Well, you were elected. Now let's go meet the troops.' He got all those people in the [executive] dining room. I don't think any of them had a clue as to what was going on. Lou threw open the door. He said, 'Well, here's your new boss.' Of course, you could just see faces that just were amazed and appalled. I don't know what all the various emotions were. Then Lou stomped out of the room," leaving Bressler and the surprised executives to get acquainted.

Bressler confirmed that the decision to go outside the railroad for Menk's successor was based on the board of directors' perception that the company needed someone who would focus on developing the nonrail assets and that the railroad didn't have the right talent to accomplish that. Bressler related that Bob Wilson, a former BN director and retired chairman of Weyerhaeuser, told him that after a few months under Norman Lorentzen, who had been named to succeed Menk as chief executive of the railroad when the company was divided into transportation and resources divisions, the board told Menk that the arrangement was not working. Menk then agreed to help find his successor outside the company.

Bressler considered Menk's ability to change directions to be one of his assets as an executive. "If you said, 'Lou, I listened, but I don't agree with you. We're going to have to do something else,' he would turn around on a dime and say, 'Okay, let's go off one hundred eighty degrees.' I always consider people like that as having a great facility. They didn't hold grudges. They didn't hold old positions. They could say, 'You're right. Let's do that.' He would turn around."

Shortly after Bressler arrived in June 1980, Richard C. Grayson, who had been chief executive of the Frisco, followed him onto the management team. The Frisco merger, although approved by the ICC in May 1980, was tied up in court, and the new management believed it needed Grayson and his acknowledged abilities as a cost cutter and couldn't wait for the merger or the possibility that it might ultimately be killed. Grayson was persuaded to retire from the Frisco and immediately was hired as president and chief executive officer of the Burlington Northern Railroad. Hiring Grayson even before the Frisco merger was completed contributed to an impression in much of the railroad industry that the BN had management problems.

"I agreed to go up there [to St. Paul] even before the merger was approved," recalled Grayson. "Dick [Bressler] was not satisfied with what was going on at the railroad. He retired a few people. We were going to spend a tremendous amount of money to prepare for the coal business."

Grayson arrived during the period when utility coal customers were furious over the increased rates the railroad was imposing. "When I got there, we had, I think, some 22 [actual or] potential lawsuits over the letters of intent [for coal transportation rates]," Grayson said. "They were all too low, and we couldn't make any money on them. Dick [Bressler] and I went and called on all these customers." With the passage of the Staggers Act, the railroad also for the first time was allowed to sign contracts with the utilities. As described earlier, the disputes were settled.

Grayson took over the BN at a time when the company believed it would have the Powder River Basin coal business all to itself. "We thought we had the North Western out of the picture," he recalled. "Larry Provo [then C&NW chief executive] agreed with Lou [Menk] that they wouldn't have the money." Grayson and the BN management didn't anticipate that the ICC would give the C&NW all the time it needed to come up with the money it required or that the C&NW ultimately would turn to the Union Pacific for financing.

Momentous things were happening when Grayson took over the railroad. The Staggers Rail Act, deregulating the industry, had just been signed. The BN was forming a holding company, initially with the idea that each of the various businesses would be required to earn its own cost of capital and that the practice of subsidizing of one venture by proceeds from another would come to an end. In addition, an almost top-to-bottom management change was about to occur at the railroad. The holding company would parcel capital to the various subsidiaries based on need and the forecasted rates of return. The idea of separating the railroad and the company's natural resource assets was still developing in the minds of the new leader.

Within months of Grayson's arrival and the closing of the BN-Frisco merger, many of the top railroad executives were former Frisco officers. "[The BN people] were a good bunch of railroad people, focused on maintenance. But they had never lived on hard times like the Frisco people," Grayson said. "I had to shake out the management. Bill Thompson [a Frisco executive who was named executive vice president of operations] could get more out of a maintenance dollar in mechanical and engineering than anyone I've ever seen. There were a lot of things we saw that they could do without." Grayson cited as an example the decision to put many more locomotives than those in coal service through the new, efficient maintenance shops at Alliance, Nebraska, which had been built primarily to maintain locomotives used for the coal business. Thompson, a big, gruff executive, was known as Big Bill to most on the BN; the regional vice president in Billings, Montana, was somewhat smaller of stature and became known as Little Bill—although he was called other, less complimentary names behind his back.

In addition to Thompson and his senior staff in operations, former Frisco executives were placed in charge of accounting and management systems. Although the number and speed of the changes appeared as a purge to some BN officials, Grayson rejected that theory. "I put John Hertog [a longtime BN executive] in as vice president of coal operations, put Bill Thompson in charge of operations, and Ivan Ethington [a longtime CB&Q and BN executive] as executive vice president over both of them," Grayson pointed out. Longtime BN executives were retained, but many found themselves in different jobs. Eighteen of some 24 executives at one of Grayson's monthly executive staff meetings in late spring 1981 had not been in their positions a year earlier. However, only two were completely new to the BN or the Frisco.

Nevertheless, so many "southerners" were showing up in the Twin Cities that an employee at the Northtown maintenance shops in Minneapolis posted a new logo on the bulletin board. Changing the B of "BN" to an F, the poster proclaimed the railroad to be the "Frisco Northern." Within just a few years, however, most of the former Frisco officers had retired, and the hardy "northerners" again were running the BN.

In part because lifetime income protection was a condition of the two major mergers the BN had been through in a decade, the company had many more employees than it needed. Although Grayson and his management team moved aggressively to furlough union workers, the "exempts," as nonunion managerial employees are known in the railroad industry, could not be forced to retire.

The country was sliding into a recession in 1981, and the BN laid off thousands of workers as it tightened its operation. Between 1981 and the end of 1983, railroad employment fell by about a third, from 55,000 to 36,000. Grayson, who felt strongly that employees should know what was happening and should hear it first from their management, made it clear that, because of fundamental changes occurring in the industry and at the BN, most of the union jobs being eliminated would not be reinstated in the future. Laid-off workers were

Grayson's "Window Plan"

Under Dick Grayson's plan to reduce administrative and managerial staff, employees had a window of opportunity to take advantage of a generous offer to leave. Employees who were 55 years old and had at least 15 years of service could take early retirement and would be paid a bonus of 180 percent of their final annual salary, up to a maximum of $100,000. Fifty-six-year-old employees received a smaller bonus, and the bonus was scaled back with each additional year of age until those above a certain age received no extra payment. The idea of the bonus, which was paid out over five years, was to provide income to employees until they were eligible to receive Railroad Retirement payments at age 62. The bonus payments, along with the company pension for which they already were eligible, meant that most managerial employees who took the offer received almost as much income as if they stayed.

Faced with working for only a nominally larger amount than they would receive by retiring, older managers headed for the exits in large numbers. One assistant vice president in St. Paul informed his supervisor on the last day the window was open that he was retiring, although he was not yet 60. He claimed that the Human Resources Department had run the numbers for him and that had he stayed he would be "working for about $1.95 a week after taxes." The BN had some 1,600 exempts who were eligible for Grayson's window plan, and more than a thousand of them took advantage of it. Because the retirees were not being replaced and the company was paying out the bonuses over five years, the railroad saved salary expense and was able to record a gain of $75 million in 1981 operating income from the reductions in salaries minus the bonus payments.

encouraged to take jobs outside the railroad even if it meant having to relocate, rather than wait for a callback that would never come.

For the officers and other exempts, it was a different story. They had to be persuaded to retire. Grayson devised one of the first "window plans" in any industry to encourage early retirement. "I figured if we would spend a little money, we could persuade a lot of people to retire for whom we didn't have any real work," Grayson said. Voluntary early retirement plans since have become standard in American business.

Grayson had a reputation as a cost cutter, but his executive skills went considerably further. The Frisco was known as a nimble, tightly managed property. Grayson, a short, stocky man who tended to wear brown suits, would not have been cast as a chief executive by any advertising agency or movie casting director, but he was an accomplished operating executive and a strategic thinker. His decision to acquire significant pieces of the Milwaukee Road as part of his Iowa corn strategy was a solution to problems that had existed for many years for the BN.

Grayson could be charming when he wanted. Not long after he arrived, the BN announced that it was considering abandoning up to 4,000 miles of light-density lines, incurring the wrath of politicians in most of the grain-growing states where it operated. As the BN was restoring some former Milwaukee Road lines to service, Grayson managed to become friendly with South Dakota governor William Janklow. Considering that hundreds of miles of track were slated for abandonment in North Dakota and the state was virtually at war with the railroad, it was an even bigger achievement when Grayson began a friendship with North Dakota governor Allen I. Olson. The two men had never met until a reception in Bismarck to open the Burlington Northern traveling exhibit of western art. Although the governor's staff had declined the invitation from the railroad, Olson was a western art aficionado and changed his travel schedule to be able to attend the reception. Before the reception ended, the governor and the railroad president were sitting on folding chairs in a corner of the room, and their relationship was on a first-name basis.

Bressler meanwhile was keeping out of day-to-day operations and management of the railroad and was concentrating on getting the holding company organized and running. Bressler, not surprisingly, pointed out that he had faith in the future of the railroads, but he saw himself as an agent of needed change. "I said, basically, that this business, given the assets in it, should be making a much better return than it was," he said. Bressler had little use for the way traditional railroaders had learned to conduct business under regulation. For instance, he surprised his people by suggesting that customers begin investing in their own car fleet.

Historically, as common carriers, railroads owned the rolling stock, and the cost of ownership and maintenance was factored into the tariffs. The only car type that was not owned by the railroads was the tank car, mostly used for carrying chemicals and petroleum products. The shippers wanted to use the tank cars for temporary storage, which sharply cut asset utilization for the railroad and couldn't be factored into a tariff. The shippers agreed to provide their own cars subject to a mileage allowance from the railroad when the cars moved.

Despite the suspicion with which Bressler was met at the railroad, over time he came to appreciate the railroad executives' abilities and devotion to their work. "The railroad employees and particularly the officers were some of the most dedicated and hardworking—most officers could be found in their offices on Saturdays—that I have encountered anywhere." he said. "I was startled—maybe 'shocked' is a better word—that an industry that was one of the first to be spawned at the start of the industrial revolution had not evolved management practices that had been adopted by so much of modern American industry."

Bressler and the career railroaders had totally different views of running a business. Under regulation, a railroad had been expected to cross-subsidize various lines of business, but the common carrier obligation—which still remains on the books—did not permit them to exit a business that wasn't earning its way. Bressler added a third option to the two that railroad executives already knew. They could raise rates to generate the required return on investment. If competition prevented that, they could try to reduce costs to generate the required return on investment. And if the first two options failed, they could exit the business, which now was much easier to do since deregulation.

The coal business is a case in point. Bressler said that soon after his arrival at the BN, he told the board of directors, "I don't see right now, if you forced me to tell you, whether we are going to make any money in this coal business. I see zero return on this enormous investment," which was the reality at the time. The board was stunned. He said, "We've got to figure out a way to turn this around. Either we have to cut back this investment, or we've got to do something to improve the return." That was like speaking in a foreign language to railroad executives who had never been allowed to think about withdrawing from a market.

Bressler told of his early effort to learn something of the railroad culture:

> When I came to the BN I knew practically nothing about the railroad business. I started out trying to go around and meet people. It was very interesting, because I met people like John Reed [chief executive of the Santa Fe] and Ben Biaggini [chief executive of Southern Pacific] and so forth. All you have to do is meet a few of those old railroad types

to get quite an interesting picture of what the industry's probably like.

Some of those individuals whom I met that year and who ran railroads at that time, in retrospect, you have to ask how could they have been so imperious as that. Of course, Lou [Menk], bless him, was imperial too, in his own right. He would take the business [rail]car out to Billings in the summertime. That was like the summer White House. That's where I first met Lou. . . . I was still with ARCO. I had never met him, and we had something going on that involved the BN. He said, "Well, you better come up and see me." He told me where he was, so I went to Billings. He parked the business car and a couple of other cars out there on a siding in Billings. That's where you met Lou in the summertime.

Menk owned a ranch at Roundup, Montana, north of Billings, which was a regional headquarters of the BN. He kept an executive office in the Billings office building.

The railroad culture shocked Bressler, who said, "[During] the first few days there in St. Paul, I asked somebody, 'I get on the elevator, and everybody else gets off. What's going on here?' They replied, 'Oh, well that's the custom. If the chairman gets on the elevator, it is expected that he has to go wherever he's going fast. Everybody else is supposed to get off.' This was a whole different world. In so many ways, it's like stepping back into the 19th century."

Bressler related another anecdote to explain the culture that he was learning. "One time we were someplace with a whole crowd of people, and I was told, 'You can always tell the officers. . . . They all wear hats.' It didn't make any difference. It might have been a hundred degrees in the shade, [but] a railroad officer never goes without his hat."

The railroad world was different from anything Bressler had experienced before. He recalled:

The first few days that I was on the job people would come in with these bales of reports and put them on the desk. I said, "What is all this stuff?" They were derailment reports and accident reports and expense accounts of people way down in the organization. I said, "What am I to do with this stuff?" I was told, "Well, Mr. Lorentzen processed it, and he signed all these expense accounts." I said, "If I'm to do that kind of thing, we're in real trouble, because I don't know the first . . . thing about derailment reports and so forth."

Bill Greenwood, who at the time was senior assistant vice president for intermodal and later served as chief operating officer of the railroad, remembered that Bressler moved quickly to change the bureaucracy:

> He did things in the first week. The CEO's office in St. Paul used to get these morning reports. Back then everything was filled out by hand and on a form. The thing was 25 pages thick. Then a bunch of other reports had kind of come from that. One morning he walked out with that inbox full of reports. There were these seven male secretaries lined up outside [of his office]. He said, "I want everybody to turn around and look at me. Everybody look. Now watch. I want to tell you what I think of this stuff you're sending." He flipped it upside down and said, "Don't ever send me anything like this again," and turned around and went back into his office.

One of the most bureaucratic aspects of BN culture that was on borrowed time was the "No Report" form that railroad officials turned in when there was nothing new to add to the numerous daily reports they filed.

Bressler said he had to confront the coal business and customer lawsuits almost from the day he arrived at the BN:

> I was trying to find out a little about the [railroad] business and the coal business. Frank [Farrell, the BN's senior vice president for law] or one of his lieutenants would give me a rundown on the list of litigation. I said, "These are all our best customers. They're all suing us. What's going on here? How can you run a business in which you're in court with all your biggest customers? . . . I'm going to go out and visit these customers.
>
> I should have taken armed guards with me, because in

some cases I was almost assaulted by some of these people whom I met, these utility customers. Of course, it was the first time that they had ever met an executive from the railroad. Nobody had ever come around to call on them other than the marketing people or a lawyer or someone of that nature.

So after a few of these visits, because Lou came to town every once in a while, I said, "Lou, didn't you ever go out and meet them?" He said, "You don't want to talk to these people." I said, "Well, of course they're all just foaming at the mouth, Lou, because they think that they were quoted one rate and then it was doubled or tripled." "Well," he said, "they didn't understand." I said, "We didn't either, did we?" He said, "I guess not." It was just incredible what I learned in those first few months.

The lack of relationship with customers—common to most railroads at that time—was a shock to Bressler. "It just blew my mind that some of those things had gone on and were going on," he said. "Of course, this disdain for customers I just found to be awful. I'd never been with a business that had that kind of relationship with its customers."

Bressler said he also discovered that the Northern Lines merger hadn't been implemented fully or culturally, much less the more recent Frisco combination: "Northern Pacific and the Great Northern . . . these people all still reflected their old heritages."

Bill Greenwood, who began his railroad career on the old Burlington and ended it as chief operating officer of the Burlington Northern, had a different view of the slow merger process. Much of the fault lay in the regulatory environment, he contended. BN executives intentionally had moved slowly after the Northern Lines merger, in a successful effort to avoid the kind of operating disruptions that had occurred in other mergers. They understood that deregulation meant the railroad would have to reduce its cost structure. They would have dealt with the cost issue even if Bressler never had come to the BN, he believed. "We had shops that were redundant. We had people who were redundant," Greenwood said. "It was time. [Since deregulation], you could now deal with it. We couldn't have dealt with this probably two years before that."

Greenwood provided an example of how regulation had forced

railroads to operate against their natural inclination and contrary to good business practices: "You had a whole segment of commerce lawyers at every railroad who backed [the pricing people] up. So you probably had 15,000 people in the industry managing this whole complicated pricing mechanism that had nothing to do with the marketplace. It had to do with responding to regulation."

The BN, Greenwood pointed out, had done a study that anticipated deregulation by several years and called for the creation of a business unit structure built around market segments instead of the traditional railroad approach based on commodities or car types. Bressler was made aware of the study. "He considered it for at least two or three minutes," Greenwood noted, "and said, 'Do it. Do it right. Do it now. Every other business is managed this way. Why wouldn't you do this? Do it.'"

Bressler had a deep appreciation of Grayson's abilities. "I recognized fairly quickly that he was probably the best talent to run the railroad that there was around," Bressler said. "He was going to retire. That was his objective—to retire. . . . So I started working on him. I said to him, 'Don't retire. Come run the railroad.'"

Once Bressler had persuaded Grayson to remain, Bressler ran into another aspect of railroad culture: every railroad in the industry was convinced that its way of operating was the one true way a railroad should be operated. "The next day I had one of these luncheons [with employees of various levels]," Bressler recalled. "All these people said, 'What on earth would somebody from the Frisco know about running the big BN?' Before, they had all been talking about the Great Northern and Northern Pacific. Now I hear the Frisco and that I had the audacity to pick a guy from the Frisco, the little Frisco." Grayson, who worked closely with Bressler, had a more positive view of him than did many BN operating executives. "Dick Bressler was one of the finest executives I've ever seen," he said.

The reaction of longtime BN employees to Bressler's choosing Grayson to run the railroad helped persuade Bressler that the railroad and its resource assets should be separated. Bressler recalled telling Grayson, "This place has been around here for a hundred and some-odd years. We'd better just break it up and move these resource businesses out of here. Move wherever you want, but you ought to move someplace."

After briefly considering moving the holding company to Denver, Bressler determined that he wanted to operate at some distance from the railroad and its headquarters, which he knew would be moved from St. Paul, although very few were aware of that in 1981. By mid-summer 1981 the holding company had been created and Bressler located it in Seattle, about as far from St. Paul as any location served by the BN. It was equally distant from Fort Worth, Texas, where the railroad eventually moved its headquarters in 1984. Seattle also offered the advantage that dividends from subsidiaries were not taxed by the State of Washington.

The relationship of the railroad with the holding company settled into a pattern. Each was relatively comfortable, although Seattle did the teaching while St. Paul had a lot of learning to do. Bressler and his small cadre of executives—fewer than 65 were employed at the holding company—didn't meddle in the day-to-day operation of the railroad, but railroad executives were expected to travel to Seattle for quarterly meetings to review how the railroad was adhering to its business plan. Budgets also had to be approved by the holding company, which controlled and dispensed capital to the various business units.

Bressler explained his thinking on the separation and the move:

> If [any organization has] been around for X number of years, it becomes quite ossified in its thinking and also in its behavior. I don't care what institution you're talking about, whether it's a railroad or a university or a church. . . . A lot of it you could lay at the feet of the fact that it's bureaucratic. The only way that you can really change (a culture) is to change the people. Of course, that's sort of a slow process. You can change people at the top, but you've got to change that culture someplace along the line. That was part of the reason for the moves and splitting up these businesses.

Jim Dagnon, retired BN and BNSF senior vice president of human resources, began his career as a union clerk on the Northern Pacific and was a union official before joining the ranks of management. He had his own perspective on the mergers and the culture of the expanded BN. "There are several things, I think, about a merger that make mergers worthwhile," he said in an interview for this book. "First is improving the franchise. That's got to be the key. It's not just pure integration and savings because of duplicate headquarters, et cetera."

Dagnon saw the meshing of the cultures as crucial to the success of a company like the BN, which had been through multiple mergers:

> Most companies do have a distinct culture. Each culture has
> its own strengths. NP, Great Northern, CB&Q, and Frisco
> had those same distinct cultures. The NP was very frugal. It
> came from Bob Macfarlane, who never spent a dime. NP
> was working on the various resources. Great Northern had
> more high fliers and big spenders who were a little more
> aggressive and a little more decentralized with less struc-
> ture. They were all decent people. So the combination came
> together. . . . [The cultures] were additive. You had a lot
> more action-oriented [culture] when you had the mixed
> team of Great Northern–NP, with the NP more cautious.

With Lou Menk and his years at the Frisco before moving to the
Burlington and then the Northern Pacific, yet another culture was
added, Dagnon observed: "We got a good taste of the Frisco culture,
and it added another whole depth of value. You got this real passion
for cost cutting and leanness as well as the understanding that it isn't
just volume. It's volume and margin, and it added another whole set
of values out of that."

As capital-intensive network businesses, railroads traditionally
had considered volume growth as the most important criterion for
success. It was a proxy for revenue. If a piece of business contributed
one cent above its direct operating expense toward covering fixed
cost, it was worth having, even if ultimately the railroad lost money
on a fully allocated basis. Bressler challenged the revenue focus of
the railroad managers almost from his first day in St. Paul. He pointed out that revenue was meaningless unless there were profits and
that the only measurement that counted for stockholders and investment bankers was return on equity or return on investment. He said
he didn't want to hear his executives talking in terms of revenue.

Alluding to the seeming takeover of the larger BN by Frisco executives, Dagnon said, "The people who could do [the cost cutting]
came in, and that's where all the stories came from about the guppies
that swallowed the whale."

Dagnon believed that the constant thread that served the BN very
well over the years was the ability to focus on crucial issues. "One of
the things that we seemed to be very good at was the single-minded
focus," he said. "We always seemed to have one focus at one point in

time, and as a collection of people could accomplish it. We got confused if there were many more than one."

He cited the period when the focus was on getting enough volume to fully utilize the railroad's capacity:

> We became single-focused on that. Then we evolved to realize, "Wait a minute. Some of the stuff we're even losing money on." Then we began to focus on margin and volume and where we were going. Whatever it was at the time we'd be single-focused on, the place would deliver. . . . It never seemed to be dictatorial. It was sort of the case that somebody gave us a direction. That's what the leader wants. We're going to go get it. Assuming those focuses matched the times and the need at the times, that ability to do it could pull you through almost anything.

Dagnon mentioned the railroad's Herculean effort to maintain operations when the Great Midwest Flood of 1993 forced thousands of miles of rail line out of service as an example of the value of single focus. "The company became single-focused, and people pulled in, a bit like a power company in a power outage," he said.

Grayson's arrival triggered a shift from single focus on traffic volume to single focus on cost cutting. "We really got the fat out with the focus on margins and cutting cost," Dagnon said. The BN also focused on the concept of velocity. "The number of turns per car and per locomotive could mean money. Slower could mean faster, but it was a single-minded focus on velocity," Dagnon explained. Velocity, in the railroad industry, is a measure not of speed but of the utilization of assets.

> "When it came time to focus on the mergers, it was whatever the merger took. It was that single-minded focus," Dagnon explained. "We're going to make this work. We're not going to make this the Penn Central. We're consciously going to mix people and layers so we don't have silos. You get to the point in every merger I've been part of where you say, 'Gee, these are pretty decent guys on the other side. They've got some of the same problems up north that we have down South or back East that we have in the others.'"

Under prodding from Bressler, the railroad began to adapt to his demand that it had to generate its own capital and no longer could rely on natural resources to support rail operations or capital needs.

Bressler was frustrated by the budget process almost from his first day at the BN headquarters in St. Paul. He recalled:

> I got around to talking with Bob Binger [who was in charge of resources before the separate subsidiaries were established] one day. He was a very reticent fellow. I asked Frank Coyne [the BN's chief financial officer], "What goes here? I just can't seem to understand what's going on in these resource businesses. I can't get anything out of Binger." "That's very difficult," Coyne told me. He said they gave Binger a budget of how much cash he had to produce. Of course, that was the secret to the thing.

Bressler discovered that Binger's reluctance to be forthcoming about the resources was based on his experience that any information he gave to the people running the railroad would be used to extract cash from his part of the company. "Of course that turned the light bulb on in terms of exactly how those businesses were run. He deliberately ran them to produce as little as possible," Bressler said. "He was absolutely right that everything he produced, if it turned up in cash, was taken away and something else was done with it. Binger's [impression] was that he just saw that money being poured into the railroad with no results. Of course, to a certain extent he was right." Shortly before the holding company was activated, Binger, the scion of a prominent Twin Cities family, retired.

Finance was a particular interest for Bressler. By his standards, the process of developing the financial plan at the BN was chaotic. He recalled: "I got the fellow who ran the real estate operation in one day. I was trying to find out how people ran these businesses. . . . We had all this property, jillions of acres. I asked him how he determined what was done. He said, 'Well, Mr. Coyne calls me up and tells me to sell some property because we need cash.' That was the way it was, too."

Bressler was determined to end the practice of using resource assets to pay for railroad capital needs. Each unit, he said, "would be changed sufficiently so that it could operate as a stand-alone entity on its own, with good management, and be a viable business."

Preparation of budgets had been equally informal. Bressler said:

The finances were kept very close. I remember toward the end of summer and the early part of fall in 1980, I'd start asking Coyne to tell me a little bit about the budget process around here: "When am I going to see a budget for next year?" "Oh, don't worry about it," he said. "It's under way." I kept pressing. He finally said, "Ray Burton does the budget. He's the treasurer." Ray's a very smart fellow, but he also kept things under his hat. So one day I said, "Ray, I understand you're in charge of the budget process around here," . . . and I asked him how he did that. He said, "Well, we work it out as to what the company has to produce, and then we present it to the board." I asked him when the operating department became involved, and he said, "Oh, you wouldn't dare ask them to put together a budget." I asked him, "How possibly then does the budget have any relationship to reality?" "Well," he said, "it probably doesn't." Well, I found that out in spades.

Burton made the transition to the holding company in Seattle but soon left the BN. After a stay at the Santa Fe, he became chairman, president, and chief executive of TTX Company, a railroad-industry-owned car leasing company.

Regarding the BN's budget process, Bressler added:

Every company that I'd ever been with—GE, American Airlines, or ARCO—had a process. It was far from perfect in a lot of places. But at least there was an understanding that the people who put together something as rudimentary as a budget were the people who were responsible for the operation. That wasn't the case at BN. In fact, the people who ran the operation hadn't the foggiest notion of what it was all about. I shouldn't say it was particularly true in the railroad, because it was true in the resource businesses too. If there was something left over at the end of the year, then everybody cheered.

The Burlington Northern Railroad was going through culture-change overload. The new leadership was trying to force change as rapidly as possible, but the company was more than a century old and its culture was deeply embedded. It would change, but not as quickly as Bressler and his team wanted. If the new leaders had not pressed so hard, though, the change would have come a lot more slowly, if at all. The holding company was demanding that the railroad support itself and no longer rely on cash flow from natural resources to sustain its capital spending. At the railroad, the new executive team was forcing change and new discipline.

The forced change was embodied in the appointment of Big Bill Thompson as executive vice president for operations. Despite his gruff persona, those who knew him found him to be a quite pleasant person. "He was tough as nails," Bressler said. "He came in to see Dick [Grayson] and said, 'You know, Dick, this railroad merged back in 1970, but they've still got shops open all up and down these lines.' He said, 'If we're going to turn this thing around, we're going to have to start closing these shops.'"

Despite the belief of many Burlington Northern executives that he was anti-railroad and that his intent from the beginning was to separate the resource assets from the railroad, Bressler insisted that he found that the railroad property was an excellent set of assets. His goal was to maximize the return on those assets.

In fact, Bressler encouraged the railroad executives to be more aggressive in adopting new technologies that offered the promise of improving operations. He had served on the board of directors of Rockwell International, a leading manufacturer of aircraft control systems based on global positioning satellites, and thought the same technology could improve the railroad dispatch system.

Shortly after he became chief executive, Bressler pressed for significantly more research and development, after learning from his senior staff that the BN had no development projects under way at the time. In the BN annual report for 1980, published a couple of months later, Bressler stated that the BN was going to be undertaking research and development (R&D) to find cheaper, less polluting, domestically available fuels to power the railroad's locomotives.

After an internal search for a research director failed to find anyone acceptable to him, Bressler went outside the BN and selected Steven R. Ditmeyer, a graduate of the Massachusetts Institute of Technology and the associate administrator for research and development at the Federal Railroad Administration. Ditmeyer, who joined the BN in September 1981, was made aware of Bressler's comments to his senior staff, and he had also read the annual report that outlined a plan for an R&D program. Ditmeyer thus was taken aback when his immediate supervisor, the vice president of purchasing and material, instructed him to go slow, to undertake only small projects, and to make sure there were no failures. "He said that this was how things got done on a railroad," Ditmeyer recalled.

In February 1982, Bressler came to St. Paul and met with Ditmeyer and the vice president to learn how the R&D program was progressing. Ditmeyer recalled Bressler's response:

> Look! When are you guys going to start spending some real money? I don't want our suppliers determining what new technologies we adopt and the rate we adopt them. I want you to push the envelope. In the petroleum industry, where I come from, we know we are not being aggressive enough if we are not hitting dry holes. I want you to hit some dry holes. Only then will I know that we have an aggressive R&D program. Furthermore, if you have any "sure thing" projects that cross your desk, I don't want you guys in R&D pursuing them. Pass them on to the folks in engineering, mechanical, or wherever, and let them implement those projects.

In essence, Ditmeyer was given a "license to fail," a rarity in the railroad industry culture.

In April 1985, Ditmeyer received a call from the executive vice president of operations, who said that he had been informed that Bressler wanted him to prepare an R&D presentation for the June board of directors meeting. Told he would have 20 to 30 minutes, Ditmeyer asked for more time because he wanted to show the directors the natural gas–fueled locomotive and the satellite-based train control system he was working on.

The executive vice president doubted Ditmeyer would get the additional time but promised to pass the request along. A couple of days later, Ditmeyer was told that Bressler wanted an hour-long presentation and a field trip to see the locomotive and the control system.

At the June 1985 board meeting, the directors saw the world's first natural gas–fueled locomotive and the world's first satellite-based train control system, called ARES, or Advanced Railroad Electronics System. ARES was installed on two locomotives running between Minneapolis and St. Paul. The board agreed to fund the installation of natural gas conversion kits on two higher-horsepower locomotives to run between the coal fields of Montana and a power plant in Minnesota. The board also agreed to fund the installation of ARES on 17 locomotives to run on the 250-mile loop of track serving the port of Superior, Wisconsin, and the taconite mines of the Mesabi Iron Range in northern Minnesota.

The gas locomotives ran successfully in 1991 and 1992, Ditmeyer noted, adding that, if implemented on a large scale, the technology would have generated a 20 percent annual rate of return. ARES was also tested successfully between 1987 and 1992, and the annual rate of return for an installation on all of the BN was calculated to be greater than 30 percent. Other capital programs offered even greater returns, however, and ARES never was implemented. A frustrated Ditmeyer returned to the Federal Railroad Administration.

Bressler summarized Ditmeyer's period at the railroad: "We hired [Ditmeyer] because he understood the kind of change [that needed to be made]. I said, 'We ought to try out something like this on the railroad.' To my knowledge, it worked pretty successfully. But when push came to shove, [the officers and directors] just wouldn't do it. It was too radical a change." The Electronic Train Management System (ETMS) that BNSF is piloting today is in many ways a descendant of the ARES project, coming more than 20 years later.

The fundamental difference between the new management and the old was that the new people saw themselves as asset managers rather than railroad operators. Walter Drexel, who had been treasurer at ARCO and vice president for planning at its Anaconda Copper subsidiary in Montana, soon followed Bressler to the BN. After a year at the holding company, Drexel was named president and chief operating officer of the railroad, and he added the chief executive title after Grayson effectively retired to become corporate vice chairman in St. Louis at the end of 1982.

Drexel was most outspoken about managing assets and in the process managed to infuriate railroad employees. As Drexel recalled:

> One of the first things I did [upon arriving at the railroad] was to have an interview with *BN on Camera* [a monthly videotaped program for employees]. I made the comment that we weren't as well run a railroad as the UP was. By that, I meant that our financial results were horrible and UP's were pretty good at that time. Of course, everybody just got all upset because they thought all they were supposed to do was run trains. Now, my idea was that you ran

trains for the purpose of making a good financial return for your stockholders.

When I went there, it was amazing to me—the red tape that was involved in [the railroad's] operation. The president of the company used to approve expense accounts. He thought he was busy because he had a bunch of paper shuffling across his desk.

You have to give Lou Menk credit. He recognized that the management that he himself had put in place, and was part of, was not going to be able to cut it in the deregulated environment.

The entire railroad industry was undergoing the first wave of cost cutting that followed deregulation. The BN's was one of the most severe, not necessarily because its costs were particularly higher than at any other railroad, but because its management, which had come from outside the industry and had little or no respect for tradition, dived enthusiastically into the task.

The number of people on the railroad payroll particularly infuriated Drexel. "I think, if my recollection is right, in 1980 there were about 60,000 employees," Drexel noted. "In 1984 there were about 37,000. The revenue had stayed pretty flat. I mean, even cutting all those people had not changed the amount of our revenue, which makes you wonder what those people were doing all that time."

Drexel was driven to increase operating income. "About 1980 or 1981 the operating income was somewhere in the range of 100 million dollars," he said. "In 1984 or 1985 it was 900 million. It irritated me that we didn't make the billion I wanted. But in that process we had to change the culture, try to change the culture."

His efforts to force a culture change didn't endear Drexel to his employees. "We were hated, and you can understand why we were, because here things had been going on for a hundred years, so to speak, one way," Drexel explained. "Revenue was guaranteed by the government. It didn't matter whether you served the customer or not for a long time. . . . You ran trains. To judge whether or not the company was successful was whether or not your trains were run on time. That was all."

Drexel made the decision to move the railroad headquarters from St. Paul to Fort Worth, Texas. Ironically, the decision, announced in mid-1983, came just a year after the company had announced that it was staying in St. Paul, following an extensive relocation study. "I guess that one of the things we did to break up the culture was to move out of St. Paul to Fort Worth," Drexel said. "I know we were strongly disliked by the people in Minnesota [for choosing to move], but I think it was the right thing to do."

Grayson had announced in 1982 that the railroad was considering relocating its headquarters. At the time, Minnesota's economic and tax policies were viewed broadly as unfriendly to business. The first study was thorough and run by the railroad's head of strategic planning. All factors—education, housing, health care, taxes—were considered, and when the study was completed, the railroad decided to stay in St. Paul. In a statement distributed to news media, the railroad said it didn't want the State of Minnesota to misread the decision as an endorsement of its policies. If the business were being started from scratch, the BN said, the railroad would be located elsewhere, but the cost of relocating the headquarters was just more than could be justified.

A year later, after Grayson retired, Drexel told a staff meeting that the railroad was moving, adding, "And this time there will be no study." He instructed Michael Donahue, the railroad's vice president of strategic planning to "put them in a building where nobody would know it was the railroad," recalled Thomas J. Matthews, who had been brought in as senior vice president of administration and human resources. "Those were his very specific instructions, as well as to find a place where [a lot of executives] would not go. Most of the management people whose function was moved to Fort Worth were offered the chance to follow the work. We had some exceptions to that, such as people close to retirement."

The decision was draconian but effective. Despite the success of the Grayson window plan to encourage early retirement, there still were entirely too many people in the headquarters building, and in Drexel's eyes they were resistant to the changes he felt must be made.

In announcing the decision to relocate some one thousand miles to the south, the BN told many managers that they would be included. But for many who were third- or fourth-generation St. Paul–area residents, it was like being told they would not be able to see their grandchildren except occasionally, and they would have to give up the Minnesota lifestyle they valued. Many sought an alternative to relocating to Texas and ended up taking an early retirement option. Some 400 employees chose not to relocate, and the savings came close to offsetting the company's cost of going to Fort Worth. In addition to breaking the old culture, Drexel saw another short-term benefit to moving the railroad headquarters. He told one executive before the move was made that when railroad executives found themselves in Texas, which had no state income tax, "they'll think they've died and gone to heaven." Minnesota's personal income tax rate had been as high as 12 percent.

Drexel, like Bressler, was an outspoken believer in asset management. "Well, that's the way we saw ourselves," he said. "I didn't know how to run trains. I didn't want to know how to run trains. I didn't put steel in the track. I didn't do anything with the ballast. We managed assets, and we managed people."

When Bressler was trying to persuade Drexel to leave ARCO and join him at the BN, he sent Drexel a pile of paper. "He sent me a lot of information on the railroad, a lot of paperwork, and a lot of annual reports and that sort of stuff," Drexel recalled. "The more you looked at it, the more your interest got piqued, or at least mine did. Now, here was an opportunity, I thought, to come in and make a mark by cutting the costs and trying to change the environment, trying to change the culture."

Drexel described what he encountered when he arrived in St. Paul:

> I found out that the culture was much worse than I had anticipated—how locked in everybody was. . . . When I first got there, I talked to them some about customers, and they just looked at me with a blank look like "What in the world is a customer? We run trains. That's what we do. We run trains." The asset that BN had was a tremendous base. I don't think there's any question about that. They had great territory, "great franchise," as the railroad people like to call it. They had a great asset base and probably had more assets—as we found out—than they needed if it was run efficiently.

Always outspoken about his views of traditional railroaders, Drexel said,

> I assumed—and I think it was correct—out of [all these]

people there were bound to be some of them who were pretty good if they were just turned loose. The thing that we immediately thought was that it was a massive, centralized operation. A piece of paper given to that St. Paul office building wouldn't get out in six months, and everybody would have forgotten what it was there for to start with. Arrogance for a hundred-plus years, I guess, was an integral part of the railroad industry, period.

Despite the turmoil caused by the effort to change the railroad culture and to reduce costs wherever possible, some things didn't change. The inexorable consolidation of the railroad industry was one of them. Despite having a reputation as an asset manager who was determined to separate the natural resource assets from the transportation, Bressler was willing to invest money in the railroad where he saw a return on investment. He was willing to make the railroad even larger, although Drexel believed it was almost impossible to manage enterprises as large and as spread out as the BN was.

THE BN PURSUES THE SANTA FE

The BN tried to expand even further in 1982 with a proposal to merge with the Santa Fe. The BN's first try to acquire the Santa Fe came while much of the railroad industry was focused on whether Conrail—successor to Penn Central and other eastern bankrupts and still owned by the federal government—was viable or whether it would be broken up and sold in pieces. Conrail had been losing about $1 million a day ever since its creation in 1976. The BN had a committee analyzing Conrail and trying to decide which lines they would try to purchase if, as it then seemed, Conrail was liquidated.
Bressler had other ideas:

> I went to call on John Reed [then Santa Fe Industries chief executive] because it was fairly apparent that a merger of those two properties—plus the fact that they had all those resources at the same time—it was a good fit. John was always in the operations room. That's where he spent his time. Then they'd have to call him. He'd have to come up, and I could tell that I was boring him because he kept looking at his watch as if he had to get back.

Our proposal made him very, very uncomfortable. When I first proposed it, I recognized that he was uncomfortable with me in talking about that. So I took Grayson with me on another visit because he knew Dick, and Dick was kind of old-shoe. They would chat a little bit about one thing or another. But Dick also recognized that would have been a good merger if we could have pulled it off. So we talked and talked. John would listen, but he would never say very much.

Reed didn't respond to the BN's proposal. Bressler described the BN's next move:

So we went down to see him again. Again it was the same sort of a pattern—a little byplay. Finally, I said, "Well, John, we're here because we thought that by now you'd have some response to us on our proposal." With that, he reaches into his pocket. He pulls out his billfold. Then there's this slip of paper, obviously written by his general counsel. He read from the paper: "The Santa Fe has no interest in a merger with the BN at this time." He folds up the slip of paper and puts it back in his pocket.

Not long after rejecting the BN overture, Reed and Benjamin Franklin Biaggini, chief executive of the Southern Pacific, announced that Santa Fe Industries and the Southern Pacific Company would merge, and it was clear that the Santa Fe would be the dominant partner, which explained Reed's reluctance to consider the BN overture. Santa Fe Industries and the Southern Pacific Company gained quick approval from the Justice Department and merged, placing the Southern Pacific Transportation Company subsidiary in a voting trust while the ICC considered the rail merger. The merger was to prove a disaster for both railroads.

Even before the Frisco merger, the Burlington Northern and most other railroads had become engaged in a fight to oppose legislation facilitating the construction of coal slurry pipelines, which would have threatened the expansion of the western coal business. In a slurry line, pulverized coal is mixed with water and is pumped through the pipe.

A consortium of utilities and construction and energy companies proposed in the mid-1970s to run a 36-inch-diameter pipeline some 1,500 miles from the Powder River Basin southeast to a large generating complex at White Bluff, Arkansas. The pipeline would have had a capacity of 25 million tons a year, which at that time would have absorbed much of the growth from the Powder River Basin. Ironically, some industry observers feel that, considering the dramatic growth of the coal business and the cost of fighting the slurry pipeline, the railroads might have been better off letting it be built.

The pipeline promoters originally approached the BN and proposed that the pipeline be built along the BN right-of-way and that the BN become a partner in the venture, with the right-of-way as its investment. The railroad's studies showed, however, that its participation would provide less income to the railroad than if it carried the coal itself.

The battle was over legislation that would have granted state and/or federal power of eminent domain—the right to take private property for a public purpose—to the pipeline promoters, something the railroads never had received during the 19th-century building boom, although railroads received state eminent domain authority and had the right to cross public lands in the West. The pipeline promoters needed eminent domain authority because the railroads refused to allow the pipeline to cross their rights-of-way.

A secondary front in the pipeline dispute was over water. Water was a crucial issue in the arid West. If the pipeline had been built, it would have required large amounts of water to be mixed with the pulverized coal. At the discharge end, the coal would have been centrifuged out of the slurry mixture and the highly acidic waste water discharged into the Mississippi River.

The developers—a consortium of Arkansas Power and Light, ARCO, Bechtel Corporation engineers, and Kansas-Nebraska Pipeline organized as Energy Transportation Systems Incorporated (ETSI)—proposed to build a pipeline to carry water from Lake Oahe, one of the Missouri River impoundments in South Dakota, to the Gillette, Wyoming, area. At one time the promoters even proposed using local sewage effluent as the fluid, which would have required permits before the effluent could be dumped into the Mississippi. The refusal of states to give up their water led to their refusal to grant eminent domain, which caused the developers to turn to the federal government.

When another group of developers in the late 1970s proposed a pipeline in the East to carry coal from West Virginia and Kentucky to utility plants in Florida, the railroad industry united in its opposition to the two-front threat to the coal business, then the largest single commodity carried by railroads. The railroads were joined in the campaign by environmental interests and by rail unions that feared a further loss of jobs. The AFL-CIO and the U.S. Chamber of Commerce, on the other hand, sided with pipeline developers on the grounds that it would create construction jobs and would lower the cost of electricity. Although the railroads succeeded several times in delaying a vote in Congress, it was virtually impossible to kill the competitive threat, as the pipeline developers would come back in the next congressional session.

The only operating coal slurry pipeline in the United States, ironically, was owned by the Southern Pacific Company, the holding company for the Southern Pacific railroad. It carried coal several hundred miles from an Indian reservation in northern Arizona to the Mojave power plant on the Colorado River between Arizona and California. There were no rail lines or highways in that area, and when the SP studied the proposed move, it determined that for the single commodity involved it would be cheaper to build a pipeline than a railroad.

Ultimately, the railroads were successful in blocking the eminent domain legislation, and when ARCO dropped out of the consortium and wrote off its initial $25 million investment, the pipeline proposal collapsed. Informed by a staff member that ARCO had written off $25 million, Drexel shrugged and said, "A dry hole." ETSI filed suit against the western railroads, charging that they had engaged in illegal restraint of trade in their efforts to block its venture. Faced with the loss of potentially hundreds of millions of dollars, most of the railroads chose to settle.

The settlement cost the BN $150 million, and Bressler remembers making the decision to settle after reading a deposition that the now retired Lou Menk had given, in which Menk lost his temper. "I loved Lou, but he would open his mouth at inopportune times. Of course, that cost us plenty," Bressler said.

The Santa Fe passed on the opportunity to settle, choosing to go to court in Beaumont, Texas. Robert D. (Rob) Krebs had been president of the Southern Pacific, then moved to Chicago when the Santa Fe and the SP decided to merge. He eventually became chief executive officer of the Santa Fe and later was chief executive of the BNSF after the 1995 BN–Santa Fe merger. He recalled the pipeline suit and settlement as one of the more bitter experiences of his tenure at the Santa Fe.

Krebs—and others who followed the trial—believed the federal district judge who was hearing the suit sided with the pipeline plaintiffs against the railroad. As he put it,

> We were winning. We had the case won. I went into court the Friday before the trial ended. [The judge] called our general counsel, and I was there too, so I went with him into his chambers. The judge said, "You know, you guys have put on a great case here. I believe you're going to win this thing hands down. If I were you, what I would do"— and this is down in Beaumont, Texas, in a U.S. District Court—"if I were you, what I would do is I would put whatever money you want in an offer to settle on the table, and it's due over the weekend. We're going to have our closing arguments the first part of next week. I'm going to give the instructions to the jury, and we'll know by the middle of the week what the answer is."
>
> So we thought about it over the weekend. We put $80 million on the table, which infuriated him so much that Monday morning, over the transom from the judge, came a partially directed verdict saying the Santa Fe was guilty. Once he sat up there with his robe on and read that to the jury, it was all over.

Fifteen years later, Krebs still smarts over the "railroading" the Santa Fe received. "I figured it's a federal court," he said. "We could have settled for $160 million, and our maximum was $150. We didn't go the extra ten, and it was the biggest mistake of my life. It cost us $320 million."

Alan Fitzwater, a former BN vice president in charge of lobbying and public affairs, has long believed that the railroad should have dropped its opposition to the coal slurry pipeline for strategic reasons. The fight over the pipeline issue occurred at the same time that the BN was trying to keep the North Western out of the Powder River Basin. The pipeline could have been financed only if the developers had take-or-pay contracts with the utilities, meaning they would be obligated to pay the contracted amount whether they took the coal or not. But once the 25 million tons of coal was under contract, the pipeline ceased to be a competitive threat because it couldn't accept any more coal.

Fitzwater, who once headed the ICC's Rail Services Planning Office, believed that the ICC was concerned only that the BN not have a monopoly on the coal business. If the pipeline were a certainty, he said, the ICC may very well have rescinded its order that the C&NW be a 50 percent owner of the coal line. If that were the case, based on coal volume moved out of the basin in the first years of the 21st century, the BNSF's coal business would be almost twice what it is and rates undoubtedly would be higher.

While ultimately the UP probably would have acquired the C&NW to gain its double-track high-speed line between Omaha and Chicago, the UP would not have been the major competitor that it is in the coal business today. Coal transportation also would be much more profitable for the BNSF because the brutal rate competition with the UP would not have driven rates down as far as they have gone.

A principal reason for going outside the company to find a new CEO in 1980 had been the board's desire that the natural resource assets of the BN be developed more aggressively. Bressler did just that. When the holding company was created in early 1981, the subsidiaries of Burlington Northern Incorporated were Burlington Northern Railroad; Milestone Petroleum; Meridian Minerals; Plum Creek Lumber; Burlington Truck Lines; Burlington Northern Air Freight, a rapidly growing forwarder; and Glacier Park Company, a real estate subsidiary. The BN was a major landowner in Seattle, Minneapolis, St. Paul, and Denver and had thousands of acres of developable land throughout the West. Investments in the railroad now were determined by the capital it could finance with its own operating income and cash flow. Each of the subsidiaries had its own management, and for the first time each was expected to maximize earnings rather than operate as a "piggy bank" for the railroad.

Jim Dagnon, who worked for many years at the railroad and then was with the holding company for three years before returning to the railroad, put the holding company issue in perspective:

> You had the railroad, you had the minerals, and you had the land, et cetera. We were spending some time managing it and making some money off it and leasing the land, et cetera. But in many ways it was really subsidizing the railroad operation to some degree, not a lot but some. When

you're doing that, it gave you a reason not to be necessarily
as efficient in railroading as you had to be. Bressler came
and pulled those out. We really began to manage and focus.
Now the railroad numbers and results are out there totally
by themselves.

Traditional railroad operating executives didn't like the loss of
the cushion that the resource assets had long provided. Dagnon,
however, saw the benefit that accrued to stockholders, particularly
after the spin-off and complete separation of the railroad from the
resources. He explained:

> You really had to focus on the railroad business, and we
> had to focus on the timber business and the trucking busi-
> ness and all the other pieces we had. If you looked at every
> one of the spin-offs that we had, the shareholders gained.
> You could have bought any one of those [initial public
> offerings], and I bought many of them, and you just gained.
> You really did. In the meantime, the railroad had to fight
> day to day. Not only did the spin-off leave the railroad with
> the debt, but [the railroad was] the cash cow. The cash cow
> managed to pay that debt down to a debt-to-equity ratio of
> 30 or 35, which is unbelievable.

Bressler never received the credit he should have for setting the
BN on the path to its current industry-leading position, Dagnon
believed. "He set the railroad off on its own in a way that it had to
perform to survive," Dagnon pointed out, "and with the cash flow
and getting the debt-to-equity ratio down we could afford to go after
the Santa Fe, and go after it before UP did."

Although the company wanted to separate the railroad totally
from the other businesses, that proved extremely difficult to accomplish.

When the Northern Pacific had gone into bankruptcy in the Panic
of 1893, the reorganized railroad that emerged in 1896 was in poor
physical condition. In order to make the new NP debt more attractive to lenders, the company pledged its natural resource assets that
stemmed from the original Pacific Railway Act land grant as security
for two new issues of Northern Pacific bonds. The indenture was
crafted to protect lenders by ensuring that the railroad would be

properly maintained and that sufficient capital investment would go to the railroad.

The two issues of bonds, one due in 1996, the other in 2046, had no sinking-fund requirements and were not callable. Proceeds of natural resource sales or operations were held by the indenture trustee of the bonds until the railroad management certified that an equal or greater amount had been invested in the railroad. In effect, every time the Northern Pacific cut a tree or mined a ton of coal, the funds were held by the bond trustee. When the company certified that it had invested an equal or greater amount of money in the railroad, the funds were released.

This was not a significant problem for most of the century after the bonds were issued, because the NP needed large capital expenditures. The growing value of coal reserves, however, made it obvious that a time would come when the company either would be pouring more capital into the railroad than was prudent or it would not be able to realize the full value of the natural resource assets. This became increasingly true following the Northern Lines merger when the NP lines largely became secondary to parallel Great Northern lines and required less investment. If the proceeds of resource operations or sales could not be used for the benefit of stockholders, the existence of the NP bonds obviously was a disincentive to developing the resources.

The bonds, however, paid a rate of interest—4 percent for the 1996 bonds and 3 percent for the 2046 issue—that was extremely low by the standards of the 1980s. The Burlington Northern needed to get the general lien released on nontransportation assets so that the holding company could proceed with their development.

The problem of the NP bonds consumed the attention of several chief financial officers and the company's outside financial advisers. One observer was quoted in *Business Week* magazine as saying, "Corporate sainthood is reserved for the person who solves the NP bond problem."

At one point, the BN informally tried to get the U.S. Treasury to issue a new bond with a maturity that matched the NP bonds. Under its plan the company would purchase the entire issue of government bonds and deposit them with the trustee. That would substitute the full faith and credit of the U.S. government for the security of the natural resource assets of the Northern Pacific as protection for the bondholders, which would have allowed the trustee to release the pledged resource assets. The government, which did not issue bonds with a maturity longer than 30 years, considered the BN proposal to be a private issue and declined to issue the debt.

BN managers then came up with a plan they hoped would get the bond owners to trade in their bonds for a new issue that had a higher rate of interest but without the onerous conditions. They proposed in 1985 to buy back the bonds at a deep discount from face value, paying for them with a new debt issue that would carry a higher rate of interest but would not have the lien on the nontransportation assets. The BN would deposit enough government securities with the bond trustee to guarantee all principal and interest payments as they came due. Bondholders liked the security of the original-issue bonds, and because bonds trade at prices based on current interest rates—bond prices fall when interest rates rise, and they rise when interest rates fall—the bondholders were not willing to accept the deep discount.

A group of bondholders sued and won a preliminary injunction that blocked execution of the plan, leading the BN to drop the plan. After additional legal wrangling, the parties negotiated a final settlement of the NP bond dispute in 1987. In the notice of settlement, the U.S. District Court for the Southern District of New York pointed out that, if the litigation had proceeded, the plaintiffs would not have gained monetarily and that the injunction had given them the opportunity to negotiate a more favorable settlement than the railroad originally had proposed.

The settlement defeased the NP bonds. The railroad agreed to pay $35.5 million into a fund that would be distributed to bondholders at the rate of $14.75 for each $100 of face value of the 1996 bonds and $45.625 for each $100 face value of the 2046 bonds. The bondholders would keep their bonds, which would continue to accrue interest but without the security of the lien on nontransportation property. In effect, the BN bought back the natural resource lien.

Once the deal was done, it was relatively easy to restructure the company. The railroad transferred the resource assets to the holding company in the form of a dividend, finally separating the natural resource assets from the rail assets. Burlington Northern Incorporated remained in existence under the plan, and its principal asset was the Burlington Northern Railroad Company. A new company, Burlington Resources Incorporated, was created. It held the former BNI natural resource companies, along with El Paso Corporation, which BNI had acquired in a hostile takeover a few years earlier.

The acquisition of El Paso Corporation is an example of

Bressler's strategic thinking. Burlington Northern Air Freight Incorporated (BNAFI), BNI's air freight subsidiary, was growing rapidly, but people who understood the business knew that if it was to remain competitive, it soon would be forced to buy a fleet of aircraft and become a carrier rather than a forwarder. United Parcel Service, which long had relied on others to provide its "lift," encountered the same problem in the mid-1980s and today is one of the world's largest air carriers. Bressler didn't see the return if BNAFI were to buy as much as $500 million of aircraft and take on the personnel and operating expenses that would go with such an investment, so he arranged a sale of BNAFI to the Pittston Company, which also owned Brinks Incorporated, for $177 million in cash. The proceeds of the BNAFI sale funded the acquisition of El Paso Corporation.

Stock in Burlington Resources was issued to Burlington Northern stockholders, and the two companies each traded on the New York Stock Exchange. Other than sharing similar names, the two entities were completely independent of each other. While the legal structure had Burlington Resources as a spin-off of Burlington Northern, in actuality the railroad had been spun off and set loose. Bressler and his principal advisers remained with Burlington Resources. In the separation process, much of the corporation's large debt was assigned to the railroad.

Meanwhile, Walter Drexel had retired at the railroad. He was succeeded as chief executive by Darius Gaskins, who had been chairman of the Interstate Commerce Commission when the Staggers Rail Act was enacted. When Gaskins left government service, he spent a year with an oil, gas, and shipping conglomerate, before joining Burlington Northern in 1982 as senior vice president of marketing and sales. A West Point graduate who earned an advanced engineering degree at the University of Michigan, Gaskins had been in the Air Force space program. When the military lost its manned space flight program to the civilian National Aeronautics and Space Administration, he resigned his commission in 1967 and went back to school, earning a doctorate in economics at Michigan.

Encouraged by his advisers at Michigan, Gaskins stayed in academia for a while, joining the economics faculty at the University of California at Berkeley. As Gaskins recalled,

> I went there, and it was OK for a year or two. Then it got a little boring, because I was teaching the same course. I was still interested in the government, but Berkeley's on the

West Coast. After three years, I asked them for a leave of
absence and went back [to Washington, D.C. in 1973] to
work at the Department of the Interior on resource policy.
Energy was a hot-button issue then because of the Arab oil
embargo that followed U.S. support for Israel during the
[1973 Yom Kippur] war.

From the Interior Department, Gaskins moved to the Federal
Trade Commission as director of its Bureau of Economics, then
moved on to the Civil Aeronautics Board, the regulatory agency for
airlines. There he was in charge of economic studies under Alfred
Kahn, a Cornell University economics professor who was working
temporarily in the Carter administration. When Kahn moved to the
White House as the economic czar, Gaskins moved to the Department of Energy. Then President Carter appointed him to the Interstate Commerce Commission in 1979, and he was designated its
chairman. "So there I was at the ICC," Gaskins said. "That was an
interesting period because we had a lot of momentum toward deregulation. Carter wanted it. The truckers were very upset."

Gaskins served as chairman of the ICC during the period when
deregulation was being debated and enacted. He also was one of the
few chairmen of the ICC whose education and professional background qualified him for the position. The ICC had been known for
many years as a sinecure for people who were owed political favors.

During Gaskins tenure at the ICC, the agency approved the BN
acquisition of the Frisco and was forced to deal with the shutdown
and liquidation of the Rock Island and then the sale of the Milwaukee, which would have been liquidated if the sale to the Soo Line had
not been possible. As rail deregulation began to move through the
legislative process, the ICC began to deal with the industry's new
power to engage in differential pricing—charging different rates to
different customers for essentially identical service.

Grayson, now president and chief executive of the BN, wanted to
bring Gaskins to the railroad, but Gaskins decided that, considering
his involvement in the BN-Frisco transaction approval, it would not
be appropriate for him to go from the ICC directly to the BN. After
a year at Natomas Incorporated in Houston, Gaskins decided he
wanted a different career path. "So I called up the two guys in the
rail industry, the two companies that had shown some interest in me

when I was at the commission," Gaskins said in an interview for this book. "One was the BN. The other was the Santa Fe."

As Gaskins told the story,

> I had a strong feeler from Dick Grayson and a strong feeler from Larry Cena [now Santa Fe president] and John Reed. Reed was gone. I called up Cena and said, "Look. I've got to decide something in 30 days. Would you ask your people if there's any interest? If there is an interest, I'd be interested in talking to you." I called up Dick Bressler. Two weeks later, Grayson and Drexel came down to Fort Worth. I was in Houston. I flew up to Fort Worth. We met at the Hyatt Hotel. We had dinner, and they offered me a job as head of marketing. I had never heard from Larry Cena, but six months later he said, "By the way, I talked to my guys and they said they didn't have any need," or something like that.

That was Gaskins's introduction to the way railroads did business. "It didn't surprise me," he noted. "I wouldn't have been surprised if none of them had any need. What shocked me was that Bressler, that these guys, offered me a job. But the interesting thing is that Bressler was probably calling the shots, but the people who negotiated the deal and everything were Grayson and Drexel."

Gaskins said he had problems getting control of the marketing department while old-BN hand Richard Gleason was vice president of marketing, but that all changed at the beginning of 1983 when Drexel became chief executive. Gaskins arrived in St. Paul during the period of Frisco control of the BN and saw the need for culture change that Bressler and Drexel had seen. He observed:

> I really did think that the only way this railroad was going to really get where it needed to be was that we had to change the culture for everybody. We couldn't just have a select group that knew what the answer was, because you could already see the Frisco guys running into trouble. They knew how to run a railroad, at least a railroad in the southeastern part of the United States—a small railroad—and they were used to yelling at people and bossing them around. But it wasn't clear they knew what they were doing with the big Rocky Mountain railroad.

Gaskins had a good working relationship with Drexel, and after the railroad moved to Fort Worth, Gaskins was named president in 1985, while Drexel remained chief executive. A short time later, when Drexel took an early retirement, Gaskins became chief executive. Gaskins furthered the forced culture change at the BN in two ways. Like Drexel before him, he had no long-term relationships, which made it easier to replace executives who he was convinced could not make the transition to the deregulated environment. He also began to bring in executives from outside the railroad industry who had a strong knowledge of the commodity businesses that were crucial to the railroad. "We had to hire people from the outside," he said. "Some of the best things we did were that we hired customers, smart customers, in the marketing department. We hired Rich Carter and Phil Weaver." Carter and Weaver were agricultural experts who had been executives with major BN customer companies.

Gaskins saw that as the start of real marketing at the BN. "What a difference it made," he said. "What a difference. We did cooperative deals with other railroads, and if I could have beaten down some of their resistance, we would have made even more progress." He cited an agreement with Canadian National that gave the BN access to the industrial complex area of Detroit, Michigan, and Windsor, Ontario, and gave the CN access to Kansas City. Prior to the agreement, neither railroad had been able to handle freight directly for its own account beyond Chicago, and because the distance from Chicago to Kansas City and Detroit was relatively short, many shippers opted to use trucks rather than unreliable rail interline service.

Not all the proposed deals were successful. "We tried and tried with CSX [Transportation] and Norfolk Southern," Gaskins recalled. "They were both—particularly CSX—frustrating to me, because I knew [CSX chief executive] John Snow very well then. I could talk to him. He's an economist. He and I would have a deal in concept, and it would never get done. It would never get done, because when he talked to his operating people or marketing people, they gave him 97 reasons why it couldn't get done."

The BN, under Gaskins and the new marketing leaders he brought in, began to do things that no railroad ever had done before. Carter came up with the idea of selling Certificates of Transportation (COTs) at auction. A certificate holder had an assurance that a specified number of grain cars would be spotted for loading at a point of its choosing by a specified date and at the price agreed to at the auction. The BN was able to gain approval from the ICC to commit up to half its grain-car fleet for the service, reserving the other half for traditional tariff grain service, a protection for smaller shippers. The idea was that the grain dealers and growers and their customers all operated in a free market where various parties were able to profit— and lose—from the supply-and-demand movements of grain prices. Only the railroad had failed to participate.

With COTs, the BN began to capture some of the opportunities. When grain demand was rising, transportation demand would increase and the railroad's grain cars would bring a higher price at the weekly auction. COTs also were transferable, so if a customer had acquired one but later had no need for the transportation, the customer could sell the COT to someone with a greater need. Gaskins pointed out, "The COTs also was the notion that we really had to get into the business development aspect, in which you're trying to get people to site facilities on your property."

Gaskins and Bressler had different views of the railroad. Gaskin described the difference:

> I saw it as an opportunity. He saw it as just something to get rid of and to drain a cow. So his view was, "You guys generate the cash. We're going invest it in oil and gas." That was his call. I don't have a quarrel with that. But it turns out with the benefit of history [that] it was not a very good choice. The pipe on El Paso Pipeline was a hell of a transmission line. The energy stuff itself was a poor investment. We never did find the right set of people to run that even though the pipeline's well run. The energy company I don't think had ever had world-class leadership in it.

A FIGHT—AND A SEPARATION

The spin-off of Burlington Resources from Burlington Northern Incorporated led to the 1989 resignation of Gaskins and the elevation of Gerald Grinstein from vice chairman of the holding company to chief executive of the railroad. Grinstein had joined the company after successfully selling Western Airlines to Delta Airlines as the airline industry also contracted following deregulation. A Seattle lawyer and University of Washington graduate, Grinstein had been one of the young lawyers who served in staff positions for Senator Warren Magnuson in Congress. Grinstein rose to chief counsel of the Senate Commerce Committee before going back to practice law in Seattle.

As Gaskins recalled, the holding company, with the help of investment bankers, planned to break itself up:

> They came up with a super plan, which was that they were going to bust the company into three parts. It was a dynamite plan. It was the best thing that ever happened to the BN railroad when we got rid of the holding company. It's the best thing that ever happened to El Paso when they got control of their destiny again. It was the best thing that happened to the real estate company and the other ones that couldn't make it, because the market proved they couldn't make it. They didn't go anywhere.

An initial supporter of the breakup, Gaskins said:

> It was clearly a good plan. I supported it. Everybody supported it. We were working towards it.
>
> Then it gets ugly, because the real estate guys and Tom [O'Leary, a BNI vice chairman] say, "We have to have a lot of property to put in this real estate company. It's got to be worth a billion dollars or we can't go to the market with an [initial public offering]." So they wanted to get a lot of the land under the railroad, not just all our property but also the land under the right-of-way. We had a knock-down, drag-out meeting, an interesting meeting. Grinstein [already in Fort Worth as vice chairman] was bitching because Grinstein loves the notion of a railroad the way it used to be. He thought it was wrong to take all the money out of the railroad. . . . He thought it was wrong to take the land away from the railroad when we're splitting it up, but there's a meeting to discuss how much of the assets are going to go from the railroad to the real estate company.

Gaskins suggested that Grinstein's resistance didn't go much beyond complaining. Gaskins recalled that Grinstein had him attend the meeting by himself to represent the railroad's interests:

> Chris Bailey [chief law officer of BNI] was running the real estate company, and all he wanted was a billion dollars' worth of land. Bressler was not stupid. He listened to the arguments. He gave me exactly what I wanted. We would

give up all the property that's not immediately associated with railroad development . . . but basically he had to give us the property under our fixed plant. We couldn't operate without that. It didn't make any sense if you gave some of the real estate under the railroad. We'd be fighting over that for years. Bressler said, "Well, so be it."

But that was not the end of the internal machinations. According to Gaskins,

But then I got the documents. The documents included giving some of the land under the railroad to the resource company to get one billion dollars' worth of land for the resource company. We were all ready to split the thing up. The documents they asked me to sign—I said, "I'm not going to sign them. . . . This is wrong. I cannot sign this document. It's not the right thing to do, and I'll put in my resignation. So unless they cave and give us the land on the railroad, I'm not going to sign it and I'll put in my resignation."

When Bressler heard that Gaskins was prepared to resign over the breakup plan, he couldn't understand. He believed that Gaskins had been given everything he asked for. "Bressler didn't know about the final details," Gaskins said. "He knew about the meeting in his office where he pronounced the rules. The devil's in the details, though."

As Gaskins remembered it, that dispute took place in June 1987. "Just after that we had a strategic planning conference," he said. "The bust-up was going to take place at the end of the year. It was pretty clear the way Bressler talked that he was anticipating that I was basically gone." Gaskins had agreed to stay until September 1989, seven years after coming to the railroad and five years after becoming president.

Setting the railroad off by itself was a good thing, Gaskins believed. "It wasn't a bad deal at all," he said. "There was nothing wrong with the debt. The railroad could service the debt, and they did service the debt. I can't say that anything bad happened because we had all the debt." He did observe ruefully, "One thing that did irritate is that the same board members who voted to dividend all that cash . . . and that voted for all those oil and gas acquisitions, the day Jerry came over, they were wringing their hands and saying, 'We've got too much debt on this property.' I said, 'Wait a minute. I never voted for these debts.'"

Grinstein, who now headed the Burlington Northern Railroad, told *Forbes* magazine after the spin-off, "The standing joke was that they [Burlington Resources] got the gold and we [the railroad] got the shaft." Grinstein, who was the one officer who had a choice of which company he would join, chose the railroad. Several members of the board also chose to remain with the railroad, somewhat to Bressler's surprise.

With debt of more than $2 billion, Grinstein focused on reducing the railroad's debt-to-capital ratio, which he succeeded in doing. But the railroad paid a price by being forced to cut back on its purchases of locomotives, the single largest capital expenditure for most railroads. The BN eventually became an underpowered railroad. The lack of a reliable up-to-date locomotive fleet affected service, and the BN had trouble meeting its customers' expectations, as well as its own. It would not be until after the BN merger with the Santa Fe in late 1995 that the company moved aggressively to renew its locomotive fleet.

The 1980s were marked by a period of contentious labor relations as Burlington Northern—like other railroads—tried to rein in costs. Total compensation took nearly one-third of every revenue dollar at most railroads. Under Walter Drexel, the company had begun a number of initiatives designed to gain greater productivity from fewer people.

The BN also engaged in an extensive program to rid itself of thousands of miles of branch lines, also part of its drive to reduce labor costs. Under railroad labor agreements, the same wages and work rules applied on branch lines as on main lines. Many light-density lines were unprofitable simply because the traffic that originated or terminated on them didn't generate enough revenue to cover their cost of operation. Operating costs generally were higher because there was more handling of cars, and gathering and distribution require more labor. Because steel rail was lighter on branch lines than on main lines, trains on the branch lines had to move at slower speeds. An 80-mile round-trip on a 40-mile branch line could exhaust the allowable on-duty time of a crew, requiring a second crew to relieve the first one and bring the train in.

In early 1981 the BN filed with the ICC its intent to abandon some 4,000 miles of branch lines over several years. A firestorm followed throughout the agricultural regions served by the railroad, because most of the lines that were candidates for abandonment were in those regions.

Today, because of rulings by the ICC in the mid-1980s that made it possible, branch lines frequently are sold or leased to short-line operating companies that have lower costs than major railroads, thus preserving the rail traffic. Even where workers are represented by rail unions, the short lines generally have less stringent work rules that allow them to operate at lower cost. In the years immediately following deregulation, however, the choice for a major railroad was simple: operate the branch lines or abandon them.

The BN move to abandon 4,000 miles of branch lines would result in the loss of thousands of rail jobs. Workers could exercise their union seniority and "bump" to jobs in other locations, but that would result in less senior workers losing their jobs. This campaign coincided with the railroad's decision to close hundreds of agencies across its system and to require that customers deal by telephone— the personal computer would come later—with a centralized customer service center. As a result of agreements made during the northern lines merger, many BN workers not only had lifetime job income protection but also could not be forced to relocate against their will. The unions took the BN all the way to the U.S. Supreme Court, which ruled in favor of the railroad's right to abandon lines whose continued operation, in the railroad's judgment, made no economic sense. Although the thrust may have been to reduce labor costs, the actual program was not a labor dispute, the court ruled. Income protection for displaced workers would be another issue for the ICC to deal with under its procedures. Management, in this case, had the right to manage its business.

The BN also moved to reduce the amount of main-line trackage it operated. One day in a meeting in his office, Drexel told an employee communications official that the railroad was operating too much trackage and would have to reduce it. "We've already started the process of abandoning 4,000 miles," the official told him. "I don't mean branch lines," Drexel said. "I mean main lines."

Perhaps there was simply a lack of faith that the railroad really could grow its business, but nevertheless the BN moved to eliminate its main lines between Laurel, Montana, near Billings, and Sandpoint, Idaho, and the line over Stampede Pass in Washington. Like the Stampede Pass line, the Montana line was a segment of the original Northern Pacific main line. It also crossed two mountain ranges and was relatively costly to operate.

The actual sale of the lines occurred after Gaskins had succeeded Drexel. Gaskins said:

> The Montana Railway was a very tough thing to get done, but the logic was that we don't need two lines across Montana. Montana's killing us. We've got an environmental problem on the southern line [the former NP main line]. We've got the worst labor relationship on the southern line than any other we've got on the whole railroad. Why don't we find somebody to buy that and operate it as a captive to us?"

The Montana line sale also was a signal to the rail unions that change was going to happen one way or another.

The Stampede Pass line was part of a parcel of lines that were sold to short-line Washington Central, while the Montana line was sold to investor Dennis Washington, who created Montana Rail Link (MRL). To make the latter deal work, the BN signed a contract guaranteeing MRL an annual minimum amount of overhead traffic—business that neither originated nor terminated on the line. The BN would hand over westbound trains to MRL at Laurel, and MRL crews would operate the trains to Sandpoint, where they were returned to the BN.

After the 1995 merger of the BN and the Santa Fe, with intermodal traffic growing rapidly and the railroad encountering congestion on its existing routes east from Seattle, BNSF reacquired the Stampede Pass line and rebuilt the tracks to open the route over the pass. The Montana Rail Link arrangement had proved costly to the BN. Rob Krebs, who had become chief executive of BNSF, sought also to recover the Montana lines from Montana Rail Link, but the BN lawyers had written a good contract, and Washington refused to sell it back. BNSF still hands a significant number of through trains over to MRL.

Only a year after the 1984 move of the railroad to its new headquarters in a high-rise office building in downtown Fort Worth—Drexel had achieved Bressler's mandate that no one know there was a railroad there—Drexel decided to take early retirement. Some sources have said he was nudged out by Bressler, who originally had brought him to the BN from ARCO and who had decided he wanted to make Gaskins the railroad chief executive. Drexel said only that he had not seen Bressler since the day he walked out of the Seattle headquarters of the holding company. He added, "Dick Bressler had the habit of falling in love with strange people. I always put Gaskins in that category. He was head of the ICC, and Dick thought that was important."

Gaskins clearly knew that none of the major railroads would be able to compete with truckers or win back traffic already lost unless the cost structure was changed. High wages were only the most visible of railroad labor costs. Restrictive work rules ran the costs up even higher. The process was marked by long, drawn-out negotiations, as railroads, the BN among them, had to deal with as many as 14 separate unions, each of which feared that another union might be able to negotiate a better deal in the periodic rounds of negotiations.

A rigid craft system resulted in less than efficient work assignments. Changing a fuel pump on a locomotive, for example, which might take one worker only a half hour, quickly became a multihour project when sheet metal workers, electricians, and mechanics all asserted their right to some of the work. Each of the workers also was guaranteed a minimum amount of time, which further increased costs. The work rules had evolved over nearly a century and were subject to interpretation. Many of these restrictions were eased in later national agreements.

Gaskins the economist frequently was frustrated by the labor situation. "It was the frustration over the whole area of not being able to get [the unions] to see that if we had too many crews, there was a whole level of business that we could not pick up, and it would be better for them than us to hurry to get it done," Dagnon said. "So with that frustration came, 'Well, if we can't do it one way, we'll do it another. So let's try to find another bridge.'"

The BN, like other railroads, was saddled with crew size agreements that went back to the age of steam locomotives and with business practices that were more than half a century old. Crew consist, as it is called in the railroad industry, is set by negotiated agreements with the unions that represent on-train crews. At the BN, it meant that every freight train usually had five crew members.

It became an article of faith in the industry that if railroads could reduce their crew costs, which were the largest single element of the operating-cost structure, they could recapture business lost to truckers. Some railroads were able to persuade their unions that if they were allowed to run with smaller—less expensive—crews, they would operate shorter, faster trains more frequently and that would bring in new business, which would provide new jobs. The deals that were negotiated allowed so-called short-crew operations only on intermodal trains carrying trailers. The railroads that achieved these short-crew agreements also committed to use them only for new business. The vast majority of other operations continued with full crews.

The BN sought similar deals and was modestly successful at reaching agreements with the unions representing workers in its southern region. But the United Transportation Union (UTU) in the North proved intractable. The BN found itself running what it called Expediter trains on part of the railroad but not across the northern tier. With four and five crew members, the Expediters were uneconomic in that corridor.

Gaskins came up with the novel idea of using the Winona Bridge Railway Company—a nonoperating BN subsidiary that owned a bridge across the Mississippi between Winona, Minnesota, and Winona, Wisconsin—as a vehicle to get around the UTU intransigence. Winona Bridge would be granted trackage rights to operate trains across the BN northern-tier corridor between Seattle and the Mississippi River. It would lease locomotives and intermodal cars from the BN, and it would hire its own crews. As a new operating railroad, the crews initially would be nonunion, although under the 1926 Railway Labor Act they had a right to organize and seek a representation election. The idea was that unionized or not, Winona Bridge would begin life with just two crew members on each train—a locomotive engineer and a conductor. The UTU, which would have lost the extra crew jobs, and just about everyone else saw through the subterfuge. The union threatened to strike, and the railroad sought an injunction in federal court. The BN lost that battle. Rather than engage in what was sure to be years-long warfare with the UTU, the company abandoned the Winona Bridge ploy. It never was able to run Expediter trains in the northern territory.

Not long after Bressler and other BN railroad executives had tried to negotiate an acquisition of the Santa Fe, it became obvious that the Santa Fe had rejected the BN's overtures because it had a deal of its own that it was pursuing. As the consolidation of the railroad industry gained steam in the 1970s and 1980s, the Santa Fe had flirtations with a number of other carriers but was unable to consummate a merger agreement. Among railroads that the Santa Fe considered as possible partners were the Western Pacific, the Southern Pacific, and even Conrail and the Norfolk Southern (NS) in the East. In the latter case, the NS was the suitor, but just as with the Bressler proposal, the Santa Fe wasn't interested in being acquired. It preferred to be the hunter rather than the hunted.

The first merger attempt with the Southern Pacific was made in 1980. "It was partly protective," said John Reed. He explained that Santa Fe executives had seen the BN-Frisco combination and the Mop-Up of the Union Pacific, the Missouri Pacific, and the Western Pacific as mergers that would be approved: "Just like everybody else in the [industry], we'd look and say, 'Who's left?' Of course, we believed that the Santa Fe and Southern Pacific—if it could have been done properly, and if you could have gotten rid of some of the excess property—could have been a pretty good thing."

John Schmidt, who had risen to prominence in the Santa Fe organization after he had won a major tax case involving old 1895 hundred-year bonds, was placed in charge of negotiating the details with the Southern Pacific people. As Reed said,

> He was a very effective negotiator and spent quite a while in California on this assignment. We thought we had things pretty well worked out, but it was not to be, at least for then. I believe we were in the middle of a board meeting when John called from California to report that he felt the SP people had backed away from previously agreed upon conditions, and he felt he could no longer deal with them. He recommended that the merger be called off, and it was.

Both the Santa Fe and the Southern Pacific were among the great companies that had built the West. In many ways, both managements were arrogant. In 1980, at least, neither company wanted to be the one to be acquired. The SP, in fact, had come very close to creating the first truly transcontinental railroad when it almost reached a merger deal with Seaboard Coast Line Industries, but that deal collapsed when Ben Biaggini, the SP's chief executive, and Prime Osborn, Seaboard Coast Line's chief executive, could not decide which company would acquire the other.

Reed declined to go into detail of the collapse of the 1980 merger talks but gave the impression that there were major cultural differences between the SP and the Santa Fe.

Shortly after succeeding Reed as chief executive officer of Santa

Fe Industries in 1983, Schmidt resumed negotiations with the Southern Pacific, and the talks this time were successful. The two companies announced they were negotiating a merger and reached an accord on September 27. By this time, though, the mighty Southern Pacific was on a financial downhill slide, and its traffic losses had become a crisis. Truckers were taking away the once-lucrative perishables business, driving the SP's market share to less than 10 percent. The onslaught of Japanese imported automobiles and Californians' acceptance of them led to closure of a number of automobile assembly plants on the West Coast, further weakening the SP traffic base. The SP also no longer could count on the annual interchange of cars with the Rock Island, which had ceased operations in 1981, or with the Union Pacific at Ogden, Utah, now that the UP's acquisition of the Western Pacific allowed it to offer single-line service between the Midwest and the West Coast.

This time there was no dispute over who would be dominant in a combination of the two huge rail systems. The Santa Fe clearly was taking over the Southern Pacific. The two holding companies—Santa Fe Industries and Southern Pacific Company—having received Justice Department clearance, merged on December 23 of that year. That would prove to be a great mistake.

The imperious SP chief executive, Ben Biaggini, then 67 years old, said he would retire upon consummation of the transaction. Schmidt, just 55, would become chairman of the combined railroads, and Robert D. Krebs, the SP's 41-year-old president, would be president.

While the two parents combined, the railroads could not be merged until the ICC granted its approval, which could take up to 31 months. The Southern Pacific Transportation Company was placed in a voting trust until the commission reached its decision. Management of the new company, the Santa Fe Southern Pacific Corporation (SFSP), was confident that it was only a matter of time until it could end the voting trust and implement the rail merger.

Even though the two railroads were operated separately, it was clear that the SP eventually would be subsumed in the Santa Fe. A few SP executives, Krebs among them, moved to Chicago. Many others, believing that their railroad careers were effectively at an end, left in what became a great brain drain. As is true throughout the business world, the most talented and employable people are often the first to leave. The SP was left with a less-than-highly regarded management team and little bench strength. This would not be a problem when the SP was merged into the Santa Fe, but it would prove to be a flaw that would haunt any other owner.

The combined railroad would be the third largest in the industry in track miles, trailing only Burlington Northern in the West and CSX Transportation in the East. Clearly, the shape of consolidation in the railroad industry would take a different direction. There would be three competing mega-railroads in the West, each with the critical mass to ensure long-term survival, instead of the two that actually exist today.

The confidence that merger approval would come quickly was based on faulty understanding of the criteria the ICC would apply. As presented to the ICC, the merged Santa Fe and SP would have had a monopoly on rail traffic across the southern tier of the United States from New Orleans and Memphis on the east to Los Angeles on the Pacific coast. It would have solely served most of the rail carload traffic sources within California.

As was the case with other rail holding companies, the intent was to separate the rail assets from the nontransportation assets. The Santa Fe Southern Pacific organized Catellus Corporation in 1984 to conduct the nonrailroad real estate activities of both railroads. Large parcels of SP land were transferred in the form of dividends to the holding company.

As an indicator of their confidence that the merger was only a matter of time, executives at Chicago-based SFSP authorized railroad operating officials to begin painting locomotives in the new livery of the merged railroad. Railroad wags said the huge initials "SPSF" on the locomotives actually stood for "Shouldn't Paint So Fast." In future merger cases it became axiomatic for executives to demonstrate their respect for regulators by stating something to the effect that "we're not repainting the locomotives yet," as an indication that they were not assuming victory before the regulators acted. Locomotive paint jobs were minor when compared with some other transgressions committed by the merger applicants. The SFSP adopted an arrogant stance toward the ICC and other interested parties. It refused to negotiate with other railroads to remove potential anticompetitive issues in advance. Schmidt went even further, threatening to abandon the unification if the ICC had the temerity to load it with conditions. The UP, the railroad's principal competitor, led the vigorous opposition of many shippers.

On July 24, 1986, the confident SFSP executives, led by Schmidt, entered the ICC's magisterial chamber to await what they fully

The ICC Refuses to Be Taken for Granted

Although the ICC professional staff had recommended approval of the Santa Fe–Southern Pacific merger, four of the five members of the commission concluded that the combination would have been anticompetitive. Only the lightly regarded Heather Gradison, who was chairwoman of the commission and clearly and admittedly was taking her economic philosophy orders from the Reagan White House, voted for the merger. The rejection of the merger, still the only modern-era merger to be turned down, was not all that surprising. Former ICC general counsel Fritz Kahn told Frank N. Wilner:

> Certainly the denial of the Santa Fe–Southern Pacific unification was aberrational. But a look at the map at the time suggests why the proposal might have been turned down. All of central California, Arizona, New Mexico and western Texas—the southern transcontinental corridor—would have belonged to a unified Santa Fe–SP.
>
> While that doesn't seem so strange in the light of the recent Burlington Northern–Santa Fe and the Union Pacific–Southern Pacific marriages, the times were different, and so was the sophistication of the proponents. The Santa Fe management was as arrogant as can be, and some of that rubbed off on their counsel, who well may have alienated the ICC sufficiently at the time of oral argument to have led to the proposal's denial.
>
> This arrogance resulted in the refusal to address the concerns of what we now call "two-for-one shippers" and an unwillingness to grant trackage rights to competitors, as other railroads very wisely did in their subsequent unification proceedings.

The ICC staff, mindful of the rapidly deteriorating fundamentals of the SP—and the slippage in the Santa Fe's fortunes—had recommended approval of the merger. The ICC did find that the benefits that would flow from unification of the Santa Fe and the SP were what the company had said in its filings, but the commission also determined that the anticompetitive effects would outweigh those benefits. A shaken Schmidt announced that the company would seek reconsideration from the ICC, and the company began negotiations to remove the issues that had blocked approval the first time.

expected to be a favorable verdict. The Santa Fe Southern Pacific Corporation executives had done more than repaint some locomotives. They already had changed corporate stationery. They were so confident that the quarterly report spoke of "a dynamic future" for "two strong compatible companies." It was obvious to everyone but the members of the ICC that the merger of the Santa Fe and Southern Pacific railroads was a done deal, but the commissioners were the only ones with votes that counted. No combination of major railroads had been rejected since the decision in 1968 against the Northern Lines merger and that subsequently was approved on reconsideration, creating the Burlington Northern.

The Santa Fe and Southern Pacific executives were shocked when the commission—by a 4–1 vote—rejected the Santa Fe–Southern Pacific merger as anticompetitive.

In recent mergers, the railroads involved have agreed—even before filing their merger application—to deals that cost hundreds of millions of dollars in diverted traffic to competitors, just to ensure that there would be fewer overt opponents and to present a "clean deal" to the regulators. Most observers believe that the refusal to deal with the anticompetitive issues before the ICC's initial rejection led to that failure of the Santa Fe–Southern Pacific combination. Certainly, the disdain that Schmidt showed for the ICC didn't help. As Frank N. Wilner wrote:

> A cocksure Mr. Schmidt initially mocked the ICC's adverse decision, declaring that "we have three strong railroads in the East . . . two strong railroads in the West, and two weak ones, and I own both" weak ones. Then he hinted at some vague congressional override of the ICC decision. Eventually he turned contrite, promising opponents the very trackage rights he earlier refused if only the ICC would reconsider its decision. Mr. Schmidt then dutifully walked the plank and resigned.

The SFSP then began negotiations with railroads that had opposed its original merger application. It also began to take actions to cut costs at the railroads. Late in 1986, in a move that other railroads had already taken—the BN had taken a pretax charge of $1.9 billion earlier that year—the SFSP took a massive $914 million write-down of assets and announced plans to abandon 6,200 miles of track and to terminate or relocate 7,900 employees of its two railroads. The trackage reductions amounted to about 15 percent of the combined mileage.

Some analysts speculated that the SFSP was trying to make itself more attractive to a potential buyer should the appeal for ICC reconsideration fail. The SFSP gave no indication that anything was for sale and continued trying to remove the barriers to merger that the ICC had identified in June. The SFSP agreed to grant trackage rights to the Union Pacific between El Paso, Texas, and Los Angeles, providing a second strong carrier in the southern transcontinental corridor. The UP, through its 1982 acquisition of the Missouri Pacific, already had a route between El Paso and the eastern gateways. The UP, which had opposed the merger, dropped its opposition and filed a statement urging the ICC to reconsider and approve the merger application.

The last-minute attempt to fix the problems of the merger created new ones. The BN, which originally had supported the Santa Fe–SP merger, became an opponent primarily because the UP agreement gave that railroad the right to offer single-line service between California and Texas, something the BN could not do. The BN, which did not compete in many markets with either the Santa Fe or the SP, viewed the UP as its principal competitor. As long as the UP could not offer California-Texas service, the BN was willing to stand on the sidelines as the Santa Fe and the SP moved to combine; they were no threat to the BN. The deal with the UP changed everything for the BN.

The SFSP negotiated a trackage rights agreement with the Denver and Rio Grande Western (DRGW) that would allow the smaller regional carrier to expand its operations west from Salt Lake City to San Francisco and other points on the West Coast, adding some 2,000 miles to its system. The SFSP also granted trackage rights to the Missouri-Kansas-Texas (Katy) over some of its lines in Texas. The SFSP believed that the agreements with the UP, the Katy, and the DRGW resolved the anticompetitive problems and filed a petition in early 1987, asking the ICC to reconsider its earlier rejection of the merger. The BN, which liked neither of the settlements, asked in a filing at the ICC why these trackage rights agreements, considered deal breakers early in the merger process, now were acceptable. The BN offered no suggestion in its filing that it would be satisfied by any conditions.

There was general dissatisfaction among the Santa Fe Southern Pacific board members with the handling of the case, and Schmidt subsequently was asked to resign. Shortly before his spring 1987 departure, Schmidt—accompanied by Frank Grossman, the SFSP's Washington lobbyist, and by a Washington political consultant— began to call on various transportation publications and others that he had refused to grant interviews earlier in the proceedings. This time he asked with considerable humility for their editorial support of the petition for reconsideration. Asked at the *Journal of Commerce* what had brought about his changed approach, Schmidt, who was visibly showing the strain he was under, replied that he had learned that although the paper had a small circulation—only about 20,000—it was read by the members of the ICC and their staffs.

In an interview with the *Journal of Commerce*, Alan Fitzwater, BN vice president for government affairs, said, "I don't think, as a practical matter that [negotiating trackage rights with the SFSP] would be consistent with the deals already struck." Making it clear that the BN now wanted the SFSP merger killed once and for all, Fitzwater also said, "They can't buy off everyone in the world . . . and still have anything left for themselves. There's nothing they could really do to lessen our opposition at this time."

The BN's filing claimed that the trackage rights that had been negotiated with the UP, the DRGW, and the Katy made the merger proposal significantly different from the one the ICC had dealt with in 1986. If the petition for reconsideration was granted, the BN said, the ICC should handle the case as an entirely new merger application. Most observers believed that the SFSP could not tolerate another year of proceedings before finding out if it could merge its two railroads. The Union Pacific's acquisition of the Katy was pending before the commission, and the BN feared that the UP could be a big winner by default if the Santa Fe–SP merger were reconsidered and approved. It suggested that, if the SFSP were reconsidered, it be consolidated with the UP-Katy application, another move designed to kill the merger.

Schmidt resigned under pressure from his board of directors in April 1987. "That left a vacuum, and the board felt that things might get a little chaotic," Reed said. He was asked to hold things together and agreed to come out of retirement and succeed Schmidt on an interim basis until a permanent replacement could be found.

The attempt to merge the two railroads proceeded. In fact, there was some feeling that Schmidt had so alienated the ICC members that his removal would enhance the likelihood that the merger ultimately would gain approval. "I was mainly a figurehead, pending the search for a new CEO," Reed said. "I think most of the board had already been favorably impressed with Rob Krebs." Krebs had been named president of the Southern Pacific at the age of 38. He had come to Chicago as an officer of the new holding company and was slated to be president of the merged railroad. By spring 1987 he was one executive who was satisfactory to both the former SP and the former Santa Fe directors. Reed added, "We nevertheless went through the process of engaging a consultant—a headhunter who presented some candidates from the industrial world—and then the board enthusiastically voted to make Krebs the new chief executive. I remained chairman until the next annual meeting in 1988."

Looking back at the failed merger of the railways 15 years later, Reed felt that the outcome may have been for the best. He observed, "The two companies had a very different culture, a different approach to service and public relations. I doubt that there would have been a very happy coexistence."

Krebs picked up where Schmidt left off and continued the effort to persuade the ICC to look anew at the proposed merger. Meanwhile, like sharks smelling blood, other railroads began to maneuver, knowing that if the merger was finally rejected, the Santa Fe Southern Pacific Corporation would be required to sell one or both of its railroads. Despite the grants of trackage rights to the UP and the Rio Grande and the submission of statements of support from shippers, the ICC denied the petition for reconsideration on June 30, 1987.

Once the merger was officially dead, the Santa Fe Southern Pacific had several options. It could sell the Southern Pacific, which already was held in an independent voting trust. It could sell the Santa Fe. It could sell both railroads and exit the railroad industry altogether. Or it could sell the whole company. The last was rejected out of hand. The company quickly announced that it would sell the Southern Pacific and keep the Santa Fe. The sale of the Southern Pacific took more than a year to accomplish, as there was spirited bidding for the SP.

The sale of the Southern Pacific, which also would require ICC approval, drew several bidders. At the same time, there were two unsolicited bidders for the entire holding company. These were from the Henley Group Incorporated, an investment company based in San Diego, California, and from Olympia and York Developments Limited (O&Y), a real estate development company in Toronto,

Canada. A quick sale of the Southern Pacific would provide the funds for SFSP management to finance its plan to keep the holding company out of the hands of either of its suitors.

By late 1987, there were two known bidders for the Southern Pacific—the Kansas City Southern Railway (RLEA) and the Denver and Rio Grande Western. The Railway Labor Executives' Association, a group of rail unions, was trying to organize an employee-leveraged buyout, as was an SP management group. The RLEA bid was intriguing because if it were accepted by the SFSP and approved by the ICC, it would make the patrician SP the first major employee-owned railroad in the industry. Guilford Transportation Industries in the East, and even the BN, at least briefly considered bidding for the "sufferin' Pacific," as the SP was known. The KCS was owned by holding company Kansas City Southern Industries, which also owned a major mutual fund management company. The holding company insisted it would have no problem financing a purchase of the Southern Pacific. Similarly, the DRGW was owned by billionaire investor Philip Anschutz, who also would have no problem financing the purchase if he were to win the SP.

Anschutz perhaps had the greatest need for the SP. The Rio Grande, as the DRGW was known, was a bridge carrier with lines running between Pueblo and Denver on the east and Salt Lake City on the west. The UP's main line paralleled the Rio Grande, and the UP, of course, extended east of Denver and west of Salt Lake City. The DRGW had to rely on connections with other railroads for a steady flow of traffic, and the UP had little interest in providing it. Although the Rio Grande, along with the SP and the BN, was a partner in what was considered an alternate (to the UP) Central Corridor rail route, railroads like the Rio Grande originated and terminated relatively little of their traffic and effectively had been condemned to slow death by deregulation. For Anschutz, however, the SP would extend the Rio Grande lines all the way to California in the west and, via trackage rights, to St. Louis in the east, expanding his budding rail empire to some 16 states. Both bidders offered to pay about $1.8 billion for the SP in cash and assumption of debt. The RLEA never was able to come up with financing and failed to submit a bid.

At the same time that it was trying to get the SP sold, the Santa Fe Southern Pacific was fending off the increasingly hostile efforts of the Henley Group and of Olympia and York to buy the holding company. Between them, Henley and Olympia and York acquired some 23 percent of the SFSP's outstanding stock. Wall Street analysts were predicting that Michael Dingman, the driving force in Henley, would attempt a hostile takeover of the SFSP, with or without the support of O&Y.

In a meeting of institutional investors, securities analysts, and reporters at the New York offices of investment banking firm Goldman Sachs and Company, Krebs announced that the SFSP intended to pay a special cash dividend to shareholders of some $4 billion, once the company restructured and completed the sale of various assets, including the Southern Pacific. The dividend pledge served to keep stock arbitrageurs in line. "Arbs," as they are known, take positions in a company when it is "in play," as the SFSP was. They hope to profit by having the final price of a transaction at a higher price than they paid initially. If no transaction takes place, the arbs would suffer significant losses, but they usually can avoid that outcome by the use of hedging techniques. The prospect of a huge special dividend was designed to keep them from selling their stock to Henley or O&Y.

Dingman told reporters that if he gained control of the holding company, he would sell the Santa Fe and keep the Southern Pacific. Henley was not about to devote a lot of time to a hostile fight for control of the SFSP, however, and soon sold its interest to yet another suitor. Itel Corporation, a Chicago-based holding company with rail interests, acquired 16.9 percent of the SFSP stock.

Itel, which had been a $90 million container leasing company that was in bankruptcy as recently as 1983, had grown into a transportation conglomerate with $1.9 billion in projected revenue by the fourth quarter of 1988. It was headed by Samuel Zell, known in Chicago business circles as "Grave Dancer" because of his proclivity to pick up troubled companies at low prices. The Itel empire included five short-line railroads, the largest container and railcar leasing company in the United States, a large marine dredging company, and a nationwide warehousing and distribution services business.

The Itel transportation services group was headed by Jack Edwards, a slick-talking deal maker who once had been a marketing executive at the Southern Pacific and later built a network of non-asset-based third-party logistics companies, buying independent businesses largely for stock in what was considered a classic "roll-up." Itel bought Henley's Signal Capital Corporation and Equilease Corporation units as well as its holdings in the Santa Fe Southern Pacific and in American President Companies for $827 million in cash and $373 million in Itel stock. American President, a steamship line based in Oakland, California, was a pioneer user of land bridge services and was the first company to operate a domestic network of trains with containers stacked on top of each other—double stack, as it now is known.

The purchase of Signal Capital, which in turn owned Pullman Leasing, added 30,000 railcars to the 43,000 already in the Itel fleet, making it the largest railcar leasing company in the United States. Earlier in the year, Itel had become the largest lessor of containers when it acquired the container assets of XTRA Corporation for $100 million. The Itel container fleet accounted for about 20 percent of worldwide capacity.

Both Itel and O&Y accepted seats on the SFSP board and became known as the eight-hundred-pound gorillas on Rob Krebs's board.

The SFSP finally chose to sell the SP to Rio Grande Industries, the Anschutz-owned holding company for Denver and Rio Grande Western Railway. A bitter Kansas City Southern, which contended it was a more appropriate owner for the Southern Pacific, mounted a fruitless battle for the railroad before the ICC.

Some consultants who had worked for the Kansas City Southern and for Anschutz believe that Krebs preferred the Rio Grande as a buyer because he knew what the SP's problems and strengths were and he knew that Anschutz was a deal maker who would sell off much of the Southern Pacific's large remaining real estate holdings and eventually sell the railroad to someone else. In that scenario, the SP would not receive an infusion of capital and never would be an effective competitor for the Santa Fe, which the SFSP intended to keep.

The sale of the SP was completed on October 13, 1988, not long after Krebs defeated the hostile takeover attempt at the SFSP. To raise the money for the special dividend, the company sold its Kirby Forest Industries and Robert E. McKee engineering and construction businesses. Several pipeline and energy subsidiaries were sold or spun off to stockholders. In 1989 the holding company changed its name to the Santa Fe Pacific Corporation.

Under Krebs's leadership, Santa Fe Pacific focused on running the businesses it still had. John Swartz, president of the Santa Fe Railway, was succeeded in July 1989 by Mike Haverty, a veteran railroad operating executive who had risen through the ranks, starting at the Missouri Pacific. Haverty's first act was a symbolic one. He ordered the restoration of the famous red-and-silver Warbonnet paint scheme on all new locomotives that were ordered, a move to solidify employee morale.

The Santa Fe, which had a good grain franchise in the Midwest and a small coal business in New Mexico, increasingly focused its efforts on the rapidly growing intermodal business of carrying containers and truck trailers. The ubiquitous 89-foot flatcar was rapidly being replaced by cars that were specially designed to carry trailers and containers with as little weight and fuel consumption as possible. Intermodal traffic reached 50 percent of Santa Fe revenue, a larger percentage than at any other railroad.

Intermodal, which once had been a low-priced service designed to stem the losses of traditional rail traffic to truck competitors, gradually was becoming a separate business line, and a rapidly growing one at that. At several railroads, yards that once had been crowded with various types of cars and had become virtually deserted over time now became dedicated intermodal yards where expensive specially designed lift devices rapidly loaded and unloaded trailers and containers. Because it was competitive with over-the-road trucking, intermodal had become a service-driven business rather than a price-driven product. The Santa Fe was in a particularly good position to capitalize on the trend because its largely double-tracked main line between Chicago and Los Angeles had capacity and was engineered to allow intermodal trains to run at speeds of 79 miles per hour. Faster trains consume more capacity because more distance must be allowed between them and preceding and trailing trains. The Santa Fe's efforts to keep its passenger service alive in the 1950s and 1960s now paid off, as it was able to offer service quality that its competitors—the Southern Pacific and the Union Pacific—were unable to match.

The Santa Fe was in a bind, however, that eventually would force it again to seek a merger partner. It relied on traffic for which there was significant competition, limiting its pricing flexibility. Intermodal, because it competed with over-the-road truckers and other railroads, was a low-margin business. It lacked the higher margin of base-load traffic that had to move by rail—huge amounts of coal and the kind of export and domestic grain business that assured financial survival for the BN and the UP.

Rather than being the start of a new golden age for railroads, as some had predicted after deregulation, the 1980s were a continuation of the tumultuous years that preceded the decade. Nowhere was this truer than at the Burlington Northern. Not only did the BN face the same problems and issues that other railroads faced, but it also endured a turbulent period of management changes that might have destroyed a weaker company.

Rob Krebs

A Focused Executive

At the close of the 20th century, Rob Krebs, the Santa Fe leader who ultimately helped initiate the Santa Fe's merger with the Burlington Northern (BN), was known for his optimism. A perfectionist, he was considered by other executives and competitors to be perhaps the most focused executive in the railroad industry. With a thorough understanding of the railroad's operations, he had a profound focus on the customer.

Krebs was a key driver in recognizing the growth potential of intermodal transportation—using more than one form of transportation to carry freight from origin to destination. By emphasizing its intermodal service, BNSF proved able both to compete with trucks and to form marketing and service alliances with its traditional competitors, serving customers whose facilities were not directly adjacent to a railroad track. By the time Krebs retired in the second year of the 21st century, intermodal was growing rapidly and was on its way to becoming the largest source of revenue for BNSF and other railroads.

At the Santa Fe, Krebs enlarged intermodal markets, focused on the on-time service performance necessary to compete with long-haul trucking, and pursued strategic alliances with trucking firms to promote intermodal growth. By the time the Santa Fe and the BN merged in 1995, intermodal accounted for half of the Santa Fe's volume. During aggressive building projects in the early 1990s, Krebs frequently used the saying "Build it and they will come" to describe his vision for continued growth. Whether he knew it or not, Krebs was echoing the sense of vision expressed by his predecessor a century earlier, Cyrus K. Holliday.

Beginning with the arrival of Dick Bressler in mid-1980, just as deregulation was about to become a reality, BN directors did what no other railroad had done until then. They put the company in the hands of people who had no railroad experience or who had spent little time in the industry or company. The practice continued until 1995, when Rob Krebs became chief executive of the newly formed Burlington Northern Santa Fe Corporation.

Bressler, who was the first to admit he didn't know any of the details of running a railroad, was fortunate to have Dick Grayson, a veteran rail executive with experience in operations and marketing, to run the railroad from late 1980 until the end of 1982. Grayson was succeeded by Walter Drexel. During the Drexel years the railroad management was in a constant state of flux, as there was no one like Grayson to run the business while Drexel focused on moving the company and forcing culture change.

Drexel was followed in 1985 by Darius Gaskins. Because he came from the outside, as had his predecessor, Gaskins was able to make difficult personnel decisions because he didn't have the ties that so frequently prevent such decisions from being made when executives have spent many years rising through the ranks together. Gaskins also immersed himself in the details of running the railroad.

Gaskins was followed by Gerald Grinstein in 1989. Bressler brought Grinstein into the company in 1987 as vice chairman headquartered in Fort Worth. He arrived at the BN during the period of contentious labor relations with a reputation of being able to get along with union chiefs. His responsibilities obviously were broader than simply to get along with the unions.

The common thread among these outsiders was that the BN board recognized that, in the deregulated world, the BN could not do business as usual and that a significant culture change was required if the railroad was to adapt successfully to the changing business environment. Hiring executives with different backgrounds and no allegiances to the culture of the past was one way of forcing that change.

The culture change was not smooth. From long experience, traditional railroad operators were wedded to a way of life and a way of doing things. In the operating departments it was traditional that managers moved up through the ranks with relatively little formal training, taking the skills and knowledge learned on the last assignment to the next. That made it very difficult to change after a lifetime of doing what appeared to be successful. Similarly, marketing executives had to learn a whole new way of conducting business, having been denied the ability to meet with customers and develop packages of services at prices they were prepared to pay. Many resisted the changes that had to be made. Learning to be flexible and adaptable were new concepts.

After deregulation, for example, railroads rushed to lock up as much business as they could under contract, not having been allowed previously to enter into confidential contracts with customers. Having been forced to deal with continual losses of traffic that left them with excess equipment and underutilized facilities, they initially tended to trade lower rates for guarantees of traffic. It was a number of years before executives realized that most contracts were committing railroads to a continued uneconomic regimen. The industry wasn't earning its cost of capital, and committing to rates that, though profitable and contributing to the fixed plant, did not bring the railroad closer to earning its cost of capital only perpetuated the situation that had led the industry to seek deregulation in the first place.

Other railroads did not go as far outside the industry as did the BN for its leaders, but all engaged in massive cost cutting and reduction of assets in order to improve their return on investment. The BN was more aggressive than its competitors and, by the end of the 1980s, was positioned to operate more profitably than it ever had before. The proof was that in the 1980s the BN came closer to achieving the ICC standard of "revenue adequacy" than most other railroads. The only railroads that outperformed the BN were the Norfolk Southern, which benefited from a lucrative, high-rate, export coal business, and smaller railroads such as the Illinois Central, which didn't maintain as much fixed plant. The BN finally achieved a lower operating ratio—one of Walter Drexel's goals—than its rival UP.

While other railroads took a more gradual approach to changing their culture, the BN under Drexel, Gaskins, and Grinstein moved aggressively to drive the change. No matter how necessary it was, though, the process frequently was painful.

Drexel, who prided himself on his abilities to manage a bundle of assets regardless of what the industry was, was perhaps the most zealous. He measured performance solely in terms of operating income and the ancillary activities that contributed to that. Although the company's operating income rose from about $100 million to more than $900 million in only four or five years under Drexel's guidance, executives who worked under him have said that the failure to achieve $1 billion in operating income rankled him more than anything else.

Drexel, who had no railroad or transportation background, was the right man at the right time when it came to reducing the head count. Rail executives at the BN and other railroads didn't hesitate to furlough workers when business was slack or to eliminate jobs when technology made them unnecessary. That was a way of life in the industry. They were considerably slower, however, when it came to reducing the "officer" head count, the nonunion lower, middle, and upper management positions. After all, these were their colleagues, and considering that people tended to stay with the railroad for their entire careers, it meant they would have to push their friends out the door. Drexel did not hesitate to do what he believed was necessary.

Tom Matthews, who briefly was chief financial officer of the railroad under Drexel and Gaskins, recalled the radically different way the business was run under Bressler at the holding company. Speaking of Don Woods, another corporate planning executive brought in from ARCO by Bressler, Matthews said, "He's a very smart guy. The way Bressler ran the company is that he had these quarterly meetings at the holding company. Don was primarily positioned as the interrogator. Bressler was the listener. There was controversy." While his career was in the ascendancy, Woods was moved from the holding company to the railroad to gain operating experience.

Woods and Gaskins, although personally cordial, became rivals, particularly when Bressler and Drexel pushed for a more formal succession planning process than the BN had been used to. "We did a successor planning deal, which I was involved in, as a matter of fact," said Matthews. "[Drexel] made Don the head of the operating department. He made Darius [Gaskins] the head of marketing and everything else." They were expected to compete to succeed Drexel.

Ironically, considering his seeming indifference to the railroad executives who reported to him, Drexel came to enjoy being chief executive of the nation's largest railroad. When Bressler asked him to give up the CEO job at the railroad so Gaskins could be promoted, Drexel decided he did not wish to be a vice chairman without portfolio. Bressler accepted his resignation.

Bressler, who found the budgeting process excruciatingly informal and chaotic by his standards, imposed a much more rigid process on the BN. The result was more of a classic General Electric, Fortune 500 company model, as Matthews described it. Regional vice presidents, for example, were required to have budgets for each of their regions. Gaskins was responsible for revenue budgeting, and the various budgets were consolidated as the process moved forward.

Contrary to the days when Ray Burton would inform Bob Binger how much cash the resources businesses would have to generate to cover the railroad's capital needs, the new process was very formal. "You went in a room, and Walter attended all of those," Matthews said. "Every line item was evaluated." He remembers one budget meeting where there was a debate over whether or not the BN should switch from wooden to concrete ties.

The new managers quickly picked up one old-culture trait. They measured the BN against its century-long rival, the Union Pacific. "The focus of the [outsiders] was that if the UP could have an operating ratio of X, then the BN would not be satisfied until it had a better operating ratio," Matthews said. "I believe in 1985 a comparison was done. The operating ratio for the full year 1985 was lower at the BN than it was at Union Pacific."

In contrast to the traditional railroad culture, the new executives forced the railroaders to look farther into the future than they ever had before and to think more broadly. No longer did their jobs revolve almost entirely around internal measurements of operating efficiency. "Bressler once said that he didn't want anybody at our level, my level included, to do anything about anything that would affect the next year," said Matthews. "If you were going to be a good executive, you were thinking well beyond that horizon and hiring other people to take care of problems this year. He would have people assess, for example, the future of the energy business as it might affect coal." Bressler believed that a chief executive did three things: strategic planning, creating the annual budget, and succession planning.

Although people who were at the BN when Bressler arrived believed that he had no faith in the railroad industry, a number of contemporary BN executives came to be supporters who believed he was misunderstood. On the contrary, Matthews said Bressler saw a lot of unexploited opportunities within the railroad.

During the takeover wave that swept American corporations in the 1980s, Bressler, on more than one occasion, said he would sell the company to anyone who came forth with a proposal that was fair and good for stockholders. Even entertaining such thoughts was anathema to most railroad executives. "There was never, in my opinion, a view that the railroad wasn't worth a lot," Matthews said. "Bressler and Drexel thought if the railroad got run like a business, there was a huge upside." Everything they did was intended to make railroad executives into good business executives.

The payoff, Matthews believed, was for the benefit of the stockholders. "If somebody researched it," he said, "and if you took the price of BN stock on the date Dick [Bressler] showed up and looked at the price of BN stock ten years to the day later, it was either the fourth or fifth best-performing stock on the New York Stock Exchange during that period of time."

One trait of the rigid command-and-control management approach of the railroad before deregulation was that it also was not a customer- or employee-focused business. As Matthews put it,

> We said when we were trying to change the culture that it
> was a militaristic, order-giving and order-taking mentality
> and therefore had no respect for the innate abilities of the
> people who worked at the railroad. They've got a couple of
> ways that they talk about the book of rules. They gave me a
> book of rules. What the hell did I have to do with anything
> in the book of rules? But you were supposed to memorize
> and follow those rules. One employee once said, "When I
> go to work for the railroad in the morning, I check my
> brains on the way in and pick them up on the way out,
> because nobody wanted me to use my brains." It was cen-
> trally controlled, and by virtue [of that] it was not close
> enough to its customers to appreciate the needs of its
> customers.

At a discussion among executives about the need to structure a culture change campaign, one operating executive said it would take military discipline. An assistant vice president who was a graduate of the U.S. Naval Academy got a pained look and said, "Guys, we teach them to think at the boat school these days."

After Drexel, there was no question that Gaskins was customer-sensitive, as was Bill Greenwood, who had been chief commercial officer under Gaskins and became chief operating officer under Grinstein. With intermodal the fastest-growing segment of the railroad business, the railroad had to become more customer-focused if it was to compete with the flexibility and service capabilities of the truckers.

Grinstein, about whom more will be learned in the next chapter, had a politician's need to be "loved," and that affected the way he continued the drive to change the culture. As Matthews put it, Bressler didn't care what labor thought of him. It just didn't bother him at all. Grinstein, on the other hand, "would have a heart attack" if union leaders called him what they called Bressler.

The culture change also was focused on lower-ranking officials. The BN established a leadership center in Arlington, Texas, a Fort Worth suburb, where every trainmaster and official of comparable rank was sent for at least two weeks every year. "They went to Arlington for leadership training," Matthews said. "This was leadership training about what it was before, what we wanted it to be, and how you manage in this culture as opposed to the way you managed in the old culture."

That was a hard pill to swallow for many in the operating department. These were managers who had served in the ranks and had been subject to the rigid—even harsh—command-and-control environment. Traditionally, a lot of managers with no formal training relied on intimidation because they had been intimidated when younger and they knew it worked on them, so it surely would work on their subordinates. The up-from-the-ranks culture was typified by many executives who proudly carried their union cards with them and who continued to pay dues in order to retain their seniority in the craft in which they originally had worked. "I was going to put on the bargaining table a proposal that if a person went into management, he had to give up his seniority," Matthews said. "Vice presidents were outraged. I created a circus. I don't think anybody should be in management and still hold seniority. They should figure out whether they want to be in management."

After 10 years of operating in a deregulated environment, with nontraditional chief executives running the business, the BN had become a railroad whose executives were less focused on rigidly following rules and traditions. They were more focused on doing the right thing and on figuring out what the right thing was, within the context of rules. They were more accountable from a financial standpoint.

As stressful as the 1980s were for the railroads, the 1990s would prove to be no less a period of change.

9

A Fight and Then Another Merger

We were seventh of 11 Class 1s, and that's not a good place to be.

ROBERT D. KREBS, Santa Fe chief executive, explaining his decision to merge with the Burlington Northern

Turning a calendar page merely changes the date. It doesn't necessarily mean the end of ongoing events. For Burlington Northern at the start of the 1990s, culture change and learning to deal with frequent management turnover still was the order of the day.

The previous decade had seen the railroad managed by three consecutive chief executive officers, each of whom had come from outside the railroad industry. The relatively rapid turnover at the top translated into frequent changes throughout the management ranks.

The Drexel-Gaskins-Grinstein period was marked by relatively rapid turnover. The operating department, which had been relocated from St. Paul to Overland Park, Kansas, went through several heads even before the headquarters was moved to Fort Worth.

Big Bill Thompson retired and was replaced by Don Woods, who initially was being groomed as a potential successor to Drexel. Woods was a corporate planner who had followed Bressler and Drexel from ARCO. He had no railroad experience.

When it became obvious to Drexel and the board that Woods was not the right choice, he was succeeded by Joe Galassi, a longtime BN executive who had begun his career before the 1970 Northern Lines merger. Galassi had an operating background and also had spent a couple of years in charge of the railroad's real estate and industrial development department during the ascendancy of the Frisco executives.

After the separation of the railroad from the natural resource assets, BN management was able to focus solely on running the railroad as a business. Compared with the 1980s, though, this period was reasonably calm. Under Grinstein, the driving goal was to bring down the railroad's debt. The debt-to-capital ratio, which was in the high 80 percent range at the separation, gradually came down to a little more than 30 percent, among the best in the railroad industry. The consensus of analysts and economists is that by lowering the debt as quickly as he did, Grinstein put the BN in a position to successfully fight off the UP in a battle to acquire the Santa Fe that would break out in 1994.

Daniel Evans, former governor and senator from Washington, served as a BN director during this period.

> "At that time, the first thing the railroad had to do was get itself financially in strong shape," he said. "I think they really succeeded in that when it came down to the Santa Fe merger. By that time, Burlington was bigger, stronger, and was the survivor. There may have been something of a reverse takeover in terms of management simply because part of that deal was having Krebs become the next chairman. That became sort of a de facto succession plan."

Now retired from the board, Evans knew Grinstein from their years in Seattle public life. "Jerry is an unusual guy," Evans said. "He has superb human skills. He gets along well with virtually anybody and really uses those skills in his management style to really coalesce that railroad and its people."

Where Drexel and Gaskins had sought culture change by forcing a change in the people running the railroad, Grinstein focused on the people who were there and tried to change their behavior and the process of managing the enterprise.

> "That it was in the hands of people who wanted to be in the transportation business is a cultural thing. . . . My thesis would be to add that the franchise is good," Grinstein said. "The culture is better and richer. . . . Even when BN had to go through what I thought were essential evolutions and

BNSF Railway is not simply a creation of the merger of Burlington Northern and Santa Fe railroads, but of more than 330 different railroads dating back to 1849. Over time, through various mergers and acquisitions, BNSF came to include these major predecessor railroads.

Under John Budd's leadership the GN purchased 14,000 cars, acquiring specialized freight cars, particularly jumbo covered hoppers to handle grain and bulk and granular commodities such as flour, sugar, and chemicals.

Interstate Commerce Commission (ICC) examiner Robert H. Murphy (left) talking with the Northern Pacific president Robert S. Macfarlane (center) and Great Northern president John M. Budd (right) during a recess at the merger hearing in Minneapolis in December of 1961.

These locomotives represent more than 100 years of service for the Chicago, Burlington & Quincy Railroad Company, from the 1860s to the 1960s.

John Shedd Reed, like so many railroaders of his generation, returned to the railroad after serving in the war, and worked his way up through the operating department ranks. He was named president of the Santa Fe in 1967, and remained at the helm until the early 1980s.

In the 1960s and the decades that followed, the Santa Fe was more aggressive than many railroads at growing the new intermodal business. Today, BNSF's intermodal business comprises about 40 percent of the company's freight revenues.

Dick Grayson, chief executive of the Frisco, acknowledged that management knew it would need to find a merger partner. He saw a great future with BN and having a cross-country route.

For the latter part of the 20th century, the Frisco was a bridge carrier, one that relied more on traffic connecting to or from other railroads than on traffic it originated or terminated itself. As the industry consolidated into fewer and larger systems, most railroad experts were convinced that the bridge carriers would be incorporated into larger networks.

Lou Menk was a leading spokesman for the railroad industry, calling for deregulation several years before the industry decided to support the movement. He also felt businesses must be good corporate citizens and instituted such policies as annual performance reviews, improved health insurance plans, a pension plan for nonunion employees, and scholarship programs for children of employees.

Lou Menk with his predecessor Bob Macfarlane.

When it came time to find a successor for Lou Menk, the board decided to go outside the organization. The search settled on Richard M. Bressler, a highly regarded executive at energy giant Atlantic Richfield Company (ARCO).

Walter Drexel made the decision to move the BN railroad headquarters from St. Paul, Minnesota, to Fort Worth, Texas. Drexel focused on managing assets and creating culture change.

Darius Gaskins succeeded Walter Drexel as chief executive of the BN. Gaskins had been chairman of the Interstate Commerce Commission when the Staggers Rail Act was enacted.

Chief Executive Rob Krebs, third from left, helped break ground for an expansion project at Corwith yard in Chicago, Illinois in October 1991.

Rob Krebs, the Santa Fe leader who ultimately helped initiate the Santa Fe's merger with the Burlington Northern. Krebs was known for saying, "Build it and they will come" to describe his vision for continued growth.

Under the leadership of Gerald Grinstein one of the driving goals for Burlington Northern was to bring down the railroad's debt. Grinstein also focused on the fundamental relationship between BN corporate leaders and field employees.

It was in the area of safety that retired four-star general John T. Chain made his most significant contribution to Burlington Northern.

BNSF Railway's corporate campus in Fort Worth, Texas includes buildings for Marketing, Operations, Administration, Technology Services and various support functions. Construction began in 1994 on the key office buildings on the campus. The four vintage business cars were later installed in front of the Visitors' Center.

The BNSF Network Operations Center (NOC) is the information hub for an efficient transportation network that spans most of the nation, with gateways to Canada and Mexico. BNSF has one of the largest computer systems in the world to control and manage the 5,700 locomotives, 200,000 rail cars and 1,400 trains that travel over its system every day.

Matt Rose, who was named the BNSF chief executive officer in December 2000, is the youngest chief executive of any of the major railroads. Rose began his transportation career in 1981, with management experience in both the trucking and railroad industries.

In January 2005, BNSF Railway introduced a new logo to better reflect its brand personality. Here, a new BNSF locomotive showcases the logo in an updated paint scheme.

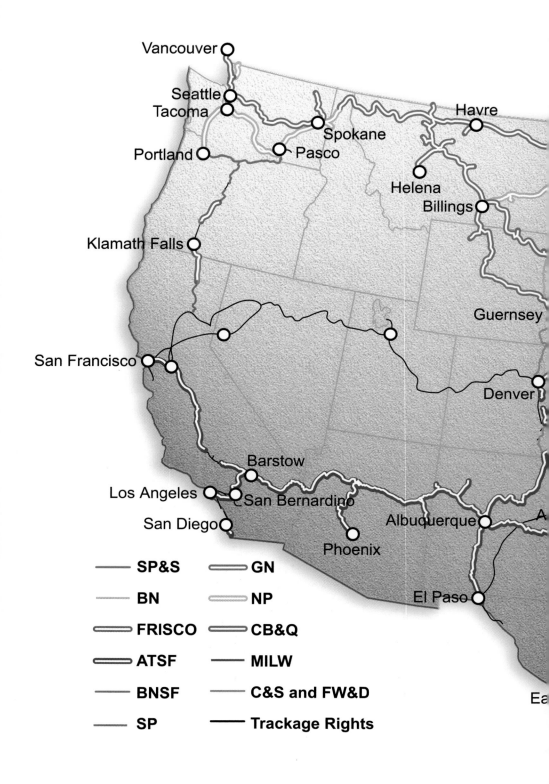

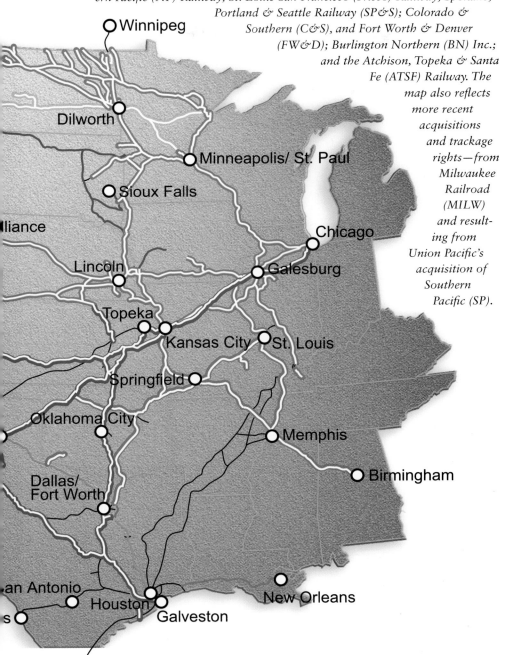

Today BNSF Railway operates 32,000 route miles in 28 states and two Canadian provinces. The BNSF network reflects the strength of its numerous predecessor railroads, including Chicago, Burlington & Quincy (CB&Q) Railroad; Great Northern (GN) Railway; Northern Pacific (NP) Railway; St. Louis-San Francisco (Frisco) Railway; Spokane, Portland & Seattle Railway (SP&S); Colorado & Southern (C&S), and Fort Worth & Denver (FW&D); Burlington Northern (BN) Inc.; and the Atchison, Topeka & Santa Fe (ATSF) Railway. The map also reflects more recent acquisitions and trackage rights—from Milwaukee Railroad (MILW) and resulting from Union Pacific's acquisition of Southern Pacific (SP).

BNSF coal train traveling through the Texas Panhandle to serve Houston utilities. In 2005, coal comprised 21 percent of BNSF's freight revenue. Prospects for BNSF's coal business continue to be positive, as utility demand is increasing for cleaner-burning, low-sulphur coal from the mines BNSF serves in the Powder River Basin in Wyoming and Montana.

A BNSF grain train curves around a frozen lake near Forsyth, Montana. This shot, by BNSF locomotive engineer Clarke Sutphin, was a winner in BNSF's annual employee photo contest and featured in the 2005 calendar.

maybe discontinuities, you had a cultural will to survive and to make this company. It was a persistence and determination about this company that I found unusual."

Unlike others who came from the outside, Grinstein had a greater appreciation of the people who were already there when he arrived. That may have been a manifestation of his political nature, which focuses on people, rather than the asset manager culture in which people tend to be ancillary to the broader goal. "In the first place, it had a large number of very dedicated people," he said. "By that I mean people who define their lives in terms of the railroad. That is an attribute that is not easy to come by. When it happens and when it occurs, it can pay in the long-run future dividends. So the people portion of the equation, I thought, was extremely important."

He also understood the need for behavior change. As he described it,

> The second piece . . . was that I didn't think there was particularly modern management technique involved. You still were calling brakemen and conductors and engineers [to duty] by moving blocks in little cases. I remember my first visit to a yard. No one made eye contact with me, and they were all seated. This was a Saturday morning. I said to whoever was with me on that trip, "What's going on here?" No one looked at me, and they're all dressed up. What am I looking at?" He said, "Well, the truth of the matter is that one of your predecessors came through here, and all the people were kind of jabbering and talking and so on. He said, 'You've got too many people. Get rid of some of them.' So they laid them off. So they all wanted to appear to be totally busy, and they're not going to make eye contact, because if they do, that means they're not busy." That's a true story.
>
> Having that experience convinced me that if you had a trusting relationship, you could really make a go of it. Bringing modern management techniques to the kinds of equipment you order and how you utilize equipment and how you control equipment and plan the run of the railroad all struck me as things that had not been applied and there-

fore the company was undermanaged. What they were
doing was to try to find shortcuts instead of taking the right
way about getting to a profitable enterprise.

Grinstein believed that if people were given the proper tools and
were properly led that they would perform better. Soon after he took
over the railroad, he began a drive to improve performance and customer service. "Service by Design" was the name of the campaign. It
was a forerunner of what most major railroads are doing today.
Instead of the traditional focus on running trains, the BN tried to
schedule individual cars, giving each a trip plan as soon as it entered
the railroad's system. Service by Design never was very successful,
partly because the railroad's computer systems of the time weren't up
to the task and partly because the people who would have to make it
work didn't fully embrace it.

An example of the problems encountered in trying to improve
service was the railroad's ability to focus on a few "hot" cars that
belonged to very important customers. A United Parcel Service trailer or container, for example, could be tracked through the system
and its handling could be expedited so that on-time delivery was virtually certain. When the vice president of strategic planning was
asked by a reporter why the railroad couldn't provide the same level
of service across the board, he responded that if the railroad tried to
do that with all its traffic, it would grind to a halt. Exception handling was the rule.

Grinstein loved the railroad and loved being its chief executive,
but some people faulted him for continuing the managerial instabili-
ty of the previous decade by a series of executive appointments that
just didn't work out.

Although it is hard to establish a nexus, the rapid changes in
management contributed to a deterioration of the railroad's safety.
Railroading has been traditionally perceived as an inherently unsafe
occupation, although it is more accurate to say that it is inherently
unforgiving. Just a momentary loss of concentration can result in the
loss of a limb or a life. All railroad managements try to achieve
enhanced safety, but traditionally their methods focused on discipline rather than on looking for root causes or improving work practices. By the early 1990s, the BN's safety record was the worst in the
railroad industry, as measured in lost-time accidents per thousand
person-hours worked.

At the same time, Grinstein was under pressure from his board to focus more on succession planning. Despite the railroad's depth of talent, Grinstein had come to the conclusion that his own successor was not among the railroad's management cadres.

Through two Omaha, Nebraska, directors—Michael B. Yanney, chairman and chief executive of investment firm America First Companies LLC, and Charles M. Harper, chairman and chief executive of ConAgra Incorporated—Grinstein was introduced to General John T. Chain Jr., the four-star general in charge of the Strategic Air Command (SAC) at Offutt Air Base near Omaha. Chain was approaching military retirement, and Grinstein offered him the position of executive vice president of operations. The railroad presidency was dangled in front of him like a carrot.

With no transportation experience at all, the Chain appointment in 1991 seemed strange to many inside and outside the BN. To insiders, it meant that a number of careers had just been cut off, and there was less opportunity to advance. Grinstein told the *Journal of Commerce* that Chain did not have to run trains, that the head of the operating department really was a planner of precision transportation service, and that Chain had spent his professional life planning precision military operations. He said Chain would bring just the right set of skills to his new position.

Chain liked to tell a story of planning for precision operations: "I could send a B-52 from here to Kosovo, have them meet with aerial tankers twice to refuel, expecting to drop a bomb, plus or minus three seconds. So precision was part of it. That was one of the things that I thought I'd find with the railroad, that railroads did run on time in this era. That was another part of the culture shock. But the big culture shock was the animosity that I found between [rank-and-file and supervisors]."

At SAC, Chain had to worry only about potential hostile action and bombers meeting with tankers at predetermined points in the sky. At the railroad, he had human behavior to deal with and uncontrollable events. A mechanical breakdown on a single-track section of railroad would quickly back up trains for hundreds of miles, throwing many schedules into disarray. Weather always was a factor, and trains did not operate above the weather. Ice and snow could foul tracks and freeze switches. Heavy rains often triggered mudslides that blocked tracks. Every railroad has to contend with such events. The better-managed railroads cope with them better and recover faster. Unfortunately, for many dispatchers and trainmasters, the uncontrollable events became an excuse for conducting business as usual.

Many rail executives, perhaps aware that railroads were built and run in the 19th century by former Civil War officers, like to talk about military-like precision. The command-and-control management concept often was an excuse for not thinking or taking initiative, the hallmark of today's U.S. military. Critics of railroads like to point out that the U.S. military today is more diversified than are the railroads, and as one former military officer who came to the BN pointed out, the military teaches the troops to think.

Chain walked right into the culture change and the turmoil that went with it. The retired general said he had expected the railroad culture to be different from what he was used to in the military, but he was not prepared for the degree of difference he encountered. Discussing the Air Force environment with which he was so familiar, Chain said:

> As a young fighter pilot, your involvement with the enlisted people was very thin: a guy packed your parachute; a guy helped you get your helmet ready; and a guy took care of your airplane, and if he didn't take care of it well, you were the one who was going to die. So you liked each other. You trusted each other, and there was a real bonding between the officers amongst themselves and the officers with the enlisted people. That stuck with me the rest of my career as I grew up in the Air Force. . . . The officer corps and the enlisted corps have to be a brotherhood. [They] can't be two separate groups, because your life depends on those.

There was no such bonding in the railroad, at least not between the ranks and management. They didn't even like each other, for the most part. Chain soon learned that. As he said some years after his retirement from the railroad:

> The first thing I wanted to do was to go out and meet the workers—the enlisted guys—to find out what they did, how they did it, and what their problems were. I hadn't been there a week, and I went up to North Dakota—Minot. When I was in SAC, I always visited the northern bases in the winter, when it was the toughest, and the southern bases

in the summer, when it was the most miserable. I wanted to share the misery.

So I'd go straight to one of our most northern bases to meet the guys who are doing this job. I host a breakfast, and there are probably 12 of these railroaders from different disciplines sitting at the table. We weren't there 10 minutes before one of them called me a scumbag. I thought, "Well, I've been at the railroad less than a week, and this is a nice way to start." I said, "What do you mean? You don't even know me." He said, "You're just another one of those guys out of headquarters. . . . You're just management; all management stinks. You guys don't like us. You hate us."

Chain tried to figure out where the animosity came from. "You talk about putting somebody back on his heels," he said. "I thought, 'Well, there's a barrier that we're going to have to work through. That isn't going to be done overnight.'"

"I'm not complaining about it," he added. "I'm just being honest about what I found, which was that I expected a different culture. I didn't expect the animosity, because I didn't know how you could possibly run an organization—we talked about running trains on time. How can you establish a process by which you run trains on time when the people who are going to run the trains hate you?"

Chain related how he then met with a group of lower-level supervisors. Here he began to get a sense of what was wrong with the culture, at least in operations. As he recalled,

> The next group I talk with are the young exempts [nonunion supervisors frequently called officers in the militaristic rail culture] who had been promoted out of the ranks. Now they are wearing a coat and tie, and they are "Mr." Instantly, after 20 years in which they've been hammering and nailing or something, now they are somebody, and they, by God, are going to treat those people who worked for them the way they were treated. So they didn't move into an officer culture. They moved into a get-even culture.

They had moved up in the pecking order. Chain said some seemed to have the attitude "Now I've been promoted; I'm going to act just like the guy I'm replacing who came out of that same culture."

Chain never was able to bridge the gap between being a four-star general and being a civilian in charge of operations. He was used to more collegial help and people following orders than was the practice at the BN. An example was when Chain learned that the railroad contract with Amtrak provided for a monthly incentive of $1 million for on-time performance. He ordered the transportation department and dispatchers to see that the BN received the bonus. No one warned him: The railroad performed on time for Amtrak, but doing so created congestion and delays to the BN freight operations that cost more each month than the bonus it received from Amtrak.

Chain did try to deal with the culture he found. "It was a strange environment, but I still had a five-year contract, and by gosh, I was going to try to do whatever I could do. I went back to the basic principles of trying to do whatever I could with the exempts."

By the spring of 1993, Grinstein realized that Chain was not the answer in operations and that he would need a new head of operations. He transferred Chain to the new position of executive vice president of safety and corporate support, where he focused on improving the railroad's safety performance. Replacing him as head of operations was Bill Francis, another longtime BN executive.

At the same time, Grinstein changed the duties of two other executives without changing their titles. Bill Greenwood, who had been executive vice president and chief operating officer and who many thought might succeed Grinstein, went back to heading marketing and sales, as he had under Gaskins. John Q. Anderson, a former McKinsey and Company consultant who had joined the railroad as head of marketing and sales when Greenwood had been promoted, similarly kept his title but was put in charge of coal marketing, at that time BN's largest single line of business.

It was in the area of safety that Chain made his most significant contribution to the railroad. "One of the big problems was safety," he said. "We weren't just the worst railroad in safety. We were twice as bad as the next worst railroad in safety."

Chain learned that there was a connection between safety and the railroad culture. "I knew that people are products of their environment," he noted, observing that the environment seemed closer to that which existed in 1855 than to current reality.

He realized that safety improvement would be a long-term project. "We've got to engage teams to include the workforce out there, [and] you then also run into the problem with the union leader, who is another huge barrier," Chain said. "To jump over that, which we did in safety—we jumped over the union leader in safety—is how we ended up busting the safety problem."

The safety problem was bad statistically, and it was costing the railroad millions of dollars in liability claims and settlements for injured workers, to say nothing of the cost in customer satisfaction. Injuries always are followed by investigations and disrupted operations.

The BN in 1991 reported 2,887 injury cases that resulted in at least one day away from work. By 1995 there was an 84 percent reduction in the figure, to 467 cases. In the same four-year period, the number of injuries that were reportable to the Federal Railroad Administration under its rules dropped 77 percent, from 12.99 per 200,000 work hours to 2.93. Back injuries were a particular problem because they were difficult to prove or to dispute. Under Chain's focus on safety improvement, this kind of injury fell 85 percent in four years. Eye injuries declined 88 percent over the same period, and there was similar improvement in every category of personal injury.

"The whole point is that railroads are in business to make money," Chain said. He observed that if the BN's safety record had remained where it was in 1991, the BN easily could have been one of the railroads that went out of business.

Railroads operate under the Federal Employers Liability Act (FELA), a tort-based system of compensation. FELA predates modern state worker compensation laws that are focused on returning injured or ill workers to their jobs as quickly as possible and that provide a no-fault system of compensation. In the railroads, sick or injured workers must prove that their employer's negligence played some part in causing their injury or illness. Most claims are settled, but enough injury cases are taken to court and enough juries have awarded huge verdicts that railroads tend to settle for an amount higher than the same incident would cost under state worker compensation programs.

The FELA system is much favored by rail unions. A virtual "FELA bar" of personal injury lawyers exists, and many union leaders owe their election to office to campaign support from FELA lawyers who, in turn, are designated as the union's "authorized" personal injury lawyers. The railroad industry tried to campaign for repeal or amendment of FELA in the 1990s, but in the face of vigorous union lobbying in opposition, they were unable even to get hearings from Congress.

During the 1990s, as worker injury costs skyrocketed, all major railroads were forced to change the amounts they accrued for payments and ended up taking special charges against earnings. Safety became recognized at the BN and other railroads as "good business." Chain described how this change came about: "Many of the exempts said, 'The reason we have a safety problem is because people aren't getting hurt. They are just trying to get money from the railroad. Therefore we don't have a safety problem. We just have an attitude problem.' That was exactly right."

He may not have expected the culture he found, but Chain quickly understood the safety problem. When he went out to the field, workers gave him an earful: "Management doesn't care. They give us crappy equipment. They make us work long hours, and they don't pay any attention. They wouldn't spend a buck to help us get anything that we need."

That of course was not true, but it was a measure of the animosity that existed at that time between rank-and-file workers and their supervisors. Chain realized that the system was flawed. "Some way, we [were] going to have to bridge this," he said.

Some in management didn't even acknowledge there was a problem. "We're last because the other guys don't report everything," one executive said. "We report ours." Of course, the same thing was said at the other railroads.

The traditional railroad approach of naming safety teams of workers and exempts had failed. Chain tried a variation, bringing in representatives from across the railroad so he could pick their brains. He described the new approach: "We sat them down in a big room in a big horseshoe. I explained that we've got people out there who really [were] being maimed, and the only way we're going to solve this is for us collectively to figure out what we need to do, what kind of equipment we need, what kind of rules we need to change so the person isn't subject to getting hurt, and what kind of teaching we can do."

Chain brought in safety experts from DuPont. The chemical company had a reputation for safe operations and had created a safety consultancy for other companies and industries. As Chain recalled, "DuPont came in and did a survey. They said: 'You guys got a mess on your hands.' But they said that they could run classes and help."

Grinstein was supportive. "He said, 'If you need that, we'll do it.' The biggest thing, I think, that DuPont did is that although they taught some nice fundamentals, the exempts recognized that management was serious about safety in that they were spending some real money to hire somebody else to come out," Chain said, observing that the BN was "a rather frugal organization."

Chain asked the employees, "If you had a pot of gold—and don't worry about stepping on anybody's toes—where would you spend it? What would you do? What rules would you change? What would you buy?" He received a mix of frivolous and serious responses.

One participant said: "Well, we've got those Kubotas out there [small, motorized all-terrain-like vehicles that carried tools and that inspectors used to travel the length of trains in yards], but the wheel base is too short. We shouldn't have bought them. We should have bought something else." Chain immediately committed not to buy more Kubotas and asked the employee what he would recommend.

Employees were skeptical, but as Chain said, "Right then, I saw to it that we never bought another Kubota." Other employees spoke up about eye injuries, and Chain responded, "Okay, we'll get so many goggles out there it will make your mind spin."

At the first couple of meetings, which were to be scheduled monthly, Chain says he reacted to everything by saying, "We're going to do it." Then, he said, "What we needed to do was put in place some rules to go along with them." One of the most prevalent causes of injury was getting on and off moving equipment. "That went back to the 1850s," says Chain. "That's how railroaders prided themselves. They got on and off that stuff. I said: 'We're going to stop getting on and off moving equipment.'" This decision was an assault on the macho self-image of the railroad worker. "Well, if they weren't getting hurt, it would be fine," Chain said. "But they were getting hurt, so we put that rule out, and I think if anything was hated, it was that rule. If anything would send a signal that we were serious about stopping injuries, that was it."

Employees pointed out that the rule meant that trains would have to be stopped, to which Chain told them: "Well, that means you stop that train until those people get on and off. I don't care what it costs us in money. I don't want anybody to get hurt, not because we're saving or losing money but because I care about that person. I care about each and every one of those people out there, and we're going to do everything we can to see that nobody ever gets hurt."

The BN was serious, and Chain dived into the safety challenge with enthusiasm. He recalled:

> Then we started spending the money. As to eye injuries, we started mandating the glasses, but we didn't say, "Just wear glasses." We flooded the system with glasses of all sizes and shapes. People were supposed to wear safety boots. We

mandated safety boots that we paid for. One of the young
people came up with his own study out of Lincoln, Nebraska, working in the shop. He did his own study on rings. . . .
He got some pictures of people who had [fingers] pulled off.
So we mandated—not me but the team mandated—that
nobody could wear a ring. That meant that Grinstein
couldn't wear a ring. I couldn't wear a ring. Even in the
headquarters we couldn't wear a ring.

The next change had to do with dust masks and beards, which
also was controversial at first, according to Chain:

I had guys come to me and say, "Jack, I met my wife when I
had a beard. I married her when I had a beard. She's never
seen me without a beard." I said, "Well, you're going to
have to either change your job or you're going to have to
shave the beard, because you've got to be able to wear a
mask if you're going to be with maintenance-of-way." By
supporting the people in the field who were coming up with
[these rules], we really did end up cracking through.

Chain believed that the BN probably saved billions of dollars, not
just millions, by the improvements in safety. The BN's safety record,
relative to that of other railroads, improved greatly.

Some union leaders and some company officials were less than
enthusiastic about the safety campaign Chain was driving. As he
recalled:

There was some anger that we weren't going through [the
union leaders]. Yet it was awfully hard for them to tell their
people, although some of them did, "Don't participate in
this." I actually had some guys in safety teams who either
switched . . . to other unions, or just said, "I'm going to
continue to support this, because it's more important than
my union membership." They saw that we were serious,
and the results proved that we were serious. These weren't
made-up results to show somebody. These were results for
the people in the field.

Chain then came up with a 2.5 Club—a reference to the industry-leading Norfolk Southern injury rate—for any group that had below 2.5 injuries per 200,000 man-hours. He noted, "Those in the 2.5 Club, without being told ahead of time, were all given five shares of Burlington Northern stock." That reward was followed up by options.

There were objections. "But fortunately Jerry was a supporter on things like that," Chain said. "I told him, 'I'll take that to the board. If we're going to be successful, we've got to reward people.'" Even though the BN ratcheted up the 2.5 Club the following year, there was cultural resistance to rewarding rank-and-file employees for working safely rather than disciplining them for violating rules.

The labor-management culture had evolved into a series of trades so that neither side would be able to claim "victory." Such trades frequently were petty and certainly did nothing to improve morale or performance. Chain cited an example:

> [During] that very first trip to Minot, one of the first things I saw was piles of snow. There were no hookups for people to plug their car heaters in. [Block heaters were a standard amenity at many employers throughout the frigid upper Midwest.] So I said to the division superintendent, "Why don't we have heater units to plug in for our guys?" He says, "If we're going to do that, we're going to trade them." I said, "What do you mean by trade them?" He said, "Well, for instance, they all want big lockers. We could trade them small lockers for putting that in there, if that's what you want, Jack." I said, "You don't trade for something that a person should have. Now you get plug-ins for these guys, and you don't trade them for it."

Although providing block heaters for personal vehicles was not a safety issue, the incident demonstrates just how petty the relationship between employees and their unions on the one hand, and the railroad on the other hand, had become. Chain recognized the importance of having the company make the workers' lives a bit easier without having to negotiate it.

Chain tried, with some success, to bring the military culture to the BN, at least in the area of safety. "You [should] want to take care of your people because you care about your people," he said. "If you take care of your people and they know you care about them, they're going to work better at the same time. It's not just that they're not going to get hurt, but they're going to do the job better and be more responsive to other things. It's changing the culture of the trainmaster going up for the long-term success that is so critical."

Grinstein was a strong supporter of Chain's efforts and a decade later still credited the retired general with having had a significant positive impact on the railroad. "[Safety improvement] was a fundamental change that had to take place inside that company," Grinstein said. "People in some way understood that until we undertook that safety immersion—baptism—that the company didn't really care about them. They were just a number." He credited Chain for the sharp improvement in safety: "He did a fabulous job. But what it said to these people was—Jack gave them safety glasses, hearing protection, and shoes."

The BN was not the only railroad where safety became a major focus. The cost of injury claims was hitting everyone in the industry, and all were emphasizing personal protection for employees. The Santa Fe, for example, began requiring the wearing of safety glasses at its mechanical shops in Topeka as early as 1975. The purchases and materials department followed a few months later. By June 11, 1976, the vice president of operations mandated that the safety eyewear program be implemented system-wide. Reportedly, at the time, Santa Fe faced some resistance from the unions over this policy. The United Transportation Union (UTU), for instance, filed section 6 notices for various issues, from ensuring a choice of ophthalmologists to claiming the cost of time spent securing the safety glasses.

Santa Fe's safety-shoe program was revamped numerous times from its start in the 1960s, with a wider selection of safety shoes and an increased subsidy offered in the 1970s and 1980s. By 1991, steel-toe safety boots were mandatory for all Santa Fe employees in safety-sensitive positions, and employees were provided one free pair a year. Similar programs continue at BNSF today, with a substantial subsidy provided for the purchase of one pair of safety boots per year.

Nothing that the BN did was unique, but changes in the BN's safety performance stood out because it needed so much improvement. When the BN took actions that were virtually routine at other railroads, it seemed as if the BN had pioneered those innovations. Regardless, they had the desired effect, and the BN's safety performance did improve.

Former BN director Evans agreed, saying the board was concerned about the cost of injuries and accidents. "Jack did a whale of a job in that respect. Our accident rate was cut in half, cut in half again, and then cut in half again," he said. "That was Jack's leadership."

A Strike Leads to Millions of Dollars in Savings

Also in 1991, the U.S. railroad industry was headed for its first nationwide strike since a four-day strike in 1982. The dispute was involved, and an understanding of the working of the Railway Labor Act (RLA) of 1926 is in order, because the strike ended up with unintended results that saved the railroads more than $250 million in annual labor expenses.

By design, the RLA strongly discourages work stoppages in the railroad industry—for unions to strike or for companies to impose their contracts or lock out employees in a labor dispute. The big agreements between railroads and unions—airlines were added to the RLA in 1935—usually run indefinitely but may be amended periodically.

When one side or the other wants to change the contract, it serves a section 6 notice on the other party, as provided for in section 6 of the RLA. That notice spells out the new wage rates and work rules that the union wants for its members or that the company proposes to implement. When an agreement is reached—and most disputes end in negotiated settlements—the settlement typically establishes a moratorium on further change and spells out when those issues next can be renegotiated. A key RLA provision is that during negotiations or mediation, each side must observe the status quo. Agreement provisions covering wage rates and work rules may be changed only after an agreement is reached or the parties fail to reach an agreement and thus become free to exercise "self-help," as the law calls it. As discussed in the previous chapter, employees may strike only in major disputes—repudiation of an existing contract, for example, or exhaustion of the negotiation process—whereas minor disputes, such as those over most alleged contract violations, must be submitted to binding arbitration.

The National Mediation Board (NMB), which consists of three presidential appointees, administers most aspects of the act. Unions and railroads negotiate without government involvement, but either side may call for mediation at any time. Depending on the politics of who is appointing NMB members, sometimes the railroads seek intervention, and sometimes the unions do. The NMB has no time limits and has the discretion to hold the parties in mediation. When the board determines that further mediation would serve no purpose, it withdraws mediation and offers both sides binding arbitration. In many such disputes, one side or the other rejects arbitration. That starts a 30-day cooling-off period at the end of which the union is free to strike and the company is free to impose its proposals or to lock out employees.

If the NMB determines that the nation or a significant region is about to suffer serious economic disruption by losing essential transportation service, it may certify that determination to the president, who may appoint an emergency board to recommend a basis for settlement. That extends the status quo for up to 60 additional days. The PEB, as such a Presidential Emergency Board is known, studies the issue and issues its recommendation within 30 days. The two sides then have another 30-day cooling-off period to negotiate, using the PEB recommendation as a template. If no agreement is reached, the provisions of the act have been exhausted, and the parties may take whatever action they see fit.

In the case of major rail disputes, by tradition, Congress intervenes under the commerce clause of the Constitution. Congress, of course, is not qualified to draft a labor agreement, so it tends to use the PEB recommendation as a template and imposes a settlement.

The 1991 labor dispute was particularly complex. A dozen separate unions were involved, each with its own parochial bargaining issues. Some issues in the dispute, which was a negotiating round that began in 1988 for a national wage and work rule agreement, went back to 1984. Rail workers had received no increase in wages since 1988, nor had railroads been able to achieve any significant productivity gains. One of the longest-running issues in the talks was health and welfare. Railroads paid the full cost of health insurance, and, with costs rising rapidly, they were seeking in their new agreement to have various new cost controls, including access to "managed care."

The railroads sought to contain health care costs in the 1984 national round of negotiations. No agreement was reached then, but both sides agreed to continue discussions, and the 1984 round ended with a new national agreement in 1986 that didn't resolve the health and welfare dispute. The next round began in June 1988, and the railroads took the position that they would not consider wages and work rules until the long-delayed health and welfare issue was resolved. The result was impasse.

Early in 1990 the Railway Labor Executives' Association, representing unions in national negotiations, and the National Carriers' Conference Committee, which represented the railroads, agreed to shorten the mediation and arbitration process of the law and go directly to a Presidential Emergency Board with all issues in the round.

That agreement was intended, in part, to get union leaders off the hook, because if they dealt with the 1984 health and welfare issue, they faced having to go to members for ratification of an agreement they knew would be unpopular, yet if they didn't deal with it, there would be no progress on a national agreement and rail workers who had gone nearly two years without a pay raise would have to go even longer without one. Union leaders had seen some of their colleagues being turned out of office if they asked their members to begin paying for health insurance.

The deal worked for both sides. By putting the health care cost issue into the government's lap, it removed a contentious issue from the table, and some negotiators hoped they then could get on with negotiating a wage-and-work-rules package that included productivity improvements. The size of train crews, for example, was a major issue for most railroads, even though some had partially addressed it in earlier negotiations at the individual carrier level. The Santa Fe, for example, had negotiated a crew consist agreement with the UTU in 1989 that enabled the railroad to operate through-freight trains with fewer brakemen. Most carriers in 1991, however, still were operating with crews of four or five.

As had been the case with many industries, the rapidly rising cost of health care had become a significant financial burden on the railroads, one they felt strongly needed to be brought under control. The railroads sought a change in the system to provide for managed care, then seen as a less costly way to provide health care for workers and their families.

The unions' initial position was that they would accept no change in health care, for which workers then paid nothing. "No single industry can solve what is a national problem," a securities analyst said at the time, referring to the health and welfare discussion. "That makes it appropriate to have a Presidential Emergency Board study and recommend a resolution of the issue."

In fact, negotiators for both sides were agreeing to disagree. By seeking a PEB, they acknowledged that they would not be able to reach an agreement on their own. Both sides agreed in advance not to take any "self-help" action—strike, lockout, or imposition of wage and rules changes unilaterally—until at least 30 days after the PEB reported on the wage and rules issue, which wouldn't happen until after it made its recommendations on the health and welfare dispute. More revealing, both sides agreed not to take any action at any time Congress was not in session, acknowledging that they knew Congress ultimately would have to bail them out. At the same time, they wanted to be in a position for Congress to step in quickly and order an end to a strike or lockout. A few months later, the nation was on the verge of the Gulf War, and neither unions nor railroads wanted to be perceived as having selfishly endangered the nation in a time of emergency.

In January 1991, with troops and material pouring into the Persian Gulf, the Presidential Emergency Board issued its recommendations. Most observers read the recommendations as essentially siding with management. Labor sources made no secret that they didn't like the report at all. The recommendations supported the carriers in their effort to change the health plan and gave the carriers long-sought work rule improvements in the agreements of several crafts. For example, track maintenance workers, who for years had worked solely within division boundaries, were to work over greater distances. This change made it economical for the railroads to buy additional highly automated, expensive track-maintenance and rail-laying equipment for newly created system production gangs.

There were several voluntary extensions of the deadlines as both sides agreed to do nothing disruptive while the war was imminent or under way, but it became increasingly obvious that a strike was the only way to resolve the settlement because it would force a settlement on union workers without their having to approve a concessionary agreement.

Both sides began to lobby Congress in anticipation of its coming role in the dispute. Unions even tried to get a more pro-labor set of recommendations, unsuccessfully seeking legislation that would postpone any action while a new panel was created by Congress to study the issue.

With the Gulf War over and all delay provisions having been exhausted, the railroad unions struck at midnight on April 17. Congress took just 17 hours to pass legislation ordering the workers back to their jobs. It imposed the recommendations of the Presidential Emergency Board on both sides, with legislative language that it should be as though the parties had negotiated the agreement.

The latter statement proved dreadful for the United Transportation Union and extremely beneficial to the railroads. At the start of the process, the railroads had served a notice on the UTU that they wanted to negotiate the size of train crews—crew consist, as it is known. The union took the position that crew consist never had been the subject of "national handling," and it refused even to discuss the issue.

PEB 219, as the deciding board was known, sided with the UTU that crew consist was a local issue and not subject to industry-wide bargaining. But PEB members expressed the view that it was long past the time for crew consist to be resolved, and they recommended that the issue be negotiated on each railroad, subject to binding arbitration if agreement were not reached within a specified period.

When Congress imposed PEB 219 on the unions and the railroads, that recommendation became law. With the parties forced to negotiate, agreements on crew consist were reached in railroad-by-railroad negotiations over the next year. To avoid protracted litigation or arbitration, most railroads agreed to a gradual reduction of jobs and income protection for the affected workers. The result was the loss of 25,000 brakeman positions and a reduction of labor expenses of about $250 million annually at the time. No other single labor reform in the industry has had as big a financial impact.

A year later, in another dispute and knowing they would not be allowed to strike nationally, the International Association of Machinists (IAM) thought it could strike a single railroad without government intervention and struck CSX Transportation. To labor's shock, the entire railroad industry shut down, locking out more than 200,000 workers. This time it took Congress three days to order the workers back to their jobs. And because it was dealing with a shutdown and there had been no Presidential Emergency Board, Congress had no template from which to work. It ordered that the two sides engage in best-and-final-offer binding arbitration, with the arbitrators choosing the best and final offer of one side or the other, as opposed to "interest" arbitration in which the final award is a blend of demands from both sides. Rather than risk being a "loser" in public, both railroad and union negotiators then managed to reach a negotiated settlement, precisely what Congress had intended.

The decision to shut down, however, was not without controversy inside the railroad industry, and suddenly the BN and the Union Pacific were headed in opposite directions.

Locking out was on the table for discussion, and the issue was whether all railroads would shut down in support of one. No one could remember the last time the entire industry shut down, and it was not certain they would do so this time. If only one railroad were struck, the rest of the industry could continue to operate. The railroad officials knew, however, that if they allowed one railroad to bear a strike by itself, they all placed themselves in the position where unions could whipsaw them into favorable settlements.

The rail chiefs did not know at that time which railroad would be struck. Grinstein recalled the incident that he referred to as a shootout between himself and the head of the Union Pacific:

> At our meeting, Drew [Lewis, UP chief executive] wanted to settle, and I didn't. Drew was thinking that they're going to pick out BN, because BN has such [lousy] labor relations. That's what was, I think, in the back of his mind, because someone turned to me in this meeting at the AAR [Association of American Railroads] or whatever it was and said, "If they strike Drew, will you shut down?" I said, "Absolutely. That's what it means. That's what we have to do." John Snow [then CSX chief executive] was siding with Drew Lewis.

The issue was complicated by political realities. Representative John Dingell (D-Michigan), powerful chairman of the House Interstate and Foreign Commerce Committee, had made it clear that Congress would not act without an industry-wide work stoppage. Dingell said Congress would not order American workers to stay on the job and take away their right to strike. There would have to be a work stoppage before Congress would legislate.

So the issue before the rail chiefs was simple: If there was a strike against one, do the railroads deal with it as a strike against all? The strike in the previous year, which was ended by Congress after just 17 hours, still was fresh in everyone's mind. "In 1992 the issue was, if they strike, do we all shut down?" Grinstein said. "Drew said no, and I said yes. We were really having a battle. John Snow was siding with Drew. I am convinced, although I have no proof, that Drew thought that we were the ones that would get struck because of BN's recent labor relations." If the UP could continue to operate while the BN was shut down, the UP could gain considerable commercial advantage.

Grinstein pointed out, however, that Jim Dagnon, the BN's chief of labor relations, had managed to change the relationship with most of the unions, adding,

We were not the bad guy at that point. We were still
thought of by the railroads that way, but I don't think necessarily by all the unions at that point, because we had a lot
of dealings with them. I think [David] Goode [chief executive of the Norfolk Southern] was with me. I know [George
W.] Edwards [Kansas City Southern chief executive] was
with me, because I remember his conversation. At midnight,
[IAM] brilliantly struck CSX. If they had not struck CSX,
my guess is I would not have known how it was going to
turn out. We were prepared to shut down if they struck
anyone, but I don't know what Drew would have done.

The BN became involved in another labor battle as a residual
issue from the 1991 strike and the crew consist issue. UTU locals,
representing some 3,500 train service employees on the northern
part of the railroad, never had served section 6 notices in the 1988
round of negotiations, nor had they given their power of attorney to
the international union to negotiate on their behalf. PEB 219 and the
imposition of its recommendations did not apply to the BN employees in those UTU units. These were the same unions that had refused
to allow the railroad to operate Expediter intermodal trains with
two-person crews several years earlier, leading the BN into its ill-
fated Winona Bridge exercise. The BN still could not reduce the size
of the crews.

The UTU locals were determined not to give up any more jobs,
especially after a federal court ruled that the PEB 219 crew consist
recommendation did not apply to them. The international union leadership understood the need to settle, but without the proxy from the
local unions it was barred by the union's constitution from getting
involved formally, nor could it overrule the locals.

Meanwhile, the railroads that competed with the BN were beginning to gain a cost advantage as they reduced the size of each train
crew and the BN trains still were crewed by four and five people.

Using a reporter for the *Journal of Commerce* as a go-between,
UTU International president Thomas DuBose would say: "Mr.
Dagnon has a choice. He can negotiate or he can litigate." DuBose
then would suggest something he might be able to do if Dagnon
would take certain action on behalf of the BN. Because of the union
constitution, the two men could not deal with each other directly at
that time.

Through the journalistic back channel, Dagnon would respond to the DuBose initiative, occasionally offering a proposal of his own. Local UTU leaders, of course, knew that eventually they would have to give the BN the same kind of crew consist agreement the UTU had given other railroads.

Finally, the UTU general chairman took a vacation and went on a Caribbean cruise. Grinstein recalled with a laugh, "They cut the deal while he was at sea." Upon his return from the cruise, the UTU general chairman was the first member of the union to sign up for the early-retirement buyout that was part of the settlement agreement.

KREBS SOLIDIFIES HIS CONTROL

With two years of difficult labor relations behind them, the railroads again focused their energies on trying to retain the traffic they had and if possible to recapture some that had been lost to competing transportation modes.

Seeing the drop in operating expenses and the increase in operating income that went with the reduction in train crews, Wall Street securities analysts began favoring railroad stocks as good investments, even though railroads still were not earning their cost of capital. Commercially, though, except for a few railroads that had special circumstances, the industry was in a slow- or no-growth environment. Railroad market share of most categories of higher-rated merchandise cargo continued to erode, shifting to truckers that offered greater service flexibility than could railroads.

Despite the entry of the C&NW into the Powder River Basin, the BN continued to enjoy rapid growth in its coal business, although margins with each new contract seemed to get thinner. The BN tried to end the vicious cycle of trading traffic between itself and the C&NW, backed by the Union Pacific, and always at a lower rate.

The Santa Fe, at this time, had a rapidly growing intermodal business between Southern California and the Memphis and Chicago gateways to eastern railroads. Trailers and containers carried by the railroad now accounted for more than half of Santa Fe revenue. The only problem was that because their service was not as good or consistent as trucking, railroads had to charge less than trucks, which meant the intermodal business was not nearly as profitable as other lines of business.

Also in early 1991, the Santa Fe relocated its headquarters from its historic building on Michigan Avenue in downtown Chicago to a plain suburban office park in Schaumburg, Illinois.

After Rob Krebs restructured what now was called the Santa Fe Pacific Corporation to fight off hostile takeover attempts, the company essentially was left with a railroad and just a few nontransportation assets. Michael Haverty, a longtime Santa Fe operating executive, had been named president of the Atchison, Topeka, and Santa Fe Railway. One of Haverty's greatest achievements was negotiating the first arrangement in which a truckload motor carrier committed to using intermodal service.

J. B. Hunt Transportation Services, the second-largest national truckload carrier, agreed to put its trailers on the Santa Fe dedicated intermodal trains. The deal provided a significant boost in revenue for the railroad, and it allowed Hunt to schedule drivers more efficiently, using the railroad particularly where there were load imbalances and saving the cost of drivers moving about the country with no revenue freight in their trailers.

The Hunt–Santa Fe service, which was given the trade name "Quantuum," was particularly significant because only a couple of years earlier a Hunt executive had told an industry conference that there was no way Hunt ever would use "substitute service." Hunt customers wouldn't stand for it, he said, because it was not good enough. The Hunt deal was a breakthrough, and many truckload carriers now use intermodal service from all major railroads. While they still compete vigorously with each other, truckers also have become major customers of the railroads.

In June 1991, Haverty resigned as president of the Santa Fe and was replaced by Krebs. It was commonly accepted at the time that with the sale or spin-off of the other assets there was no need for two presidents and that the company was Krebs's more than it was Haverty's. Haverty later became chief executive of the Kansas City Southern Railway.

The Santa Fe was able to reach Memphis by connecting with the BN at Avard, Oklahoma. The Avard connection was crucial to the Santa Fe, but it was a secondary route for the much bigger BN, which had acquired the route through the Frisco purchase in 1980. The former Frisco line was a light-density single track line that handled relatively little BN traffic and by the early 1990s had become a candidate for downgrading.

The Santa Fe and the BN developed a voluntary coordination

agreement for handling the Santa Fe's traffic through the Avard connection. The Santa Fe marketed eastbound traffic originating on its lines, while the BN would market westbound traffic originating in its territory. Early in 1994 the arrangement was upgraded to a haulage agreement in which the BN would handle Santa Fe trains between Avard and Memphis, but the Santa Fe would handle the marketing in both directions.

For the BN, however, the addition of a couple of trains a day in each direction did not change the economics enough to justify the dedication of managerial or physical resources to the service. The Santa Fe was receiving less than satisfactory service and was losing competitive intermodal business to the Southern Pacific, which had a longer, but single-line, route between Southern California and Memphis that went through San Antonio and Houston. Santa Fe chief Rob Krebs made several visits to the BN headquarters to seek greater cooperation, but the incentive was just not there. It would not be until the BN and the Santa Fe merged and the Avard-Memphis line became a single-line route that it would get the attention and upgrading necessary to make it a competitive route.

As network businesses, railroads needed every bit of revenue they could get, and most railroad executives understood that if a piece of business provided anything more than its direct cost, it was helping cover the fixed cost of the system. This led to the continuation of the practice that began with deregulation in 1980 of locking up business in exchange for rate concessions.

The railroads—and the BN and the Santa Fe both were active in putting as much business as possible under contract—did secure their revenue base. But because contracts tended to be at rates that didn't cover fully allocated costs, they actually contributed to the inability to earn the cost of capital. Unable to increase margins by pricing, the industry still was focused on increasing margins by cutting costs.

No one knew when it would happen, but there was a sense in the railroad industry and on Wall Street that there would be more railroad mergers. There still were more railroads and rail infrastructure than the available business could support. The industry essentially was down to four major carriers in the West (the BN, the Santa Fe, the Southern Pacific, and the Union Pacific) and three in the East (Conrail, the Norfolk Southern, and CSX). In addition, the Kansas City Southern, the Illinois Central, and the U.S. subsidiaries of the Canadian National and the Canadian Pacific had Class 1 status but were considered large regionals at best. The Union Pacific had effective control of the Chicago and North Western and was moving before the ICC to make it official.

The BN had nibbled without success around the edges of the sale of the SP by the Santa Fe Southern Pacific Corporation after the failed attempt to unite the SP and the Santa Fe in 1987.

Grinstein recalled going to Denver in 1988 to meet with Phil Anschutz to discuss a possible joint purchase of the SP by the BN and Anschutz's Denver and Rio Grande Western. "Darius [Gaskins] and I went and met with Phil Anschutz, and I had a separate meeting with Phil," said Grinstein. "We met with him in that office with all the Remington sculptures and all the American art, western art." Anschutz owns one of the world's finest collections of western art and displays much of it in the offices of his private investment company.

"We discussed with him the possibility of joint venturing on the SP, and he was very ambiguous about the discussion," Grinstein said. As discussed previously, the Rio Grande was doomed as an independent railroad. The SP was in bad physical, financial, and managerial shape, but it served some growing markets that made it attractive to several potential buyers. For the BN, it would provide access to all Pacific Coast ports the BN didn't already serve; it would allow single-line service between Texas and California, which the UP didn't have; and it offered a better route between Texas and the upper Midwest than the BN had.

BN executives, with the benefit of hindsight, had come to realize that buying the Frisco in 1980 probably was the wrong acquisition strategically—purchase of the Missouri Pacific, which had been available, might have been a better strategic fit with its system. Bob Downing thought that the Katy, which could have been bought relatively inexpensively, would have been a better move for the BN. Grinstein noted: "A big mistake the BN made was not buying the MoP. It was a huge mistake."

Grinstein didn't waste time looking back, however. "Call them 'strategic misjudgments,'" he said. "Whatever they were, they were things that the company has survived, and given its culture and its franchise, [the BN] can become the premier railroad."

The BN had doubts that if it had bid for the SP, it could have gotten the acquisition approved. The Rio Grande also was a good fit if there was a joint bid, because it closed a gap between the BN at Denver and the SP at Salt Lake City. If the second central transcontinental corridor had been under one management, it might have been an effective competitor to the Union Pacific. "I had another meeting with [Anschutz] a few weeks later," Grinstein said. "Again, I said to him, 'I would be interested in doing it.' By the way, I had talked to some other people. I had talked to Mitsubishi about possibly joining with us, because they were making a lot of investments in the United States."

A joint venture might have made sense for the BN, but Anschutz obviously had his own plan in motion. "Phil already had his plan in mind, but he wasn't sharing it with us—or with me. He was very closed-mouthed about it. Maybe that's right. Maybe you should be," Grinstein mused. Anschutz was known as a deal maker, and it was generally accepted that he intended to sell the combined Rio Grande and SP, whereas a joint acquisition with the BN, which intended to remain in the railroad business, would have prevented him from the kind of financial dealing that he liked. He also would have had the BN as a partner, and he tended to be a mostly independent businessman.

There was no way that the BN and the Union Pacific ever could combine. There would have been too many competitive issues to overcome, and culturally the two western giants were more suited to war with each other than to peacefully coexist. So, with the Southern Pacific off the table as a possible acquisition for the BN, that left only the Santa Fe as potential partner in the West.

About this time Grinstein was under growing pressure from the BN board of directors to get his succession in order. He still was a few years from retirement—he would not be 65 until mid-1997—but the turmoil in the management ranks over previous years had convinced the board that Grinstein's successor was not then on the payroll.

In early 1993 there were sporadic rumors that the BN and the Santa Fe were discussing a possible merger. As Grinstein later said, the talks were on-again, off-again, and at one time were off for several months. A merger of the two railroads had certain attractions. The BN and the Santa Fe were a good fit strategically, and Krebs, who was just 51 years old that May, would solve the BN succession problem.

During one of the lulls when it appeared that Krebs, Grinstein, and their advisers would not be able to reach an accord, Grinstein turned to Richard K. Davidson, president of the Union Pacific Railroad, and offered him the BN presidency with the assurance that he would succeed Grinstein as chairman and chief executive in the future.

Former BN director Daniel Evans confirmed that the BN had tried to hire Davidson. At that time the UP was headquartered in

Omaha, and its holding company was in Bethlehem, Pennsylvania. Davidson had not been Drew Lewis's first choice to succeed him. "Davidson was ready to leave [the UP]," Evans recalled. "We were looking at Davidson as a heck of a guy." At least an informal offer was made to Davidson, and when he informed the UP board that he planned to leave, the board instructed Lewis to name Davidson president of the holding company and to move him to headquarters in Bethlehem, clearly making him Lewis's successor-in-waiting. Lewis would reach mandatory retirement age in 1996.

Davidson was a highly regarded executive. "[Getting Davidson] obviously would have been marvelous, leaving the merger totally out of it," Evans said. "The merger might not have happened." Evans continued:

> We were close. If he had been hired, then it would have been an interesting thing if we then went back into a merger set of talks with Santa Fe. Suddenly, Krebs has no place to go. I don't know whether that would have been enough to tip that, whether Krebs was strong enough. . . . So it would have been interesting to see what would have happened. Actually, I think it might well have been that if Davidson had come aboard and replaced Jerry and the merger had gone ahead, it would have worked even better than it did. I think Davidson would have brought people. With Rob [Krebs] there, though, it meant you had his group of board members, the Burlington group of board members. . . . The ones who were close to Rob were very close to him. I think that helped him.

It's only speculation, but Davidson would have been aligned with neither side, although he briefly would have been the BN chief executive. "That's why I say I think it might have been easier for a guy like [Davidson], who was really skilled, to come in and meld those two corporations together," Evans suggested.

Merger talks did get the board's focus off of a successor to Grinstein. "We were pushing him to get—as time went on, as he got closer and closer to retirement age—we think you've got to get this thing going. That slowed down some, because once we got into the negotiations for the Santa Fe merger, that changed the whole dynamics of succession planning."

The BN and the Santa Fe finally reached a merger agreement and announced to the world on June 30, 1994, that they planned to combine. In a joint announcement from Santa Fe headquarters in Schaumburg, Illinois, and BN headquarters in Fort Worth, Texas, the two companies said they were creating a rail network covering the midwestern and western United States, able to provide shippers with single-line service connecting all principal West Coast ports with major midwestern and western markets and with ports and markets in the Southeast.

Santa Fe shareholders were to receive 0.27 of a share of Burlington Northern common stock for each Santa Fe share. Initially, the two companies expected the merger to be an all-stock transaction with no cash changing hands. Separately, the Santa Fe announced that it would distribute to its shareholders, by the end of September 1994, the remaining stock it still owned in the Santa Fe Pacific Gold Corporation. The distribution was to be a dividend and was not dependent on the merger.

The merger partners said that the BN, which would be the surviving corporate entity, would change its name to Burlington Northern Santa Fe Corporation, and the merged railroad would be called the Burlington Northern and Santa Fe Railway Company.

Grinstein would be chairman and Krebs would be president and chief executive officer of the new company. The Grinstein succession problem had been solved. One industry analyst commented that the BN was paying several billion dollars "to hire Rob Krebs as CEO, and it's getting a railroad thrown in for good measure."

In their press release, the two railroads pointed out that the combination of the Burlington Northern and the Santa Fe was a predominantly end-to-end merger with very little overlap between the two systems, and that would benefit shippers. The merged BN-Santa Fe network would provide single-line service across the southern transcontinental corridor from central and Southern California to the southeastern gateways of Memphis and Birmingham.

Midwestern grain shippers could look forward to new single-line access to the West Coast and Gulf ports, as well as enhanced shipping options to Canadian and Mexican gateways. As did most other railroads beginning the process of seeking regulatory approval, the BN and the Santa Fe touted the increased efficiency of single-line service for many customers that previously had to rely on connecting service between two railroads. The Santa Fe's strength in intermodal traffic would complement the BN's strength in coal and grain.

The BN had considerably more on its plate in 1993 and 1994

than just merging with the Santa Fe. The BN tried to enter the growing Mexico-U.S. market when it announced the start of rail-barge service between Galveston, Texas, and the Mexican port of Coatzacoalcos in April 1993. The BN was the only major western railroad that did not have direct rail service to Mexico, and the North American Free Trade Agreement meant that considerably more traffic would move between the two countries.

The BN had tried earlier to begin its own single-line service to Mexico, using trackage rights it negotiated with the South Orient Railroad (SO) that ran between Fort Worth and the Mexican border at Presidio, Texas. The South Orient once had been part of the Santa Fe.

What the BN didn't know was that the South Orient operated over less than 10 miles of the Southern Pacific's main line between Alpine and Paisano, Texas. The SP sued the BN and the SO, contending that the South Orient's trackage rights could not be transferred to a third party. If the service had to be offered as joint or interline service between the BN and the South Orient, it would not be nearly as attractive as the BN originally estimated. Rather than fight an extended and expensive battle in court over the trackage rights, the BN dropped the arrangement.

The rail-barge service never was financially successful. The BN shipped mainly grain to Mexico and ran into the problem that the cargo was a commodity with constantly changing values and demand while the tug and barge operation across the Gulf of Mexico was a fixed-cost proposition. Other railroads have had similar lack of success running railcars across the Gulf to Mexico.

Also in 1993, the Midwest was hit by devastating flooding in July and August. Every railroad that had tracks near or along the rivers—especially the Mississippi, the Missouri, and the Osage—endured weeks of service disruption as hundreds of miles of track were under water or washed out. The railroad industry suffered millions of dollars in damage to its facilities but managed to keep freight moving, even though it was at great cost. Railroads, as they traditionally do in times of national crisis or disaster, forgot their rivalries and extended as much help as they could to each other. The Santa Fe, for example, moved some of its premium Chicago-Los Angeles intermodal trains by what its operating people called the "Polar Route"—across the northern tier on Burlington Northern and then south to Stockton, California, where the train returned to Santa Fe track.

Early in 1994 the railroad became the launch customer for a new generation of locomotives that could pull heavier loads at lower cost. The BN ordered 350 EMD SD70MAC alternating-current (AC) locomotives from the Electro-Motive Division of General Motors Corporation. The AC traction motors had fewer moving parts and offered the promise of lower maintenance costs. Although, at nearly $2 million each, the new units were more expensive than the then-standard direct-current (DC) traction locomotives; they had sufficiently more pulling power, so three of the new units could replace five of the old. The BN planned to use the new locomotives in its still-growing coal service.

There was one last management upheaval in 1994. Greenwood, in charge of all commercial activities, and Francis, in charge of operations, became involved in a ruinous rivalry. Both executives were popular and had cadres of officers who behaved as disciples. When it became clear that they could no longer work with each other and the railroad was on the verge of managerial paralysis, Grinstein was forced to act. Over the Memorial Day weekend, he informed both men that they were being retired. The railroad announced their departures on the Tuesday following the holiday.

THE BN AND THE SANTA FE STRIKE A DEAL

The proposed BN-Santa Fe had a market value of $2.7 billion, based on the exchange rate and the market prices of the two railroads' common stocks on the date they announced the deal. The BN and the Santa Fe filed their notice of intent to merge—a required procedural step—with the Interstate Commerce Commission on July 8, 1994, and said they would ask for expedited handling by the agency.

The ICC had another western combination on its plate at the same time. The Union Pacific was seeking to take complete control of the Chicago and North Western and had asked the commission for permission to acquire the rest of the C&NW stock that it didn't already own. The UP already was a powerful competitor for both the BN and the Santa Fe, and the addition of the C&NW would make it more so. The UP would be able to operate a more efficient single-line service between Chicago and Southern California, something only the Santa Fe could do in 1994. The UP would be able to route coal traffic more efficiently by eliminating the need to turn traffic back to the C&NW at Council Bluffs, Iowa, and by gaining access as far north as the Twin Cities, the UP grain franchise would be enhanced.

Clearly, the consolidation of the railroad industry still had a way to go. The successful conclusion of the UP-C&NW and BN-ATSF mergers would leave the West with three major systems, while the East already was down to three major systems. When asked why he had agreed to merge his railroad into the BN, Santa Fe chief executive Rob Krebs said: "We were seventh of 11 Class 1s, and that's not a good place to be." In an interview for this book, Krebs said:

> Santa Fe was a great railroad for what it was. But it didn't have the breadth of coverage for one thing. It was an 11,000-mile railroad. It was a big triangle. Chicago was one corner, Texas another corner, and all of California was the other corner. Over 50 percent of the business was intermodal. First of all, it seemed to me that what our customers were looking for was one-stop shopping, and [railroading is] a network business. The greater the network is, the more valuable it is to customers. The network we had was a great network for what we did, but it just need[ed] to be [filled out]. It's the same reason I thought that ultimately we're going to hear of transcontinental mergers. . . . We are a better, more valuable company to our customers as part of a bigger network. So that was the first thing.
>
> The second thing was that I wanted to diversify the traffic base. BN was a unit-train railroad, at least much more of a unit-train railroad. If you took coal and grain, I'll bet you they were about 50 percent of the BN's business. So you put them together, and not only do you get great geographic coverage, but you also get a traffic base.

The Santa Fe had a strong franchise in wheat grown in Texas, Oklahoma, and Kansas, but it was forced to carry the wheat either to Gulf of Mexico ports or to barge transfer facilities along the rivers. "Kansas, Texas—it all went to the Gulf," Krebs said. "Of course, we didn't get to the Pacific Northwest. We didn't get to Seattle or Tacoma or those gateways up there. We didn't have any access to that part of America's agriculture."

Krebs also saw financial advantage to combining the Santa Fe with the BN:

> The other reason why I wanted to do the deal was the synergy involved. The railroad industry always has a hard time

approaching earning its cost of capital. Every time you put two organizations together, you have the Noah's Ark syndrome. You don't need two presidents. You don't need two marketing departments. You don't need two law departments. You can go on and on and on. We had identified $500 million worth of synergies, a good two-thirds of which came from reducing redundant overheads. We made those and more. So, I knew that would provide a better financial return for both companies, shareholders. So those were the reasons. I would think they all came true.

BN and Santa Fe lawyers, planners, and operating officials spent the summer of 1994 preparing the voluminous merger application, which included an operating plan for the combined railroad, financial projections, and statements of support for the transaction from shippers, civic parties, and any other groups that had an interest. The two companies were not to have a smooth path to merger, however, as the Union Pacific moved suddenly in early October to acquire the Santa Fe for itself, starting a hostile takeover fight that would last until early 1995.

Drew Lewis and Dick Davidson flew the UP corporate jet from Bethlehem to Schaumburg on Wednesday, October 5, and called on Krebs late in the afternoon. Lewis proposed that Krebs withdraw from the BN deal and agree to have the Santa Fe acquired by the UP. Krebs had a fiduciary obligation to his stockholders to get the best price possible in any sale. Once he and the Santa Fe board had agreed to be acquired in June, the company was "in play" as the Wall Street financial community liked to say.

Lewis made an oral offer that was contingent on the UP's getting Interstate Commerce Commission approval, but Krebs insisted that the UP buy the Santa Fe up front and put the railroad in trust, as the Santa Fe had done with the Southern Pacific. That would have transferred the risk that a merger might be rejected from the Santa Fe to the Union Pacific and its stockholders. The UP offer was valued at $3.4 billion, but as it was presented, Santa Fe stockholders might have to wait nearly three years before seeing any money.

The Santa Fe-BN deal also required ICC approval, but the two railroads, route structures were end-to-end, and the merger didn't present nearly as many anticompetitive issues as a Santa Fe-UP merger would. Approval of a Santa Fe-BN merger was considered a foregone conclusion.

"[Drew Lewis] just wasn't willing to pay, though," Krebs recalled. "If he had paid what he offered the day he walked in my door, he would have ended up owning the Santa Fe."

After being rejected by Krebs, Lewis and Davidson headed back to the airport and called Grinstein to arrange a meeting that same evening. Grinstein recalled that day: "[Lewis has] got a difficult road. In any event, Drew came back. He calls me up, and he said, 'I just met with that——. And I'd like to meet with you.' Of course, I refused to meet with him. So then starts this battle between the UP and the BN."

Grinstein noted that the UP had a proprietary sense about the Santa Fe. A former UP chairman, he said, told a BN board member: "The Santa Fe is our railroad. It does not belong to you. It would never fit with you."

Grinstein continued: "Shortly thereafter—that thing had some ebb and flow to it in the battle, and you never knew where it was going to come out—at one point, Phil [Anschutz] called me and wanted to meet. We met and talked about it. His proposal was, of course, 'Give this thing up. You were so much better off with the SP.'"

Krebs would have given up the BN deal, but the UP refused to relieve the Santa Fe stockholders of the risk that the deal might be rejected. While publicly sticking to the BN merger, Krebs made it clear that if the UP would buy the Santa Fe outright, it could have the smaller railroad.

The UP's proposed combination with the Santa Fe muddied the already murky railroad merger waters. It would have created the nation's largest railroad, with annual revenue approaching $7.5 billion. It would have included more than 26,000 miles of track, more than 4,800 locomotives, and nearly 98,000 freight cars.

Despite having two suitors, the Santa Fe was not the only railroad involved in merger. The Illinois Central Corporation, then the tenth-largest railroad, had announced in July that it was buying the Kansas City Southern Railway in a stock swap valued at $1.63 billion. The KCS-IC deal eventually collapsed. And, of course, the UP's petition to allow it to exercise minority control of the North Western still was before the ICC.

Wall Street likes nothing more than a contested takeover. Word of the UP's offer sent the Santa Fe's stock up nearly a dollar per share on October 6 in extremely heavy trading. More than 10.1 million Santa Fe shares changed hands. UP stock, on the other hand, dropped by $1.875 a share on heavy volume, as the initial Wall Street reaction was not enthusiastic. BN stock declined 50 cents a share, as the consensus was that it would have to improve the terms for the Santa Fe if it were to prevail.

The BN and the Santa Fe had planned to file their merger application just a few days after the surprise UP bid. Proxies for both companies' shareholder votes were already at the printers, and a vote on the merger was tentatively scheduled for November 16.

The UP-BN rivalry, which had manifested itself in so many ways over the previous century, was classic. The UP, with 17 percent of railroad industry freight revenue, was the largest railroad, and if it could acquire the Santa Fe, it would remain the largest. If the BN won, however, at $7.1 billion in revenue, it would become the largest U.S. railroad.

Lewis didn't accept Krebs's rejection of his offer. He wrote to Krebs and the Santa Fe stockholders, saying: "I was disappointed by your unwillingness to consider our proposal. We view this transaction as a strategic imperative. Accordingly, I am writing to submit the following proposal to combine our companies."

The Santa Fe and the BN each prepared for the corporate version of war. Grinstein and Krebs held telephone board meetings with their respective boards, and the BN repeated its "commitment" to consummate the merger. "The board reaffirmed its intent to file the Santa Fe merger application with the Interstate Commerce Commission," the BN board stated in a news release.

Even as word still was circulating that the UP was trying to capture the Santa Fe, the UP filed suit in Delaware against the BN, the Santa Fe, and members of the Santa Fe's board, seeking a judgment that the BN-Santa Fe merger agreement could be terminated by the Santa Fe in order to allow it to accept the UP's proposal, and seeking an injunction requiring the Santa Fe to negotiate with the UP. In an effort to avoid the kind of costly litigation that had resulted when Texaco Incorporated broke up a merger between Pennzoil and Getty Oil Company several years earlier, the UP also asked for a ruling that it had not wrongfully interfered with the contractual relations of the BN and the Santa Fe.

The Santa Fe had no immediate public reaction, but Grinstein released a statement in which he pointed out that the BN-Santa Fe merger itself was a "direct response to the dominant position that UP has in the West." Pointing out that the UP already had gobbled up three railroads since deregulation and had a pending action to control the Chicago and North Western Transportation Company before the ICC, Grinstein accused the UP of trying to use its market power to become even more dominant.

The initial reaction of executives at other railroads and of Wall Street analysts was that Lewis was in a win-win position. "If they get [the Santa Fe], they win. If they don't, they complicate the BN-Santa Fe deal," said one senior railroad executive. There had not been a hostile railroad takeover battle in 40 years.

Financial analysts and executives of other railroads doubted that a UP–Santa Fe merger could be approved by the ICC. There was a consensus that the UP's principal goal was to break up the BN–Santa Fe merger or at least to raise the price significantly for its principal competitor.

While the BN and the Santa Fe had been proceeding on a schedule that would have their merger completed by 1996, the UP told securities analysts that it estimated it could implement a Santa Fe merger by 1998. Several analysts observed that the two-year time difference cut into the real value of the Union Pacific's bid. There was speculation that the BN actually was acquiring the Santa Fe cheaply and that a 10 percent increase would bring its offer closer to the value offered by the UP.

The BN and the Santa Fe proceeded with their application, although both delayed their shareholder votes on the merger. First the UP, then the BN, raised their offers for the Santa Fe. In early December, the BN and the Santa Fe asked the ICC to suspend activity on their merger application. The battle of words between the BN and the UP continued into the winter.

On January 12, 1995, there was a wave of stock trading when a rumor swept Wall Street brokerage trading rooms that the UP had decided to drop its bid. The UP stock rose while the BN and the Santa Fe stocks each fell on heavy volume. All three stocks remained actively traded.

The rumors that the UP was giving up, which proved to be unsubstantiated, stemmed from moves by the Clinton administration to abolish the Interstate Commerce Commission. The rumors had the ICC authority over rail mergers being transferred to the Justice Department's Antitrust Division, where it was believed that no merger involving major railroads with the parallel overlap of the UP and the Santa Fe could gain approval, because no merger could pass a Clayton Antitrust Act test of market concentration. When hearings that led to the termination of the ICC were held, the administration had decided to keep rail merger approval authority either with the Department of Transportation or a new agency and not to allow it to go to the Justice Department.

Rumors aside, the BN and the UP couldn't even agree on how the ICC should be eliminated. The UP supported transfer of rail merger authority to the Department of Transportation (DOT), perhaps, as some critics suggested at the time, because the UP believed it could more easily influence the DOT. The UP's Drew Lewis was a former secretary of transportation in the Reagan administration. The BN, on the other hand, was willing to see the Justice Department inherit the ICC's merger authority. BN legal analysis suggested that the Justice Department would act more quickly and would be just as likely to approve a BN-SF merger, but much less likely to approve a UP-Santa Fe merger.

The delayed vote of the BN and the Santa Fe shareholders was rescheduled for February 7.

The UP stood on its sweetened offer from November 8 of $17.50 a share for 57 percent of the Santa Fe stock and 0.354 UP shares for each of the remaining Santa Fe shares. By late January the UP offer had a blended value of $17.24 a share for the Santa Fe. The BN, which had been forced to increase its original offer, would pay $20 a share for one-third of the Santa Fe—the BN and the Santa Fe would jointly buy back stock in a partial recapitalization—and 0.4 shares of the BN for each share of the remaining two-thirds of the Santa Fe. The blended value of the BN offer was $20.27, or $3.8 billion for all of the Santa Fe.

Santa Fe stock was trading on the New York Stock Exchange at $17.50 a share. The BN offer was worth a bit less because it would not pay for the Santa Fe until the merger was approved. It is axiomatic in the investment community that delay diminishes the value of deals. The situation was fluid because of the price changes of the three stocks. The BN's offer, for example, gained in value in the first week in January when a $3 a share run-up in BN stock added 80 cents a share to the value of its offer.

The UP finally did what Krebs had demanded initially. It agreed to close on the deal as soon as the Santa Fe would agree to a merger, taking the risk of government rejection of a UP-Santa Fe merger by putting the Santa Fe in a voting trust.

By January, it was estimated that more than 60 percent of Santa Fe stock was in the hands of institutional investors, and another 10 to 20 percent was held by arbitragers, two groups that have no emotion when it comes to mergers and acquisitions. Both groups were waiting for the UP to make another move, possibly increasing its offer by another $1 a share.

The UP needed to do more than throw money at the Santa Fe, however, because unless it could force the Santa Fe to the negotiating table, its willingness to outbid the BN would mean little. The Santa Fe's board steadfastly refused to negotiate with the UP, even when the UP offer was worth more than the BN's. Acknowledging its fiduciary responsibilities, the Santa Fe's board provided information so the UP could prepare a higher bid, but the two companies did not talk at a senior level. The UP appeared ready to stand pat in the bidding and to count on the Santa Fe shareholders to reject the BN merger.

The BN was able to rely on the fact that Santa Fe shareholders were not voting on an either-or, BN or UP merger choice but were voting only yes or no on a Santa Fe merger with the BN. A rejection, no doubt, would have dropped the Santa Fe's stock price to around $12.50, where it had traded prior to the merger announcement the previous June. The BN was betting that the institutions and arbitragers—who were tiring of four months of uncertainty and wanted to cash out—would vote their controlling interest in the Santa Fe in favor of the BN merger.

The battle for the Santa Fe ended in late January when Drew Lewis announced that the Union Pacific was dropping its bid. All the UP had to show for the bitter four-month battle was the satisfaction that it had forced its rival to pay an additional $1.2 billion for the Santa Fe. From an all-stock transaction, the BN had moved to a package of $500 million in cash and more stock. The Santa Fe also was $750 million deeper in debt as a result of the stock buyback, and the BN would assume that debt.

Many on Wall Street and in the railroad industry believed that the UP's goal all along was to raise the cost of the merger, but the UP convinced investors and their counselors that it was serious when it agreed to pay for the Santa Fe immediately and to put the company in a voting trust while the government considered the merger application. The voting trust shifted the risk of rejection from the Santa Fe shareholders to the Union Pacific. The UP never had been able to force the Santa Fe board or management to the negotiating table.

Always ready with a quip, Grinstein told the *Journal of Commerce*: "My main thought is we ought to go straight to the movie and skip the novel. This makes the *Perils of Pauline* blush, it had so many ups and downs."

Grinstein thought the UP ultimately was swayed to drop the fight because of regulatory issues it couldn't overcome. "It would be very difficult to get approval for an acquisition of 12,500 miles when you have about 4,000 miles of overlap," he said.

The UP surrender was not at all surprising when related events were considered.

The UP's hopes were dashed by testimony that Gail McDonald, then ICC chairwoman, gave before a House committee considering the fate of the commission. McDonald told the committee that the ICC would move to a 180-day schedule for considering railroad mergers.

That was a radical change from the 535-day so-called expedited schedule it had established for the BN-Santa Fe proceeding. The schedule was expedited because under the law the ICC could take up to 31 months to process a merger case. At an analyst meeting in January, Krebs called the schedule "a joke."

McDonald's testimony made it clear that the UP was risking more than it could afford. When considering mergers that must be approved by government regulators, companies must make a number of assumptions. The UP's best case set of assumptions when it began the hostile takeover fight was that it would receive the blessing of the ICC and would end up with the Santa Fe, giving it a southern transcontinental corridor to go with its central corridor. The worst case analysis was that three years would pass before its merger would be rejected. Reconsideration requests, court challenges, and other delays would extend more than four years before it would have to divest the Santa Fe.

The Santa Fe would be in a voting trust during that period, but the UP would own it and the profits the Santa Fe earned would belong to the UP. By then, if the UP actually had to divest the Santa Fe, its loss would be limited to the cost of the capital it committed to buying it in 1995. That would be a considerable sum—perhaps $300 million annually, though offset by Santa Fe earnings—but it was probably worth the risk when considering the benefits of owning the Santa Fe.

The decision of the ICC, in its efforts to avoid shutdown, to process the merger in only six months worked against the Union Pacific, radically changing the risk-reward considerations. While the BN would be at risk only for the $500 million it would pay to buy 13 percent of Santa Fe stock in the recapitalization, the UP would have been at risk for its entire $3.5 billion. The prospect of a forced sale within a year was more than the UP could tolerate. Analysts at the time were saying that the Santa Fe would bring only $13 a share in a forced sale, a loss of more than $1 billion for the UP.

Once the battle for the Santa Fe ended, the BN-Santa Fe merger approval process went smoothly. The ICC resumed consideration of the merger application on March 9, after a three-month suspension.

The BN and the Santa Fe negotiated trackage and access rights with the Southern Pacific to address some competitive issues, such as the Colorado-Texas corridor. The latter agreed not to oppose the merger before the ICC. The SP, which had a nice business moving low-sulfur, high-heat-value coal from western Colorado to Texas utilities, had handed off the coal trains to either the BN or the Santa Fe at Pueblo, Colorado. Because the coal traffic was attractive to both the BN and the Santa Fe, the SP received favorable interline rates. With both routes south from Colorado to Texas in the hands of one railroad, and that railroad the principal hauler of low-sulfur coal from Wyoming, the SP feared it would be at a competitive disadvantage. Trackage rights to operate its trains into Texas satisfied the SP. Similarly, the SP was granted trackage rights from eastern Kansas to Texas that promised to put it into the grain business for the first time.

Final ICC approval came on August 23, and the BN and the Santa Fe became the Burlington Northern and Santa Fe Railway (BNSF) on September 22, 1995.

Even before the BN and the Santa Fe completed their merger, the UP had turned in a different direction. Within weeks of dropping its bid for the Santa Fe, the UP began merger talks with Phil Anschutz, who controlled the Southern Pacific. The capital-starved SP was a much less desirable railroad than the Santa Fe was, but it offered the UP its "Holy Grail" of a southern transcontinental route, a strong network throughout California, and a potentially faster single-line route from Southern California to Chicago and to the Memphis gateway to eastern railroads.

Whereas the Santa Fe had been well maintained, however, the SP was in poor condition, and it would take several billion dollars to bring its lines up to their potential. The SP also had a notorious lack of locomotives, and many of its locomotives needed major maintenance overhauls because they had been used so heavily.

In a replay of the Mop-Up merger of 1980, the UP based its case for acquiring the SP on the argument that the commission had just allowed its principal competitor to become larger and to access more customers more efficiently, and thus it was only fair to allow the UP to compete. By the time the regulators began actually working on the application, though, they no longer were the ICC. Congress had finally agreed to abolish the nation's oldest regulatory agency, but, effective January 1, 1996, it replaced the ICC with a new agency, the Surface Transportation Board (STB). The STB had much less power, a smaller budget, and fewer employees than the ICC. It also had just three commissioners, as they continued to be called.

Creation of the STB was one victory the UP could boast over what now was BNSF. BNSF was quite willing to let rail merger authority go to the Justice Department. The UP, supported by the SP, mounted an aggressive lobbying campaign to keep merger authority out of the Antitrust Division. The decision went right down to the wire of Congressional adjournment for the Christmas–New Year holiday, and even after Congress acted, there was uncertainty as to whether President Clinton would sign the measure. However, he did so, as the clock ticked toward New Year's Day.

Ever since the fiasco of the Santa Fe-Southern Pacific merger, it was clear that merger applicants would be expected to remove as many anticompetitive aspects of their deals as possible even before the regulators considered their applications.

The UP and the SP had serious competitive issues. They were the dominant railroads serving the rich chemical-producing and -shipping area along the Texas and Louisiana Gulf Coast. The Santa Fe got into the Texas chemical territory, but not as extensively as either the UP or the SP. Similarly, the UP and the SP were the only two railroads that served the central transcontinental corridor between Colorado and California, and the only two that served the corridor between Texas and the Midwest. There was so much overlap, in fact, that many experts predicted the UP-SP merger would be rejected.

The Kansas City Southern saw an opportunity to expand its franchise by acquiring track or at least trackage rights from the UP and the SP. The UP, however, wanted to resolve all the competitive issues in one negotiation. So, unknown to the KCS, the UP and the SP entered into talks that resulted in giving BNSF trackage rights over more than 3,500 miles of the UP and SP lines and selling another 350 miles outright to BNSF.

So, just days after its own creation, BNSF suddenly found itself nearly 4,000 miles bigger, as the competitive balance to the UP along the "chemical coast," and with guaranteed access to any shipper that would have gone from service by two railroads to service by just one as a result of the UP-SP merger. The trackage rights that BNSF had received connected it between Colorado and California along the central corridor. It had also gained rights to operate its trains between the Texas Gulf Coast and Memphis. The gap between the BN and the Santa Fe in California also was closed.

When the trackage rights deal was announced, Krebs said more than $800 million of the UP and SP traffic had been opened to BNSF and he expected to get 50 percent of it.

The trackage rights agreement revealed the first disagreement between Grinstein and Krebs. It became clear that the two men would not work together for long.

Krebs believed that the UP-SP merger was going to happen no matter what position BNSF or anyone else would take and that the massive trackage rights agreement was the best that BNSF could do. Some observers also believed Krebs thought that, by not making trouble for the UP-SP merger, he would be currying favor with regulators for the transcontinental merger he saw coming next. If he believed that, events would prove him wrong.

Grinstein argued within the company that BNSF should oppose the UP-SP merger, seeking line divestitures rather than trackage rights. He didn't believe trackage rights would solve the competitive problems. In December, Grinstein told *Forbes* magazine that he didn't think the trackage rights would cure the UP-SP problems, infuriating the UP and SP lawyers, some of whom believed the Grinstein interview was a breach of the contractual agreement.

Grinstein would not be around long for the work of combining the BN and the Santa Fe, though. In December 1995 he announced his retirement as chairman of the board, about a year earlier than had been expected. About the apparent break with Krebs, Grinstein said, "He and I were totally different people. My vision of the company was entirely different from his. What I would have done would have been very different." Years later, Grinstein still declined to say more about the relationship.

The timing of his departure, however, worked for Grinstein. "At that point I had a first grandchild about to be born and my wife dying to come to Seattle," he noted. "I happened to have liked Fort Worth, by the way, strangely enough. But the primary reason was . . . I did become nonexecutive chairman at Delta [Airlines]. I was willing to take that on, but Rob [Krebs] and I were two different people with different values and different everything."

Both men realized that they probably never would have been able to develop a good working relationship. As Jim Dagnon, who was in charge of human resources, said, "Grinstein's decision to retire made the transition to Krebs's leadership that much easier."

Dagnon recalled a conversation he had with Grinstein, for whom he had worked at BN before the merger:

> Jerry came to me one day and said, "Jim, I really need to leave. Rob needs the freedom that he has to have to run this place." He said, "Our styles are different. Rob's going to run a great company. He's going to run this really well. He doesn't need me sitting on the board and criticizing his style or whatever's different. Jim, will you go work with the board of directors to work out a deal for me to go away?" The board was concerned because they heard some things about Rob's style too. They knew Jerry to be a people person. That's what the Burlington board really wanted. Rob's reputation was different than that. What they ended up getting and finding was that Rob was just as caring about the people as Jerry was. That's what the transition was. . . . The board did not want Jerry to leave. They wanted him to oversee the transition. I went in and told them exactly that Jerry felt Rob needed the freedom. Jerry, being Jerry, would speak his mind if he didn't like it, or his body language. Jerry can't hide anything if he had to. Rob deserved to be free. So after I got the board to agree, I went to Rob and I told him this story. I said, "Jerry wants to leave, and he asked me to work with the board to get it done. Here's what I've done. You're my new boss."

Krebs did not immediately get the post either, as a veteran BN board member was named chairman. Krebs would get that title to go along with those of president and chief executive officer within the year.

Many shippers, industrial groups, and government agencies continued to oppose the UP-SP merger, including the Justice, Transportation, and Agriculture Departments, which each filed in opposition and appeared before the STB. The agency dismissed the objections and approved the merger on August 12. It closed on September 11, 1996.

There now were two very big rail systems blanketing the West.

RAILROADS RUN ON TRACK—AND INFORMATION?

By the time the UP and the SP combined, the BNSF was well along in implementing its merger plan. First, the combined information technology suite had to be reworked so there was one system where there had been two. A major capital spending program was undertaken that invested $9 billion in the railroad in just four years.

Charles Feld had joined the BN in 1992 as its chief information officer in a unique arrangement. He never went on the payroll but was a consultant who brought in his own team to revamp the railroad's information technology. Feld came from Frito-Lay, the snack food division of PepsiCo Incorporated, and the BN was his first client.

Snack foods may not have much in common with railroading, but the logistics demands meant that Feld was well qualified to handle railroad IT (Information Technology). Frito-Lay had 40 manufacturing plants and 4,000 distribution points, plus salespeople, raw materials, and finished goods to worry about, and its raw materials and products were perishable.

"What we did [at the BN] was that we were the opposite of the outsourcing paradigm," Feld said. "So if a company was having a lot of technology problems—if that technology was expensive, slow, or frustrating, which most companies are and have been—they would tend to keep their leadership team and outsource the machines, the programs, and everything else. So they'd keep five or six people at the top."

Feld brought a completely different approach to the problem the BN was having with IT. As he described it,

> My contention was that [that typical approach] was a mistake and that usually the five or six people at the top were the problem, not the programmers and not the machines. Therefore, if you were to hire five or six people from the Feld Group, we'd go in and run the company. The out-

source leadership team would keep everything else. It made sense to outsource the network or the data center. That would be okay, but you don't just package up your problems and send them to somebody else.

McKinsey and Company consultants had worked at Frito for years and also were doing some work for Grinstein at the BN, which is how Grinstein and Feld became acquainted. "BN had pretty gripping systems problems," Feld recalled. The railroad headquarters were in downtown Fort Worth. The IT function still was in St. Paul, and the operating department was in Overland Park, Kansas. According to Feld, the distance between functions created insularity.

Feld said that the BN systems were dysfunctional when he got there:

> There was no one thing, but companies either have their systems working for them or working against them. The systems were working against the BN when I got there. Basically, if you went into their dispatch, their customer support centers, their yards, or anywhere, the most important piece of technology was the telephone. The computer was sitting there, but if you wanted to know where anything was, you'd have to pick up the phone and call the yard, if [the train] just left, and say, "Did it leave?" Or if somebody was looking for something, they'd use the phone because the systems didn't reflect the physical picture of where things were.

The BN's problem wasn't much different from that at other railroads. Despite the existence of wayside readers that would note the passing of a train and computers that listed every car in a train, the railroad still was not able to tell a customer precisely where its car was. The best it could do was to respond to a car location query by telling the customer where the car had been at a particular time in the past. That past sometimes was minutes, but sometimes it could be a day. Nor was there any way of knowing that a train actually had left a terminal.

Discussing the problems he inherited, Feld explained:

> If a train left the Havre, Montana, yard, heading toward

Spokane or something, it was supposed to have left, but you
don't know if it left. You don't know where it is, because
the way the systems were structured was that people didn't
have to enter the data. There was no way of knowing. By
the way, people didn't have time to enter the data because
they were so busy in the yard. When a train would depart,
they wouldn't put it in the system. They would wait five or
six hours, because they were so busy. They would come
back five or six hours later and say, "All these trains depart-
ed." This train could have arrived at the next yard already.

The problem became serious as the railroad began to focus on customer service, which required tracking individual cars more than
trains.

After Feld was on the job about a year and a half, the BN-Santa Fe
merger came along. "I think Burlington Northern was really starting
to cook in 1995, because we had put some systems in place. We had
changed the organizational structure," Feld said.

The work Feld was doing for the BN was readily adaptable to the
new BNSF, as the merged railroad had to combine computer systems. Krebs ran a real-time railroad; the Santa Fe was far more
dependent on merchandise traffic than was the BN. Krebs saw the
opportunity right away, Feld said.

In the early 1990s, the Santa Fe had created its own advanced
transportation management and scheduling system, known as the
Transportation Support System (TSS). This was truly a revolution-
ary, industry-leading transportation platform, which allowed for a
trip plan for every car based on customer expectations for service,
and it was one of the assets that made the Santa Fe an attractive
merger partner. Portions of the TSS program were later sold to
Deutsche Bahn and to Canadian National.

Feld had assumed that Krebs would put the Santa Fe's head of
information technology in charge of the merging systems, basing the
effort on the Santa Fe's TSS, and that he would leave when the merger took place. But Krebs surprised him. "He called me and said, 'I
really want you to do this job because I think you're the most qualified, not because you're BN or Santa Fe,'" Feld recalled.

BNSF soon had process discipline in its information technology,
Feld said. "The discipline when we started doing the Santa Fe merger, the way Krebs ran it, was that if you didn't depart a train, you

couldn't arrive a train," Feld explained. "It was impossible in the computer system's logic. It would just set up big flashes and say, 'You can't do that,' because if it didn't depart Havre, how could it be in Spokane?"

Krebs decreed that merger implementation would be accomplished in two years and persuaded Feld to look upon the IT project as his next two-year consulting engagement rather than a continuation of the BN consultancy. Feld acknowledged that he was torn "because I was very committed to Jerry [Grinstein] and not overly excited about the Santa Fe culture." When Krebs asked Feld to stay, it surprised a lot of the Santa Fe systems people because the Santa Fe had better systems than the BN had.

Feld determined that the traditional "take one from column A and one from column B" approach was not the right way to go.

> "What we did is that we looked at each of the systems, and clearly the Santa Fe had the best transportation system. So we made that part of the new merged system," Feld said. "We didn't go in and look at their equipment distribution and their locomotives. We took the whole thing in, because that's where people make mistakes—when they try to take the best of breed inside. There were parts of the BN transportation system that were better than the Santa Fe's, but that's the mistake you get into. You don't need to hermetically seal. Then you've got to have a lot more interfaces."

The rollout of the new combined systems actually was accelerated. "The rollout—because it was changing on equipment and it was changing processes for people—was very, very tough on the BNSF," Feld said. "What we had to put in place was 'This was the BN. This was the Santa Fe. This is the BNSF.' We had a two-year journey we had to put together." In the end all the unified systems were in operation within 21 months.

Initially, to outsiders, it appeared that the smaller Santa Fe had taken over the larger BN. A lot of employees on the BN said they were reminded of the Frisco merger 15 years earlier. The appearance of a Santa Fe takeover was in part because at the time the merger was announced, the BN created a much more lucrative "change-of-control" package for more of its executives than did the Santa Fe.

More than 100 BN executives were given two years in which they could decide of their own volition to leave, with up to three years' compensation, if they didn't like working in the merged company. The Santa Fe, on the other hand, had extended the plan—which was intended to keep executives from leaving while the merger was pending—to a smaller number of executives and provided for only two years' compensation. When the merger took place, more BN executives than Santa Fe executives found they could afford to retire—and did.

The BN-Santa Fe merger implementation went relatively well—spectacularly well when compared with other mergers that occurred around the same time. Well before the merger, the BN had built a new Network Operations Center in north Fort Worth, so it was a relatively simple decision to combine the Santa Fe operations with the BN's in the new facility. Krebs quickly moved to expand the suburban facility, vacating most of the downtown Continental Towers Office Building that Walter Drexel had leased.

Krebs recalled one of his first visits to the NOC, a huge multistory dispatch center that looked like it could be used to manage the NASA space program:

> Grinstein had me come down and look at it. I remember my comment. I walked into this place, and I looked at it. I was stunned. I think my comment was "Oh, s——t!" But it was built, and there was nothing you could do about it. So it was clear to me that operating headquarters was going to be here. Once I figured the operating headquarters was here, you've got to have everybody else here too. I don't believe in having operations here and the executives in some other city or in some tower, not even downstairs or downtown.

Krebs made it clear that he wanted to create a new company, not just meld two existing companies and their cultures. He agreed with Grinstein at that point to build the marketing building, but he soon ordered architectural changes to include the executive offices and boardroom where the original plans called for a viewing gallery over the NOC. "My goal was to get rid of the $9 million a year we were spending downtown, and we've got, I think, two floors left out of 30," Krebs said.

Considering all the turmoil the BN had gone through over the previous years with top executives from outside the industry trying to drive culture change, Krebs came in with the advantage that he was known and respected as a top railroad executive. He was in a better position than his predecessors had been to force change. Putting the two railroads in a new headquarters assisted in the process.

"That's another thing that helped us change the company, because it was neutral ground," Krebs said. "It wasn't old BN. It wasn't old Santa Fe. And it's a nice looking place."

Despite some cars of freight that managed to be sent back and forth past their destination and were dubbed "Flying Dutchmen" by the press, the integration went smoothly. Four years later in another merger case, Krebs filed with the Surface Transportation Board a thick book that "laid out every promise we made in our [merger filing] and how we charged through the barriers or beat the hurdles in every category—safety, service, investment, improvement in the facilities, everything," Krebs said, not without some pride.

Although both railroads had been successful on their own, there still was a lot of work to do. Krebs described the situation:

> I'll tell you what surprised me when I showed up down here was how undercapitalized we were. We didn't have the capacity, and in the Powder River Basin the UP was in there grabbing market share from us. We couldn't provide service. We were holding trains. We couldn't get the grain to the Pacific Northwest, because we didn't have the track capacity and we didn't have the locomotives to pull. The Santa Fe was in reasonable shape, but that's where we were growing. So the southern Transcon [as the Santa Fe referred to its Chicago-Los Angeles line] needed a lot of work too.

A little more than a year after the BN and the Santa Fe completed their merger, the expanded UP system suffered a service crisis of greater magnitude than anything seen in the U.S. rail industry since the World War I congestion. "Of course, then the UP came along, and they dumped about 10 percent [several hundred million dollars, worth] of their business on us for a while," Krebs said. "We still got maybe 40 percent of that because of the rights we got. You have to figure that as part of their merger we picked up the equivalent of a Class 1 railroad. My guess is that our business on [the trackage rights] is probably north of $400 million and approaching $500 million [annually]."

The capital spending program was in three "buckets," as Matt

Rose—then senior vice president of operations and now chairman, president, and chief executive officer—told *Railway Age*. There was the money that had to be spent on locomotives to make up for the years of underpurchases by the BN. There was the "normal" capital spending that had to be undertaken just to be able to serve the existing business of the railroad. And, finally, there was "expansion" capital to enable the railroad to handle growth. The last category included double-tracking the Transcon, new and expanded terminals throughout the system, signaling, and communications.

Securities analysts dubbed the capital spending program as "Build it and they will come," a line inspired by the motion picture *Field of Dreams*. The analysts, who tended to view many corporate activities from a short-term perspective, were critical of the huge capital spending program, mostly because they wanted to see more free cash flow that would fund either a dividend increase or stock buybacks.

Although BNSF had gained significant traffic and revenue from shippers that were able to switch carriers during the UP service collapse, the traffic gains were not permanent. Once the UP was in a position to handle its normal business, much of the diverted freight went back to the UP.

By 1999 BNSF began reducing its capital spending. For one thing, it had largely completed the catch-up spending that had been necessary. Also, growth was slow, which meant the railroad was in danger of having more capital invested in the business than could be justified by volume or revenue. The double-tracking of the Transcon was suspended, leaving gaps in Kansas, Oklahoma, Abo Canyon in New Mexico, and the Texas Panhandle that could be completed in the future when traffic volume justified the cost. That work since has resumed.

With the shortage of good power that BNSF had inherited from the BN now eliminated, the railroad sharply cut back its orders for new locomotives. From more than $2 billion right after the merger, annual capital spending dropped to $1.5 billion. BNSF capital spending still was sufficient to ensure that the railroad would be able to handle all the business it had, as well as the new business it was likely to receive, and to do it efficiently.

Krebs and Matt Rose, who succeeded him, both began telling analysts and shippers that the railroad would reduce investment to align assets with the level of business. They suggested there would be another round of line eliminations by sale or lease to short-line operators, but little was done in that area over the next couple of years.

Krebs, like his predecessors, drove management change. But unlike his predecessors, he combined their zeal with his knowledge of railroading and its culture. Under Krebs as the new chief executive, there was a significant shakeout in management as the new team chose from executives in each railroad. Their task was made easier by the change-in-control arrangements that allowed those who were not chosen to leave with financial security.

Surprising many who knew him, Krebs also drove the development of a new BNSF culture. He even surprised himself. "I wasn't much on cultures until I got here and I realized how different the two were between BN and Santa Fe," he said. "I don't think you can overestimate the differences. We had angry people."

The Santa Fe had a reputation of being a cohesive unit of tough, single-minded executives. The BN, on the other hand, was considered "softer," less disciplined. The BN people would hold meetings and seemingly reach agreement, but they would begin questioning everything as soon as the meeting ended.

Acknowledging his reputation as a driven, focused executive, Krebs added: "The other thing is that I got warmer and softer over time. So I gave them the land to put the child care center there. I agreed to put the employee exercise facility in and put a cafeteria over there, as well as to take an old building and fix it up to do that. It's a nice place to work."

Not long after the merger, Krebs turned to the noted Aspen Institute think tank to help focus the executive team on culture and how to develop one for BNSF. The BNSF group was at the Colorado conference center for seven days. "We took a senior management group and their wives," Krebs said. "We sat down and we did the readings that the Aspen Institute has about liberty, equality, community, and efficiency."

Feld, who had an outsider's perspective, said: "I think the reason [Krebs] agreed to go to the Aspen Institute is that he was not happy with the BN culture, but he also wasn't happy with the Santa Fe culture. What he wanted to do was create a BNSF culture. He was very explicit about that. I think that most of his Santa Fe people who were on the executive team thought he was just saying it because it was politically correct."

Railroad people who knew Krebs as a young trainmaster—who carried a gun when he was assigned to high-crime East St. Louis— and a rapidly advancing hard-charger at the Southern Pacific, still

The Aspen Institute Helps Create a BNSF Culture

Rob Krebs understood the need for change following the BN-Santa Fe merger. "This was a much bigger railroad," said Charles Feld. "He couldn't personally run it himself like he ran the Santa Fe. He needed to have other people who could think and not be afraid to think. So I think it was heartfelt. He just didn't know what to do. I think the Aspen Institute was the first step. I don't think it was conclusive, but it was a first step in opening the door to the dialogue that we then entered into as an executive team, because it sent a pretty strong signal."

Krebs expressed his pride in the Aspen Institute exercise in the Rocky Mountains of Colorado:

> Well, I was trying to get this management group away and to get them together. The Aspen Institute has this program in which you read everything from Hobbes to Machiavelli to Martin Luther King Jr. to Galbraith. It's based around four concepts that the guy who started the Aspen Institute after World War II ostensibly to make sure that Hitler never got control of anything again . . . a person of that mentality. He founded this thing to develop and understand the qualities that made the United States great; those being liberty, equality, community, and efficiency.
>
> So the Aspen Institute has the executive program where people go there from all different kinds of companies. They do these readings, they sit around and [employ] the Socratic method, or whatever it is, and they talk about them. So I said, "Okay, I want to do that, but I want to change things three ways. The first thing I want to do is to just be BNSF people."

Told that the institute had never done that before, Krebs responded: "I know, but you can do it. This is team building. I think we can learn from your process, but I think also I want a team to lead, and I can't do it if I don't have my whole team."

Krebs wanted the Aspen Institute program tailored for BNSF's needs. "The second thing I want is to go through the regular program, but instead of going skiing in the afternoon, we'll go skiing a little bit," he told the institute's representatives. "Then I want to get back together, and I want to discuss each one of these qualities and how it applies to BNSF." He also insisted that the spouses of his executives be included as equal participants "because what I was trying to do was—I was sure everybody was going home at night and they were saying 'Oh, this guy Krebs is doing this.' Or 'I don't understand these guys from the BN.' All the pillow talk—I wanted the response from the pillow to be 'Well, I've met those guys, and they're pretty nice guys. Are you sure you're right about that?'"

The Aspen Institute wasn't really ready for what Krebs wanted. "We walked in and there's this round table and there are all these chairs around the back of the room," he recalled. "I said, 'Well, what's that?', He said, 'That's where the wives sit.' I said, 'No, no, no. I want them right up here at the table.'"

The first meeting worked so well, Krebs said, "that we had three or four more sessions in which we brought in all the vice presidents and the key people in human resources and labor relations." He continued:

> I went to every session. I didn't stay for the whole thing. What was really interesting was that they would sit around afterwards in the afternoon. They'd say, "Now, liberty, equality, community, efficiency. That's four axes. You draw Santa Fe. Was it high on liberty, or is it high on efficiency?" For Santa Fe, liberty was way down, and efficiency was way out there. "You draw it for BN." BN was "All liberty—it was great. Efficiency, well, we got around to it. It was okay. We cared about it."

One session was devoted to studying the culture of the Union Pacific, and the BNSF executives decided they didn't want to have the same culture. "We got into shared values we should have and what kind of style we wanted to have," Krebs said. In addition to deciding which features of the BN and the Santa Fe they thought should be retained in a new culture, Jim Dagnon said:

are surprised to hear of the Aspen Institute program, particularly that Krebs was so personally involved. It appears to have paid off for BNSF, though, as most observers agree that among modern-era mergers BNSF developed its own culture more rapidly than had happened ever before.

"We had this giant catharsis, where everybody started saying, 'This is how I feel about this,'" Krebs said. "When we were all done, there were three pivotal questions that had to be answered. One of them was whether we were going to be centralized or decentralized. Another was whether Krebs is going to be Darth Vader or Mary Poppins."

Krebs pointed out that the Aspen Institute method does not give participants answers. Participants are supposed to develop their

"We decided which items on the UP we didn't want to replicate. The word 'arrogance' is one that came up. We said, 'They're arrogant.'"

One thing both cultures had in common was the railroad culture of working long hours and focusing on the business at hand. The executives got into philosophies of good and evil. Feld recalled initially that there was a lot of "What are we doing here?"

Feld said that, in trying to figure out what kind of a culture BNSF should have and how to attain it, the group at the Aspen Institute explored issues like these: Would people get up in the morning and work hard at their jobs just because it is a part of an inherent desire to do good? Or do they only do it because they're getting paid and, if they don't do it, they're going to get fired.

> "Essentially, what it does is that it begins to set up your beliefs, because you do different things from a management point of view if you believe people are inherently good as opposed to if you think they're lazy. It was right down the middle," said Feld. "The guys, including Krebs, from the Santa Fe side believed that people were inherently bad and that the reason they performed and did the right things in society and in companies was because there were rewards and punishments. [The BN guys] believed that people are inherently good and only do bad things when they are threatened."

The spouses participated fully at Aspen. Feld told of one spouse who turned to her senior executive husband and said: "'That's the way you treat your kids.' This was not just about railroads. . . . It was about philosophy of life."

own. But the discussion leader for the BNSF group finally said, "I've had enough. I'm through. I'm finished. I'm going to give you the answer to these three questions. The answer to should you be centralized or decentralized is both. Should you go after bulk or intermodal? The answer is both. As to Krebs being Mary Poppins or Darth Vader, the answer is both."

Many people inside and outside BNSF saw Krebs change after the merger, and many of them were surprised.

> "I think he changed," said Feld. "It's not like he was always that way. He changed with this merger. I met him before the merger. I worked for him right at the merger and for two

years. I watched him change over time. It was not easy for him to change." Feld continued: "Rob was very predictable at first. He became more unpredictable, in a positive sense, because he came with his idea of what was right and what was truth in the Santa Fe way, as did his lieutenants, the guys who were my peers. I think the difference between Rob and the rest of the group was that he was a learning machine."

Krebs soon got an example of the need to push a BNSF culture where it hadn't existed before. At the Santa Fe he had made it a practice to visit railroad facilities and employees. He recalled:

> I'd go out every month. I'd go to two or three places. Then, after the merger, I started doing that on the BNSF. I went up to Havre, Montana. I figured I was going to hit the new territory. I walked into that meeting with these employees. I made my little spiel, and then we opened it up, because usually at least two-thirds of the meeting is people talking and my listening. It took me five minutes to figure out that the people up there had never accepted the merger of Great Northern and Northern Pacific. Those people in the field still say, "He's GN, and he's BN or NP." I finally said to them, "Hey, you guys are one merger behind. That had to be. Those companies wouldn't exist." That's when I decided culture was as important as capital expenditures. That's why we went through that process.

Dagnon, who had been through several rail mergers, admired the way Krebs pushed for a common culture. There were former BN executives, he said, who resisted some of the changes: "[They'd say,] 'After all, we bought them.' But we heard the same thing at the Burlington merger. We heard the same thing when Rob came at the Santa Fe, that 'Hey, wait a minute. We acquired them. Why are they running the show?' Again, it's this utilization of the talent and taking the culture. One thing I credit Rob for was that we did no planning. He and Jerry [Grinstein] got together, and they put the team together."

The failure of the Santa Fe–Southern Pacific merger nine years earlier had left railroad lawyers convinced they never again would allow detailed merger planning to occur before the ICC approved the combination.

MERGER IN THE EAST—AND THEN THERE WERE FOUR

In October 1996, only five weeks after the UP and the SP combined, a takeover war broke out in the East as CSX announced it had agreed to acquire Conrail, the now profitable railroad that had been created out of the eastern and midwestern bankrupt railroads of the 1970s. Conrail blanketed the Northeast between Boston, New York, and Philadelphia in the east and Chicago and St. Louis in the west. It had a rail monopoly in the New York–New Jersey megalopolis, the nation's largest-consuming market.

Eight days later, the Norfolk Southern, which had lusted after Conrail for years and already had made three attempts to buy it, counterattacked with its own acquisition offer.

The CSX-Conrail deal initially was a stock transaction. The conservatively managed NS went to its investment bankers and built a war chest of more than $20 billion. Krebs quickly saw the potential for BNSF to be part of the first transcontinental railroad in the United States.

Norfolk Southern and CSX fought over Conrail for more than four months and finally agreed to buy it and split its operations between them. The rounds of bidding, however, had upped the price to $10 billion cash—more than had ever been paid for a railroad—with the NS taking 58 percent for $5.8 billion and CSX getting 42 percent for $4.2 billion. CSX and the NS both ended up with seriously weakened balance sheets, which, along with a difficult time splitting Conrail and meshing its operations into their own, made it impossible for either to engage in another round of rail mergers—at least not for some years.

Krebs's idea was that if BNSF, which already had been merged for more than a year, were sold to Norfolk Southern, it would have a several-year advantage in the market over the UP, which just then was starting to absorb the SP into its system. Krebs's logic was that if the NS stopped fighting CSX over Conrail, it would get trackage rights from CSX or would be able to purchase a line into the huge New York–New Jersey market and still would have its strong balance sheet and the money it was planning to spend in the fight over Conrail.

If the UP had responded by moving to acquire CSX so it could have its own transcontinental system, Krebs believed, it either would have had to wait a couple of years until the SP integration was complete or risk trying to integrate three large systems simultaneously.

Krebs was not alone in seeing the strategic advantage of a BNSF-NS linkage. Philip Anschutz, who had become vice chairman of the UP board and the largest individual investor in the entire railroad industry as a result of the SP sale to the UP, hopped on his private Falcon 50 trijet and flew to Norfolk. At a brief meeting in the Norfolk Southern hangar at Norfolk International Airport, Anschutz delivered a succinct message to David Goode. "Stay on your own——side of the river," the canny deal maker said, referring to the Mississippi River, which divided eastern and western railroads. Anschutz clearly understood that a BNSF-NS merger at that time could put the UP—and his investment in it—at a competitive disadvantage.

A few months later, the UP suffered what it called its "service crisis," which extended from mid-1997 to mid-1998. Shippers and the news media referred to it as a meltdown. The UP said it hadn't realized how fragile the SP infrastructure was, and when there was a surge in traffic in 1997, the system just couldn't handle the business. The congestion began in the Houston chemical complex, but soon trains were parked all over the UP system. Even railroads that were not directly involved, like BNSF, were affected. First, they had to operate through and over the same congested areas, particularly on the trackage rights. Second, because freight was not being handed off at interline points, a shortage of cars developed throughout the industry.

The UP meltdown and the 1999 service failures of the NS and CSX would have an unanticipated effect on BNSF.

KREBS CALLS IT A CAREER

By 1999, Krebs, who had been named president of the Southern Pacific in 1980 when he was just 38 years old, had been running major railroads for 19 years. He had told his wife he planned to retire by the time he was 55, and already he was two years beyond that target. He told an associate that he had enough money and that he was "working for my kids" and had been for a number of years.

Unlike so many executives throughout the industry who have to be shoved out the door, Krebs was ready to retire. In an interview while he still was chairman of the board, he said:

> I've done so many recapitalizations, mergers, and bust-ups. You get tired after a while. Not only that, but also you get stale. So I told my wife I was going to retire when I was 55. The [BN-Santa Fe] merger came along, and I didn't make it at 55. I'm going to make it by 60.
>
> I understood right at the very beginning when we came down here and created BNSF that I had to find a successor. That was the most important thing I could do—not the most important—but it was one of the most important things, especially if I wanted to get out. So I looked around for the best person, and he just happened to be 40 years old. I think that's wonderful. I'm glad he wasn't 58. In fact, probably, if he was 58, he wouldn't have been a potential successor, because whoever that person is has got to have enough time to do something.

Krebs was referring to Matthew K. Rose, a rapidly rising young executive he had identified as a potential successor and to whom he had begun giving increasingly important positions.

Rose had come to the BN in 1993 and was named vice president of vehicles and machinery in June 1994. Promotions came quickly. He was named vice president of southern region field marketing for the merchandise business group in January 1995 and was appointed vice president of chemicals following the BN-Santa Fe merger in September. From May 1996 until August 1997, Rose was senior vice president of the merchandise business unit, one of three BNSF business groups.

Less than two years after he was put in charge of operations, Rose became president and chief operating officer, responsible for all operations and marketing activities. A year and a half later, in December 2000, he was named president and chief executive officer. When Krebs retired in March 2002, Rose was elected chairman.

True to his word and his desires, Krebs left completely and did not stand for election to the BNSF board of directors at the 2002 annual meeting.

On December 20, 1999, BNSF and the Canadian National

Matt Rose

Youth Will Be Served

Matthew K. Rose, age 45, is a leader who brings to the railroad a greater understanding of the need for change than more traditional up-through-the-ranks executives might be expected to have.

Rose's background is different from that of other railroad executives, most of whom have spent their entire careers with the companies they lead. He spent years in the service-driven trucking industry and brought a strong customer-service orientation to BNSF. Before joining the Burlington Northern, Rose was vice president of transportation for Triple Crown Services (a Norfolk Southern subsidiary), which provides a truck-competitive retail freight service using specialized vehicles that can operate on both tracks and highway. Earlier, he held various positions with Schneider National, the nation's largest truckload motor carrier, and with International Utilities, a trucking conglomerate. He began his railroad career in 1981 as a corporate management trainee with the Missouri Pacific and was appointed an assistant trainmaster.

Rose heads BNSF at a time when the railroad culture is changing more radically and rapidly than at any time in the last century and a half. Historically, railroading has featured a command and control management structure and culture. Going back to a time when labor (in the person of the train crew) was taking the owners' capital out of the immediate control of the entrepreneur, the railroad always has worked with sets of very explicit rules and procedures. Penalties for violating rules were severe. Reflecting the changing times, today's rail workers are not as willing as their fathers were to accept either the harsh discipline or the demanding nature of their jobs. Change comes slowly in the railroad industry, but the more-progressive leaders like Rose are trying to foster a more cooperative and even collegial culture.

Matt Rose was as different from Rob Krebs as Krebs had been different from Jerry Grinstein. Krebs, however, told how he decided in 1997 that Rose should succeed him:

> I looked around for qualities. I wanted somebody who was aggressive. I wanted somebody who was energetic. I wanted somebody who had high standards. I also realized that I had to have somebody who was acceptable to the organization. I wasn't exactly acceptable when I came down here. There were a lot of people who said, "We don't need Krebs down here." So those were the qualities I was looking for, and I saw them in Matt Rose. That's why I put him in the operating job.

The position was senior vice president and chief operations officer. In that position, Rose was responsible for coordinating transportation, maintenance, quality, purchasing, labor relations, and information services activities.

Rose had been in marketing positions most of his career and lacked hands-on operating experience. Krebs described the July 1997 meeting when he informed Rose that he was in line to succeed him:

> He came in here and sat down. I said, "Matt, I've looked around the company at our management talent, and I think you are the person who is probably the most suited to succeed me." He said, "I think that's really funny, because I haven't had any operating experience." I said, "Well, Matt, I just want to tell you that, effective at the beginning of the month, you are the senior vice president of operations." He said, "Oh." So he did that for about a year and a half, and we stepped him up [to chief operating officer]. It's been a wonderful, orderly transition.

shocked the transportation world when they announced a plan to combine the two railroads into a system that would blanket most of North America except for the U.S. Southeast.

The resulting 50,000-mile system, covering the U.S. West and stretching from Vancouver to Halifax in Canada, would have 67,000 employees and annual revenue of $12.5 billion. Both companies had maintained tight security, and rumors that a deal might be pending didn't even start to make the rounds of competitors until just a few days before the December 20 announcement.

Optimistically, the two companies said they hoped to have Canadian and U.S. government approvals by mid-2001, but in an early sign that approval might not be so smooth, Linda Morgan, then chairwoman of the Surface Transportation Board, reacted by saying, "I am surprised by the timing of this proposal. Railroads, together with their customers and employees, have not yet fully adjusted to recent mergers, and this proposal may represent the beginning of another round of major rail mergers. The board will have to review carefully all of the ramifications of any such application that may be filed."

The companies said the all-stock deal, with no premium paid to either side, was a merger of equals that valued the CN at about $6 billion and BNSF at $13 billion. BNSF shareholders would own about two-thirds of the company.

To comply with Canadian law—the CN had been owned by the Canadian government until 1995, when it was sold to private investors—a holding company based in Canada and with a majority of Canadian directors would be created. The new holding company would own the two railroads, which, after regulatory approval, would be operated as a single integrated system.

The combination of BNSF and the CN was an end-to-end merger, with virtually no overlap. Very few, if any, customers that had competitive rail service would lose it. The two railroads had strong balance sheets, and each was operating at relatively high efficiency. At the time of the announcement, the CN and BNSF were the most efficient railroads in the two countries, with ratios of operating expenses to revenue of 73 percent for BNSF in the third quarter of 1999, and 71 percent, the best of any North American railroad, for the CN.

As had been standard in rail mergers, executives of BNSF and the CN told securities analysts and reporters that the transaction would benefit customers by providing more efficient single-carrier service to more points than before.

As proposed, Krebs would become nonexecutive chairman of North American Railways (NAR), the holding company. Paul M. Tellier, CN chief executive, would be president and chief executive of NAR; Matthew K. Rose would be chief executive of BNSF; and E. Hunter Harrison, CN executive vice president and chief operating officer, would be chief executive of the CN. Harrison had begun his railroad career on the Frisco and had become a regional vice president of the BN before a restructuring in the late 1980s forced him out of his job.

Tellier said $300 million in cost synergies had been identified, one-third each from more-efficient use of locomotives and cars, purchasing and procurement, and "back-shop" general and administrative savings. A few weeks later, the synergy figure was raised to $500 million.

Other railroads initially had muted reactions, but in an indication of things to come, the Union Pacific, which was the CN's largest interline partner, said in a statement: "We are obviously still studying the implications of the CN-BNSF announcement. An immediate area of concern is how this will be viewed by rail shippers who have already expressed strong reservations about further rail mergers. We will be meeting with our customers to solicit their views and decide what Union Pacific can do to protect their interests, particularly in those areas where competition would be adversely affected by the proposed connection."

Wall Street was less than enthusiastic, hammering both railroads' stock on the day of the announcement. BNSF stock fell $2.19 a share, or 7.71 percent, to $26.19, and CN's fell 69 cents a share, or 2.31 percent, to $29.06, both in heavy trading on the New York Stock Exchange.

Senator Charles Grassley (R-Iowa) said he was concerned about further reduction of competition in transportation and that Congress would take a close look at the transaction. Shippers, still smarting over the service failures that followed the UP-C&NW, UP-SP, and Norfolk Southern-CSX-Conrail transactions, expressed concern at the possibility that they would have to deal with another rail consolidation.

Ironically, the BNSF-CN announcement came only a month after the STB had declared the UP-SP service crisis to be over. It also came while the Norfolk Southern and CSX still were struggling to return service levels to normal after their difficult division of Conrail and the absorption of its operations into their systems.

Within days, the STB said it was scrapping its long-standing policy of reviewing merger applications on a "one at a time" basis and notified the CN and BNSF that they would be "expected to address the effect of the proposed transaction, and any likely subsequent transactions, that would produce further significant consolidation in the industry." The CN and BNSF would be "expected to submit evidence on the cumulative impacts and crossover effects that are likely to occur in the wake of the proposed transaction, should it be approved," the agency said.

Also within days, the muted reaction had become a firestorm of criticism of the proposed merger. Both partners were caught by surprise.

Tellier said he had learned several things from the attempt to merge the CN and BNSF. "To this day we have never met a shipper, an analyst, or shareholder who has told me this was not a good idea," said Tellier, who later moved on to be chief executive of Bombardier, one of Canada's largest manufacturing companies. He continued:

> It was an idea ahead of its time. We were the two strongest railroads [based on] our performance, our balance sheet, and so on. Therefore, Dick [Davidson of the UP] and the others, who were led by Dick, felt that they could not allow this to happen. Then John [Snow, then with CSX and later U.S. secretary of the treasury] got into the picture. John is extremely skillful in Washington, given his background and his contacts. The powerful lobby that the UP has and the combination of those two worked very powerfully to derail this. If we had to do it again, I would have tried to bring [the other railroads] in earlier, and I would have tried to take them into my confidence. But when you are a publicly traded company, it's difficult to do this. It's very difficult to do this. I made the phone calls. We had agreed, Rob [Krebs] and I, who was going to talk to whom by when. I ended up talking to most of the CEOs. If I had to do it again, I would have done it differently, but it's difficult. I got burned. So therefore if I had spoken to David [Goode of the Norfolk Southern], to John, and so on maybe, especially in the case of David, this outcome would have been different. My biggest surprise was [that] I was relying very much on BN to get the job done in Washington.

BNSF doesn't believe it dropped the ball politically, but its Canadian partner clearly thought otherwise. The CN now sees itself as a player in the United States as well as in Canada, as Tellier pointed out:

> We have organized a Washington office since [the BNSF merger effort]. I'm working with people like Haley Barbour [a prominent Republican operative who was elected governor of Mississippi]. Today we do have access, if we have to, to key governors and so forth. But I was assuming that this would be done. If I had to redo it, I would have organized this Washington office and this Washington lobby before I did.
>
> I would never again in my life announce a deal four days before Christmas, because when you do something significant like this, you've got to work it. You've got to run all of it to touch bases as quickly as possible so that you say to Wellington or you say to Fidelity [two large institutional investment firms], "Give me a chance. Hear me out. I'll be here. I'll be here tomorrow afternoon. I'll be there on Thursday morning."

Unfortunately for BNSF and the CN, visiting with key constituencies was delayed, which gave opponents time to marshal their forces. "Exactly," Tellier emphasized.

> "It's the same with Washington. You fly in. You go and see Senator Lott, Trent Lott [R-Mississippi]. You say, 'Listen. I'm the major carrier in Mississippi. This is good for you, and here is why.' But Christmas break and so on, so we hit the road, Rob and I, flat out for about 48 hours. Then there was downtime for Christmas. We started to maintain the momentum early in January. We were already losing. We were on the defensive."

By the second week in January 2000, BNSF and the CN realized they were in a real fight. Four major railroads—the Union Pacific, the Norfolk Southern, CSX, and the Canadian Pacific—began a campaign to persuade shippers to support them in opposing the proposed merger. The Gang of Four, or the Four Amigos, as the press quickly dubbed them, published an "Open Letter to Railroad Customers" in paid advertisements in several newspapers. The letter was signed by the chief executive officers of each of the four railroads.

> "We have serious concerns with the potential impact of the BNSF/CN merger on the future structure of the rail industry," the chief executives said in the ad. "We agree with the [Surface Transportation Board] that the BNSF/CN proposal may trigger another round of railroad consolidations, resulting in two large rail systems serving North America." The letter also raised the possibility of even more mergers. "No major member of the rail network can afford to stand still while another becomes disproportionately larger," the presidents wrote. "We believe that another wave of mergers would be premature," they said, alluding to the service problems that had followed previous rail mergers.

It soon became clear why the other railroads were so vehemently opposed to the BNSF-CN combination. From their perspective, the timing was dreadful because the opponents weren't in a position to play in the merger game themselves. Speaking to securities analysts, CSX's John Snow candidly pointed out that his railroad and the others had terribly weak balance sheets, which was why they didn't want to be forced into mergers to compete with the combining BNSF and CN.

The weak balance sheets were self-inflicted, however, and resulted from the opponents having paid huge premiums for their recent acquisitions. The UP's ill-fated 1994 attempt to prevent the BN from buying the Santa Fe had cost the BN nearly $1 billion more than it originally had offered and the Santa Fe had been willing to accept. After the UP had forced railroad valuations up, its 1995 purchase of the Southern Pacific Rail Corporation carried a purchase premium of more than $1 billion, and the ensuing bidding war between the Norfolk Southern and CSX over Conrail cost the two buyers a purchase premium of more than $2 billion.

The service collapse that followed the UP's early attempt to integrate the SP into its system led to huge operating losses, a cut in the dividend, and the issuance of convertible preferred stock. Similarly, the problems of integrating Conrail operations into their own cost the Norfolk Southern and CSX untold hundreds of millions of dollars in additional operating expenses and lost revenue opportunities.

Unable financially to engage in mergers of their own, the UP, the NS, and CSX didn't want to face the prospect of having to compete against a combined BNSF-CN that would be solidifying its position and locking up market share while they watched helplessly.

In a moment of candor, Snow told analysts in January 2000 that he was not opposing the BNSF-CN transaction on its merits. "It might even be a good merger," he allowed.

Under the merger rules that the STB used in 2000, the BNSF-CN transaction appeared to meet the public interest test for approval. The opponents thus did the only thing they could. They tried to sabotage the deal by preventing it from ever getting into the regulatory process.

Krebs used his quarterly earnings meeting with analysts in New York in January to spell out the advantages of the merger and to state that he saw little chance that BNSF and the UP would reach an accommodation. "I don't see any possibility of a deal with UP," he told the analysts. In a seemingly light remark, Krebs demonstrated that he had acquired the same animosity toward the UP that BN executives had nurtured for a century. Responding to a question about why BNSF and the CN were doing their merger at a time when other railroads found it very troublesome, Krebs said, "I don't have to fulfill Union Pacific's manifest destiny to be the biggest railroad."

By February, BNSF and the CN were working hard to persuade shippers that the merger would be good for them. At the same time, the Four Amigos were campaigning for the STB to order a moratorium on any Class 1 mergers.

The CN and BNSF said they would guarantee shippers equal or better service after they were combined. The move was intended to win shipper support for the merger. In addition, the CN and BNSF said they would guarantee route options for shippers, keeping existing gateways that connected with other railroads open after their combination was effective. They also promised a rail alternative for those shippers that otherwise would have one rather than two railroads to use after the combination.

In an effort to stem the criticism of their proposed combination, BNSF and the CN began negotiations with individual shippers and groups representing shippers. No public announcement ever was made, but word began to leak out that BNSF and the CN were prepared to extend some form of competitive access to shippers in exchange for their support of the combination. Competitive access had become a major issue for many shippers that had lost competitive options as the industry went through its wave of consolidation.

Meanwhile, the Surface Transportation Board ordered a one-day hearing on the future structure of the railroad industry. So many interests asked for time to appear before the three commissioners that the proceeding was extended to four days in early March of 2000. Although the BNSF-CN transaction was not specifically to be the subject of the hearing, the sessions were conducted in the shadow of the planned merger.

The long list of witnesses included representatives of rail labor organizations, intermodal companies and associations, regional and short-line railroads, Amtrak, chemical and plastics shippers, and logistics companies. Many of those who testified—from railroad chief executives to shippers to port and local interests to federal government agencies—addressed the yet-to-be filed BNSF-CN deal.

The chief executives of all U.S. and Canadian railroads were focused on the immediate prospect that another rail merger could trigger a new round of mergers that would leave only continent-wide systems. Witnesses representing shippers advised the board to work to inject more competition in the industry when dealing with future merger cases.

Opponents of BNSF and the CN pleaded for an extended moratorium on further rail mergers, something they had been advocating before the hearing. Krebs and Tellier argued for prompt STB consideration of their merger application, which they planned to file with the STB within just a few weeks.

"There is no bad time for a good merger, nor a good time for a bad merger," Tellier told the commissioners. He accused his rail competitors of having "reacted in a very emotional manner."

Hitting directly at the service failure issue that had many shippers so angry at the prospect of another merger, Krebs said, "Mergers are part of the answer to better rail service. A moratorium would destroy [rail] values that can never be replaced."

Fighting the growing sense that a moratorium on further rail mergers might be imposed, Tellier and Krebs both urged the STB to "raise the bar." Tellier testified, "You, the STB, tell us what the standards are."

The Union Pacific stood to be the big loser if BNSF and the CN were to combine to form the largest rail system in North America. A lot of southbound traffic that flowed on the CN from Canada and the automotive complex in Michigan to the UP at Chicago would have been diverted to BNSF. The Norfolk Southern and CSX didn't have traffic losses to worry about, but they did have the legitimate concern that if they were forced into another round of mergers at that time, they would be the acquired rather than the acquirers, and because of the huge debt each had taken on in buying its share of Conrail, they would not receive a very high price. This was particularly galling for the NS, considering that just three years earlier its balance sheet was so strong it could have bought BNSF.

For the Four Amigos, the other alternative was even more unthinkable. None could bear the thought of allowing BNSF and the CN to merge and gain a several-year foothold in the market, offering customers more options and being able to handle more of their transportation needs.

At the hearing, it became increasingly apparent that the idea of a moratorium was gaining strength with the members of the STB. The opposing railroads acknowledged that they had asked shippers to testify against any further rail mergers at that time. BNSF and the CN also solicited supportive witnesses, but not in as organized a campaign.

After the first two days of the hearing, Tellier approached a reporter and said in his French-accented English: "Let's see if I've got this right. These guys [CP, CSX, NS, and UP], they screwed up their own mergers, and now I get beat up for it?"

Within a week following the conclusion of the hearings, the STB issued a ruling imposing a 15-month moratorium on any combinations among Class 1 railroads while it developed new merger rules that it believed would be better suited to the conditions of a highly concentrated industry. The agency soon released a notice of proposed rule-making, soliciting views on how the rules should be changed.

Pointing out that there was no provision in the Interstate Commerce Act for a moratorium on mergers, BNSF and the CN first sought reconsideration by the STB and then filed suit, appealing the board's order in the D.C. Circuit Court of Appeals. BNSF and the CN also asked the court to stay the STB order while their appeal was being considered, a move that would have forced the regulatory agency to accept their joint application for permission to combine.

Tellier, in the CN's appeal, said: "The notion that the two most efficient railroads in North America cannot combine now to improve their business because the other major railroads are having trouble running theirs has the effect of protecting competitors, not rail competition, and clearly is against the public interest."

Krebs was equally outspoken, saying: "If Chairwoman Morgan's radical decision stands, the effect would be something unheard of in any industry. For a period of 15 months, industry participants will be denied the opportunity to realize service efficiency improvements that a carefully conceived and well-executed combination can provide shippers, shareholders, employees and the public."

BNSF and the CN apparently had been persuasive in negotiating with some shipper interests. Ed Emmett, then president of the National Industrial Transportation League, which represents shippers, said his reaction to the moratorium was one of disappointment and puzzlement, adding, "This decision appears to have been made more out of confusion, not of purpose." Emmett told the *Journal of Commerce* that the STB seemed more concerned about protecting competing railroads than about helping shippers achieve the benefits of a good merger. "The STB is always accused of not taking the side of shippers, and I think the agency and some observers may wrap this in the mantle of a shipper-friendly decision, when in fact it was done more because of the other Class 1 railroads," he said. A former ICC commissioner himself, Emmett said the rule-making could have been carried out simultaneously with consideration of the merger.

Secretary of Transportation Rodney Slater applauded the decision to revise merger rules but objected to the moratorium. "We are disappointed that the board ordered a 15-month suspension of all merger activity, including a proposed consolidation of the Burlington Northern Santa Fe–Canadian National Railroads," he said.

The two railroads were not alone in their stance that the STB was claiming authority that it didn't have. The Western Coal Traffic League, which represents coal shippers and frequently battled BNSF on rate and other issues, filed a notice of appeal to the STB decision. The coal group had not taken a position on the merits of the merger but questioned the legal authority to impose a moratorium without considering the pros and cons of the proposed merger. Other shipper groups ultimately joined the appeal, some making the argument that a 15-month delay would be damaging to shipper interests by denying them the commercial advantages that a merged BNSF-CN system offered.

In justifying its moratorium decision, the STB repeatedly expressed concern about the duopoly that would be created if the rail industry consolidated to just two transcontinental systems. The

The BN Goes Outside the Railroad Industry for CEOs—the Only Railroad to Do So

The selection of three consecutive chief executive officers who came from outside the railroad industry and who had no railroad operating experience helped accelerate the culture change that Dick Bressler and the BN board of directors believed was necessary.

Under Walter Drexel and his successor, Darius Gaskins, the forced change was consistent if not easy. Neither man had the personal relationships that develop inside railroads and other traditional businesses. When they found an executive who was slow to change or otherwise did not fit their idea of how the railroad should be managed, they offered a severance package and sent the individual on his way.

The culture change continued, but under Gerald Grinstein it didn't have the aura of a planned campaign, which probably was just as well. Whereas Drexel and Gaskins had consciously tried to force change and didn't have a lot of emotional baggage about dismissing executives or forcing people to retire, Grinstein's background was considerably different.

A lawyer by training, Grinstein had spent years in Washington as chief counsel to Senator Warren Magnuson and later as chief counsel of the Senate Commerce Committee, which Magnuson chaired. After leaving Washington, Grinstein practiced law in Seattle and became chief executive of Western Airlines, one of the smaller trunk carriers that would not survive airline deregulation. Grinstein received high marks for successfully negotiating the merger of Western into the larger Delta Airlines.

With Western gone as an independent airline—Grinstein joined the Delta board and later became its chairman and chief executive—Dick Bressler saw an opportunity to bring Grinstein to the railroad. Grinstein said he still thought he had been chosen initially to be a vice chairman for the wrong reason. "I don't think Dick [Bressler] was interested in my labor skills at all," he said. "I think he saw a deal maker who had just sold an airline to another one and that I would understand that the railroad was just another business deal. . . . In effect, what I'm saying is that I think he picked me for the wrong reason, because I was crazy about the railroad."

Very intelligent and personable, Grinstein was known for being quick with a quip and had an infectious good humor about him, particularly with outsiders, whom he immediately put at ease.

Grinstein also had the political philosophy that because one makes enough enemies in the normal course of politics, one doesn't need to go out of one's way to create new ones. He also believed that one should never pick a fight that doesn't need to be fought.

At the railroad, this manifested itself in a reluctance to force people out even after it had become obvious to most others that it was necessary for the good of the company. Instead of firing longtime executives, Grinstein sometimes followed the Washington practice of "layering" the management. Instead of forcing people to retire, he gave them new titles and shifted their responsibilities. New people were brought in with slightly different titles. This classic form-over-substance approach allowed the BN to deny that people were being fired. When Grinstein ordered that two of the railroad's most senior longtime executives be retired over the Memorial Day weekend in 1994, it was a measure of how serious the problem had become.

Grinstein also had a bubbling enthusiasm for the railroad. Years after he retired, he said in an interview for this book: "It's a wonderful company, and the fact that it has survived so much and is still in the position it's in is a tribute to what a good company it really is and the people in the company."

position was ironic because it was the STB that already had created a duopoly of BNSF and the UP in the West, and a duopoly of the NS and CSX in the East. The issue of duopoly had been raised by opponents in the UP-SP merger and when the NS and CSX sought permission to divide Conrail between them, but those concerns had been rejected by the STB.

Morgan was chairwoman during each of the recent merger cases, all of which had been approved. Some rail merger critics, including the president of a Class 1 railroad, had predicted when the BN and the Santa Fe combined that an inevitable process leading to just two railroads had begun.

The federal appeals court rejected the appeals, saying that the STB had established a basis for the moratorium. As in so many cases, the courts traditionally defer to the expertise of regulatory agencies, as long as they give interested parties due process. The four-day hearing had been all the process the STB needed to satisfy the legal standard.

Only days after their appeal was rejected, BNSF and the CN announced that they were calling off their combination. They decided that 15 months was too long to keep stockholders in limbo.

Looking back, Krebs acknowledged some miscalculations. "Where we were naive and where we were wrong was the emotional response," he said. "Customers could not separate what had just happened to them at Conrail and Southern Pacific from what had happened with CN and the IC [a merger that was implemented extremely smoothly and with no service disruptions] or was happening with BNSF. I'll be the first to admit we had some problems with BN and Santa Fe, but nothing like what happened at the SP or at Conrail."

A year after having given up on any hope of merging with the CN, Krebs said:

> I figured people would look at that and say, "Okay, well this makes sense to us." It's certainly a pro-competitive merger, and we would have support to get it done. Wrong. First of all, customers were so fed up with mergers that they didn't want to have any more. The UP and the SP [really caused that reaction]. I also didn't think the eastern guys' [Snow's and Goode's] reaction would be as strong as it was. Again, it shows you what a good merger it was going to be. So I didn't realize we were going to get ganged up on like we did. I also didn't understand . . . I guess I misread Linda Morgan. I thought she would be calmer about the whole thing. That's what killed us, because what it became was a political deal.

A retired CN vice president perhaps put the BNSF-CN defeat in perspective, by paraphrasing Machiavelli: "They forgot that your enemies will come after you with more zeal than [that with which] your friends will support you."

IO

The Present

It's All about Service

I'm in favor of a healthy railroad industry. In the long run, it doesn't help anyone to have an unhealthy railroad industry.

ROGER NOBER, chairman of the Surface Transportation Board, May 2003

Following the Surface Transportation Board order on April 17, 2000, which created a moratorium on combinations among Class 1 railroads, the agency spent some 15 months developing new merger rules.

With their own merger dead, BNSF and the CN went back to operating their respective rail systems as efficiently as possible. Both companies were ahead of their competitors in disciplined operations and customer focus, which placed them in a position to provide more and better service to customers and to maintain and even improve their competitive positions.

Unlike their major competitors that had suffered through costly service crises following mergers, both of the would-be partners had demonstrated that rail mergers could be carried out efficiently and relatively quickly. The CN, for example, had acquired the Illinois Central in 1999 and had integrated its operations with no problems; then it had acquired the Wisconsin Central in 2001 and integrated it even more smoothly. BNSF, a much larger, more complex system, had some minor difficulties in implementing the merger of the BN and the Santa Fe, but most of the problems emanated from the integration of new computer systems to replace those of the formerly separate railroads.

As discussed earlier, BNSF excelled in having quickly created a

BNSF culture to supplant the separate identities of the BN and the Santa Fe. Alluding to the notorious Penn Central merger of 1968, in which the century-old enmity of the Pennsylvania and the New York Central carried over to the merged railroad, former BNSF chief executive Rob Krebs said, "I think we brought the management group together as one group instead of green versus blue."

In his railroad career, Krebs was president of the Southern Pacific at a time when Southern Pacific still was a major system. He then was chief executive of the Santa Fe following its abortive attempt to merge with the SP, a time when he had to fight off hostile takeover attempts by raiders more interested in the company's real estate and other assets than its railroad business. Finally, after fighting off the efforts of the UP to acquire the Santa Fe, Krebs merged his company into the BN.

To many in the industry who knew him as an extremely focused, even cold, executive, Krebs became a different man as he headed toward his own retirement. Those who worked with Krebs said his biggest attribute turned out to be his ability to change. His perception that a new culture must be developed as quickly as possible probably was his greatest contribution to BNSF. Even Krebs could joke about having become a "touchy-feely" kind of executive. The Aspen Institute program discussed in chapter 9 surprised some, and his concentration on creating a new culture rather than simply melding two surprised many.

Relations in the once-clubby railroad industry were strained after the imposition of the merger moratorium, as Krebs of BNSF and Paul Tellier of the CN believed their competitors had ganged up on them unfairly in blocking the BNSF-CN combination. Krebs believed that the opposition of the Gang of Four—as the chief executives of the Canadian Pacific, CSX, the Norfolk Southern, and the Union Pacific became known—was particularly unfair. After all, he reasoned, he had acquiesced to the UP-SP merger and negotiated trackage rights at a time when he could have opposed the transaction and perhaps would have been granted ownership of certain lines if the STB had been forced to condition that merger with line divestitures. He had hoped for reciprocal consideration from his colleagues.

Yet, as had been the case throughout the history of the industry, the railroads simultaneously were vigorously competitive with each other and highly interdependent on each other. In fact, had the BNSF-CN combination proceeded, North American Railways Incorporated would have been less dependent than other railroads on connecting carriers, a factor that no doubt contributed to the response of other railroads.

During Krebs's last months as chairman of the board—he already had handed the reins to Matt Rose as chief executive officer—he reflected on the inherent strength of BNSF even without the CN combination. "Why are we where we are today?" he asked rhetorically. "First of all, we made a good merger, and it was a financially good merger too. No one spent a lot of money to buy the other one. We were a stronger company financially the day after we merged than the two companies were the day before."

Like so many railroad executives who had learned their craft and achieved executive office during the era of regulation, Krebs was convinced that cutting costs was the first priority for any railroad. As the BN and the Santa Fe had done separately, BNSF had bought back some of its common stock even while it was investing some $9 billion in four years. He saw no dichotomy in shrinking the capital base by buying back stock and at the same time investing new capital in the business. "We started off on a good, strong financial footing," Krebs said. "I think we spent the money to provide service. The downside of that is that puts more capital into the business."

When the new STB merger rules were promulgated in mid-2001, most of the lawyers and consultants who represent railroads and their customers agreed that none of the preceding mergers would have been stopped had the new rules been in effect when those transactions were being considered. As this is written, no railroads have put the new rules to the test by trying to merge. Most rail executives and observers believe that it is only a matter of time, however, until final consolidation of the railroad industry occurs in North America, resulting in two gigantic systems that will blanket the continent and will compete with each other in every region.

The new rules, as adopted by the Surface Transportation Board, place a heavier burden on merging railroads to satisfy the regulators that the kind of service problems experienced after several recent mergers will be avoided in the future. And because the next major merger is expected to set off a final round of rail consolidation in the United States, the new rules demand considerably more information from the merging carriers, including proof that the merger would not reduce competition.

The issue of competition is particularly important, as rail mergers generally have resulted in a reduction in rail-to-rail competition, and the STB and the ICC before it have followed a policy of preserving competition where it existed but not creating new competition. It was that policy that led to BNSF's gaining nearly 4,000 miles of trackage rights in the Union Pacific–Southern Pacific merger to preserve options for those shippers that originally had been served by more than one railroad.

In announcing its new rules, the STB said it intended to offset merger-related reductions in competition by requiring "competitive enhancements," such as reciprocal switching arrangements, trackage rights, and efforts to eliminate restrictions on interchanges by short-line railroads. In fact, merging railroads would be expected to consider the so-called downstream effects of their combination and to identify potential service and competitive issues and advise the agency how it could remedy such problems.

The board also said "the quantity and quality" of competitive enhancements that would be required "would depend on a variety of factors, such as merger-related competitive harms for which feasible and effective remedies could not be devised, and the amount of public benefits that could be expected to flow from a particular transaction."

The idea that future rail mergers should be required to enhance competition, as suggested by the STB, rather than simply avoiding a reduction in competition, sent shudders through the rail industry. Rail mergers historically have been designed to enhance the competitive opportunities for the merging railroads, with little thought given to enhancing overall competition. Edward Hamberger—president of the Association of American Railroads, the Washington-based industry association that represents all of the major railroads—reacted to the revised merger rules by saying, "We continue to believe that new rail mergers should not be subject to a standard requiring enhancement of competition, but instead should remain subject to the test of whether a merger preserves competition. Conditions relating to competition should only be focused on remedying competitive harms, if any, that may result from a merger." The president of the AAR is employed by the railroads and never takes a public position that has not been agreed to by the railroad chief executives who make up his board. While BNSF and the CN could agree on little with the UP, the NS, CSX, or the CP, they could agree on their antipathy to the STB policy calling for enhanced competition in future mergers.

Although the railroad industry has hundreds of reciprocal switching and trackage rights agreements, the vast majority of these agreements are voluntary. The idea that government might mandate such agreements is anathema to private railroads that have been free of government regulation for little more than two decades. The trackage rights that were negotiated for the Southern Pacific in the BN-Santa Fe merger and for BNSF in the UP-SP merger were voluntary, although in each case they were included as conditions for approval in the final merger ruling.

The railroads fear mandatory use of their property by competitors on two grounds. First, they know that such access would cost the owning railroad some traffic, and much of the retained traffic would move at lower rates. Second, if the competing railroads were unable to reach agreement on the fees to be paid for reciprocal switching or trackage rights, the STB would move to set the charges. That would open the possibility that owning railroads would not receive fees high enough to cover the full cost of ownership, effectively forcing them to subsidize competitors. Such an environment would discourage needed capital investment, the railroads contend.

The new rules did promise to raise the cost of future mergers. The more competition that is agreed to or mandated, the less revenue will be available to the merging railroads. At some point, combining carriers will walk away from a merger if they determine that the loss of income from traffic that would be diverted to competitors outweighs the anticipated gains of the merger. That was the logic behind the decision of the Northern Pacific and the Great Northern to abandon their merger in 1930, after the ICC approved a merger into the Great Northern Pacific, but conditioned the merger on divestiture of each railroad's 50 percent interest in the Chicago, Burlington, and Quincy.

The STB said the tightened merger standards reflected the reduction in Class 1 railroads that already had occurred, as well as the fact that mergers no longer were needed to eliminate excess rail capacity. Therefore, the board said, its definition of the public interest had shifted to a focus on avoiding service problems that were disruptive to rail customers.

Among the major railroads that were to be covered by the new merger rules, only the Union Pacific unequivocally supported the STB. The UP stated on numerous occasions that it opposed more rail mergers, a position that was consistent and made good sense from its perspective. It was unlikely that the UP, as the largest railroad in North America, would be allowed to initiate the final round of mergers. For the UP to gain regulatory approval of a merger with another Class 1 railroad, it probably would be required to accept conditions that effectively would negate the advantages of the merger by costing it more traffic than it would gain. On the other hand, just as it had done following the BN-Frisco and BN-Santa Fe mergers, the UP would be in a position to plead for merger approval in a subsequent filing, on the grounds that equity demanded that regulators allow it to compete with its larger, merged competitors.

By mid-2001, when the new rules went into effect, the other Class 1 railroads still were not anxious to embark on another round of mergers. The Norfolk Southern and CSX still were struggling financially with the aftermath of their joint $10 billion purchase of Conrail and the ensuing service problems that resulted from the dismemberment and division of that railroad. Service quality at both railroads, however, had returned to more-normal levels. The other railroads, although they had improved their operations, still were not in a strong enough financial position to play in the merger game. Addressing the North American Rail Shippers Association annual meeting in mid-2002, David Goode (chairman, president, and chief executive of the Norfolk Southern) and Ike Evans (then president and chief operating officer of the UP) stuck to the industry mantra that railroads have to focus on providing improved service and adding value for customers without resorting to mergers. Evans took the opportunity to point out that the UP has given up length-of-haul to marketing-alliance partners, taking the long view that such alliances help both rail partners and their customers.

Although on the surface the merger moratorium resulted only in the collapse of the BNSF-Canadian National combination, proponents of the moratorium may have perceived other, more salutary effects. With no major rail consolidations since the Norfolk Southern and CSX purchased Conrail and divided its operations between them, the industry by mid-2003 had experienced more than four years of relative stability in which individual companies focused on improving operations and strengthening balance sheets.

The Union Pacific, for example, in 1999 finally overcame its service crisis that followed the acquisition of the Southern Pacific in 1996. It recaptured some of the traffic it had lost to BNSF in 1997 and 1998, as freight tends to move by the most efficient service route available, and the UP had the best access to the growing and profitable chemicals traffic originating along the Texas and Louisiana Gulf Coast. The UP also resumed the capital spending program it promised to undertake during the UP-SP merger, as it continued the process of integrating the SP into its enlarged system.

Similarly, by 2002 the Norfolk Southern and CSX had completed the integration of Conrail operations into their systems. Operations at both of the eastern giants returned to normal levels, and most of the kinds of customer service complaints that were heard in 1999 disappeared. Some customers that previously had single-line service from Conrail now had to deal with interline service between the NS and CSX, however, so not all customers saw the breakup of Conrail as an unmixed blessing.

Although all of the railroads that had been involved in the last round of mergers since the BN-Santa Fe in 1995 used the merger moratorium and subsequent time to strengthen their balance sheets, none had returned to premerger levels by mid-2003. The UP still had outstanding $1.5 billion in convertible preferred stock that it sold to an offshore trust in 1998, and although it increased its dividend in early 2003 and began redeeming the convertible preferred stock, the dividend payout to stockholders had not been restored to the level that existed before the service crisis. The Norfolk Southern, which spent $5.8 billion for its 58 percent of Conrail, also was forced to cut its dividend payout rate. In addition to restoring operating efficiency, it concentrated its efforts on reducing debt and returning the debt-to-capital ratio to traditional levels. Prior to the Conrail purchase, the NS had boasted the lowest ratio of operating expenses to revenue among major railroads and had the strongest balance sheet and safety record in the industry. CSX Transportation, alone among the railroads involved in mergers, changed its operating management and focused on improving service. CSX Corporation sold most of its non-rail subsidiaries to reduce debt.

In early 2003, with the railroad as its principal remaining subsidiary, CSX announced it was closing its Richmond, Virginia, headquarters and was consolidating the holding company at the CSX Transportation headquarters in Jacksonville, Florida. That decision came only weeks after longtime CSX chief executive John Snow resigned to become the secretary of the treasury in the George W. Bush administration. Michael Ward—who had been made chief of operations at the railroad in April 2000, during the height of the Conrail-related service problems—was named chairman, president, and chief executive of CSX Corporation. He earlier had been named president of the railroad.

The merger moratorium may have cost the Canadian National its opportunity to forge the largest North American rail system, but the railroad managed to accomplish a smaller merger during the moratorium period when it purchased Wisconsin Central Limited and its subsidiary railroads in 2001. The CN had stated that it would proceed with the transaction only if the Surface Transportation Board decided it was a "minor" transaction that was not affected by the moratorium. The Wisconsin Central (WC), which was neatly and quickly integrated into the CN system, filled a geographic hole in the CN's network, providing a good route between Duluth, Minnesota, and Chicago, where it connected with CN lines from eastern Canada and the Illinois Central, which had been acquired in 1999, as well as other railroads. Prior to the WC acquisition, the CN had relied on trackage rights over BNSF to connect Chicago with its western Canada system.

The railroads that had so vigorously opposed the CN and BNSF in their merger attempt had argued that the moratorium was necessary so they could focus on improving operations instead of being forced into an ill-timed round of mergers. When the STB granted them the moratorium they sought, they did just that. Former STB chairwoman Linda Morgan told the author she thought the railroads did the right thing by focusing on improving operations rather than merging. "A lot of what the railroads have done [since the merger moratorium began] is take out embedded costs that they hadn't been paying any attention to, improving their operations so that the [system] velocity was up, their dwell time was down, and before you knew it, there was better car and locomotive utilization and less yard handling," she said.

While the Canadian National generated a lot of attention because of its shift to a "scheduled railroad" operation, Morgan pointed out that all railroads gained. "Look at NS. Look at their Thoroughbred Operating Plan," she said. "Here's a railroad that everybody always viewed as the best operating railroad, yet they were running their operations with all kinds of inefficiencies in it. When they stepped back and peeled away and sort of started all over again, they discovered that they didn't need to be doing it the way they were."

A principal customer benefit of merger always has been the prospect of more-extensive single-line service. Merging railroads traditionally hold out single-line service as an opportunity for their customers to expand their market coverage by extending their economic and efficient geographic reach. Single-line service, because it eliminates the need to transfer customer freight from one railroad to another, also is more efficient and less costly. The BN-Santa Fe merger, for example, provided a more efficient single-line service between Southern California and eastern railroads at Memphis than previously had been possible. It allowed the new BNSF to compete for traffic that it couldn't handle as well before the merger. Prior to the merger, the Santa Fe had to rely on the BN to get its trains to the Memphis gateway over a secondary BN line, while the BN had virtually no presence in the huge import-export trade through Southern California.

SERVICE INNOVATION SUPPLANTS COST CUTTING

Before the BNSF merger and the SP acquisition by the UP, the SP had the only effective single-line service to and from Memphis and Southern California, but its route was several hundred miles longer than the joint BN-Santa Fe route. The UP also could offer single-line service, but its circuitous route through Salt Lake City and much of the Midwest was not competitive.

In combating BNSF and the CN, the other major railroads had argued that they could develop marketing and service alliances and joint service agreements that would provide rail customers with the benefits of single-line service but without the severe service disruptions that had marked previous mergers.

During the merger moratorium, the railroad industry, including BNSF and the CN, did develop a host of new services. One of the first such offerings was between the CN and the Canadian Pacific and had been announced even before the BNSF-CN combination was canceled. The CN was granted trackage rights over the CP for paper and forest products traffic from eastern Canada into the U.S. Northeast, while the CP gained the right to route intermodal trains through a new CN tunnel between Sarnia, Ontario, and Port Huron, Michigan, that provided a more efficient route between the industrial heartland of eastern Canada and the U.S. Midwest. As was usually the case with voluntary trackage and haulage rights agreements, the deal worked for both railroads at virtually no competitive risk or cost for either. The CP has very little business east of Montreal and carried little paper or forest products traffic to the eastern United States, so the trackage rights to the CN presented no competitive threat while it provided revenue from the trackage rights fee to the CP. On the other hand, the CP gave the CN revenue that helped pay for the expensive new tunnel, while it did not threaten the CN's traffic base.

South of the U.S.-Canada border, the "deals" came at a fast and furious pace. BNSF was a leader in developing new customer-focused services, an unsurprising development because BNSF was the industry leader in intermodal, the most service-sensitive line of business. Intermodal shipments begin on rubber tires on highways, and the easiest thing is to leave them there to their destination. Railroads must provide superior service at lower rates if they are to convince shippers to transfer loads to rails for the long haul.

BNSF began to offer service guarantees over a number of routes. Unlike in the past, however, where service guarantees were built into contracts and the customers tended not to pay for them specifically but did guarantee volume, BNSF offered the guarantees as a premium service available to any customers and for which customers paid a premium. Traditional tariff service, which never had included service guarantees, still was available for customers that chose not to pay the premium or did not require the service assurance. From 2000, when the service guarantees first were made available, BNSF expanded its guarantees over its own system and began to offer them in conjunction with eastern railroads.

The industry trend toward alliances included interline movements of refrigerated goods between produce-growing regions in the West and consuming markets in the Northeast and Southeast. Alliances were aimed at specific commodity movements and did not commit any railroad to any greater relationship with its partner. While BNSF and the Norfolk Southern had a long-standing cooperative relationship, for example, that did not prevent the NS from entering into similar and competing alliances with the UP.

The alliances worked as long as there was capacity to handle the traffic, and as long as each member of the alliance believed it was receiving revenue to justify its commitment of capacity and the management resources to handle it.

One rule that was adopted by the STB with little opposition from the railroads would require merging railroads to prepare a service assurance plan, much as they had been required to prepare an operating plan and a safety plan for the combined properties. Under the service assurance plans, which BNSF and the CN had volunteered to submit under the old rules before their merger was abandoned, the carriers would be required both to commit to given levels of service and to tell customers and regulators how they would rectify service failures if they did occur. Before the moratorium was imposed, BNSF and the CN had committed to guarantee that every customer would receive service at least as good as it had received from BNSF and the CN separately. BNSF and the CN also committed to retain all existing gateways even if a customer chose to interline with a competitor rather than use the combined BNSF-CN service.

A Tale of Two (STB) Chairmen

The merger moratorium and new rules were a product of the Surface Transportation Board while Linda J. Morgan headed it. It was during Morgan's tenure as chairwoman of the Interstate Commerce Commission that the BN and the Santa Fe merged, and later after the STB replaced the ICC, Morgan oversaw the UP-SP and Conrail transactions. The service crises that followed the latter two cases, though, appeared to color her view of rail mergers in general. During the hearings that led to the merger moratorium, Morgan virtually ignored Krebs's testimony in which he pointed out how BNSF had achieved every commitment it had made in its merger application.

Transportation writers and others who deal regularly with the STB sensed that Morgan was reacting to congressional criticism when she imposed the merger moratorium. Many shippers that had suffered through the earlier service failures had contacted members of Congress to express their views that they didn't want any further disruptions that might come from another merger. As discussed in chapter 9, a number of members of Congress spoke out against the BNSF-CN transaction. Morgan was known to be politically astute.

The STB was created at the end of 1995. The Interstate Commerce Commission Termination Act that created it called for the new agency to be reauthorized every three years. Under pressure at varying times from unhappy shipper groups and from rail unions unhappy over the agency's willingness to approve abrogation of negotiated union agreements in order to achieve the benefits of merger (known as cramdown), the STB never was reauthorized. It was refunded under continuing resolutions, however, and threats to block reauthorization proved to be hollow. Although Morgan was cognizant of the issue, she continued to implement the law as she interpreted it, telling congressional hearings on several occasions that if Congress wanted regulatory policy changed, it should change the law.

Roger Nober arrived at the STB and succeeded Morgan as chairman of the agency in December 2002. Both were lawyers and had similar backgrounds, although they were of different political persuasions. Like Morgan, Nober had been a longtime congressional aide before joining the regulatory agency. He had been a staff member to Republicans on the House Transportation and Infrastructure Committee and was appointed to the STB by

President George W. Bush. Morgan had been general counsel at the Senate Commerce Committee when Democrats controlled the Senate and had been appointed to the Interstate Commerce Commission by President Bill Clinton in 1994. By early 2003 the railroads were providing generally consistent service, and the "heat" from shippers and their lobbying groups was considerably less on Nober than it had been on Morgan.

More important, perhaps, was that while Morgan tended to interpret the act that the STB administered in ways that were favorable to railroads, she never could ignore populist views against rail consolidation. Nober, on the other hand, demonstrated from the beginning of his tenure a laissez-faire attitude toward further rail mergers that was consistent with the pro-business positions taken by the Bush administration.

In one of his first public discussions of rail policy and regulatory issues, Nober hinted at a more relaxed approach to rail mergers under his leadership. While saying he supported the merger rules that had been developed during the 2000–2001 moratorium, Nober did suggest that he was not sold on the requirement that merging railroads should identify potential competitive issues and that the STB should take a "downstream" perspective towards mergers, anticipating other mergers that might be triggered by an application before the board.

Speaking to an investor group, Nober said it wasn't his agency's role to predict the future. "That's a difficult burden to meet," he said. The new chairman of the STB also said that he would not necessarily look favorably on concerns that another merger could set off a chain reaction of bad service and higher rates. "We'll look at the merger, and not look at every problem that a shipper has ever had with a railroad," he said. "This [merger approval process] will not be used as a means for looking at every complaint."

In a statement that rail executives had not heard in many years, Nober said that railroads, while not a perfectly competitive industry, are private companies and that it was not necessarily the STB's job to regulate all disputes that come up regarding carriers. "I'm in favor of a healthy railroad industry. In the long run, it doesn't help anyone to have an unhealthy railroad industry," Nober said. Such free market thinking had not come from the federal government since before the original Interstate Commerce Commission gained the authority to disapprove rail rates at the beginning of the 20th century.

BNSF and the CN, assuming that their merger would at least receive consideration by the STB, had engaged in negotiations with various interests in the hope of both eliciting support and mitigating opposition. Had the moratorium not been imposed, the two railroads were willing to guarantee some form of competitive access that many rail customers were demanding be imposed on the railroad industry. No merger, no competitive access.

Other than forcing planners to think in greater detail about how a merger would affect their service, the rule did not seem to be as significant as many shippers thought. The service failures that followed the merger of the UP and the SP or the division of Conrail between the Norfolk Southern and CSX had been completely unforeseen. It was unlikely that future rail planners would be any more prescient than their predecessors.

In fact, as the UP-SP service collapse had occurred while the Conrail transaction was under consideration, some rail customers called on the STB to delay approval of the NS and CSX purchase of Conrail. In testimony supporting the transaction filed in December 1997, James McClellan, NS senior vice president of planning, explained what had happened in the West and pointed out that the UP's problems were unique to its system and that the same kind of problems would not occur in the East. McClellan said there would be unforeseen circumstances in implementing the Conrail division, but because they could not be anticipated, nothing would be gained by delaying the approval.

With just two major systems in the West and two in the East, the next round of consolidation undoubtedly would combine eastern and western carriers in end-to-end mergers. With fewer facilities to be closed or rationalized, the opportunity for disruption and congestion would be less than in previous mergers. Morgan, who presided over some of the largest mergers in rail industry history during her tenure at the Interstate Commerce Commission and then the STB, has said that she believes there will be another and final round of mergers, but she hopes that it will be for different reasons from those in the past.

Historically, rail mergers were driven by the prospect of increasing operating earnings by taking redundant costs out of the combined systems and by capturing some traffic that was moving on other carriers. A final round of consolidation will be good for the industry if it is driven by a desire to do more for customers and to grow the business as a result, Morgan stated.

Shortly before she left her government post, Morgan reflected:

> I'm of sort of a mixed mind on consolidation right now.
> Some of it may be that I'm still smarting from the last
> round and the [service] difficulties that ensued, and having
> been told everything was going to be fine. Then it ended up
> not being fine. There is only so much a government agency
> can do to make something fine. After a point, it is in some-
> body else's hands. . . . But there is a part of me that worries
> that the automatic embracing of consolidation that has
> gone on in this industry causes people not to look for other
> ways of providing service. I think that has been what has
> been going on. I think that, without getting into the merits
> of the moratorium one way or another, the moratorium
> period allowed people to think of other ways of achieving
> the same sorts of benefits.

Despite the moratorium, Morgan's record demonstrated that she
was not antimerger. She did have reservations about the reasons for
mergers, though, saying she feared that too many rail executives
have looked at mergers as their only option to solve deeply embedded problems:

> It doesn't mean that consolidations are bad. It just means
> that [I would feel better] if I could create an environment
> and feel comfortable that people were looking at all options
> for making the systems better and not just saying, "Well,
> because consolidation seems to have worked, we're going to
> do it that way," and not looking at these other alternatives.
> That's not just with respect to consolidation. I think it's
> with respect to how they deal with communities, how they
> deal with their customers, how they deal with one another,
> and how they deal with their employees.

Morgan believed the BN-Santa Fe merger was "really the beginning of the last round." She continued: "At the time, it looked like a
good merger to me. There were a lot of people supporting it. The
record certainly was not dictating something other than approval. It
was your typical end-to-end kind of merger in which you were going
to open up markets that were going to connect. You were going to
meld [disparate] commodities into one company. It made a lot of

sense."

The UP-SP merger, which had more competitive issues and problems than any other recent merger, was almost a foregone conclusion once the BN and the Santa Fe combined, Morgan explained. "It was going to happen," she said. "First of all, I had one merger that was already approved. So I had to achieve some sort of competitive balance in the West, on top of the fact that SP was in financial disrepair." The SP was in violation of loan covenants throughout its last year as an independent company, and loan trustees waived their rights on the condition that the sale to the UP proceed. As a result, BNSF ended up with nearly 4,000 miles of trackage rights and the equivalent of two Class 1 railroads in additional business, as it became the vehicle for maintaining competitive balance throughout the West.

Looking to the future in mid-2002, Morgan said:

> My sense is that this industry will bring itself to another [merger] round [because there is a cultural predilection toward mergers]. We can have an academic discussion about whether further consolidation is a good thing or a bad thing, but then I always have this other discussion, which is the "Big P," that is, politics. Is the timing right? We get back to BNSF-CN. I think the timing was not right there for a lot of different reasons. I do think the industry has to care about that because if your timing is off, you can lose so much.

As was seen during the public hearings that resulted in the moratorium, one of the key reasons the rail merger movement was at least temporarily halted was the perception that the industry was abusing its power. Actually, some rail customers had objected to railroad market behavior almost before the ink was dry on Jimmy Carter's signature making the Staggers Rail Act of 1980 into law. These were customers who believed that, because of the nature of the goods they shipped, they had no alternative other than to use rail service.

Under the regulatory scheme that existed prior to 1980, these shippers of bulk commodities did not pay what railroads considered their proper share of rail fixed costs because railroads did not engage in differential pricing, charging different customers different rates for similar service.

Under regulation, rates were cost-based, whereas they became market-based under deregulation, with railroads charging what the traffic could bear. Charging all the traffic will bear—up to but not beyond the point where the traffic wouldn't move at all—is charging the right price. Charge less and the customer retains revenue the railroad could use. Charge more and the railroad gets no revenue because the traffic doesn't move.

Rates for grain shipments provide an example of the rate-making flexibility that railroads gained by deregulation. In the case of BNSF, its rates are higher for moving grain from Montana and North Dakota to export terminals in the Pacific Northwest than for moving Nebraska grain to the same destinations, even though Nebraska grain is carried a longer distance and passes through Montana. The railroad always has explained the disparity in rates by pointing out that there is direct competition at these Nebraska origins from trucks and Union Pacific to many markets including the Gulf, which holds export grain rates down. Nebraska grain shipments contribute less to the UP or BNSF fixed costs, while North Dakota and Montana shipments make a larger contribution to those costs for BNSF. The explanation falls on deaf ears in Montana and North Dakota, where local elevator operators and growers do not accept that demand should be a factor in rates and that rates are artificially low in Nebraska. From their perspective, grain rates are too high in Montana and North Dakota.

Another major factor in the evolution of the rail industry over the last 20 years has been the effect of mergers and consolidations. From the rail carriers' viewpoint, these mergers have brought great efficiencies, reduced costs, improved service, and lowered rates. Some shippers claim one result of the recent round of mergers has been a significant reduction in rail-to-rail competition. In 1980, when the Staggers Act was passed, there were nearly 40 Class 1 railroads, and even the largest systems faced competition throughout their territories. More than two-thirds of all rail shipments then moved over the tracks of two or more railroads, often in inefficient, costly, and disjointed routings. Customers could impose a certain amount of rate or service discipline on railroads by "short-hauling" them, routing traffic from an origination to the junction with another railroad and giving the longer haul to the second carrier, at the expense of service and efficiency. In fact, the 1980 system reflected a balkanized, inefficient network with high costs.

Deregulation and the inexorable consolidation of the railroad industry resulted in lower rates, better service, and a more viable privately-funded rail network, despite the perception in some quarters that there had been a shift of market power from the customer to the carrier. With the rail industry down to just seven Class 1 railroads, each of the remaining carriers covers much more geography, and many inefficient gateways and circuitous routings that previously existed between railroads have been rationalized. In the approvals of rail mergers, the ICC and the STB consistently required points served by two rail carriers before a merger to be so served after a merger, but the myth is often repeated that rail mergers created single-served points.

Railroads have had to deal with increasing truck and barge competition for more than half a century, with a vast government-funded interstate highway system, and a still diminishing market share of intercity freight. Although the railroads argue that there are no captive customers—that shippers have geographic, material, modal, or other options—many rail customers reject that position. In fact, the Staggers Act protects so called captives served by only one rail carrier with a complaint remedy addressing rate reasonableness and a threshold above which regulation continues. The threshold—180 percent of variable cost—is high enough that much rail traffic is completely exempt from regulation, as Congress intended. Even when a rate is above the threshold, however, a complaining customer has the burden of proving that the railroad has market dominance over the traffic, and if it can establish that, it then must prove that the rate is unreasonably high. Both shippers and railroads view the other as having fared better in the regulatory arena in rate cases in the two decades since deregulation.

Most rail shipments now move under transportation contracts, particularly when exempt traffic is included. By statute and because a contract is evidence of an arm's-length agreement between the customer and the railroad, there is no regulation of rates under contracts at all. The STB, and the ICC before it, have determined that where a carrier has a single line route from origin to destination or where a common carrier rate from origin to destination is published and available for rate challenge, as on most coal shipments, for example, there is no regulatory authority to require railroads to quote rates from a junction with another railroad if the railroad can carry the traffic as a single-haul. This has created what is known as bottlenecks. For coal shipped to Texas utilities, for example, both the UP and BNSF can originate in the Powder River Basin in Wyoming. But usually only one has tracks into the generating station, and that railroad invariably refuses to quote a rate from its nearest junction with the other that would allow the other carrier to provide competition, and presumably a lower rate (or bottleneck rate) on the long haul from the mine to the junction.

Shippers that once had inordinate market control over the railroads and view their market power as lessened under deregulation have tried to get Congress to overrule the STB and amend the Staggers Act to require the publication of rates to the bottleneck. They want the railroads to be forced to quote rates to interchanges despite the structural changes the industry has undergone (a requirement that has never existed), and they seek what they call competitive access, on the grounds that if more rail-to-rail competition existed, they would see lower rates. Published tariffs could be challenged under the law, and many shippers believe those rates would be more likely to be successfully challengeable under the STB's regulatory standards.

What shippers call the fine tuning of deregulation, however, railroads see as re-regulation. Forcing competition where it doesn't naturally exist would inject government back into the transportation decision-making process, and represent an unjustified taking of the railroad's property and investment, the railroads say. If a railroad were ordered to open its facilities to a competitor, for example, the railroads acknowledge that rates would come down, making it even less likely that the capital-intensive railroads would be able to earn their cost of capital, because the rates would not cover the ongoing cost of investment in rail infrastructure and maintenance.

Thus, there also would be the issue of how much one railroad could charge a competitor for using its property. If it were free to charge a rate that covered all of its cost of ownership, there would be little incentive for a second carrier to compete for the traffic. If the government were to set the rate, on the other hand, railroads would unlikely be allowed to recover their tremendous full long-term costs, an effective return to the days of regulation. So far, the railroads have prevailed on Capitol Hill, and Congress has shown little interest in refereeing a commercial dispute between large, sophisticated businesses and in returning to the days when railroads were unable to maintain their physical plant with private capital, teetering on the edge of bankruptcy as they were pre-Staggers, particularly as future investment will be needed to meet growing demands for service.

The bulk shipper lobby came closest to success in 1985, when it claimed that the ICC was not regulating even where it had the authority to do so. Heather Gradison, then chairwoman of the ICC, had been quoted as saying that she didn't care what Congress said, that she was following a mandate from the White House to carry out deregulation. Many observers believe the failure of the Santa Fe's planned merger with the Southern Pacific was in part a reaction to the efforts to rein in the commission legislatively. They theorize that the Santa Fe and the SP were "the last ones through the door" and that the door was slammed in their faces because the ICC felt a need to demonstrate to Congress that it didn't always give railroads what they wanted. Ironically, Rob Krebs earned a footnote in rail history as the only executive to be involved in the only two mergers in modern times to be rejected by the government.

By the late 1990s, when customers were dealing with service failures in much of the country, the competitive-access issue heated up, at least rhetorically. While mainstream shipper groups such as the National Industrial Transportation League avoided taking extreme positions, several grain, chemical, and other bulk shipper associations were under no restraints. Fortunately for the railroads, however, those committees of Congress that had jurisdiction over railroads saw no reason for making legislative changes in a law that had restored railroads to financial health.

The major efforts to improve service in which all railroads were engaged no doubt contributed to Congress's reluctance to meddle. By 2002, railroads were beginning to obtain rate increases based in part on the value of their service, as many shippers demonstrated they were willing to pay more for good service. The old maxim "Shippers talk service but buy price" was proving to have been part myth. Until the railroads developed their focus on service, shippers had been forced to buy on price largely because they had no other option.

There are some who believe that, just as the merger of the Santa Fe and the Southern Pacific may indirectly have been derailed by shipper pressure, the BNSF-CN combination was in part killed by shipper discontent and the perception by Morgan and her fellow commissioners that it was not a good time politically to allow another major rail merger. The railroad mergers that took place just prior to the BNSF and CN agreement to combine had resulted in a firestorm of shipper criticism over service failures. The STB had not been reauthorized, and in early 2000 Morgan was concerned about political ramifications of railroad market behavior almost as much as she was concerned about the economic issue. There was a concern—no one knows how real it was—that reauthorization of the STB might be tied to shipper-stimulated legislation that would mandate competitive access.

Regardless of whether another, final round of rail consolidation occurs, it now is virtually certain that after more than 150 years and the combination of some 389 railroads, BNSF will be one of the rail industry survivors. As recently as 1996, Rob Krebs was willing to sell BNSF to the Norfolk Southern, which at that time had a strong balance sheet and was able to raise capital more easily than any other railroad. The subsequent Conrail transaction, however, weakened both the NS and CSX to the point where neither eastern railroad today has the financial ability to acquire one of the western giants.

BNSF, on the other hand, is at the 10-year mark since its last merger as this is written. Its operations are more efficient than at any time in history. The company continues to strengthen its balance sheet, paying down debt and using free cash flow to buy back stock and increase its dividend. It has concentrated on creating a safer environment for the people working on the railroad and in the shops, recognizing that accidents not only are costly to the company but also affect the quality of service provided to customers.

BNSF's safety efforts since the merger have increasingly focused on a partnership approach with the labor unions. The Safety Summit agreement with the Brotherhood of Locomotive Engineers and Trainmen (BLET) and the United Transportation Union (UTU) provided for labor-appointed safety coordinators on all operations divisions and for peer work practice observation programs, paired with a less-punitive approach to discipline that allowed for "alternative handling" of many rules violations. Safety participation agreements are also in place with most other labor organizations at BNSF.

An outgrowth of the Safety Summit has been a joint work/rest team including BNSF leaders, as well as labor leaders from the UTU and BLET. This team has drafted a number of work/rest agreements designed to reduce fatigue and improve quality of life for train crew employees. Operating crews, for example, traditionally have been subject to call 24 hours a day, seven days a week. BNSF has pioneered a number of studies of work/rest cycles, retaining experts from outside the industry to help structure the studies. The most important result has been an "overlay" agreement that provides employees with scheduled rest days. This agreement has been locally ratified and implemented at more than 200 pool and extra board locations. Another agreement guarantees crew members eight hours of uninterrupted rest before being called out for another run.

Yet another agreement eases the employee's transition back to work after a week's vacation. Under this arrangement, the worker will not be called before 7 A.M. on the day after the end of a vacation, even though the official end of the vacation is at midnight.

Where the former BN had a period of rancorous relations with the unions that represented its employees, the new BNSF has worked to overcome that and to create a new relationship with its workers. National, industry-wide labor negotiations draw lots of attention, but many agreements that are crafted between unions and individual railroads go virtually unnoticed. BNSF, for example, now provides a 401(k) retirement plan and profit sharing for many union workers in addition to the national Railroad Retirement System pensions.

The safety programs have paid off. In the 10 years since the BN and the Santa Fe merged in 1995, the number of derailments has declined by 23 percent. The employee injury rate since the merger has been reduced more than 34 percent.

BNSF, having implemented its merger smoothly, was in a position to take the lead in developing new service options. In the first years after the millennium, the company introduced an array of new service offerings, each designed to attract business from a specific targeted market. In a relatively short period of time, BNSF announced the start of guaranteed intermodal service; carload service improvements on the north-south I-5 Corridor between Seattle and Southern California, where BNSF competes directly with the Union Pacific and operates part of the route over UP lines; guaranteed carload service in select lanes; and a guaranteed transcontinental temperature control service in conjunction with the Norfolk Southern.

Guaranteed intermodal service in select lanes was offered in May 2000. Initially it was easier to guarantee intermodal performance. The rail portion of intermodal involves an entire train moving from one origin to one destination, and rail performance is measured by the time a trailer or container is available for a drayage contractor to pull the load from the rail terminal. Carload business requires pickup at a customer's loading dock, handling in one or more yards, and then handling in a destination yard and local delivery to a consignee dock. Once the redesign of the carload network was under way, though, removing as many time-consuming and costly operations as possible, service guarantees could be offered on carload traffic as well as on intermodal shipments.

In 2003 BNSF announced an improved cross-border container service in conjunction with Ferrocarril Mexicano (Ferromex), a Mexican railroad. The new service reduced transit times between Mexico and major North American markets, including some in the Northeast and Canada. Significantly, the seven- and eight-day door-to-door transit between Los Angeles or Chicago and Mexico City or Guadalajara competed with over-the-road shipping. Rates, which were designed to make the service attractive to customers, included customs clearance.

On the I-5 Corridor service, named for the interstate highway that parallels the rail line, BNSF invested in track upgrades that allowed it to handle cars and freight with a total weight of 286,000 pounds, an increase over the previous maximum of 263,000 pounds. This allowed customers to ship up to 11.5 additional tons per car. Prior to the BN-Santa Fe merger, shipments between the Pacific Northwest and California were routed circuitously through Denver, Colorado, and had to clear the Rocky Mountains twice. Neither the BN nor the Santa Fe was an effective competitor to the former Southern Pacific and its single-line service. The new BNSF service reduced transit times by three and four days.

Using the promotional slogan "It's on time or it's on us," BNSF developed a guaranteed on-time service early in 2002 for carload shipments in a number of key traffic lanes. The service was expanded late in that year to seven lanes, including three from the Pacific Northwest to Arizona and Northern and Southern California, and two from Northern and Southern California to the Midwest. The railroad previously had offered the service guarantee from the Pacific Northwest to the Midwest and from the Pacific Northwest to Texas.

Ever since deregulation, BNSF and other railroads generally have absorbed inflation on behalf of their customers that had sufficient market power and competitive options to drive rates lower in exchange for volume commitments. Average rail rates, in both constant and inflation-adjusted dollars, declined steadily, and the benefits of service improvements accrued to the customers. In the BNSF approach to guarantees, though, shippers could purchase a guarantee of on-time service for a 15 percent premium. BNSF promised to provide a 100 percent refund for any load that arrived at the destination after the agreed-upon transit time. On-time performance, which previously was measured from terminal to terminal and was of little value to customers, is measured from the time a customer releases the car to the time it is spotted at the consignee's dock. BNSF also posts typical transit schedules at its Web site.

BNSF not only was the first railroad in the industry to offer a full money-back guarantee but also was the first to offer an equipment guarantee program that allows customers to secure the supply of specific car types, including centerbeam flatcar, boxcar, refrigerated boxcar, gondola, and bulkhead flatcar.

Like other railroads, BNSF also was making it easier to do business with it. For many customers, railroad business procedures appeared designed for the benefit of the railroad rather than the customer. Trucking companies were much more customer focused, which contributed to their ability to make some of their inroads into rail traffic. In recent years, as the Internet became a standard for conducting business, BNSF made it much easier for a customer—and just as important, for a potential customer—to arrange for transportation.

As railroads improved their operating efficiency and could provide more consistent service, it became possible to offer guaranteed service involving more than one railroad. BNSF and the Norfolk Southern teamed up in late 2002 to provide coast-to-coast carload service guarantees for temperature-controlled commodities moving between the Pacific Northwest and locations in the Midwest, the Northeast, and the Southeast. The new service carried a $500 premium, but BNSF and the NS promised to reimburse customers double that amount if the shipments failed to reach their destination by the agreed time.

Until the railroad had a high degree of consistency, offering guaranteed service would have been too costly. Ironically, one of the reasons the ICC had objected to contracts and guarantees during the days of rigid regulation was the perception that railroads might collude with shippers to have service failures as a way of giving an otherwise illegal rebate. The regulators never conceived that railroads might use guarantees to gain business.

To ensure timely distribution of periodicals and advertising material, many publishers and advertisers set up logistics systems in which they ship from printing plants to regional centers before turning their material over to the U.S. Postal Service for final delivery. In 2002 BNSF began offering guarantees for shipment of printed material between Chicago and Phoenix and between Richmond, Virginia, and San Bernardino, California.

BNSF customers made more than 10,000 shipments under guarantees in the first three years the programs were in effect. Although the number of shipments and the revenue from them was small, providing this service allowed the railroad's marketing and sales forces to differentiate BNSF from competitors. BNSF continued to expand the markets and lanes in which guaranteed service was available, targeting over-the-road trucking. High-service motor carriers charge a high premium for guaranteed service, using team drivers to overcome federal limits on the number of hours drivers can be behind the wheel. Even with the premium for the rail guarantee, BNSF's rates still are lower than the competing truck rates.

BNSF's focus on new and innovative services is part of the company's strategy to grow the business by gaining new customers. For many years, railroads have grown only by the amount of growth experienced by their regular customers. As they served mature industries, their volume and revenue growth was slow. Most of the revenue growth in U.S. transportation accrued to the trucking industry, with its greater flexibility and more-reliable service.

From a low of 37.5 percent of intercity freight ton-miles in 1980, the rail share recovered to 43.7 percent in 2004. Trucking, however, accounts for 90 percent of the revenue. If BNSF and other railroads are to earn their cost of capital, they are going to have to grow at a faster rate, capturing traffic that now moves on highways. At the same time, they are going to have to be able to get more revenue from their current customers. That will happen only when customers are satisfied that rail service is both consistent and reliable.

It is taking a new kind of leadership to move railroads into the future.

Epilogue

I think what you'll end up seeing is just the overriding principle that less is better.

MATTHEW K. ROSE, chairman, president, and chief executive of the Burlington Northern Santa Fe Corporation, May 2003

In the first decade of the 21st century, American railroads are experiencing a tectonic shift in their business. BNSF Railway is in the forefront of that shift.

For more than half a century, railroads were forced to contend with a regulatory system and business environment in which they maintained capacity in excess of the business they were called upon to carry. This resulted in a situation in which customers (shippers) were the beneficiaries of the supply-demand equation in the economy. As long as there was excess capacity, customers could and did demand lower prices from their vendors (railroads). With excess capacity, railroads found it virtually impossible to withstand pressure for lower rates. How that resulted in the railroads' inability to generate sufficient revenue to support necessary capital spending programs has been amply discussed.

Ever since the deregulation movement of the late 1970s and early 1980s, however, railroads have been removing capacity through attrition and abandonment. At the same time, the U.S. economy inexorably grew. Then globalization came along and provided more than a spike to the growth; it raised growth to an entirely higher plane. Now the railroad industry no longer has excess capacity.

During the period of excess rail capacity, competing trucking companies benefited from the expansion of the highway system and a payment formula that allowed truckers to charge lower rates and still make a profit. More recently, though, as the nation began to grapple with societal issues such as providing health care for an aging population, educating children in a technologically changing environment, and providing housing for a growing population, highway building received a lower priority. At the same time, the Interstate Highway System was aging, and more money was being used to maintain and improve existing roads than to build new capacity. Additionally, hours of service for truck drivers became more restrictive, and truckers were further affected by growing urban congestion on highways.

These trends created a "perfect storm," and by mid-2003 the nation began to realize that there was no excess capacity either in rail or highway transportation. The supply-demand equation was changing from one favoring customers to one favoring vendors. Railroads began to raise rates, although the existence of contracts covering most of their business meant that the process would take several years. Some railroads that were effectively out of capacity used pricing to ration their capacity, driving customers whose fixed-plant contributions were smaller to other railroads or to other modes.

BNSF, which had invested heavily in track programs and acquisition of new, more-powerful, fuel-efficient locomotives following the 1995 merger that created it, was able to handle the growth in its business—and to accept customers turned away by its competitors. Equally important, BNSF was able to raise rates because its principal competitor, the Union Pacific, was unable to compete for the same business and no longer contributed to the vicious cycle of lower rates in which both companies had engaged.

Those who remembered Rob Krebs and his "Build it and they will come" approach to capital spending began to recognize that he had been correct all along and that BNSF was reaping the long-term benefit of its huge capital spending program of 1996–1999.

By 2004 BNSF was reporting record revenue and growing profits, and its stock was selling at new highs as investors recognized its increasing value. The railroad continued to add capacity incrementally, which brought it further benefits. In a virtuous cycle, BNSF continued to take new business, and its customers accepted its higher prices.

Economic fundamentals have not changed. Railroads still invest a larger part of each dollar of revenue in their fixed plant and facilities than do companies in other industries. The long decline of the industry, however, appears to have ended. Rail traffic, for the first time in generations, is growing faster than the economy as a whole. Highway competitors, facing their own capacity constraints, are less of a commercial threat. The rail share of intercity freight movement climbed above 43 percent in 2004 and was the highest in more than 40 years.

No longer the dominant form of transportation that it once was, the railroad industry now is reinventing itself. Since the end of most government regulation, railroads survived by cost cutting that resulted in the elimination of more than half the jobs in the industry, 44 percent of route miles, 30 percent of the locomotive fleet, and half the freight cars. The cost cutting, in turn, enabled them to retain customers by offering lower prices. It can be said that ever since deregulation the railroads have been cutting their way to prosperity.

Driven by the reductions in employment and assets, however, the railroads have become significantly more efficient, the only real route to prosperity. The best measurement of that improvement is that the industry has set records for the transportation it has produced, as measured in revenue ton-miles. Since deregulation, for example, revenue ton-miles have increased 63 percent. Much of the increase, however, reflects the growth of coal and intermodal transportation, both of which are long-haul businesses that drive ton-miles higher.

Globalization has been a mixed blessing for railroads. On the one hand, global trade has contributed to the rise of intermodal, the great railroad industry success story. Millions of maritime containers now arrive annually at ocean ports, carrying finished goods and components to be combined into domestically assembled manufactured goods. Intermodal now is the largest commodity that railroads carry, exceeding even coal, and BNSF is the industry leader in intermodal. On the other hand, globalization has contributed to a shrinking domestic manufacturing base and the rail traffic it long relied upon.

Railroads always have produced low-cost transportation. For a long time, though, they were not as successful at producing consistent transportation, a failure that was costly to railroads and their customers.

If a shipment is scheduled to take seven days, for example, pricing experts can figure what rate should be charged, and customers can determine the inventory they need and factor that into their cost. But if variability results in the shipment being delivered in five days one time, seven days another time, and nine another, all calculations go out the window. The customer must maintain inventory for the worst performance, nine days. Variability also increases railroad costs because it requires additional locomotives, cars, and crews to move the same amount of freight.

If railroads are to become a growth industry, though, they must develop a new business model that reflects the changed economic environment in which they operate. No single change in the way they do business will ensure prosperity. They must make it easier for their customers to do business with them. They must become much more reliable and consistent.

Many manufacturing and distribution facilities do not have direct rail service today. For a railroad to receive business from these facilities, it must offer intermodal service that makes it profitable for the shipper to use it. The railroads, particularly BNSF, have succeeded in making intermodal attractive from a service and price standpoint. In many cases, once-competing truckers have become the railroad's customer, using intermodal to alleviate their own capacity problems.

Coal transportation, still BNSF's second-largest business, will provide significant revenue for many years, as long as coal is the principal fuel for generating electricity. Coal transportation is profitable but also highly competitive. Coal also has environmental issues, and changes in government policy can affect its use. Whether coal is burned or not is out of the railroads' hands, but BNSF will carry its share of the coal that is burned.

Grain also is a trainload business at which BNSF excels. About half the grain grown in the United States is available for export, and when the ocean freight rate differential causes customers to export grain to Asian destinations from the Pacific Northwest rather than from Gulf of Mexico ports, BNSF will carry more grain longer distances and will generate more revenue and greater earnings. Just as with coal, though, the volumes to be moved are out of the railroads' hands. Export markets are determined by political considerations, international currency exchange rates, weather, and other factors that BNSF cannot control. Grain, like coal, provides good base-load volume that helps support the capital structure, but it is not the driver of growth that it once was.

Intermodal clearly represents the future. Like coal and grain, intermodal is a trainload business. It enables BNSF and other railroads to compete for the business of manufacturers that do not even have direct rail service and to carry freight that may be destined to distribution centers and warehouses that do not have rail service. BNSF executives estimate there is potentially $8 billion of volume (in

2003 dollars) for which the company may compete, business it is not carrying now.

The non-trainload carload business still is significant. It is for the most part profitable, and because it tends to be freight that cannot practically move by another mode, it is resistant to price pressures and has higher margins. So-called loose-car railroading has higher costs because cars must be taken to shipper facilities and spotted for loading, then picked up and pulled to rail yards for placement in trains, with the entire process reversed at delivery. In its continuing effort to remove embedded costs, BNSF has redesigned its carload network to reduce the number of times each car is handled en route. Unlike most traditional cost-cutting exercises, it is a more fundamental process intended to determine what infrastructure can be supported.

The railroad needs to find the processes that remove as much work as possible from the carload business by concentrating as much of it as possible in the fewest facilities. Operationally this may appear to be traditional cost cutting. From a broader logistics perspective, though, it is a way to provide improved service that will justify charging higher rates because more value is being provided to customers.

The Canadian National is considered by many to be on the cutting edge of the kind of change that railroads must adopt. It applied discipline to its own operations and to its customers and operates a largely scheduled railroad. Along the way, the CN found that discipline reduces variability in operations and results in greater consistency, which in turn results in the need for fewer crews, locomotives, and cars.

Building on the success of scheduled operations, the CN found that it could guarantee car supply for customers because it knew where its cars were and when they would be available for reloading. The scheduled-railroad concept has reduced costs significantly and has allowed the railroad to charge higher rates because its service has more value. The CN says the quality of revenue has improved, a euphemism for not having to discount as much to keep the business it has. At 67.9 percent in the third quarter of 2003, the CN also had the lowest ratio of operating expense to revenue of any major railroad in North America.

Following the CN's lead, other railroads are developing systems to bring greater discipline to their operations. BNSF is going further, focusing on process change that includes cost cutting rather than concentrating narrowly on operations.

Matt Rose, who became BNSF chief executive shortly before his 42nd birthday, is the youngest chief of any of the major railroads at the time of this writing. BNSF appears to have its management in place for a long time, a desired situation for any institution forced to deal with fundamental change. Perhaps because of his relative youth, Rose is driving change while other railroads are more slowly adapting to it.

Rose believes there will be further mergers, although he is careful not to predict when. In a panel discussion before a meeting of rail shippers, he candidly acknowledged, "The level of service at railroad interchange points is unacceptable at the current level. . . . The fact is, mergers in the past have been effective in reducing rates and improving service." Rose has stated in other settings that additional mergers may well be several years away but still are a possibility.

While other railroads have trumpeted the virtues of marketing alliances and improvements in interline operations, rail history shows that such arrangements tend to work best when there is excess capacity in the system. The virtual failure of the joint Santa Fe-BN intermodal service between Southern California and Memphis is an example. Prior to the merger with the Santa Fe, BN managerial and capital priorities were directed to other areas and business that generated greater income, so the BN never provided the Santa Fe and its customers with satisfactory service. Once the railroads were combined, however, priorities changed, investment was made, the service improved, and business grew.

Matt Rose is the only rail chief executive officer who has spent a significant part of his professional life outside the railroad industry. Thus he brings a different set of experiences and perspectives to the job. As an executive with the largest truckload carrier in the motor carrier industry, he participated in the growth of that industry and saw firsthand how trucking benefited from just-in-time and quick-response business practices, largely at the expense of the railroads.

If there is another—and final—round of railroad mergers, they will be driven by the need to provide better service and do more for customers than did past mergers, which were driven by strategic considerations of increasing density and reducing cost. Making a railroad bigger will not be the principal driver. The BNSF-CN combination was stopped by a combination of other railroads and government regulators, but it was an excellent example of a merger that was driven by customer service considerations. As an end-to-end merger, it would not have resulted in savings nearly as great as were realized in some other mergers. But the resulting increase in single-line service would have allowed the combined railroad to increase revenue by carrying much of its customers' freight longer distances. Also, many customers, by gaining more-efficient single-line service, would have gained the ability to extend their markets to new areas and customers.

Like so many companies in other industries, today's railroad industry is much more focused on its core capabilities. Cars no longer are built in railroad shops but are purchased from companies that specialize in building cars. Rose has served notice on suppliers that he wants them to change along with their railroad customers.

Rose pointed out that half the current employees will be eligible to retire within 10 years. With a growing business, the emphasis will be on finding and retaining enough qualified workers rather than on cutting those already employed. He expects the railroads to focus their drive for greater efficiency on strategies like purchasing locomotives and cars with all maintenance included and performing less maintenance and fewer component rebuilds in railroad shops, due to improved preventive maintenance.

Greater efficiency will dictate that railroads, like companies in any industry, continually seek to streamline work—for instance, by reducing handling of carload traffic at intermediate terminals or improving the blocking of trains at the origination to reduce handling down the line. The focus on efficiency also means defining and structuring work so as to ensure that the smallest number of positions can perform the greatest amount of work most effectively. In the past, such focus tended to result in layoffs, but in the future it is more likely to result in more training and greater job security for those who take jobs in the railroad industry.

Even though most government regulation ended a quarter of a century ago, railroads still have a way to go to wring out excesses from their economic structures. One way is to perform less handling of customers' freight. BNSF is in the forefront of remaking itself into a trainload operator, with nearly 70 percent of its operations being solid trainloads moving from a single origin to a single destination. This includes coal, most grain, and intermodal traffic.

Railroads today are considering contracting out functions that are not part of the core business, such as telecommunications, which may well be more efficiently handled by a company specializing in that field. In some cases, railroads may also contract out functions that are closer to the essence of railroading, such as industrial switching and terminal operations, and they may even sell or lease branch lines that clearly have economic value but can be operated more efficiently by companies that specialize in the gathering and distribution of smaller quantities of freight. Rose summed it up, saying, "We're going to go into another era now of reducing expenses. At the end of the line, the common thread will be, how do you get your ongoing maintenance capital down to protect and grow free cash flow? I think what you'll end up seeing is just the overriding principle that less is better."

The BNSF chief executive sees the need for major railroads to continue to achieve greater density, leading to a shift of more infrastructure to the regional and short-line railroads. "You'll see more and more parts of the network become short-line," he said. The more-successful short-line operators have inherently lower cost structures than do the major railroads. While they may operate their trains at lower speed to the main-line junctions, saving on capital investment, they frequently put more resources into developing local business. The most successful short-line operations have been growing at twice the rate of Class 1s.

BNSF, like all major railroads, is navigating uncharted waters. Fundamental economics haven't changed since the Aurora Branch ran its first trains outside Chicago more than 150 years ago. It still is a network business in which success goes to those that can put the greatest density of traffic on their lines. Unlike the days of rampant expansion, though, today's railroads, and particularly the BNSF, are working to create the greatest capacity with the least expenditure of new capital.

Efficiency, as has been discussed previously, results in greater effective capacity. BNSF is in the forefront of railroads using remote control operations (RCO) technology to perform yard and terminal switching operations. Initially seen as a way to eliminate some switch crew jobs, RCO has proven to be even safer than traditional switching in which an engineer controls the locomotive from the cab of the locomotive, from which ground workers frequently cannot be seen.

BNSF is also working to develop an operational Electronic Train Management System (ETMS) that will make over-the-road operations safer and also may contribute to greater capacity. ETMS, like the ARES experiments two decades earlier, allows an onboard computer to operate the brakes automatically if the train exceeds a predetermined authority limit, approaches another train too closely, or exceeds authorized speeds. If ETMS moves beyond the experimental phase and is widely adopted, it would allow dispatchers to reduce the physical separation between trains, thereby "creating" new capacity. It also would enable more-efficient scheduling of passes and meets of trains moving at different speeds.

BNSF is not the only railroad seeking the answers, but because of the cultural changes it has undergone over the last two decades and the continuing ability of its current management to deal with change, it may have the flexibility and adaptability to find those answers before others do.

NOTES

CHAPTER 1

Much of the information on Russell Sage comes from *Iron Wheels and Broken Men,* a book about the robber barons by rail historian Richard O'Connor.

Sig Mickelson, a onetime president of CBS News, wrote a dissertation, *The Northern Pacific Railroad and the Selling of the West,* on the Northern Pacific Railroad's programs to stimulate immigration into Minnesota and Dakota Territory as a means of selling large parts of its 50-million-acre land grant.

Information on the Northern Pacific's crossing of Indian territory and its reliance on the U.S. Army to protect its construction crews and its trains comes largely from *Northern Pacific: Supersteam Era, 1925–1945,* by Robert L. Frey and Lorenz P. Schrenk.

H. Craig Miner—author of the definitive history of the Frisco, *The St. Louis–San Francisco Transcontinental Railroad: The Thirty-fifth Parallel Project, 1853-1890*—provided the information on Thomas Hart Benton and his vision of trade with Asia.

CHAPTER 2

Many of the Ripley quotes are from Keith L. Bryant Jr.'s *History of the Atchison, Topeka, and Santa Fe Railway.*

Ralph W. Hidy, Muriel E. Hidy, Roy V. Scott, and Don L. Hofsommer wrote *The Great Northern Railway: A History,* the definitive history of the GN. Their work provided much of the data and many of the quotations attributed to GN executives, data on GN congestion and operating difficulties during World War I, and descriptions of and quotes attributed to John Budd.

Richard C. Overton wrote several books on the Chicago, Burlington, and Quincy Railroad and provided much of the data and many of the quotations attributed to its officers during the period prior to its merger into the Burlington Northern. Among them were *Burlington West: A Colonization History of the Burlington Railroad; Perkins/Budd: Railway Statesmen of the Burlington;* and *Burlington Route: A History of the Burlington Lines.*

Frey and Schrenk provided much of the data and numerous quotations about the Northern Pacific in their book *Northern Pacific.*

CHAPTER 3

The anecdote of difficulty finding workers during World War II was taken from *The Great Northern Railway,* by Hidy et al.

CHAPTER 5

The quotation from Ralph Budd's 1945 speech to the Chicago Association of Commerce and Industry comes from Overton's *Burlington Route.*

Passages describing the "Big John case" and the incident involving the Chicago, Burlington, and Quincy's termination of a passenger train at Hemingford, Nebraska, are from *Comes Now the Interstate Commerce Practitioner,* by Frank N. Wilner, and are used with the permission of the copyright owner, the Association for Transportation Law, Logistics, and Policy.

CHAPTER 6

The discussion of the problems facing the U.S. railroad industry in the 1970s comes from Frank N. Wilner's *Railroad Mergers: History, Analysis, Insight* and is used with his permission.

Bibliography

Berkman, Pamela, ed. *The History of the Atchison, Topeka, and Santa Fe.* Lincoln, NE: Bison Books, 1988.

Bradley, Glenn D. *The Story of the Santa Fe.* Palmdale, CA: Omni Publications, 1995.

Bryant, Keith L., Jr. *History of the Atchison, Topeka, and Santa Fe Railway.* New York: Macmillan, 1974.

Daughen, Joseph R., and Peter Binzen. *The Wreck of the Penn Central.* Boston: Little, Brown, 1971.

DeBoer, David J., and Lawrence H Kaufman. *An American Transportation Story: The Obstacles, the Challenges, the Promise.* Greenbelt, MD: Intermodal Association of North America, 2002.

Douglas, George H. *All Aboard! The Railroad in American Life.* New York: Paragon House, 1992.

Friedlaender, Ann F. *The Dilemma of Freight Transport Regulation.* Washington, DC: Brookings Institution, 1969.

Frey, Robert L., and Lorenz P. Schrenk. *Northern Pacific: Supersteam Era, 1925–1945.* San Marino, CA: Golden West Books, 1985.

Gray, Carl. R., Jr. *Railroading in Eighteen Countries: The Story of American Railroad Men Serving in the Military Railway Service from 1862 to 1953.* New York: Charles Scribner's Sons, 1955.

Hidy, Ralph W., Muriel E. Hidy, and Roy V. Scott, with Don L. Hofsommer. *The Great Northern Railway: A History.* Boston: Harvard Business School Press, 1988.

Klein, Maury. *Unfinished Business: The Railroad in American Life.* Hanover, NH: University Press of New England, 1994.

Kolko, Gabriel. *Railroads and Regulation: 1877–1916.* Princeton, NJ: Princeton University Press, 1965.

Law and Contemporary Problems: Railroad Reorganization. Durham, NC: School of Law, Duke University, 1940.

Lewty, Peter J. *Across the Columbia Plain: Railroad Expansion in the Interior Northwest, 1885–1893.* Pullman: Washington State University Press, 1995.

Martin, Albro. *Enterprise Denied: Origins of the Decline of American Railroads, 1897–1917.* New York: Columbia University Press, 1971.

———. *James J. Hill and the Opening of the Northwest.* New York: Oxford University Press, 1976.

———. *Railroads Triumphant: The Growth, Rejection, and Rebirth of a Vital American Force.* New York: Oxford University Press, 1992.

Mickelson, Sig. *The Northern Pacific Railroad and the Selling of the West: A Nineteenth-Century Public Relations Venture.* Sioux Falls, SD: Center for Western Studies, 1993.

Miner, H. Craig. *The St. Louis–San Francisco Transcontinental Railroad: The Thirty-fifth Parallel Project, 1853–1890.* Lawrence: University Press of Kansas, 1972.

Morgan, David P. *Diesels West: The Evolution of Power on the Burlington.* Milwaukee: Kalmbach Publishing Co., 1963.

Morris, Edmund. *Theodore Rex.* New York: Random House, 2001.

O'Connor, Richard. *Iron Wheels and Broken Men: The Railroad Barons and the Plunder of the West.* New York: G. P. Putnam's Sons, 1973.

Ogburn, Charlton. *Railroads: The Great American Adventure.* Washington, DC: National Geographic Society, 1977.

Overton, Richard C. *Burlington Route: A History of the Burlington Lines.* New York: Alfred A. Knopf, 1965.

———. *Burlington West: A Colonization History of the Burlington Railroad.* Cambridge, MA: Harvard University Press, 1941.

———. *Perkins/Budd: Railway Statesmen of the Burlington.* Westport, CT: Greenwood Press, 1982.

Railroad Facts: 2002 Edition. Washington, DC: Policy and Economics Department, Association of American Railroads, 2002.

Rose, Joseph R. *American Wartime Transportation.* New York: Thomas Y. Crowell Co., 1953.

Salsbury, Stephen. *No Way to Run a Railroad: The Untold Story of the Penn Central Crisis.* Boston: McGraw-Hill, 1982.

Saunders, Richard. *The Railroad Mergers and the Coming of Conrail.* Westport, CT: Greenwood Press, 1978.

Stover, John F. *American Railroads.* Chicago: University of Chicago Press, 1997.

Wilner, Frank N. *Comes Now the Interstate Commerce Practitioner.* Annapolis, MD: Association of Transportation Practitioners, 1993.

———. *Railroad Land Grants: Paid For in Full.* Monograph. Association of American Railroads, 1984. http://www.aar.org/GetFile.asp?File_ID=144 (accessed January 2005). Washington, D.C.

———. *Railroad Mergers: History, Analysis, Insight.* Omaha, NE: Simmons-Boardman Books, 1997.

Wood, Charles, and Dorothy Wood. *The Great Northern Railway: A Pictorial Study.* Edmonds, WA: Pacific Fast Mail, 1979.